"Rubertone offers a critical, humanistic, detailed, and nuanced approach to the central role of Native people both in the past and in the 'emerging modernity' of the city of Providence.... Through an archaeological and metaphorical approach to the city in the nineteenth and twentieth centuries, *Native Providence* eloquently presents a microscalar look at Indigenous lives.... The book reveals an important method, devised with mastery, to destabilize and overcome erasure. It serves as an example for similar cases all over the world."
—Marianne Sallum and Francisco Silva Noelli, *Historical Archaeology*

"Rubertone's archival research is impressive, and her reading of documentary evidence—of what it reveals and what it does not—is a model for how to find Native people in the archives, particularly Indigenous subjects that are sometimes only found in traces."
—Laura M. Furlan, *Journal of Anthropological Research*

"[*Native Providence*] intricately weaves together the biographies and movements of everyday Native individuals and families as they made their lives in the city of Providence."
—Christopher J. Slaby, *Western Historical Quarterly*

"Meticulous archival research.... This social history of survivance offers a fresh perspective on urban Indian ethnic identity in a southern New England city across two centuries."
—J. H. Rubin, *Choice*

"Patricia Rubertone deftly undermines the myth that cities don't have Indigenous histories or presents, and she challenges the notion that Native people whose homelands are often called 'New England' have disappeared. Through painstaking archival research, conversations with community members, and attention to the local landscape, Rubertone has produced a readable and usefully disorienting account of one historic city's encounter with both settler colonialism and Indigenous survivance."
—Coll Thrush, author of *Indigenous London: Native Travelers at the Heart of Empire*

"This is the best treatment of the urban experiences of Indians in New England to date and a model of historical recovery for the broader, burgeoning subfield of urban Indian studies."
—David J. Silverman, author of *This Land Is Their Land: The Wampanoag Indians, Plymouth Colony, and the Troubled History of Thanksgiving*

"*Native Providence* is a magnificently grounded, humane study of Indigenous resilience and adaptation. It recovers the complexities and contradictions of Native individuals and families who worked to make the city their own place and navigated the pressures and exclusions of settler colonialism to create their own forward-looking modernities. It places Native people and voices at the center and in doing so provocatively reorients us to a seemingly familiar city."
—Christine M. DeLucia, author of *Memory Lands: King Philip's War and the Place of Violence in the Northeast*

"Revelatory—an entirely new way of looking at this old 'thoroughfare' city. . . . Rubertone's innovative work . . . stands out as a model of historical archaeological analysis and practice—an embodiment of the hopes of the discipline's founders that the skillful inter-reading of archaeological collections, geographical evidence, and what James Deetz called 'docufacts' can contribute to analyses that transcend the study of any one of these bodies of data separately."
—Kathleen J. Bragdon, *American Antiquity*

Native Providence

Native Providence

*Memory, Community, and
Survivance in the Northeast*

Patricia E. Rubertone

UNIVERSITY OF NEBRASKA PRESS | LINCOLN

© 2020 by the Board of Regents of the University of Nebraska. All rights reserved. Portions of chapters 2 and 3 are from "Archaeologies of Native Production and Marketing in 19th Century New England," in *Foreign Objects: Rethinking Indigenous Consumption in American Archaeology*, ed. Craig N. Cipolla, 204-21 (Tucson: University of Arizona Press, 2017), and "Memorializing the Narragansett: Placemaking and Memory Keeping in the Aftermath of Detribalization," in *Archaeologies of Placemaking: Monuments, Memories, and Engagement in Native North America*, ed. Patricia E. Rubertone, 195-216 (Walnut Creek CA: Left Coast, 2008).

The University of Nebraska Press is part of a land-grant institution with campuses and programs on the past, present, and future homelands of the Pawnee, Ponca, Otoe-Missouria, Omaha, Dakota, Lakota, Kaw, Cheyenne, and Arapaho Peoples, as well as those of the relocated Ho-Chunk, Sac and Fox, and Iowa Peoples.

First Nebraska paperback printing: 2023
Library of Congress Cataloging-in-Publication Data
Names: Rubertone, Patricia E., author.
Title: Native Providence: memory, community, and survivance in the Northeast / Patricia E. Rubertone, University of Nebraska Press.
Other titles: Memory, community, and survivance in the Northeast
Description: Lincoln : University of Nebraska Press, [2020] | Includes bibliographical references and index.
Identifiers: LCCN 2020007610
ISBN 9781496217554 (hardback)
ISBN 9781496236869 (paperback)
ISBN 9781496223999 (epub)
ISBN 9781496224002 (mobi)
ISBN 9781496224019 (pdf)
Subjects: LCSH: Indians of North America—Urban residence—Rhode Island—Providence. | Indians of North America—Rhode Island—Providence—Antiquities. | Indians of North America—Cultural assimilation—Rhode Island—Providence. | Narragansett Indians—Cultural assimilation. | Cultural landscapes—Rhode Island—Povidence. | Indians of North America—Rhode Island—Providence—Genealogy. | Indians of North America—Rhode Island—Providence—Biography. | Providence (R.I.)—Genealogy. | Providence (R.I.)—Biography. | Providence (R.I.)—History.
Classification: LCC E78.R4 R83 2020 | DDC 974.5/00497—dc23
LC record available at https://lccn.loc.gov/2020007610

Set in Lyon Text by Laura Buis.

The cover illustration, *Still Here* by Gaia (2018), is a mural created in partnership with The Avenue Concept and Tomaquag Museum honoring the indigenous heritage and peoples of Providence. The artwork shows Lynsea Montanari (Narragansett) holding a black-and-white picture of Princess Red Wing (Narragansett-Wampanoag), an educator, historian, and activist. Reproduced with permission of the artist; photograph by Patricia E. Rubertone.

In memory of William S. Simmons

We have the same blood running through our veins that we had before we sold our lands. Now let the same sun shine on us that shines on others. That is all we ask.

>**Joshua H. Noka** (Narragansett), in *Fourth Annual Report of the Commission on the Affairs of the Narragansett Indians, 1884*

If some of these old roofs could talk,—they would laugh at some theories of the "vanishing American."

>**Princess Red Wing** (Narragansett-Wampanoag), in *Narragansett Dawn* (August 1935)

The earth pushes through the pavement in the city ... [an] urban and material landscape where no sacred sites are thought to exist, and a sacred stream may still trickle waiting to heal again.

>**Leslie Marmon Silko** (Laguna Pueblo) in Goeman, "From Place to Territories and Back Again"

Contents

List of Illustrations | xi
Preface | xiii
Acknowledgments | xix
A Note on the Maps | xxiii

Introduction: Narrating Indigeneity in a "Thoroughfare Town" | 1

1. Fox Point: A Waterfront Homeland, Encounters at a Stopping-Over Place, and Indigenous Legibility | 29
2. Lippitt Hill: Homelands of the Hill and Hollows, Unholy Water, and Traditional Knowledge | 71
3. Upper South Providence: Homeland at the Crossroads, Churchgoing, and Community Making | 111
4. Lower South Providence: Habitations by the River and Bay, Mobility, and the Urban Imaginary | 155
5. Mashapaug Pond: The Pond Lands, from Planting Fields to Industrial Transformations | 195
6. Federal Hill: Homeland above the River at the Town's Doorstep, Commonplace Streets, and Uncommon Labor | 239
7. Johnston: Homeland at the Borderlands, Powwows, and Urban Mythscapes | 283

Epilogue: Imagining Past, Present, and Future Urbanity | 325

Appendix: Native Residents of Providence Homelands | 335
Notes | 347
Bibliography | 389
Index | 417

Illustrations

1. Map of Native Providence homelands, ca. 1850–1950 | xxvi
2. Map of the Fox Point homeland | 28
3. Deed to Providence, 1638 | 31
4. Clarence Freeman at the Providence Checker and Chess Club, 1890 | 65
5. Map of the Lippitt Hill homeland | 70
6. Sarah Baxter 1874 advertisement | 89
7. Frederick Thomas's house, 51 Bates Street | 95
8. Dedication of the Canonicus Monument at North Burial Ground, 1883 | 99
9. Map of the Upper South Providence homeland | 110
10. Central-Classical Redevelopment Project's new Classical High School | 116
11. Canonicus Monument, Upper South Providence | 118
12. Indian Council of New England at the Pond Street Church, 1923 | 125
13. Map of the Lower South Providence homeland | 154
14. Site of the former Chestnut Street Methodist Church | 164
15. Sunday services at the Narragansett Indian Church, August Meeting, 1925 | 179
16. The Roger Williams Homes, 1940s | 187
17. Map of the Mashapaug Pond homeland | 194
18. Mashapaug Pond | 198
19. Leroy Perry, Providence, 1924 | 203
20. Nancy Elizabeth Prophet aboard the ss *La France*, 1922 | 211
21. William H. Proffitt, Benedict Street, 1940 | 216
22. Map of the Federal Hill homeland | 238

23. Moses P. Dailey, 1913 | 241
24. Collage of Weeden family photographs | 251
25. Fannie Kendall, 1871 advertisement | 256
26. Hipses Rock, ca. 1890 | 282
27. Powwow grounds on the Tillinghast farm | 289
28. Indians at National Algonquin Indian Council powwow, Johnston | 290
29. Dolly Onsley | 294
30. Onsley home on Morgan Avenue | 294
31. Bird's-eye view of Providence, 1882 | 328
32. Broad Street tag on map of endangered sites | 331

Preface

This book had its beginnings in my research on colonialist monuments and myths of Native disappearance in southern New England. I wondered why Native people had attended dedication ceremonies for monuments that denied their modernity. I suspected that their presence at these events was intended to refute Euro-American assumptions about their extinction and also to acknowledge the continuing importance within Native communities of places overwritten by memorialization. I did not know who these Native people were or where they lived. When these monuments were raised, the tribal status of Native peoples across the region had been terminated and, with few exceptions, their communal land rights extinguished. Did the Native people who attended these events still live near their ancestral lands? The program from the dedication exercises for the Canonicus Memorial in Providence's North Burial Ground—a monument I studied and wrote about—indicated that a Narragansett did the unveiling. Another presented a bouquet to the Indian commissioner. Both lived in the city, not far from monument, and had last names that resonated in the tribe's history. In photographs of the dedication, faces in the crowd, except those in the foreground, are difficult to discern. If they were clearer, would it be possible to identify other Indians at the ceremony?

More important, were there other Native people who called Providence their home by choice during the late nineteenth and early twentieth centuries, when these monuments were being built? Besides wanting to find out if they were there, I wanted to know about their stories of survivance. Were they born in this city? Did they move here? How did they find one another and build a community? Did they move back and forth between the city and rural spaces of their tribal reserves when life, on balance, seemed less precarious somewhere other than where they were currently were living? Were there transits from the city to maintain ties with family and friends left behind and with historically meaningful places? Did some travel within the broader indigenous world for other reasons? Did Providence become a new place of community and belonging filled with its own memories? What were the possibilities for reframing Providence history through Native people's experiences, I wondered—where would I begin? There would certainly be challenges, since Native people generally are not a part of modern Providence's written history.

I had previously conducted research on cities and on Native American histories, but these two interests had never intersected. Early in my career, I did archaeology *in* the city—or in spite of the city—in New York's least urbanized boroughs, where traces of Native occupation predated indigenous people's urban experiences by thousands of years. I have also done archaeology *of* the city, in Providence, an approach that takes the city itself as its evidence and inspiration. In that earlier research in Providence I examined a four-block area between North Main Street, formerly known as Towne Street, the principal thoroughfare of the seventeenth-century settler colony, and Canal Street, built on land reclaimed from the town's cove—an area that was imagined as devoid of Native people and their history. At the time, I had not yet learned that an "Indian skull" and associated bones had been discovered nearby during improvements to North Main Street in the early 1800s, or that Roger Williams had as his servant a young Pequot War captive. Never did I anticipate that I would one day embark on a study of the Native history of Providence, a city I have now lived in longer than I lived in New York. It is here in Providence that my scholarly interests in the urban and indigenous life have come full circle.

It is here, residing in the ancestral homelands of the Narragansett and Wampanoag peoples, that I wrote *Native Providence*, a book that indigenizes this city's history. Native people were never really out of place here, or new to the urban scene. Some were here all along, even after settler colonists took most of their land to build the city. Others moved here. Their children were born here. Their children's children were born here. Generations were here. Providence is an indigenous city because it sits on indigenous land, but also and significantly because of its indigenous residents. They resisted dispossession and reinserted themselves in the urban space, only to be displaced again and again by development projects that valued societal and economic benefits over human costs. With these odds stacked against them, and often too resolute to leave, they were still here. You might say they were resilient, or that they had no other place to go that was as familiar or perhaps less dangerous and alienating. They were old-style Native people who called themselves "Indians" or full-blooded members of their tribes. Others were indigenous cosmopolitans who navigated the complex terrain of their ancestry as deftly as they did the city streets. Some were called basket makers, on the understanding that their basket making alone defined them. They had different life courses and varied stories of resistance.

The book I have written is not an archeology *of* the city in a literal sense, but it is an archaeology of the city in a metaphorical sense, in that it compensates for historical silences and attempts to understand why these ruptures exist. It queries historical evidence in archives and expands the notion of what constitutes an archive of knowledge. It values place-based knowledge that resides in oral accounts, and images and objects that recall family and community histories. It attempts to understand city living by focusing on the particular spaces where Native people lived—where they were raised or born, played, dated, married, kept house, loitered, visited friends, and attended wakes. These were places of emotional attachments.

When I visited these places I saw evidence of persistence, but mostly of transformation. Houses and vast swaths of neighborhoods that once stood in the paths of highways and urban renewal projects no longer existed. They had been erased, much like the histories of the Native people who had inhabited them. What were the human costs of these acts of physical destruction, and more broadly of the accompanying paper genocide? Could I approximate what had been lost besides streets and houses? I wondered if it would be possible to retrieve deeply human and intimate stories of the Native people who lived in the city's neighborhoods during the nineteenth and early twentieth centuries, some in houses that had been destroyed—and if so, could those stories help us understand the human costs of urbanization and development for the Native people who called Providence home? What did it feel like to be ignored in the annals and records of the city and as residents of neighborhoods considered expendable? Weren't the births and weddings they celebrated worth remembering? Weren't the infants whose deaths were mourned in those houses just as important as the Native children taken into English colonists' homes as indentured servants or adopted out of their tribal communities? What about the lives of Native women who worked as laundresses—laboring over tubs of scalding water, washing other people's clothes, hanging them to dry, and ironing them in front of a hot fire—trying to make ends meet and, often, provide for their children as single parents? Weren't they a significant part of this history? Weren't the lives of Native men who drove teams, loaded and unloaded ships, hauled coal, and served in wars, stories in everyday courage? Didn't they matter? Were there other untold stories of survivance?

It took a long time to learn these place-based stories, and I have not learned all of them. I spent countless hours poring over and grappling intensively with different sources. Many sources that seemed resistant, at least initially, to revealing much information about Native lives turned out to be instructive in ways that I did not expect. What they concealed was as enlightening as what they disclosed. At the start of my research I tracked down names and addresses of Native residents, only to have to recheck them later in what was a tedious process that required enormous patience and a high tolerance for ambiguity. But what I wanted to accomplish in writing this book involved more than finding Native people and saying where they lived. There were other questions I had and other records I wanted to look at.

Because documentary evidence on Providence's Native residents in the first half of the nineteenth century is relatively sparse, most of the Native people I write about appear in later and generally more detailed records. Alternative sources such as visual records, archaeological evidence, preserved botanical specimens, and estate inventories of clothing, household furnishings, and other material things proved to be especially beneficial to the imaginative, speculative, and emotive work needed to reinterpret their experiences. So did the knowledge and memories that contemporary Native people with connections to the city shared with me about their relations and their own lives, in conversations at various venues, by phone, and occasionally by email. These exchanges were not initiated by descendant communities nor were they ethnographic or journalistic interviews. Yet our conversations and the relationships they were built on have already led to discussions of other projects. As much as I hesitate to characterize the research for this book as collaborative, I also would not describe it as interdisciplinary or ethnohistorical or, as I said, archaeological, although it shares elements in common with the creativity and resourcefulness of those approaches. Rather, I have drawn from and combined multiple strands of evidence to weave together past and present in these chapters about Native Providence and the people from Narragansett, Wampanoag, Nipmuc, Pequot, Wabanaki, Mi'kma'ki, and more distant indigenous homelands who were not expected to be here but were, and still are today.

In his acclaimed 2018 novel *There There*, Tommy Orange writes about what it means to be Native in a modern city, when Native people feel more at home walking in the shadow of a downtown building than a mountain or forest, more familiar with hearing the sound of a distant train than a wolf's howl, or more used to smelling gas, wet concrete, and burned rubber than the scents of cedar and sage. Being Indian has never been about returning to the land, Orange points out, because Native land is everywhere—in Oakland, where he was born and raised, as it is in Providence. To be Native in the city, he says, is to keep telling stories. In the same way, to write about Native Providence means telling stories about the Native people who have lived in its urban spaces.

Acknowledgments

As I glance at the loose-leaf binder where I initially kept my notes; the fifteen or so Hollinger document boxes, one for each chapter, filled with folders arranged topically and alphabetically by individual, and others on mapping, urban renewal, Native ethnobotanical practices, historical plant specimens, drafts, and more; all the computer files; and the stuffed drawers of my file cabinets, I realize how much research went into this book. Mostly, though, I realize how many individuals and institutions contributed to what I have tried to accomplish in *Native Providence*.

I first want to acknowledge the generosity of my late colleague, mentor, and friend William Simmons, to whom this book is dedicated. Bill was a son of Providence, a walking encyclopedia of this city, and a distinguished scholar known for his research on the Native Northeast. On walks and drives in and around the city, he shared his knowledge of its streets. His enthusiasm for connecting the historical record with the present by drawing from multiple lines of testimony and listening closely to the voices of ancestors speaking through contemporary generations of Native people was infectious. I have tried to follow his example seriously.

I am grateful to Tall Oak (Everett G. Weeden), a Pequot-Wampanoag, for our continuing conversations about the knowledge and memories he has long stewarded and for making family histories and struggles palpable. I am honored to include his artwork in this book. Paula Dove Jennings (Narragansett) told me about her mother, Eleanor Spears, her great-grandmother, and other women in her family with connections to Providence. Dawn Dove and Lorén Spears shared a poem from their deeply personal and reflective journals on Mashapaug Pond that is reprinted in the epilogue. Derek Henries (Nipmuc), whose family history in Providence goes back generations, was generous with his time and knowledge. I regret that I did not have the chance to meet his father, Ron Little Crow

Henries, whom he recalled with such fondness. Donna Edmonds Mitchell, who also passed away before I finished writing this book, lived and worked in Providence. I met her when she was an administrator in the Africana Studies Department and active in Native Americans at Brown. I treasure memorable afternoons driving with her through the Native neighborhoods of Providence's East Side and her Watuppa homeland, where she later resided, while listening to her stories and seeing her determination to continue on her family's path of survival.

At the Providence City Archives, Britni Gorman and Caleb Horton, and previously Paul Campbell and Claire Bestwick, gave invaluable assistance, as did Kenneth Carlson at the Rhode Island State Archives. Phoebe Bean, Michelle Chiles, J. D. Kay, and Dana Signe-Munroe at the Rhode Island Historical Society Library helped answer my questions in person and with their behind-the-scenes research on manuscript and graphic collections. Charlotte Taylor and Timothy Ives at the Rhode Island Historical Preservation and Heritage Commission facilitated access to site files, and Paul Robinson, former state archaeologist and commission member, to the commission's vaults. Mack Woodward, another former commission staff member, provided information on the city's architectural history. Thanks also go to Peter Asen and Mark Ouellet at the Providence Housing Authority, Mike Lepore at the Providence Redevelopment Agency, Marilyn Massaro, formerly at the Roger Williams Park Natural History Museum, and Andrew Smith at the Rhode Island Supreme Court Judicial Records Center, all of whom graciously pulled together materials for my visits or supplied electronic copies of requested materials.

I owe much gratitude to Thierry Gentis, Rip Gerry, and former staff member Nathan Arndt at the Haffenreffer Museum of Anthropology at Brown University; Alison Bundy, Timothy Engels, and Holly Snyder at the John Hay Library; and Timothy Whitfeld and Rebecca Kartzinel at the Brown University Herbarium. Marlene Lopes, recently retired, Andrew Davis, and Molly Bruce Patterson in Special Collections at Rhode Island College's John P. Adams Library and Nanci Young at the Smith College Archives were extremely helpful in making their collections accessible.

Thanks also go to staff members at other museums, libraries, and repositories both large and small. Ann McMullen and Nathan Sowry at the National Museum of the American Indian advised on digital collections. James McGrath at the Cyrus Dallin Art Museum in Arlington, Massachusetts, offered insights on Dallin's sculptures and the museum's archives. Kate Wells at the Providence Public Library and librarians at the Connecticut State Library, the Cranston Public Library's Central and Oak Lawn Branches, the Knight Memorial Library, the Marian J. Mohr Memorial Library in Johnston, the Nantucket Historical Association Research Library, and the Westerly Library helped search their holdings, often digging deep into rarely accessed material. I am also indebted to individuals at the Beneficent Congregational Church, the Indian and Colonial Research Center, Johnston Town Hall, North Burial Ground, and the Warwick Historical Society who made my visits worthwhile. Others at the New London Historical Society, the Stonington Town Clerk's Office, and the Maine Historical Society were equally helpful. Special thanks go to Louis McGowan, the former president of the Johnston Historical Society, an expert guide to the society's collections, and to Elise Carlson, the current president, Steve Merola, and Anthony Ricci. Elli Panichas of the Neutaconkanut Hill Conservancy made valuable suggestions before and after we hiked the restored trails of the hill that she has steadfastly attempted to preserve.

Along the way, researchers have shared comments and sources for which I am most grateful. They include Christine DeLucia, a gracious colleague with a keen sense of ethical obligations, with whom I share a deep interest in landscapes of memory in the Native Northeast, and Holly Ewald, Russell Handsman, Jeff Howe, Robert Kelley, Jason Mancini, Alexandra Peck, Robert Preucel, Harald Prins, Leah Morine Rosenmeier, David Silverberg, Coll Thrush, and Ann Valk. Marguerite DeLoney and Isabelle Williams, former Brown University undergraduates, and Madeline Kearin, a doctoral candidate (now a PhD) in anthropology, helped gather information from select printed sources, online databases, and the Brown University Herbarium. I am especially indebted to Lynn Carlson, the geographic information systems manager at Brown University's

Environmental and Remote Technologies Lab, for creating the maps for this book from lists (and revised lists) of addresses, and for conversations about how geospatial imagery can engage community memories. Julie Hagen, a freelance copyeditor, formatted extensive notes and the bibliography and responded to my queries with incredible and steadying patience. My editor, Matthew Bokovoy, offered wonderful suggestions and unfailing support and guided me with intelligence and skill. Thanks also go to Heather Stauffer for her efficiency and kindness, to Ann Baker and the entire editorial, design, and production team at the University of Nebraska Press, and to Monica Achen, a discerning copyeditor.

Financial support for this project has come from multiyear Humanities Research Fund awards from Brown University's Office of the Vice President for Research and from sabbatical leaves, for which I thank my department and the dean of the faculty. I also thank the staff of my department for administering those funds, and Eric Scantlebury, a systems manager at Brown University, for advice on computing issues.

My staunchest support has come from my family and friends, who nudged and cajoled me about why this book took so long but understood that there are no shortcuts to any places worth going. Kathi and Danny Devlin and Nancy and Tom Healy are always there for me, whether I am near or far. Pat Rubertone is wise and sensible beyond compare—he is still my best teacher.

A Note on the Maps

The maps in *Native Providence* are intended as guides for readers. The first step for creating these maps was to identify Native residents in censuses, vital records, military documents, and reports on New England's tribal communities, such as the published accounts of the Narragansett detribalization hearings and John Milton Earle's 1861 survey of Indians in Massachusetts. I tracked names across multiple documents, including city directories, and checked them against public ascriptions of identity that ranged from "Indian" to "Black," "mulatto," "colored," "Negro/Indian," "white," "red," or "other type"; only rarely were Native residents identified by tribal affiliation. If an individual was not consistently identified as "Indian," but family name, birthplace, and residence suggested Native cultural or ancestral identity, I included that person as Native. Alternatively, if the family name, birthplace, and residence of individuals identified as "Indian" by census takers and other record keepers—usually based on what they looked like—did not seem to support Native cultural or ancestral identity, I did not include them as Native.

Although my aim was to be inclusive, I certainly missed some Indians and where they lived. Points on the base map (fig. 1) do not represent all the houses where Native people in the study area lived in the nineteenth and early twentieth centuries. Mapping Native households presented additional difficulties because street addresses were not generally recorded before the mid-nineteenth century, streets were often renamed or may no longer be in existence, and houses were renumbered or not shown on city atlases. Some addresses simply could not be plotted or their locations approximated. Yet the base map conveys unprecedented evidence of Providence's modern Native homelands.

The chapter maps are geographically smaller in scope than the base map. They delineate the streets and plot the locations of addresses where the Native individuals and families discussed in the Fox Point, Lippitt Hill, Upper South Providence, Lower South Providence, Mashapaug Pond, and Federal Hill chapters lived. The chapter maps do not show all of the addresses mapped for a particular homeland on the base map, nor do they represent the homelands as bounded spaces. The names of individual residents are intentionally left off, but the streets they lived on and often their house numbers are mentioned in the text. There is no chapter map for Johnston because the Native people identified in that homeland lived in a family enclave within a two-street area.

Beyond serving as navigational tools, these maps of Providence streetscapes were created to open conversations about other Native people who might have been neighbors and to imagine still more aspects of their dwelling in the urban landscape that may challenge settler-colonial narratives. The chapter maps and base map were created by Lynn Carlson, manager of Brown University's Environmental and Remote Technologies Lab, who provided geographic information systems (GIS) expertise and technical support to help visualize the geography of Native households and neighborhoods.

Native Providence

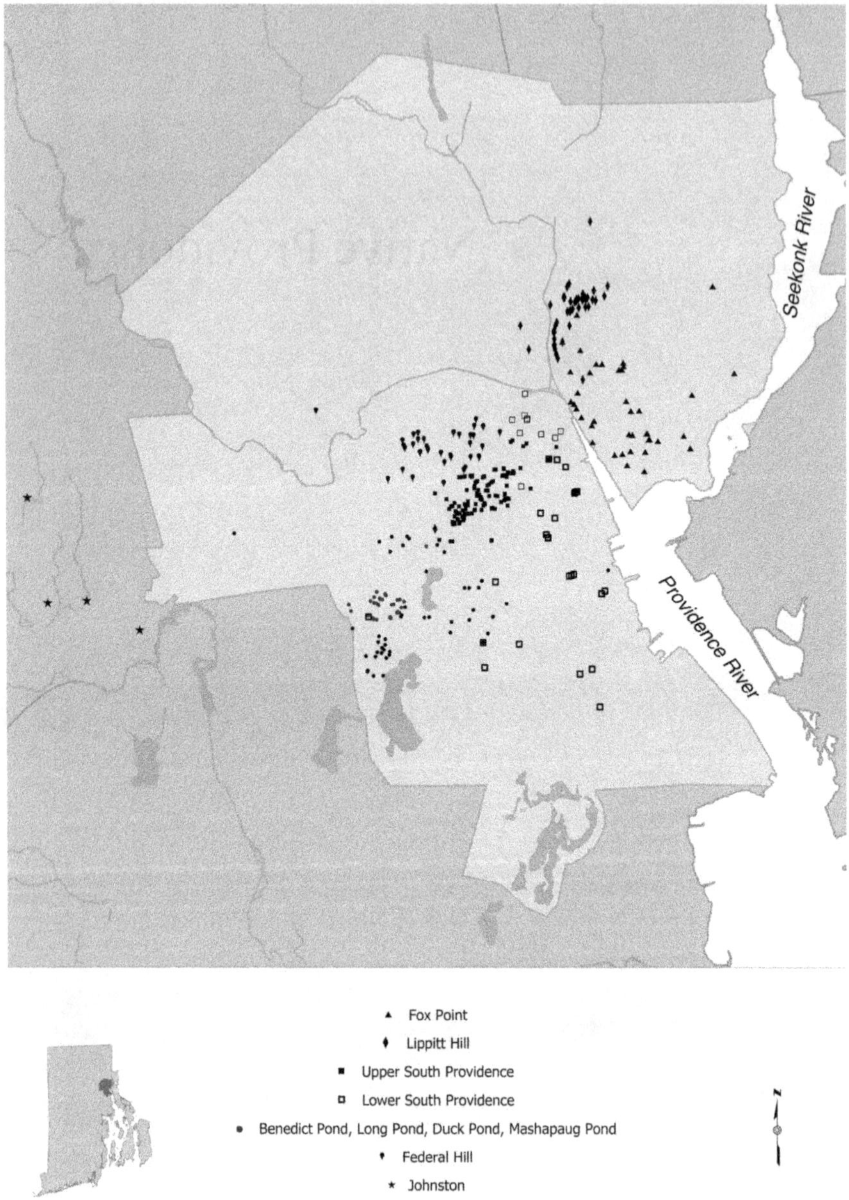

Fig. 1. Map of Native Providence's homelands, showing the locations of households, ca. 1850–1950. Map by Lynn Carlson.

Introduction

Narrating Indigeneity in a "Thoroughfare Town"

"By Golly, 'Twas an Indian" read a headline in the *Providence Evening Bulletin* on March 30, 1943. The article reported that just after daybreak a few days earlier, the public relations officer of Rhode Island's Council of Defense had spotted an Indian wearing beaded trousers and moccasins and carrying a tomahawk on North Main Street. Appearing "out of the blue," the Indian "gravely hodded [sic]" and continued walking. When the officer spoke publicly about the encounter, he was met with "talk of pink elephants and little men in Lincoln green." A high school student cleared his reputation by informing the newspaper that the officer had not seen a ghost, but a real Indian. "The Indian seen coming along North Main Street last Saturday was Chief Sunset on his way to the Rhode Island School of Design's Action Class, where he went through some characteristic motions for the students' benefit." The student said that the chief, whom he illustrated in an accompanying sketch, was "rather old," but still agile enough to do a war dance for the class "complete with war whoops." Chief Sunset was Edward Michael, "one of the six or seven Narragansett Indians left in Rhode Island." Rather than "roaming the woods with a war whoop," he lived at 91 Bates Street, worked in a laundry, and did odd jobs.[1]

Edward Michael was not a phantom, nor did he appear out of the blue. He had lived in Providence for more than fifty years. As an Indian, he was not supposed to be there. Dressed in full regalia and bearing a tomahawk, an artifact that was as much a statement of difference between "savagery" and "civilization" as a disconcerting reminder of adversarial colonial relations, he fulfilled Euro-Americans' broad cultural expectations of what an Indian looked like in a distant past, but clashed with modern surroundings.[2] To make him even more incredible, he was not only an Indian, but "a real Narragansett too." Native people called by that name had been declared extinct in 1880, before Edward Michael resided in Providence. Simply stated, he could not be Indian and modern. To be urban as well was even more incongruous because it confounded expectations about being Indian *and* about cities.

Throughout the Northeast, the most rapidly urbanizing section of the United States by the mid-nineteenth century, urban histories rarely mention living Indians. They appear in the annals written by early European colonists as welcoming the newcomers and enabling their colonial ambitions, and then suddenly disappear as a consequence of disease, war, and what were considered their own moral frailties in metanarratives of their inevitable decline. They occasionally reappear in historical anecdotes and interviews with survivors and as archaeological evidence unearthed during construction as urban development accelerated. They again come into view in accounts of American Indians who moved to U.S. cities after World War II because of the Bureau of Indian Affairs (BIA) relocation program aimed at assimilating them into urban life. Consequently, little can be learned about Indians in northeastern cities from urban histories. They are barely seen and their stories are vastly undertold.

Yet American Indians were undeniably present in northeastern cities, despite what the paucity of research on them would suggest. Cities, as the apexes of physical, social, and cultural transformations set in motion by settler colonialism—a structure premised on indigenous dispossession and its replacement by majority societies of European descent—represent the modernity that indigenous people have been denied.[3] Narrating absence, as the historian Jean O'Brien (White Earth Ojibwe) writes, was an ideological project that formed, limited, and inhibited views of Native people who might have been neighbors, rather than "romanticized constructions of generalized Indians doomed to disappear."[4] As neighbors, they were much more intricately woven into the fabric of cities than modern urban history and local histories have acknowledged. Dispossessed from land that northeastern cities were built on, except for ancestral places that they tenaciously held on to, many carved out new spaces for themselves and their families in the urban landscape. Taking diverse pathways from multiple ancestral homelands, they reconfigured New England Indian Country by extending its social and geographical boundaries beyond reservations or reserves—as the lands set aside for Indians by treaties and provincial laws were called locally—and the countryside. Within cities they created urban homelands, places of long and enduring residence where they were joined to one another through family, work, and a sense of community based on shared experiences, while continuing to be linked to the people and places they had left behind. Urban homelands were not ethnically homogeneous enclaves, but were instead neighborhoods were there was a Native presence, underobserved by history writers and official record keepers, that defied the effacement of Indians from the spaces of lived urban history.

Native Providence is about the lived realities of Native people in Providence during the nineteenth and early twentieth centuries, a time of tumultuous change for southern New England's Native communities. Its main arguments are, first, that there was a viable Native presence in Providence, and second, that a granular approach focused on indigenous lives within particular urban homelands is crucial to comprehending city living. Spatial divisions of cities into neighborhoods are one of the few universals of urban life, from the earliest towns to modern cities, according to the archaeologist Michael E. Smith.[5] Cities are best understood as assemblages of neighborhoods that exist on the ground as well as in collective imaginations. As opposed to constructing an overarching urban narrative, the more modest level of neighborhood analysis provides a lens into the sites of social life, each with its own conditions and individual experiences. *Native Providence* shifts attention to these urban localities and those who inhabit them, without losing sight of the city itself and larger political and economic structures. It weaves the intellectual currency of the spatial turn in the social sciences and humanities—which invokes space as fundamentally interconnected to social and historical phenomena—with the intimacy of anthropology that emphasizes detailed, in-depth accounts of everyday life to illuminate the spatial orders of new and ancestral geographies on the urban landscape.[6]

This book also builds on work by scholars who have begun to write indigenous peoples into urban space and to question cultural expectations in the dominant society about their place in modernity. Whereas the tendency has been to portray Indians in North American cities as post–World War II phenomena, concentrating on problems of homelessness, poverty, alcoholism, and sexual abuse considered rife among "urban Indians," a problematic term in itself, many recent authors take a different stance.[7] Their scholarship historicizes indigenous people's experiences in modern cities, recovers how their labor contributed to town building, and probes how ideological and legal structures responsible for their exclusion from urban histories make Indians living in cities the exceptions rather than the norm. These studies restore Native agency, not just in terms of examining American Indian political activism nurtured in cities, but also by exploring smaller and less overt acts of resistance that indigenous people routinely engaged in against social injustices and rejections.

Additionally, increasing scholarly attention to indigenous transnationalism and cosmopolitanism reveals the various experiences of indigenous people who, under a variety of circumstances, traveled to and resided in London, Paris, Málaga, Tangiers, and other cities of the Atlantic world and Pacific Rim. The urbanization of indigenous people that has long been under way and is accelerating rapidly in the United States and other parts of the settler-colonial world presents compelling reasons for readjusting the lineaments of modernity. Chronicling how indigenous people survived in cities, whether for better or worse, helps us to understand how they made their lives within structural inequalities of racialized and gendered social systems shaped by settler colonialism.[8] A historical perspective adds to the realization that they had agency rather being hopelessly trapped in a world not of their own making, an awareness that increases when studying the particular spaces of indigenous people's urban experiences. *Native Providence* owes an intellectual debt to the authors who have written about Indians living in cities and have more broadly redressed oversights in colonial and academic history, writings that have significant effects on Native people's struggles over land, resources, and basic human rights.[9] Few, however, have focused exclusively on a New England city and the experiences of indigenous people who were omitted from urban narratives even when they were in plain sight. I have attempted to do so in *Native Providence*.[10]

Providence, like many settler-colonial cities in the Northeast and across North America, suffers from historical amnesia about the presence of Indians in the urban landscape. Imagining cities as spaces devoid of indigenous bodies, minds, and histories was as much a part of town building as expropriating indigenous territory, as the historian Coll Thrush notes.[11] Originating as a compact waterfront settlement situated on Native land at the head of Narragansett Bay, Providence experienced unprecedented population growth during the nineteenth century that was fueled by foreign immigration and migration from its surrounding hinterlands. Within the stream of rural migrants leaving the countryside for the city were Native people, whose participation in this diaspora was barely acknowledged. The majority came from Native communities in southern New England whose tribal status was formally terminated from the late 1860s to 1880. Although the procedures for tribal dissolution varied widely, the rationale—mainstream ideas about assimilation and progress—and the end results were identical. Nearly all Native communities in Connecticut, Massachusetts, and Rhode Island lost their tribal status and land base. Having forfeited their communally held land, and facing the uncertainties of U.S. citizenship, many moved to the region's towns and cities to find work and start new lives. Some had already done so decades before their legal status as members of an Indian tribe was taken away and their reserved lands were divided into individual allotments or sold outright.

The number of Native people who moved to Providence from large tribal reservations or those such as the Narragansetts' in Charlestown, Rhode Island, and those of the Mashpees and Gay Head Wampanoags in Massachusetts, is not known with certainty. When proposals for these reservations' termination began to gain strength in the 1860s, their in situ populations were about 300, 400, and 200, respectively.[12] Of the

301 individuals on the 1881 roll of Narragansetts entitled to a share of the purchase money from the sale of the reservation after Rhode Island abolished tribal relations, 45 are identified as Providence residents.[13] The figure is probably low, given that individuals were left off the list, including some who were living in the city at the time of detribalization. Groups with small tribal reservations, such as the Eastern Pequots and the Mashantucket Pequots in the Connecticut towns of North Stonington and Ledyard, the Troy-Watuppas in Fall River, Massachusetts, and the Nipmucs from the Dudley-Webster area of central Massachusetts, as well as those without reservations, had more modest populations, most not exceeding 100 individuals.[14] In the 1861 report on Massachusetts Indians by John Milton Earle, the commonwealth's Indian commissioner, some members of these and other tribal communities are identified as living in Providence.[15] A city of moderate size, Providence had the third-largest urban Indian population in the country by the first decade of the twentieth century after Muscogee, Oklahoma and greater New York City.[16]

Incorporated in 1832, when Andrew Jackson was president of the United States and "Indian" was not a category recognized in the U.S. Census conducted two years earlier, Providence had an indigenous presence that preceded the early nineteenth century.[17] In the rhetoric of Jackson's policy of Indian removal that targeted tribes in the southeastern United States, Indians in the Northeast, whose fate was allegedly sealed at the hands of seventeenth-century European colonists, served as a lesson in historical inevitability, in which "civilization" prevailed over "savagery." Surrounded mostly by whites and deprived of resources, Native peoples of the Northeast were no longer considered a threat to the nation's security or a serious obstruction to its economic advancement. Who could bemoan their demise when prosperous cities and towns buzzing with commerce and industry were replacing the region's primeval forests and woodlands? What Jackson, civic leaders, and the general populace failed to acknowledge was that Indians had inhabited northeastern cities from early colonial times. In Providence, as in other urban localities, their persistence was part of their complicated resistance to colonial erasure.

In the seventeenth century, Roger Williams, who founded Providence, championed religious liberty, was a friend to the Indians, and named Providence in honor of the divine intervention that had guided him and his followers to the spot, added another sobriquet to this indigenous place by calling it a "Thoroughfare Town." It was where colonists, including Williams, entertained Indians who dwelled in and passed through the town.[18] Indians frequently visited Williams, most often the Narragansett sachem Miantonomo, who kept his "barbarous court" at his host's house and took some pleasure in staying with him.[19] An Indian boy, a captive taken in the Pequot War of 1637, lived with Williams as his servant. The boy's father was possibly a sachem from Sasquaukit, an indigenous homeland near modern Fairfield, Connecticut, and his mother and two siblings were among the women and children brought to Boston as human spoils of the war. Williams had requested the child from John Winthrop, the governor of the Massachusetts Bay Colony, writing that he was "Truly thanckful" for "the litle one with the red about his Neck." Williams sent someone to bring the boy to Providence, promised to take good care of him, and asked that he be given a name.[20] That name was Will, a shortened version of Williams. It was by his new name—and not the indigenous name that he had given by his clan in a naming ceremony—that Williams identified him in his letters. It was also by this name that Will might have been known to his new English neighbors, if they chose to refer to him by any name at all.

King Philip's War (1675-76), which Colin Calloway calls the "great watershed" in New England Native and colonial history (an assessment widely shared by tribal communities and within scholarly circles), disrupted the fluid movement of Native people in Providence's congested indigenous landscape.[21] Beginning as a localized uprising against Plymouth Colony led by the Pokanoket-Wampanoag sachem Metacom, also known as King Philip, the conflict escalated into a regional civil struggle that pitted Natives against English colonists and, to a lesser extent, each other. Over the course of fourteen months, the colonists' settlements were destroyed and Native communities decimated in a war that wreaked incalculable losses and whose participants inflicted unimaginable cruelties. On March 29, 1676, less than five months before the war officially ended with the killing of Metacom, Narragansetts and other Indians attacked Providence, then a modest forty-year-old English hamlet where most colonists resided in home lots situated along a single street paralleling the water, and left behind the smoldering remains of houses, barns, and fields. Few houses were spared, with estimates of the number burned ranging from twenty-nine to as many as fifty-four, a figure equivalent to the number of home lots owned by proprietors along the settlement's main street. Although the raid heightened tensions between Providence's English colonists and their Native neighbors and left behind a landscape scarred by war, Indians still hovered in the town and on its outskirts. Starving Native children crossed into the colonists' orchards to find food, and according to legend, one Native woman ventured into a garrison near Providence's western border, where she was given some milk and in return wove a small basket from bark and wool that she presented to her benefactor.[22]

Seeing the destruction of Providence, an angered Williams walked to the edge of town, where he met with Narragansetts to seek answers for what he perceived as their disloyalty. Pointing to his own house, which he had watched burn to the ground, he reminded them and the Cowesetts, Wampanoags, Nipmucs, and Qunticoogs of the Connecticut Valley gathered there that he had "Lodged kindly Some Thousands of You these Ten years." He asked the Narragansett leaders "why they [had] assaulted" the colonists "With burning and Killing who ever were kind Neighbours to them." They answered that the colony had acted hostile and forced them to retaliate, and that "God was [with] them" and had forsaken Providence's townspeople. Williams angrily responded that God had enabled the English to drive the Wampanoags and King Philip out of their country and the Narragansetts out of theirs, and to destroy "Multitudes of them in Fighting and Flying, In Hungr and Cold etc.: and that God would help ... Consume them."[23] Yet despite Williams's claims and predictions, Native peoples had not been completely displaced, nor would they be eradicated from the lands that Providence was built upon.

At the war's end, Indian captives and those who surrendered poured into Providence, creating a refugee crisis of unparalleled proportions for the settler colony. Those both young and old were sold into involuntary servitude within the colony for nine-year terms, and later on a sliding scale in an attempt to regulate their treatment. Under the graduated system, the maximum term of service was for individuals under the age of five, who had to serve until they were thirty; the minimum of seven years was reserved for those thirty and older.[24] The colonists justified limited servitude as a humane compromise compared with enslavement or execution, and rationalized it as equitable retribution for Native people's role in the war, as a means for their redemption, and as a source of much-needed labor for postwar reconstruction. Shares from the sales of Native men, women, and children, paid in specie, wool, Indian corn, clothing, and fatted sheep, went to key colonists who had defended the town during the war. Williams, who had helped to devise and oversee this system of involuntary servitude—which was not binding beyond Rhode Island and kept many displaced Native people in Providence and in the households of its English settler colonists—was among them. Known enemy leaders received harsher treatment. Chuff, a badly wounded Indian, named for his surliness and believed to be a ringleader in the war, was threatened with death at the hands of an angry mob "for his mischiefs to our Howses & Cattell" if authorities did not dole out "Justice against him." A hastily convened court condemned him and he was shot by a firing squad in front of colonists and other Indians standing by, who were awaiting their sentences.[25]

Whether free or unfree, Native people remained a visible presence in Providence. Those who lived independently, both on and off of pockets of ancestral land, adjusted their routines of hunting, fishing, planting, and socializing to a reconstructed and urbanizing landscape. One account reported that there were more of them than colonists on the road leading to Providence from its western borderlands even a quarter century after King Philip's War.[26] Indentured Native servants listed in estate inventories also offer evidence of a continuing indigenous presence. Among these inventories is that of Stephen Hawkings, dated 1711, which mentions "an Indian girle, servant" and "some small bedding for ye Indian" along with cows, yearlings, a mare, sheep and young lambs, four small swine, a Bible, and other possessions.[27] Although the circumstances that led to this individual's servitude are unknown, many Native children were bound out to serve pauper apprenticeships or were abandoned as foundlings on the doorsteps of the colonists' homes because of their families' economic hardships resulting from debt and land loss. In some cases Native women who were indentured servants gave birth in the colonist households in which they worked, and their children would inherit their status. From a young age these Native children would assist with menial chores and run errands, much like Williams's Pequot servant, Will, but not necessarily with assurances that they would be treated decently or be taught skills that would help them survive in a colonized world.

Hannah [Tuntiachchee], the favorite child of a widow living in Providence, who was "placed and bound" to Martha Sheldon, also a resident of the town, to perform household work in the best manner that she could, according to a document in the Providence Town Papers. She was to be instructed in English domestic practices and given linen undergarments, woolen hose, shoes, and other apparel suitable for work days and holidays that she could take with her when she turned eighteen and her indenture ended.[28] All these provisions were promises that Hannah would be prepared to reenter town life outside the boundaries of her confinement. In another case Job Taubabwahhoman was bound out at the age of six to Peter Burlingame of Providence, who promised to teach him English husbandry.[29] Whether identified as servants or by some uncertain designation, the lives of indigenous children, women, and men unfolded in close proximity to Providence's Euro-American settler colonists, with whom they shared their kitchens, garrets, and backlots, or whom they passed on the town's streets.[30]

The shared landscape did not mean that Native people were welcomed in Providence, even if they provided much-needed labor in rebuilding the town. Eighteenth-century town records indicate that in attempts to curtail their access to the townscape and its resources, some were warned out. Many of the unwanted were unmarried women with young children. Some ordered to leave Providence were cited for negligence in fulfilling their duties or improper conduct in the households where they worked. Their failure to comply with orders to leave resulted in forced removal, because local officials considered the poor and transient a potential economic burden on the town and a risk to the moral and social order. Still, many of the banished returned. Sarah Gardner, an "Indian woman," defied the authorities' orders for twenty years and kept returning to Providence, where some of her children were bound out as servants. Other individuals accused of transgressions, whose stories can be traced from available evidence, returned again and again because of family connections, job opportunities for their children, and the support offered by a growing community of free people of color. Faced with dismal prospects for their own survival and their children's future, they showed staunch perseverance that enabled them to carve out lives for themselves and their families in a town that, though an Indian place, did not necessarily want them.[31]

The social tensions simmering under the surface in this thoroughfare town come to light again in the diary of a white woman from Philadelphia, Susanna Lear, who visited Providence in 1788. She reported that an "Indian Chief" rode in a carriage from Boston with her and her traveling companion, Mary Woodrow Binney, the sister-in-law of Avis Binney Brown, the wife of Nicholas Brown, her host in Providence. She wrote that she first felt very much afraid of him but admitted that he turned out to be "the most agreeable company." The unnamed "Indian Chief," who entertained his traveling companions with his clarinet, anecdotes of France, where he received a Western liberal education at the expense of the Marquis de Lafayette, and accounts of "the manners and customs of his own nation" was Peter Otsiquette, an Oneida. The return of Otsiquette, who spoke fluent English and French, made news when he arrived in Boston. Yet he was left alone when the two women got out of the coach. Described as being forlorn that he was not included in their plans, he sent a note about an hour later saying how much he wished to see them again. They responded with an invitation to dine with them at the Browns' home on Benefit Street. The "Prince" arrived dressed in a scarlet coat trimmed with gold lace and "really made a very good figure."

Introduction 11

At their host's request, he danced a cotillion with Lear after dinner. Lear remarked that his dancing was "by far the best of any person" she had seen attempt the cotillion's intricate steps and changes—though his "War dance" drew far less praise. The festivities continued into the evening at another house, where the "Prince" was called upon to perform the war dance, and resumed a few days later at a party out of town. Entries in the diary suggest that Lear was infatuated with the person she referred to only as the Indian chief, as were other ladies who, she claimed, were "all in love with him" and vying for his attention. But she wrote that she was the one he complimented, called on "three or four times a day," and asked for "her name on paper"—a memento he assured her he "would not part with while he lived." Soon after these encounters Lear returned to Philadelphia. She married about two weeks later, though there is no mention of her betrothal in her diary.[32]

The "Indian Chief" was in an unexpected place, where his presence seemed strange as well as frightening to Euro-Americans, and his urbanity confounded their expectations. They were unprepared for an Indian to be educated, talented, and charming. Nor did Lear and the other ladies expect to be attracted to him. His so-called war dance "was very terrible" because it did not mesh with the surroundings and because it was considered impossible that an Indian could execute both the movements of a cotillion and a Native dance. Asked to perform the war dance a second time to convince the party-goers that someone like him could know such a dance, regardless of the degree to which it conformed to age-old customs, he complied, perhaps because he too had something to prove. Initially excluded from the plans of his fellow travelers, he reinserted himself in their lives, confronting their racial anxieties and the asymmetries defining social relations between Native Americans and whites by challenging their expectations that he could not be Indian and modern.

Native Providence picks up the story of Native Americans after the city received its charter. In the decade before the turn of the nineteenth century Providence was a small town with fewer than 6,400 residents, of whom about 476 were minorities. By the time of its incorporation the population was 17,000. The number of free and enslaved people of color, which included persons of Native descent, had grown to 1,214. When figures compiled from the 1910 U.S. Census ranked Providence as "one of the chief Indian residential cities in the United States," it had 173 Indian residents, compared with the 25 recorded in the previous decennial census. Boston, which counted 51 Indians in its population, came in a distant second among New England cities. The *Providence Journal*, which reported these figures, stated they were unreliable, citing the tendency of "mulattoes with straight hair to call themselves half-breed Indians" and the willingness of census takers in most cases to record them as such. Besides, it was "well known locally that the Narragansett Indians of Washington county have largely intermarried with negroes." Two such individuals, erroneously identified as Indians in the 1900 U.S. Census, were counted in Westerly, a small, citified hub near Charlestown, "which was never a Narragansett Indian town," an opinion hardly shared by Native families living there.[33] The higher number of Indians in Providence, though a relatively small portion of its population, was questioned. How could the city possibly have the third-largest Indian population in the United States when New England Indians were extinct? How could they be Indians if they had intermarried with neighbors of different ethnicities, or if they were "straight-haired mulattoes of mixed white and negro blood"?[34] Although censuses do not provide exact population counts, and their racial classifications were subject to the vicissitudes of recognition and preconceptions about Indianness, the equally disturbing subtext in these comments concerns the presence of Indians in New England's cities. These were places where they were not supposed to be, let alone in numbers at odds with historical understandings of Providence and the Native Northeast. If urban indigeneity was an anomalous condition, as the Dakota scholar Philip J. Deloria reasons in his influential book *Indians in Unexpected Places*, then why were there significant numbers of Indians in Providence as well as other U.S. cities?[35] Their presence and its historicity as exceptional require further scrutiny.

That censuses provide limited and not entirely dependable records of Native Providence cannot be disputed. Many scholars agree that they missed or misrepresented Native people. Indians generally mistrust them because, historically, they typically accrued few benefits from being counted. Shaped by the politics of legibility that set the boundaries of classification within predefined identities, censuses often hid Native people beneath other racial labels. Well into the twentieth century, racial categorization depended more on the judgment and perception of enumerators and less on self-identification, and this was especially true for Native people who lived outside of tribal communities or who resided in multiracial households or in locations thought to be predominantly white.[36] Thus, residents of Native ancestry and cultural identity whose physical appearance baffled non-Native recorders might have been overlooked as Indian more often than they were counted. Issues of underrepresentation and misrepresentation aside, however, censuses cannot be dismissed. Similar to other textual sources, they are a key part of the history of colonialism, and one of its consequences.[37] Used critically and responsibly, these lists, along with accompanying records of other information such as nativity, occupation, and residence, as well as marginal comments jotted down by enumerators, are invaluable to unraveling complicated stories that are about much more than statistics.

These are stories about place and about how Native peoples' lives were entwined with specific locales in the urban landscape. These are stories about urban homelands that for many Indians during the nineteenth and early twentieth centuries became their home away from their reservations and traditional ancestral lands. *Native Providence* examines these social and cultural landscapes on the premise that Providence was not simply a thoroughfare town of Native sojourners, but a place where Indians of different tribal affiliations lived, worked, and socialized. The city was built on indigenous land, and the physical and material remains, legends, and place-names of Indians intruded into the present despite being increasingly masked by cadastral erasure and urban development. These were reminders of the city's indigenous pedigree that settler colonialism attempted to replace and sometimes strategically recruited, while living Native people fared much worse. They were ignored in civic and social histories of Providence and often miscast in official documents that refused to recognize that Indians were enmeshed in the urban landscape, even as they struggled to create what Gerald Vizenor (Anishinaabe) characterizes as "an active presence over absence, deracination, and oblivion."[38] The urban chapters of their survivance, to use his term, are a continuation of their complicated stories of resistance and accommodation, rather than the conclusion of a colonialist narrative about their inevitable decline, assimilation, and disappearance. Providence, like other cities in the United States, was not a last stand for Indians any more than reservations marked the final possibility of social, cultural, and political homelands for them.[39] Native people inscribed these spaces as indigenous in as many ways as possible, but in a modern city this might not have been obvious because the houses they rented or purchased were not of their design and the mass-produced goods they used made the materiality of their households similar to that of their non-Native neighbors of comparable means.

The existence of Providence's Native homelands contradicts assumptions about how Indians dwelled in urban space, if at all. Living off of reservations and drastically reduced tribal land bases, places where they were expected to be, they had increasingly become "scattered to the winds of heaven."[40] Within cities, among the least-expected places to find Native people in the decades around the turn of the twentieth century, their manner of dwelling was also thought to be dispersed and random, lacking spatial coherence with ancestral, mythic, or sacred landscapes. *Native Providence* argues that this was not the case. Inscribed into this urban landscape were discrete concentrations of Native people who made Providence their home, and places where their presence was continuing and their attachments were deep. Recovering these homelands is easily thwarted by preconceptions about the ruptures to Native life in cities that suggest casual rather than stable residence. Such perceived chaos stems from early European settler colonists' assessment of how lightly indigenous people dwelled on the land—a view that would be invoked repeatedly over the centuries to dismiss Native presence and claims to localities. Deemed newly arrived mid-twentieth-century migrants, isolated survivors of displaced peoples, or travelers who performed their

Indianness in theaters, armories, and drawing rooms, living Indians were typically depicted as unanchored in urban space. The difficulty of discerning their urban homelands is compounded by patchy information in public records in which identity, as discussed, is calculated by phenotype. Although tribal members tended to marry within their own group or with members of another tribe, considerable numbers married individuals of other ethnicities, many of them African Americans, and had children whose ancestry confused the presumptions of outsiders. From the perspective of critical race theory, racial ascriptions imposed by institutional structures have profound consequences for how indigenous histories are perceived. With household members classified as mulatto, Black, colored (an unspecific identifier used in opposition to both "white" and a specific tribal identity), or occasionally as white, Native homes might have been unrecognized and undercounted. Even non-Native residents of the city who might have acknowledged that some of their neighbors were Indians might also have doubted those neighbors' authenticity.

Recovering Native histories in fine-grained urban spaces requires a multifaceted approach that draws on a wide assortment of historical records and values a variety of epistemologies, as advocated in calls for decolonizing research practices.[41] Each record and way of knowing offers a pathway to retranslating Native people's lives that is rarely straightforward and can lead to dead ends as well as new routes of inquiry. Principal archives that hold Rhode Island's reports on the Narragansett Indians, histories of the colony and municipality, early town papers, court documents, military lists, maritime logs, U.S. custom house records, newspapers, and maps have been important to my research. Their holdings of vital records, wills, probates, petitions, deeds, city directories, and the occasional diary, as well as state censuses, have been especially valuable in identifying Native people, culling information about their lives, and locating where they lived. So have institutions with less comprehensive collections, such as town libraries, local historical societies, tribal and anthropological museums, and state and municipal agencies that are off the beaten track of most research itineraries. Their underexamined scrapbooks, newspaper clippings, accession records, technical reports, and in some cases cardboard boxes stuffed with unsorted announcements, programs, letters, and other miscellaneous ephemera that at times seemed hardly worth sifting through offered crucial insights. During countless hours spent at these less well-recognized archives, the eloquent words of the anthropologist Michel-Rolph Trouillot kept me going. He writes of the need to study not just orthodox sources or accounts of professional historians but also those "of artisans of different kinds, [and of] unpaid or unrecognized field laborers who augment, deflect, or reorganize" the former's work.[42] Almost as daunting in their sparseness as mainstream archives were in their scope, these other archives accentuated the unequal distribution of archival power that has undergirded the separation of indigenous people from modern urban history.

Stories and family albums that Native descendants generously shared with me were also significant in decentering assumptions that Native people were absent in nineteenth- and early twentieth-century Providence. Their stories, as the anthropologist William Simmons faithfully reported in his pathbreaking book *Spirit of the New England Tribes*, offer their own perspectives on what was *and* is meaningful in their lives, compensating for silences in the colonizers' written accounts and the terseness of their statistical reports. Common tropes running through the stories passed down from generation to generation, and from country people to city folk, undermine claims of vanishing Indians and forgotten cultural knowledge by revealing Native people's understandings of landscapes that had become crowded with strangers and new buildings.[43] Other collections of transcribed oral histories and the extraordinarily rich literary traditions of New England's indigenous peoples also furnish compelling evidence supporting this contention.[44] So do stories that I have heard New England Native people recount at public events, or that they have disclosed in intermittent conversations. Photographs that I have been privileged to see show family members dressed in Native regalia and in ordinary or formal contemporary clothing, as well as in candid and staged shots. These black-and-white prints and faded reproductions of newsprint gave me an intimate window into the subjects' lived experiences, their family values, and their engagement with the modern world. They evoke personal and family histories and connections to urban spaces, although, as is typical of old photos, not everyone in them could be identified. These photographs and stories provided insights that otherwise would not have been attainable and led me to push the research in directions I would not have thought possible.

This book's attention to Native people's lived experiences within the specific spatial contours of the urban landscape could not have been written without visiting the sites of these homelands. Elizabeth Fenn, the Pulitzer Prize–winning author of *Encounters at the Heart of the World: A History of the Mandan People*, wondered how she could write about a place that she had not seen, a problem that she remedied by visiting North Dakota to get a sense of what the Mandan homeland might have been like centuries ago when it was the center of Native life on the plains of midcontinental North America.[45] For anthropologists, venturing outside of the archive is typical. Visiting places that have been prodigiously written about or mentioned in lone archival fragments is crucial to anthropologists' understanding of history, as it increasingly is for many historians. Encounters with the local reveal textures of place that might not be recorded in documents—especially when these spaces have been re-envisioned or repurposed. As Keith Basso writes in *Wisdom Sits in Places*, by visiting places, researchers can discern much about them that they would not glean from other kinds of research. Traveling to hundreds of named localities in the Cibecue region of Arizona with White Mountain Apache consultants as his guides, Basso learned that places are inseparably conjoined with history and identity. Place-making, as he writes, is a way of constructing the past—of altering and recasting historical understandings—even in societies without the professional services of revisionary historians.[46] Visiting places I had only read about in documents, heard about in oral histories, or seen in old photographs was an essential part of my research.

These site visits included many different places in the Native history of Providence: houses, schools, churches, cemeteries, a park, a town square, a railroad station, a livery stable, a pond, a quarry, and the streets themselves. Docks and coal yards, meeting halls, hospitals, old-age homes, and prisons also can be counted among the imbricated places in the city's indigenous history, though I did not visit them as part of my research. Given my interest in urban homelands, the core of Native life within the city, I attempted to visit as many houses as I could. I walked or drove down the city's streets looking for the addresses that I had identified as homes of Native people, pausing long enough to take in the streetscapes and imagine what they might have been like during the nineteenth and early twentieth centuries. Some houses were still standing and seemed to be relatively unaltered on the outside. Others had been or were in the process of being remodeled. A few were boarded up. Many had been replaced by parking lots, housing complexes, and industrial parks. Some neighborhoods had been cut off by the freeway more than a half century ago, and in some houses and churches had been demolished to make way for a new high school, a concrete testament to high modernism that is today as much a canvas for graffiti as it is a center for secondary education. On a small traffic triangle on Providence's west side where I had expected to find a monument to Canonicus, a seventeenth-century sachem who once ruled by consensus over Providence, there was nothing but a shadow of its plinth. My search for this imposing boulder was as futile here as it had been when I visited its original location in North Burial Ground on the city's east side. Crisscrossing downtown streets, I looked for the church where William Apess (Pequot), a writer and activist, preached in the nineteenth century, only to discover a vacant lot.

On other occasions, I visited Providence's westernmost homelands on road trips that took me out of my urban comfort zone. Pulling into a parking area behind a shopping strip, I found a pond whose shores were known to have been the site of a flourishing indigenous neighborhood. Now, signage written in different languages warned against fishing in polluted waters that belied the pond's rich yet turbulent history. I drove six or seven miles from downtown Providence to visit indigenous landmarks in the city's most distant Native homeland. An ancient quarry, or what was left of it, situated between commercial buildings and a state highway and barely protected by a chain-link fence, had fiercely survived. Farther away was a gathering spot that had been the setting for powwows in the early decades of the twentieth century. As at most Native stomp grounds, there were no visible remains that called attention to the dancing, feasting, and displays of cultural skill that had drawn indigenous people from the city's other homelands here, year after year, to meet up with neighbors they might not have seen that often.

After several unsuccessful attempts, I also managed to visit the much-storied rock across from the site of the powwows that defined the northwestern limits of early colonial Providence, thanks to the current landowner, who had cleared its surroundings of impenetrable brush and poison ivy. A short distance away, I hiked up to the summit of Neutaconkanut Hill, where I stopped to take in its commanding view of the city. The uplands' deep ravines, bubbling springs, and stalwart rock outcrops that some believe were linked into regional ceremonial landscapes were reminders of an earlier indigenous Providence, and also of a past that yielded to a present in which Native people persisted, negotiated their identities, and believed in future possibilities.

Toggling between archival and oral evidence helped me uncover the lived experiences of Native people that have remained elusive in urban narratives of Providence and in the colonial histories of the indigenous Northeast. The on-the-ground evidence added another vantage to the research, bringing to light how indigenous homelands have been eradicated in processes of spatial erasure that have persisted long after the expropriation of land for early town building. I had no illusions that the city's nineteenth- and early twentieth-century indigenous homelands would be intact and their buildings unchanged. Landscapes, urban or otherwise, are always in flux. Examining redevelopment plans alone was inadequate for assessing the nature of destruction, and for gauging the ongoing and often equally violent physical and environmental transformations unrecorded in written documents. As continuing structures of settler colonialism, cities compromise and destroy places of indigenous habitation and memory, though these outcomes are typically not spoken about in discussions of the racialization of urban geographies and its impact on communities of color.[47] The "narrative estrangement" of indigenous people from modernity made them the invisible victims of the processes of later urban development.[48] Assumed to have been dispossessed, with their lands confiscated in the initial stages of settler colonialism, they were thought to have been spared from further colonialist insults. Yet they were still there, and the urban places where they lived continued to be invaded, though the tactics varied. Seeing what had been done to their city homelands by urban renewal projects, highway construction, and environmental pollution provided glimpses of the degree to which the spaces of indigenous peoples' lives in Providence had been unalterably changed and their histories of place revised.

Although contested and racialized urban geographies in relation to Native peoples in the present is an important topic that demands attention, I argue that coming to terms with the human impacts stemming from the intersection of race, place, and power is not just a problem germane to struggles of the twenty-first century. In Providence land clearance projects not only began early but also occurred often. Dozens of houses that were home to Providence's Native people and other marginalized peoples were torn down in race riots at the town's north end that ushered in a new era of municipal order in the 1830s. Forty years later, nearly 150 houses in a waterfront neighborhood were razed because of mounting fears that living conditions there created a perfect environment for the spread of cholera. Many of the city's ponds, which were attractive settlement, fishing, and gathering places for Indians going back thousands of years, lost much of their ecological vitality as a consequence of industrial pollution and began to be filled in by the city during the late nineteenth century to make way for more urban real estate. Although they were no longer viable fishing and collecting places where Native people could supplement their livelihood or follow age-old routines that kept them close to the land, these once watery spaces continued to be locales where they lived, regardless of the degree to which new regimes of power and shifting priorities had changed them. All of these civic-engineering projects occurred before the middle decades of the twentieth century, when urban renewal reached a feverish peak and resulted in an unprecedented wave of destruction that demolished large sections of the city that housed its Native population, displacing many families. As late as the 1960s, there were no historical preservation laws mandating cultural-impact assessments and archaeological investigations that might have led to the recovery of tangible evidence of these neighborhoods' material and architectural histories.

To paraphrase the title of Eric Wolf's epic *Europe and the People without History*, the people of Providence's Native homelands were people without urban history.[49] They did not exist because they did not appear in written histories of the city and could not be found in official records. Regrettably, the houses of the city's most vulnerable, erased by the visions of urban developers, planners, and engineers, were not considered to have been places where Native people lived. These assumptions are a manifestation of policies and practices of settler colonialism that persisted long after early colonizers mapped finely drawn boundaries onto expropriated Native territory and built towns in which indigenous people were considered to be out of place. The spatial erasure caused by urban development reinforces the need to map Native homelands and redeem the stories of the indigenous people who lived in these places. I have attempted to do this for Providence.

Native Providence is not a history of the city that merely includes Indians. Nor is it an attempt to retrieve how these lands were known to indigenous peoples who lived there when English settler colonists arrived, assuming that layers of history could be peeled back to reveal a pristine landscape. Instead, it tells Native-centered stories of discrete urban locales, what I call urban homelands, in nineteenth- and early twentieth-century Providence. As a place-based study of Native peoples' experiences, the book gives significant attention to the diverse pathways that brought individuals and families to Providence and sometimes back to their rural hometowns and tribal reservations, contra the opinion that relocation eroded connections to outlying communities. Rather than tracing regional networks or totalizing the experiences of city-living Indians, *Native Providence* concentrates on the local and small scale and on collective and individual experiences, on the understanding that settler colonialism and its attendant effects, couched in progress and urbanism, can be gauged most immediately at these analytical levels. Its character-rich, place-based studies foreground ordinary people rather than highly visible Indian diplomats, war chiefs, star athletes, or performers, though some Native people of the city's homelands gained national and international recognition in sports and the arts. Others were well known in their local neighborhoods because of their street presence and willingness to talk to anyone who would listen, much like individuals whom Jane Jacobs describes as public characters in *The Death and Life of Great American Cities*.[50] I take the position that all Native lives matter—and that those of Natives in nineteenth-century New England, "a people pitied or despised if they were noticed at all," as Barry O'Connell remarks, deserve special attention, as do New England Natives in the early twentieth century.[51] To write about them is to value them, however difficult this task might be. Constructing detailed accounts that bring forth their experiences and render emotions palpable, while attending to the empirical, results in counternarratives that disturb and dislocate the discourses in urban histories and expose the complexities and contradictions in statistical reports—neither of which communicates all that was important to Native people. Although extracting meaning and emotion from documents, at least the majority of them, is an endeavor fraught with enormous challenges, the names of indigenous people, even the most marginalized and seemingly inconsequential, are often knowable. So are the stories of their struggles, resistances, and hopes that are etched into the spaces that they created for themselves on the urban landscape. Character-rich, semi-biographical studies embedded into landscapes of everyday life, as other scholars have argued, are preferable to representations of social worlds that tend to render indigenous people anonymous, faceless, and passive.[52]

This book is organized around maps of Native Providence. Each chapter focuses on a particular neighborhood enclave or urban homeland where Native people lived, on the reasoning that human beings dwell in place-worlds defined by some limited stretch of space. In cities social life occurs mostly within neighborhoods, where people live, work, move to, and visit. They are the primary locales of Native people's experience in a city and the sites of their most intimate, day-to-day encounters. The very existence of these homelands, each with its own spatial and social history, illustrates how Native people were entwined in urban life. Each chapter showcases a subset of the individuals and families who made these places their home, to provide evidence of their presence in Providence and, especially within specific localities, to challenge the prevailing idea that Native people, if they were in cities at all, were either haphazardly distributed across the urban landscape or "unhoused."[53] Some individuals are discussed in more than one chapter because they moved across the lived and perceived borders of these homelands. Each chapter also comments on Indian places that antedate European colonial settlement and urbanization and their material traces that accidentally intrude on or coexist in the urban landscape, and on transformations wrought by urban renewal and landfilling projects. *Native Providence* is about the indigenous people whose lived experiences within these spaces in the city mattered deeply to their individual and collective histories and to the history of the city.

The chapters, arranged around place rather than chronologically, span the geography of Providence, which remained relatively stable, give or take changes in municipal jurisdiction, during the study period. They cover swaths of time corresponding to the indigenous histories of particular homelands during the nineteenth and early twentieth centuries that are shaped by lived realities and the evidentiary trail. Consequently, some narratives unfold in the nineteenth century and others in the early twentieth, without narrowly conforming to a linear chronology. Building on this spatial scaffolding, the chapters explore Native enclaves on the east side of Providence that the Narragansetts referred to as Moshassuck and that English colonists renamed "The Neck"; on the west or "Weybosset" side, a transliteration of the indigenous place-name Wapauysett; and in the hilly upland farther out that formerly defined the city's limits.

Key patterns emerge from the stories of the indigenous, men, women, and children told in this book. Most were full-time and long-term residents who had made place-shifting journeys from their tribal reservations or off-reservation homes, but others had deeper roots in this reimagined indigenous place. Although they had a wide diversity of individual experiences, Native people found each other. Whether along the waterfront or train tracks, at busy intersections, near ponds, amid factory complexes, or on narrow side streets not far from the residences of the city's leading political, business, and social figures, they lived close to family members. Extended kin typically occupied the same house or apartment or were nearby neighbors, as were other Indians. They mostly rented, though some owned their own homes. Some renters moved frequently, if only within a few blocks. Others remained at the same address for years or even decades, as did some homeowners, indicating a high degree of residential stability not generally associated with Indians living in cities. Some Native households were neighborhood hubs that seemed to have had special significance in community networks.[54] Neighborhood churches were also gathering places, as were Providence's meeting halls, museums, monuments, and powwow grounds.

Not only were family ties sustained in transit to and within the city, but many Native residents also maintained relationships with communities residing on tribal reservations or in off-reservation enclaves. On visits they carried news back and forth between Providence and these communities. Some returned to their former reservations when the disappointments of urban life became intolerable, only to move back to the city later because the economic opportunities there were better or because their ties to the urban Indian community were as strong or maybe stronger than their ties to former reservations and other enclaves. Others left the city for the countryside, never to return on a permanent basis. Although the attitudes of Native residents toward Providence are thinly documented in written records, except for the occasional diary, memoir, or transcribed testimony, the choices they made about where to live in the city, their decisions to return after having left willingly or unwillingly, and their interactions with each other and with non-Natives speak volumes about being indigenous in Providence. In instances when their voices can be heard, they comment on the city's sights and sounds, which some considered more comforting than the desolation they felt in the countryside. Others found contentment in pockets of the city that seemed more rural. Those who left Providence to escape discrimination and the demeaning jobs they were obliged to take expressed feelings of loneliness when they found themselves in far-flung places. The city's Native homelands tugged at them, even while a sense of community transcended the city and other terrains of indigenous life. Home and away, rural and urban were not binary positions but were what James Clifford characterizes as articulated sites of indigeneity, a nonreductive way of thinking about the diversity of indigenous cultures and histories.[55] Providence's Native homelands, though not acknowledged to have been part of its increasingly diverse cultural mosaic, were as much sites of indigenous resistance and survival as other places where indigenous people persisted.

Long after Miantonomo and "his barbarous court," Will, Hannah Tuntiachchee, Sarah Gardner, and a Mohawk chief were Indians on the streets of Providence, others lived on in the city. Edward Michael, Chief Sunset, was just one of them. I have assembled the stories of their lives and experiences within the city's homelands. These place-based stories of Native Providence suggest that other North American cities have untold indigenous histories of recent times, as do cities across the settler-colonial world. I suspect that these are neither short creation tales about early indigenous-European encounters paving the way for urban development, nor narratives of merely the post–World War II decades. Rather, they are undoubtedly longer and more complicated epics about ongoing colonialism in which Native peoples were not merely "friend Indians" or enemies, nor the downtrodden or the pathologized, as they were later depicted, but were neighbors, coworkers, and fellow congregants who actively engaged in modernity. Indigenizing urban histories requires more than references to indigenous place-names, archaeological traces of deep pasts, and public displays of regalia, as important as these are as reminders of a Native presence in settler-colonial cities. Stories of urban homelands told through the lens of the creative, difficult, and successful adjustments that Native people made to city living forefront their experiences in urban histories. There are undoubtedly stories of Providence's Native homelands that remain to be told, individuals I missed in various archives, and interpretive uncertainties in the cultural translations of past lives that I have sketched. At the heart of *Native Providence* is a humanistic understanding of place that situates indigenous men, women, and children within a modern city. The homelands in which they dwelled in the city were crucial to how they experienced city life, celebrated milestones, reckoned with loss and disillusionment, and plotted their future.

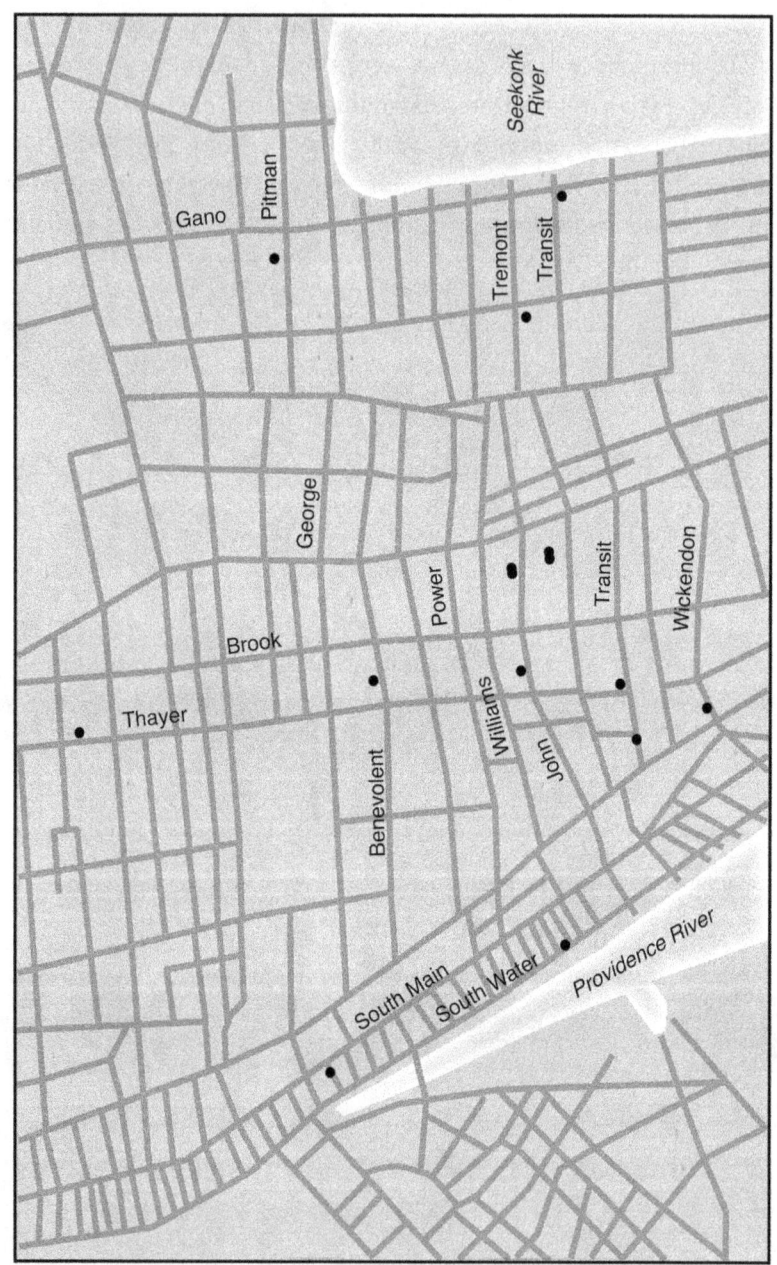

Fig. 2. Map of the Fox Point homeland, showing the locations of selected Native households. Map by Lynn Carlson.

Fox Point 1

*A Waterfront Homeland, Encounters at a
Stopping-Over Place, and Indigenous Legibility*

Situated at the southernmost tip of the land lying between the Providence and Seekonk Rivers, Fox Point figures prominently in the city's creation story. It was there, in the late spring or early summer of 1636, that Roger Williams and his companions came ashore in search of a permanent resting place after leaving Massachusetts and a temporary home they had made on the easterly shore of the Seekonk River.[1] In the iconic founding story they crossed the Seekonk and landed at a craggy spot, later called Slate Rock, where Natives shouted, "What cheer, Neetop?" These words, echoing across nearly four centuries, have been interpreted as ones of welcome. From this sanctified rock, buried deeply under sand and gravel in alterations to the Providence shoreline in 1828 and almost completely destroyed by a blast of dynamite in 1877 meant to salvage it from the depths of invisibility, the colonizers proceeded around the headland known as Tuncowoden, the indigenous name for a steep hill "shaped like a pounding mortar."[2] Sailing west past low bluffs to Foxes Hill, later obliterated by development projects that re-envisioned the city's waterfront and infrastructure, they entered the Moshassuck River.[3] At a freshwater spring on the east side of "this broad and beautiful sheet of water, skirted by a dense forest," they decided to stop and settle in. The lands upon which they built their settler colony, which Williams named Providence, had come highly recommended by governors John Winthrop of the Massachusetts Bay Colony and Edward Winslow of Plymouth for its "Freedome and Vacancie."[4]

In Providence's settler creation story, Fox Point was passed over for a location a mile or two to the north of where Williams and his followers first stepped onto indigenous land. The reasons why they decided to sail around Tuncowoden and Foxes Hill and up the Moshassuck River are unknown. Advised to abandon an earlier settlement in Seekonk because it was within the jurisdiction of Plymouth Colony, where Williams would have risked deportation, Fox Point, just across the geopolitical border of Narragansett territory, possibly did not seem secure enough. Rumors, illness, and the sheer exhaustion of being homeless might have influenced the decision to push ahead a little bit farther around Foxes Hill to a more sheltered location. The content of the conversation between colonizers and Narragansetts at the landing spot, conducted no doubt in awkward pidgin phrases and animated gestures, is not preserved in surviving records. Nevertheless, one could guess that it contained messages from Native interlocutors that this territory was not vacant land, contrary to the advice that Williams had received from his councilors. Neither an uninhabited wilderness nor a recently emptied-out space, this indigenous landscape was a place-world mapped precisely with knowledge about the specificity of indigenous traditions of past events and current practices.[5] Far from being an unoccupied and undifferentiated territory, particular locations would have been filled with Native people's stories about historical incidents and their present circumstances in an increasingly colonialized world. What the colonizers comprehended and what their settler creation story implies without revealing salient details is that the Narragansetts, on the advice of their chief sachems, Canonicus and Miantonomo, directed Williams and his party to venture beyond Tuncowoden to find a place to stay. They interpreted these instructions as verbally conveying to them rights to the lands of Providence that they later formally secured with a deed (fig. 3).

The area that became known as Fox Point was not just a stopping-over place for Native people. It lies between the headwaters of two rivers, and its once numerous streams frequented by runs of trout and salmon, a thick mantle of trees and dense underbrush, and swamps filled with diverse fauna and flora made it an attractive settlement place.[6] It was also a gateway where Natives traveling from nearby and distant homelands came to trade, lingered, and sometimes stayed, temporarily or permanently. Archaeological evidence of Native occupation from before and around

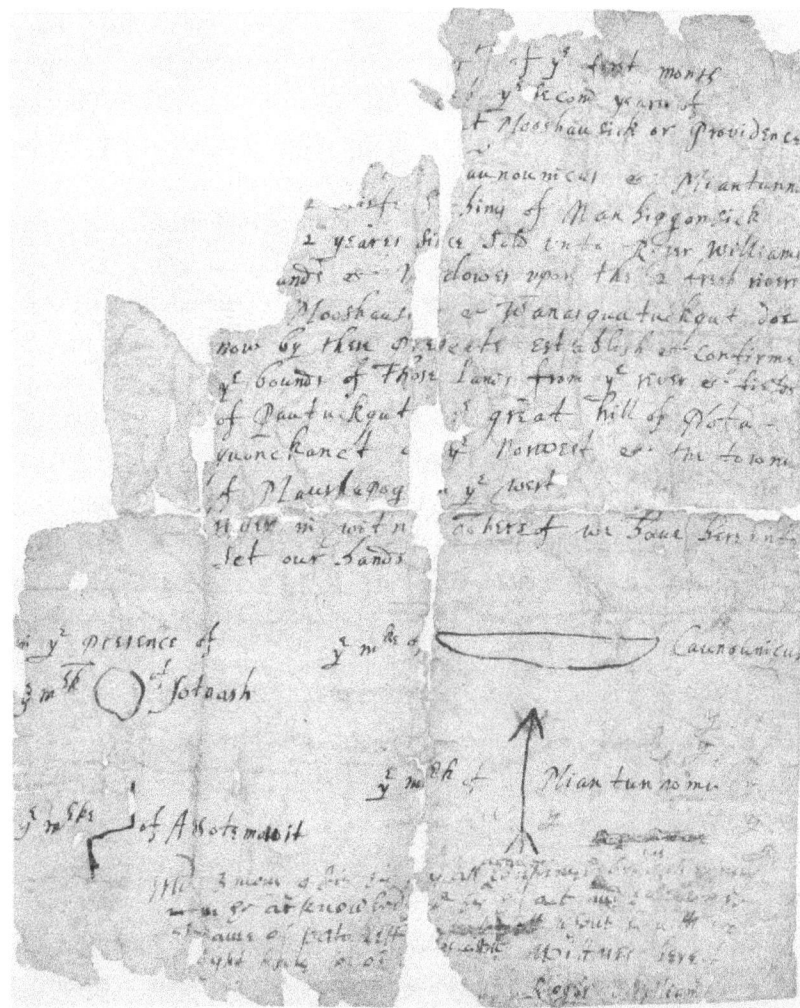

Fig. 3. The 1638 deed to Providence confirming earlier agreements between Canonicus, Miantonomo, and Roger Williams about land ownership and use rights. Courtesy of the Providence City Archives.

the time of European arrival provides tantalizing clues of "taskscapes"—places where Native people lived, hunted, fished, collected plants and raw materials, and interred and remembered the dead.[7] A fragment of a pestle, bifacial tools, an arrowhead, and deer bones excavated in the early 1890s on Pitman Street, not far from the Seekonk River, are cases

Fox Point 31

in point. At the intersection of Brook and George Streets archaeologists found traces of a small campsite beneath the pavement of a parking lot in exploratory investigations prior to the construction of a new building on the Brown University campus in the 1980s. The encampment was probably one of many that would have been left behind by Native people who stopped along this ancient stream running under the aptly named Brook Street or along others that also flowed into Narragansett Bay and the open ocean beyond. Near the southern end of Benefit Street, not far from Foxes Hill, a human burial was exhumed in a cellar hole sometime during the mid-nineteenth century. Reported by Dr. Usher Parsons, a physician, antiquarian, and collector of Indian bones, the grave was in all likelihood not an isolated burial. Its proximity to a Native "village" that once existed at Foxes Hill hints of a communal burying ground that would have been a site of internment as well as remembrance.[8]

These and other archaeological traces, along with vestigial indigenous place-names such as Tuncowoden, which resonates with the metaphor of the "common pot" that Lisa Brooks says Northeast Native peoples used to evoke the power of home, serve as reminders that Fox Point was a Native place.[9] Physically overhauled by dual processes of decay and renewal, this indigenous space was radically transformed to conform to ever-changing visions of the cityscape. Urban renewal projects began with the massive clearance of Fox Point's crowded waterfront in the 1870s in response to public health concerns that its squalid conditions were a breeding ground for diseases such as cholera that hit the neighborhood's residents and those living near the Moshassuck River at the city's north end especially hard.[10] A resurgence during the national economic depression triggered by the finanacial collapse of 1873 posed additional dangers to the city's security. Enlisting the labor of over a thousand unemployed men, the city filled swampy runoff, tore down 146 dwellings and slaughterhouses, and leveled Foxes Hill, and in the process cleared nearly 400 acres for urban expansion.[11]

Despite the extent to which the neighborhood's physical landscape was altered, its structures demolished and partially overwritten with new construction, and its streets realigned under the guise of slum clearance and development, Fox Point continued to be a homeland for Native people. They made their homes there during the nineteenth and early twentieth centuries, and were afforded some security and protection within a changing and uncertain urban world. Even into the later twentieth century, when a series of scathing studies targeted Fox Point's residential areas for planned obsolescence and eventual clearance, citing a multitude of problems about quality of life, it was a Native homeland where certain street names and addresses evoked a sense of belonging and others could seem unwelcoming.

However, much like the transformations of the neighborhood's natural landforms and buildings, Fox Point's Native people have also been largely erased from its written history. References to a Native American presence other than in the city's settler creation story are rare, even though the neighborhood has been known as ethnically mixed since the nineteenth century. It was a section of the city where people of color, including Native Americans, descendants of enslaved and free African Americans, and Cape Verdean, Southern and Eastern European, and Irish immigrants lived as neighbors, interacted, and intermarried. It was where sailors during the 1820s from different homeports and countries often stayed at a boardinghouse run by James "Uncle Jimmie" Axum, a retired African American seaman, and his wife, Hannah (Narragansett), on Transit Street.[12] The Axums' business acumen and Jimmie's musical talents with a "fiddle and tambourine," along with a steady supply of liquor that kept sailors entertained "throughout the day and evening" spread the boardinghouse's reputation beyond the neighborhood.[13]

Fox Point was also where William J. Brown, the grandson of Chloe Prophet (Narragansett), who purchased and married an enslaved African American man, was born in 1814.[14] In his memoir, he writes that his family moved from his natal home at the corner of Power and William Streets to a two-room apartment with a "garden filled with various kinds of vegetables," which was closer to the waterfront and the Axums and considered to be "quite a genteel tenement" for a family of six, especially one of color. His new home, a gambrel-roofed house with red-painted clapboards and benches on each side of its brass-knobbed door with seating for three persons, offered a different streetscape than the few wagons, occasional carriage, and some neighbors whom he might have seen on his old street. The forging hammers of the neighborhood's brass foundries created a banging heard from sunrise until sunset, except during the dinner hour—a sound that was like music to his six-year-old ears but not to his mother's callers, who said that they could not think or speak above the noise. Up and down South Main Street, the busy thoroughfare running south of the seventeenth-century colonists' home lots, were carriages and teams and sailors "in their varied condition, working men coming and going from their labor, and the men of note." In the distance was Narragansett Bay, "alive with its ships, brigs, schooners, crafts, and small boats, sailing to and fro."[15] With ships arriving and leaving port, business at the grog shops was lively and streets were filled with boys carrying pitchers and decanters of rum and spirits to the wharves to quench the sailors' thirst.

Much like Providence's other homelands, Fox Point during the nineteenth and early twentieth centuries was not an exclusively Native American neighborhood, and its Native residents did not all have the same tribal affiliations or life experiences. They did not live in a tightly circumscribed, ethnically homogeneous enclave, but on the same blocks or on close-by streets where the population was ethnically mixed. Here any racial tensions that existed with non-Native neighbors might have been defused by the common struggles of their working-class lives, which at times might have made the differences among them seem less relevant.[16] Although Native Fox Point residents' manner of dwelling did not prevent them from being viable members of a Native community, it did frequently make them invisible or misunderstood by outsiders, even those within their own neighborhood or on their own blocks.[17] In an oral history interview, Yvonne Smart, a woman of Cape Verdean and European ancestry who was raised on Brook Street from 1941 to 1952 and maintained ties with Fox Point after she moved away, acknowledged the presence of Indians in the neighborhood and how they were often misjudged: "Fox Point had Native Americans there too. There was a lot of intermarriage between Cape Verdeans and Native Americans and

African Americans. People don't often talk about that.... [W]e always knew people who ... were Native American.... [W]e didn't call them Native Americans, we always called them Narragansetts. Now we find out they weren't all Narragansetts.... We always knew the Indians."[18]

Native people were part of the neighborhood. Fox Point was their urban homeland. It was where some settled when they came to live in Providence, owned homes that they held onto, and lived for the duration of their lives. Some were Narragansetts who had moved to Fox Point years before detribalization or had been born in Providence. Others later moved to Fox Point from different ancestral homelands. Some Native men were mariners or worked in shoreside industries on the city's docks just a short walk away. But mostly Fox Point was a place where Native people, regardless of their tribal affiliation or occupation, could count on finding some family members or extended kin from their own or other ancestral communities. By attending to their stories, it is possible to discern the importance of this urban homeland in their lives as a space where they would not be alone—despite separations from their previous homes and, for some, intervening journeys that might have taken them away from Fox Point for months at a time.

Home Ownership and Small Acts of Defiance

Anstriss Nichols was among Fox Point's Native residents whose name appears in the report of the commissioners appointed by the Rhode Island General Assembly and charged with determining Narragansett tribal membership for the purposes of distributing proceeds from the sale of the reservation to the state. She was born in Providence about 1800 and lived there for almost all her life. Her claim to a share of the $5,000 sale money, like those of other applicants, was judged on the basis of genealogy, the frequency of return visits to the reservation, and participation in tribal affairs, specifically the March elections of tribal officers and the annual August Meeting, a time-honored green-corn festival for reunion with family and friends, as Ethel Boissevain writes.[19] Published transcripts of public hearings, as tribal members insist, were not accurate accounts of what took place; and what was discussed at closed meetings has never been fully disclosed. Tribal elders told of physical confrontations, people coming and going during the hearings, and disinterested stenographers taking notes sporadically. Many claimants, whether rightly or wrongly, were left off the final list, ostensibly because they did not meet the criteria for tribal membership. Anstriss Nichols was one of them.

When her name was registered for consideration as a tribal member, she was identified as the daughter of Henrietta Jackson. Cooper was given as her maiden name. In sworn testimony at a public meeting held in the village of Carolina on July 14, 1880, the second of six public hearings, she stated that her mother, Mary M. Jackson, and her grandmother belonged to the tribe, though she had not visited the reservation before attending the first meeting two weeks earlier.[20] The U.S. Census of that year identifies her mother's place of birth as "Narragansett Indian" and father's birthplace as Virginia. Connected to the tribe on her maternal side, her life was centered in Fox Point. She married William S. Nichols, an African American mariner, in Providence when she was about twenty years old. But other than the date of their marriage nothing is known about how she met her husband, when their courtship began, or her early life in Providence.[21] Soon after they married, they were living in the southerly part of the city's east side. She gave birth to a daughter, Harriet Frances, about 1827, and a son, Benjamin Robinson, about 1833, though neither of the births was recorded. Another son, named after his father, was born in 1831 and lived only a few months beyond his second birthday.[22] In 1829, William purchased for $645 a lot and dwelling house situated between Arnold and John Streets in Fox Point that would be their home for the rest of their lives.[23] For William, the rest of his life would be only another eleven years. Anstriss would live fifty more years, most of them in the home she continued to occupy after William's death.[24] It was where she raised her two surviving children and headed the household as a widow except for a brief interlude from about 1850 to 1855, when she and her son moved to Fall River, Massachusetts.[25] A few years after returning to Providence, Benjamin was listed as living with his mother at 5 Thayer Street (between Arnold and Fox Streets), where he remained for about ten years.[26] In 1866, he married Emma Proffit of Cranston, Rhode Island, whose surname (variously transcribed) was shared by other individuals of Narragansett descent who resided in Providence.[27] Harriet, who was divorced, moved back to the family home on Thayer Street by 1868 and lived there until her death at the age of fifty-six in 1883.[28] On August 11, 1885, two years after she lost her daughter to cancer, Anstriss, blind and suffering from kidney disease, was admitted to the Dexter Asylum, an institution for the poor, aged, and mentally ill on Providence's east side, by the overseer of the poor. She died there of influenza and pneumonia in 1890, at the age of ninety.[29]

Censuses and city directories suggest that the family's attachments to the house on Thayer Street came with ownership, but were made even stronger by their shared experiences. Anstriss's son continued to live there until he was nearly forty years old and married, except for when he and his mother were in Fall River. Her daughter, a music teacher, came home to live there after her divorce. The family, who had owned the house and lot at 5 Thayer since Harriet was a toddler, was not impoverished. They led a relatively comfortable life, at least for a time, that contrasts sharply with representations of Fox Point as a rundown and poor slumland during the nineteenth century. Yet, hints of the family's financial stress first appear in records from the middle of the 1830s. Starting in 1834, William Nichols made a number of real-estate investments, purchasing lots in the city's north end near Olney Street and a parcel on Federal Hill on the city's west side. He resold two of the lots—one on Lippitt Hill and the other on Federal Hill—after about a year for slightly less than the purchase price in the case of the Lippitt Hill property and for a bit more than the purchase price for the parcel on Federal Hill, though on balance he recouped the sum of his initial investment.[30]

The financial risks foreshadowed by William's real estate investments came to fruition when his estate was declared insolvent.[31] A parcel of land at the north end of the city that he purchased in 1838 was sold at a public auction five years later, with Anstriss quitclaiming any right and title of her dower in the property.[32] Articles of William's personal property were inventoried by an assessor for the probate court, to be sold at "not less than their appraised value" to satisfy his creditors and to provide an allowance that would enable Anstriss to support her children and maintain the home on Thayer Street. The inventory of his personal estate provides a glimpse into the texture of life inside 5 Thayer Street and the material conditions of Anstriss Nichols's life at about the time when her family's relative security was ruptured by William's debts, the resulting loss of income, and ultimately his death.[33]

The inventoried possessions within the modest two-story, wood-framed structure suggest that the home could hardly be described as austere or shabby. The more formal of the two first-floor rooms had a mahogany dining table, seven flag-bottomed chairs, a cane-bottomed piano stool, two carpeted stools, a stand, and a workbox. The table, the room's main piece of furniture, and the stand were listed as having covers that would have been decorative as well as protective. The floor was covered with a carpet and rug, and the windows with white curtains. The flag-seated chairs would have been arranged around the room's edges, and the mahogany-framed mirror and large and small pictures, two of each, would have hung on the walls. Pairs of plated and shell candlesticks and three china mugs would have been prominently displayed on the mantle above the fireplace. The bellows and hearth brush would have been kept below.[34]

The other first-floor room (the west room), situated at the Thayer Street end of the house, was multipurpose. There were calico curtains covering the windows, a carpet in the entry, and in the room itself, a mahogany bureau, a maple table, a clock, a looking glass (mirror), and an assortment of ordinary tables and chairs. There were glass and composition lamps and candlesticks for lighting. The fireplace was fitted with iron dogs (andirons) and a set of brass fire tools. Equipment such as clothes horses (drying racks), flat irons, and a cast iron basin for doing laundry would have been placed nearby. Other furnishings in the room were for entertaining, such as japanned waitees (lacquered serving trays), a stool, a set of seven blue and twelve white cups and saucers, four teapots, sugar bowls, and six silver teaspoons. There were also thirty-four plates and fourteen dishes, ten pitchers, six plated tablespoons, a dozen and a half common (or everyday) forks and spoons, a dozen ivory-handled knives and forks, decanters, tumblers, glass dishes, salt cellars, a castor and bottles (a caddy equipped with condiment bottles), a cooking stove and utensils, and tin plates, all of which would have been used in preparing and serving meals for the family and invited guests. China jars and stoneware pots would have been used for storage of teas and foodstuffs.[35]

The objects listed in the upstairs part of the house, which served as the family's sleeping quarters, were glass lanterns, a piece of carpet, window curtains, a cylinder stove, two leather trunks, three chamber pots, laundry equipment such as tubs, buckets, pounding boards, washboards, hangers, and a clothes line, as well as a basket, and items such as chairs, a stand, washstands with bowls, pitchers, soap dishes, and two bedsteads. One of the bedsteads was cherry, and the other was painted yellow. They were fitted with feather beds, hair and straw mattresses, and bolsters and pillows. These bed furnishings would have been covered with the family's cotton sheets and cotton and linen pillowcases, and layered with blankets, coverlids, a spread or comforter, or the white counterpane listed in the inventory.[36] Compared to other coverings placed over the sheets, white counterpanes were a distinctive kind of decorative bed covering. Embellished with a raised design woven directly into the fabric or embroidered onto it, white counterpanes were meant mostly for display rather than warmth. They made a material statement about a family's, particularly a woman's, social aspirations and values during the eighteenth and nineteenth centuries.[37] They would have been placed on a bed to be admired by female guests who were invited into the private quarters of a home not typically seen by other visitors. But to read these coverlets merely as indicators of social aspirations would be to ignore that they also carried other messages, not the least of which was to remind the women who owned them of the risks of placing too much emphasis on entrapments of wealth and refinement.

This room-by-room inventory of household items offers a snapshot of Anstriss Nichols's home in Fox Point and the array of consumer goods that she and her husband had acquired by the time of his death. Many were stylish things that showed their refined and cosmopolitan tastes.

The mahogany furniture on the first floor, previously a luxury item found only in Providence's best homes, had become more widely available in a range of prices in the 1820s and 1830s, putting objects made of this once rarified material within the reach of people from a cross-section of economic means who desired respectability from its associations with gentility.[38] The silver teaspoons, ivory-handled forks and knives, japanned waitees, matched sets of cups and saucers, teapots, and decanters additionally show the extent to which Anstriss Nichols's home, whose footprint occupied most of the house lot, was a place for family as well as for visitors.

Within each of the rooms, there was an eclectic mix of the family's nicest things along with more modest, ordinary things. In the dining room inexpensive rush-seated chairs and stools covered with slightly more expensive carpet upholstery were mixed with the mahogany table.[39] In the west room paraphernalia for serving tea, consuming alcoholic beverages, and setting a refined table were placed alongside mundane kitchen and laundry tools. But the contents of the upstairs provide the most intimate and stunning revelations about the interior of Anstriss Nichols's home, exposing an aspect of everyday life that archaeologists and museum specialists seldom study because many material items found in sleeping quarters are so perishable. As crucial to the renewal, nurturing, and perpetuation of the family as the dining room and all-purpose kitchen and living room, the upstairs sleeping area was a private space, where the family kept its collection of bedding—the blankets they used for warmth, the sheets they stored in leather trunks, and the white counterpane that Anstriss Nichols displayed on the cherry-wood bedstead.

In the family's private quarters there was also a basket. Although the appraiser did not provide a description, wood splint and straw baskets were popular household items by the early nineteenth century. They were woven in different shapes and sizes, mostly by Native women, who stamped them with color dyes in designs characteristic of their geographical regions, tribal communities, and own artistic styles, and sold them to Euro-American consumers.[40] Some baskets, smaller in size than a trunk but larger than a workbox, had lids and were used for storage.[41] That the basket was listed next to the entry for trunks suggests that it might have been lidded. But without knowing the proportions of its form, the widths of its splints, or its decorative style, its origins cannot be identified. Yet, its provenience within Anstriss Nichols's home provides compelling contextual evidence that it was hers regardless of whether it had been purchased, bartered, gifted, or made by her using basketry techniques that she had learned from her Narragansett grandmother and mother. She would likely have possessed these skills even though she had been born and raised in the city, given that it was not uncommon for Native women with urban backgrounds to have knowledge of traditional practices.[42] There is no record of precisely what the basket looked like, how it was lined, or what it contained. In spite of the missing information, what is known about the basket suggests that it, along with the counterpane, embodied Anstriss Nichols's complexly layered identities as a modern and Native woman.

Although the inventory provides remarkable insights into everyday domestic routines, social interactions, and what were possibly small acts of defiance, it gives an imperfect picture of the materiality of Anstriss's life as a widow after her husband's estate was settled. It is unclear if all of the "goods and chattels" in the inventory were actually sold and if so, whether they were sold at their appraised value. The laundry equipment that would have provided her with the tools to do her own family's and other people's wash, as she possibly did before her husband's death, might not have been sold in its entirety. Glaring omissions of clothing, sewing needles and other textile equipment, cooking pots, and toys imply that the inventory was incomplete. Regardless of what home goods and personal items Anstriss was left with, it is fair to assume that she would have made fewer new purchases on her modest widow's allowance. Some things that remained in her possession after the settlement would have eventually become worn and frayed, and might have been discarded without being replaced. Beddings and curtains might have been mended and rush and cane seats rewoven, perhaps by Anstriss herself. Additionally, she might have given furniture and household items that she no longer used and that were increasingly less relevant in her life to her children when they married and started their own homes.

The transformation of the household after the early 1840s is not simply a downward spiral of gradual decline and decay. Other furnishings were brought into home when Harriet moved back to live with her mother toward the end of the Civil War. Harriet's postmortem inventory lists a card table and ornamental table, stuffed chairs, a rocker, a sofa, a cane-seated chair and a camp chair, fancy pillows, pictures, mottoes (needlework on fabric or cardboard with sentimental and instructive verses), vases and other accessories, a looking glass, a piano, a mahogany guitar, a foot stool, a box, books, and sheet music and music books. Interspersed among the existing furnishings, these things would have created a genteel Victorian setting in the first-floor rooms and infused the space with the intangible elements of music and literacy to renew the spirit of the family home after the war and some otherwise difficult years. Also recorded are a bureau, a bedstead, a feather mattress and bedding, a wash bowl, a pitcher, a match box, a soap dish, a trunk, some small items of furniture, lace curtains and shades and other window curtains, an ingrain carpet (a popular type of carpet woven as two layers with designs on each side), a marble slab, a card receiver and stand, and small looking glasses or mirrors. In addition, there were Harriet's silk and cashmere dresses, a silk cape and cloak, skirts, hats, a muff, and other fashionable clothing that alone would have nearly filled the upper floor of the house with the material signatures of Victorian gentility.[43]

Despite their incompleteness, these inventories of household goods and personal possessions in Anstriss Nichols's home over a forty-year period reveal differently composed domestic assemblages inflected with experiences that varied by generation, gender, and relative income. Although the family was not wealthy and Anstriss struggled financially after her husband's death, what is known about their domestic space from the inventories does not fit accounts of most homes of so-called people of color living in the city's homelands or on its outskirts during the nineteenth century. A visitor to an out-of-the-way cabin "not two hours' walk" from Providence described it as having a bare floor, little furniture except for two or three chairs and a table without a cloth, and a stove of the simplest pattern. This cabin was spartan compared to Anstriss Nichols's home even as it might have appeared during the leanest of times.[44] More significantly, the furnishings in Nichols's home suggest a domestic scene that was at odds with characterizations of Fox Point that invariably focus on its overall filth and squalor and the generally deplorable conditions inside its homes. Although the inventories do not provide direct information about the quality of housekeeping, the presence of equipment for carrying out mundane household chores and performing more refined domestic rituals suggests that Anstriss, well into her widowhood and insofar as her abilities in her later years allowed, kept the type of home that was typically beyond the gaze of muckrakers and state officials.

More than the household furnishings and other real estate, the land and house at 5 Thayer Street that William Nichols left to his heirs were assurances for the future once his debts were settled. It was property to hold onto because it was their home. But besides its more profound connotations, 5 Thayer Street provided a negotiating tool that Anstriss could use when uncertainties threatened the family's well-being and when unexpected expenses would tax her already limited finances. This was apparently the situation in 1850 when her son, then a minor over the age of fourteen, petitioned the Municipal Court of Providence to have her become the guardian of "his person and estate." The request allowed Anstriss to raise $200 by mortgaging his portion of the Thayer Street property to cover the expenses of a horse, a cab and harness, and clothing that he owed to a livery stable and merchants in Fall River.[45] As Benjamin's guardian and the principal in the loan agreement, she was responsible for repaying the mortgage. John E. Jackson and Caleb Rodman, both of Providence, cosigned as sureties, pledging to assume the debt obligation if she defaulted.

Their ties to Anstriss are not entirely clear. John Jackson, who shared her mother's last name, might have vouched for her because of a family connection, though threads of their relationship are frustratingly elusive in documentary records.[46] Rodman is a popular Narragansett surname that appears in various records pertaining to the tribe, including the 1881 detribalization report.[47] Like Jackson and the majority of surnames of Native people in the nineteenth century, it was a permanent and heritable patronym resulting from settler colonialism's attempts at transforming customary indigenous naming practices to allow officials to identify Indians unambiguously.[48] The name Rodman can be traced to one of South Kingstown's earliest English families, who gave their surname to the indentured Natives and enslaved African Americans working on their large agricultural plantations and in their factories. Whether imposed in the brusqueness of colonial possession or in paternalistic gestures, Rodman, similar to Champlin, Hazard, Weeden, and so many other English-derived names, became attached to generations of Native people and is testimony to their enslavement.[49] These names would have also alerted Native people to the existence of a wide kinship web that existed even in unexpected places. They were among the surnames listed in directories under a separate section for "Colored Persons" during the twelve-year period following Providence's incorporation, when as few as three or four individuals who might have been Native American had names that were Anglicized.

Without unraveling the intricacies of Caleb Rodman's genealogy, it is impossible to trace his connections to Anstriss Nichols prior to when his name is linked to hers in papers of her son's guardianship. He was born in Charlestown about 1816 and appears in Providence directories from the early 1840s to the early 1870s, and in U.S. Census schedules from 1850 to 1870. In the city directories of the 1840s he is listed in the Colored Persons section as residing in Providence's emerging downtown commercial area and working as a drayman hauling goods in flatbed wagons across the city.[50] Around the time that he cosigned the loan, he was living on Union Street in a household he shared with a woman from Virginia and her extended family.[51] His brother, Samuel Rodman, lived two doors down. Samuel was an "Indian Doctor" and a vigorous defender of Narragansetts' rights to their ancestral land. He was adamantly opposed to citizenship on the understanding that it would not carry equal rights.[52] Caleb later moved to Carpenter's Point on the Cove

Lands not far from Lippitt Hill, and then to Potter's Avenue at the west end of Providence. In 1860 he was in Pawtuxet, a section of Warwick, with a family headed by a single mother.[53] Less than five years later he returned to Providence and boarded on Potter's Avenue, apparently with the same family.[54] In 1870 he moved in with Edward S. Cone and his first wife, Frances Richmond, members of the Narragansett Tribe, and four of their children, George, Mary, Sarah, and Anna, who were living at Long Pond.[55] Over the next few years, he was back in the Cove Lands living on Gaspee Street near the Smith Street Bridge, a gathering spot for men looking to pick up daywork.[56] His last recorded address was his brother's home on Pine Street.[57] These strands of evidence connect Caleb Rodman to Providence's Native homelands and to the families who called these places home. Although his relationship to Anstriss Nichols is murky, clues in surviving records suggest that they were linked through a network of mutual support and common struggles both rooted in and transcending residence.

After the loan was secured, Anstriss and Benjamin left Providence for Fall River. Other than the brevity of the time they spent in Fall River, during which they lived in a home that was not theirs and Benjamin worked as a laborer, little else is known about their circumstances in that city. They would return to Providence and their house in Fox Point after a few years and resume their lives there. Benjamin put aside his aspirations of being a hackman and became a hairdresser, a semiskilled occupation that offered respectability and the promise of a modest income.[58] He practiced his tonsorial talents in barbershops at Market Square on the city's east side and on Eddy Street across the river. Anstriss continued "keeping house," a term that connotes her everyday housework as much as is does her efforts to hold onto the family home in the only homeland she really knew. While her husband was alive, her family seemed to have enjoyed relative stability and security. They acquired property and material goods. Their children were schooled; and their daughter learned to play the piano and would become a music teacher. But William's untimely death threw their economic situation into a tailspin from which they never fully recovered. For Anstriss, any semblance of domestic tranquility was suddenly replaced with the realization that she now had to assume complete responsibility for keeping the house, feeding and clothing her children, paying expenses, and dealing with life's other uncertainties.

In her new role as head of the household, she was remarkably resourceful. Legal documents bearing her X-mark and a signature that others may have helped her write indicate that she appeared before the Providence municipal court in two separate cases to seek her rights as a widow and protect her family and home. Further, with these inscriptions she acted to prevent the loss of her home, not in the context of a treaty but in municipal institutions of the state, destabilizing the assumed binary between traditional and modern.[59] At about eighty years old, she traveled to the Narragansett Reservation in Charlestown for the first time to assert her eligibility, based on her lineage, for a share in the proceeds from the sale of tribal land that could help to supplement her income in some small way. For Anstriss, who had never lived on the reservation, the verdict hinged not on her place of birth or where she lived, but on failing to maintain tribal relations in ways that satisfied the criteria for tribal membership as set by the detribalization commission. She was part of a more extensive community of Narragansetts who lived apart from the reservation and had created and embedded themselves in urban homelands, where they rekindled family and tribal ties—and to the extent that time and money allowed, reconnected with friends and kin in Charlestown.

Within the next few years the home life that Anstriss Nichols had tenaciously struggled to preserve in Fox Point would be again shattered when her daughter died. Harriet's death was a profound personal loss, as the death of a child at any age would be to a parent, especially one preceded by the pain and suffering associated with a terminal disease. But there was also another kind of emotional toll that Harriet's death took on Anstriss. Her death led to the loss of material things that Harriet had brought into the Thayer Street home they shared that had to be sold to cover the costs of the funeral and other expenses. These things were not merely indices of Harriet's conspicuous consumption; they also spoke of her educational opportunities and professional achievements, and, in no small way, of Anstriss's parenting skills. Their sale took away material expressions not only of the family's social aspirations, but also these women's experiences and the home that had enabled and nurtured them. Having acted in ways that staunchly defied the muteness of Native women and all women of color in nineteenth-century America, Anstriss, alone, elderly, and in declining health, could no longer maintain or hold onto the home at 5 Thayer Street that had been such an integral part of her identity and survivance. In 1885, she finally left her Fox Point neighborhood, which records suggest she had rarely strayed from for any extended period.

Dispersed and Still Together:
Rights to a Name and Place among Strangers

Few, if any, of the homes of Fox Point's Native residents were family owned and occupied for more than fifty years, as Anstriss Nichols's house was. Rather than being the dwelling places of single families for the duration of the household's life cycle, some were stopping points that served as gateways into the Native urban community. These houses provided stability for Native people who were not born in Providence like Anstriss Nichols, but who had relocated from tribal reservations or rural villages and towns with the hope of making better lives for themselves. In an unfamiliar urban space that was both daunting and alienating, Fox Point was where they could find housing for short or longer periods of time and individuals and families from their ancestral homelands, as did many Narragansetts whose names are mentioned in the 1881 detribalization report. The houses of friends and family already living Fox Point and the apartments or rooms they rented became safe havens where newcomers would be welcomed and given shelter, food, and emotional support, not to mention avoid the pain and trauma of seeming homeless.[60] Their experiences offer insights into another aspect of life in Providence's urban homelands, especially Fox Point, which had been points of entry into the nascent city since, if not before, Roger Williams and his followers steered across the Seekonk River.

Among the Native people to whom Fox Point was a stopping-over place was Amos Brewster (Narragansett). In 1850, when he was about fifteen years old, he was living in Griswold, Connecticut, with his father, George, a farm laborer, his mother Olive (née Cross) (Narragansett), and seven siblings ranging in age from three to twenty-two years old.[61] He was the second-oldest child and one of only two sons. About ten years later, the Brewsters moved to South Kingstown, a largely agricultural area that, like the southeastern Connecticut countryside they had left, was becoming increasing industrialized. In South Kingstown, Amos found work as a day laborer, his father as a stonemason, his mother as a washerwoman, and his sister Lois, who was a year younger than Amos, as a domestic servant. Along with the change in residence came a change in how the family's racial identity was perceived. In the 1860 U.S. Census they were reclassified as "mulatto," a generalized label reserved for individuals thought to have mixed ancestry.[62] Although relocation had its uncertainties, the family seemingly regained some stability in their lives. Still, the next few years would bring about additional significant changes.

In 1863, Amos Brewster registered in the Civil War draft on the side of the Union as a resident of South Kingstown.[63] In January 1864 he enlisted in the Twenty-Ninth Regiment of the Connecticut Colored Infantry in Norwich for the town of Griswold and served for three years.[64] Military records offer rare glimpses of him and his life during this narrow time frame that otherwise would have gone unnoticed. They describe him as having black hair and eyes, a colored complexion, and standing five feet ten inches tall.[65] They track his movements from when his unit was deployed, ordered to march to Annapolis, Maryland, and called into service in one of the war's final and deadliest military engagements to when he was in military hospitals. They also indicate that he rose to the rank of sergeant.[66]

A letter written by Cpl. John O. Cross, a fellow soldier in Twenty-Ninth Regiment who shared Olive Brewster's maiden name, to his wife stated that he and Amos were well. The good news that Cross passed along hints at relationships that linked families of Native descent from Griswold together and into wider social networks regardless of where they were located at any particular moment.[67] Although unscathed by war at the time when Cross wrote to his wife, Amos Brewster was wounded in late October 1864 and spent the next six months recuperating in a U.S. military hospital in Virginia. In May 1865 he was transferred to a hospital in New Haven, Connecticut, and he mustered out in July. His injuries resulted in the loss of three toes on his left foot.[68] Although the extent to which his injury compromised his mobility and ability to fully resume agricultural work is unclear, at the end of the war he returned to what was now his mother's household in South Kingstown and resumed work as a farm laborer. Some of his sisters still lived at home, but two of them, Betsey and Sarah, had married and went by the surnames Olney and Weeden, respectively.[69] By 1870, Amos was living with a Black farmer, the farmer's family, and a white fisherman, his wife, and two children in a mixed-race household, and working as a hired farm hand. The farm was the next one over from where his sister, Betsy Olney, her husband, and their five children lived.[70] Around 1872, Amos gave up farm labor and country life and moved to Fox Point.

He lived briefly on Williams Street, but mostly on John Street a few blocks away. The house at 72 John Street, which is still standing, is a wood-framed, clapboard-sided building that historic preservationists have described as a Federal-style structure three bays wide, with a center entry at ground level, that rises two and a half stories above a raised basement.[71] It was a house I had walked past many times not knowing anything about its Native history. Similar to many historic houses in the neighborhood, it had been rescued and rehabilitated in initiatives that provided investment incentives for middle-class housing.[72] Despite the efforts of city officials, planners, and developers to save historic architecture, no attention was given to preserving the connections that these spaces might have had to Native people. This should not be surprising, as this history was generally unknown and historical preservation in Providence and in other cities across the Northeast and the indigenous world is premised on the assumption that urban spaces are de-indigenized. Consequently, the preserved Fox Point landscape is devoid of references to a Native American presence, except for place-stories entrenched in the city's creation story. Its Native residents, if they are considered at all, belong to a separate past that does not overlap with that recalled by historical preservationists, though Native peoples were (and are) part of the cityscape and stakeholders in its history.

Amos Brewster lived at the John Street address from 1870s to 1887 with his wife Sarah, whom he married in South Kingstown in 1873. She kept house and he worked as a teamster, as he had since moving to Fox Point. Childless, they shared their home at the rear of the house lot with a boarder, a washerwoman in her mid-fifties, whose relationship to them other than cohabitation is unknown.[73] Maria Blunt, one of his younger sisters, lived in a house at the front of the lot with her husband Robert, an African American, and William C. Weeden, the son of Louisa Weeden, who worked as an "elevator boy." The John Street address was apparently known among some Native people as a spot on the urban landscape where the tenants could help them secure leases and find jobs, as well as give them a sense of being at least tenuously rooted to the neighborhood.[74] The rear of the John Street address that was Amos Brewster's home for thirteen years, for example, had previously been the home of Edward Cone (Narragansett), a fellow teamster, and his son Charles.[75]

Although the move to Fox Point marked an abrupt transition in Amos Brewster's life in terms of his surroundings and circumstances, his ties to his family remained intact. His sister Maria, her husband, and their nephew were his nearest neighbors. It was a template for urban living that provided assurances of security to offset the uncertainties of making a new home in a city where Indians appeared mostly in narratives of the past, and where the majority of people were not Indians. This was certainly true on this stretch of John Street, where Amos Brewster, his sister, and their nephew were the only individuals of Native ancestry and where Amos's wife, his boarder, Robert Blunt, Silvia Offee (the owner of the property), and her daughter were the only other people of color.

Aside from racial and ethnic differences, there were commonalities among the residents other than living on the same street. According to information in the 1880 U.S. Census, all were working class. Most men were employed in building trades. Some were small-scale merchants and clerks who, like Robert Blunt, a barber, may have fared slightly better economically. There also was a porter, a stable hand, a blacksmith, a sawyer, a policeman, and a few who did odd jobs. The majority of the women, including Sarah Brewster, were described in the census as "keeping house." A few, like Maria Blunt, were listed as laundresses, who might have brought their work home, or as live-in servants, who worked for families on the block. Two women were schoolteachers and another was a dressmaker. Although spanning a spectrum of jobs from semi-skilled to unspecialized and from entrepreneurial to civil service, the shared working-class lives of the street's residents might have mitigated any strained relationships percolating from racial and ethnic differences. That most of the women were identified as "keeping house," a designation that in today's parlance would be the equivalent of calling them homemakers, also speaks to shared experiences that cut across racial and ethnic lines.

Amos Brewster was registered as a claimant to a share of the purchase money from the sale of the Narragansett reservation on June 26, 1880, at the first of six public hearings to determine tribal membership and rights to the proceeds. Five months later, he submitted an affidavit in which he responded to questions distributed to doubtful claimants like himself, stating that he had been to the reservation only two or three times before moving to Providence. He went to the August Meeting, an important annual gathering, the year before he relocated, but had never voted in tribal elections. As much as he would have liked to attend the Narragansetts' regular meetings every year, he indicated that he could not afford it. He figured that he would not get much from land that he thought "came through his grandmother," which he went to see about the year prior to filing his claim of tribal membership—perhaps not even enough, I suspect, to compensate for the loss of pay and the cost of travel.[76] Ultimately, his name was not on the final list of tribal members who each received $15.43 from the sale. In the climate of detribalization even common threads of residence and occupation on John Street might not have adequately ameliorated tensions over race and tribal identity that rippled across Rhode Island and Providence's Native homelands.

Maria Blunt's application was also rejected. When she registered as a claimant, it was noted that, though she was a resident of Providence and was not married to an Indian, she visited the "reservation every year." She said that she did not "care anything about money" but wanted to be recognized as a Narragansett. This was a right that she and other Narragansett Indians, including other Brewster siblings, would be denied.[77] Louisa Weeden, who in 1880 lived with her husband and two daughters, Bertha and Alice, in Narragansett Pier, a village and seaside resort with Narragansett families about fifteen miles from Charlestown, visited the reservation yearly.[78] In a sworn written statement to the detribalization commission for its penultimate November meeting, she said that she had last visited in 1878 and had been there five or six times within the last ten years on business concerning her land, but did not participate in March meetings to elect tribal officers or sell any of her interest in her private land.[79] She died on March 5, 1881—just four months after learning that she was not on the final tribal membership list.[80]

Betsy Olney, who had stayed in South Kingstown with her husband and their sons, also asserted her birth right as a Narragansett. According to the 1880 U.S. Census taken on June 9, a few weeks before the Commission of the Affairs of the Narragansett Indians held its first meeting to register the names of claimants for the purchase money, she worked as a laundress and her husband Giles, identified as an Indian five years later, did farm labor.[81] In the information given to the commission she indicated that she had visited the reservation, sometimes two or three times a year. More than an occasional visitor, she had traveled there many times during the last decade to attend meetings and to look after her lands, as her sisters and brother had done.[82] Yet she also was omitted from the tribal roll.

The Brewsters, who had lived apart from the reservation community at Charlestown, had taken different routes in their diaspora from southeastern Connecticut across southern New England. These known facts, along with information in the 1881 report of the investigating committee and the conclusions reached, fail to account for how they lived as indigenous people apart from their ancestral homeland. The meager details reveal little about how Amos and Maria lived as Narragansett descendants in Providence's Fox Point homeland. To surmise that by living away from the reservation that they had drifted away from it socially might not be an accurate assessment. For them as well as other Narragansett descendants, memories of the detribalization hearings and the often contentious indictments by white officials and some Indians remained fresh a decade later and would not be easily forgotten even many years later. Along with persistent prejudices that common residence and occupation could not always overcome, these experiences of discrimination faced by all who were denied the right to a tribal name would have created obstacles for being Indian on John Street.

What is known about Amos Brewster's life in the Fox Point homeland is derived matter-of-factly from censuses, vital statistics, military records, and city directories rather than from first-person narration, except for the words transcribed in the detribalization report. These statements, though not autobiographical, reveal his voice as well as Maria's, providing a telling commentary on their struggles with ideologies of extinction and race and what it meant to be Native American in nineteenth-century New England. For the Brewster siblings and many Narragansetts who had never lived on the reservation in Charlestown, these challenges to their identity were double-pronged. They were not only about being Indian; they were also about being Narragansett, which for some also meant being urban. Both were undervalued and would have no doubt subjected them to innuendos or worse and rendered them unnoticed. This in turn left unanswered questions about what happened outside of the Brewster and Blunt hub on John Street, where one could be only "white," "Black," or "mulatto," and rarely Indian, let alone someone with a distinctive tribal heritage.[83]

Soon after his wife Sarah died in 1888, Amos Brewster left John Street. He moved across the Providence River to the city's west side. Maria Blunt and her husband had moved from Fox Point a few years earlier, relocating to same Upper South Providence neighborhood where Amos would live out the rest of his life. He remarried in 1889.[84] His new home was located on a block dominated by an iron foundry among the small wood-framed houses and multifamily tenements. Decades into the twentieth century, other New England Native people would also move to the west side of the city and sometimes back to the east side. Like Fox Point, these other homelands were not ethnically homogeneous enclaves, though some had more Indians who lived there longer or in closer proximity. Yet as in Fox Point, the presence of indigenous people from tribal communities in the Northeast with different lineages and multiple heritages would have compensated for any deficits, and served to expand social networks and add to the resiliency and persistence of Providence's Indian community.

Before he resided at 70 John Street in the late 1860s, Edward Cone had lived on South Main, near the city's waterfront that would later be the core of Fox Point's Cape Verdean community. He had lived apart from the Narragansett reservation since about the 1840s. In testimony given in the detribalization hearings, he said that he moved his family back to Charlestown to stay with his wife's relatives because he had difficulty finding a place to live in Providence in the years after his son Charles was born in 1848. He farmed in Charlestown for about two years, during which time his wife gave birth to another son and he petitioned for land near that of his mother-in-law. His unsuccessful petition led to his decision to return to Providence, where he found work as a porter on Market Square, as a laborer, and as a teamster. He stated that he had attended all tribal meetings and adhered to the tribe's requests at other times, and defended the legitimacy of his parent's marriage and his skin color. His responses to grueling questioning exposed concerns over tribal identity and race that underscore the limitations of inferences about tribal membership based on phenotype. He described his mother, who was not a member of the tribe, as "cross-blooded," like him and his paternal relatives, though Brister Michael, a member of the tribal council, called her a "nigger woman." When another council member said that Cone should be judged as African on the basis of his skin color, he replied that there was not much difference in the color of their skin. The exchange makes clear that as a criterion for distinguishing between Native people living in the city and or on or close to reservation land, skin color created false expectations that were inconsistent with family and tribal understandings of identity. Compared to his skin color, Edward Cone's place of residence raised thornier issues of belonging, as it did for others who were not content to burrow in on the reservation.[85]

The size of teams that he drove and the amount of money he possibly made as a teamster did not endear him to many Narragansetts who remained on the reservation and followed a rural way of life. He had voted in Providence elections on some real estate qualifications and had cast a vote for Thomas Doyle (1827-86), a three-time mayor of Providence from the 1860s to 1886, but claimed to have never voted in two places during the same year. His participation in debates over crucial matters concerning the tribe was as real as his connection to Providence and its homelands, but not without controversy. By his own admission, he kept in touch with other Narragansetts in the city, notifying them of developments concerning the state's petition to terminate legal relations with the tribe. Some were his neighbors and others were relatives and friends. "I was one of the first to act, and thought I should inform all the members, even in the city of Providence, of this fact, and require that they should go forward and help direct or devise ways and means by which we should sustain our tribal rights."[86]

Cone, a former member of the Narragansett tribal council, was on the 1881 tribal list, as were his children and other family members. Fox Point was a stopping-over point in his urban journey as it was for them. His sister Mary Jane Cone lived in Fox Point from the late 1870s to the early 1880s. She resided on Fremont Street between Governor and Gano Streets, close to the Seekonk River and Tockwotten Point, and on Williams Street in a house next door to Amos Brewster in 1874.[87] She later moved to Thayer Street, north of Anstriss Nichols's home, and then to Lippitt Hill, where she had lived briefly during the early 1870s. For Sarah C. Cone, Ed Cone's daughter with Frances Richmond, Fox Point was a temporary home in her seemingly troubled and all too short life. Although brief, her stop there was not merely an incidental lay over. She gave birth to a son in late November 1885 at the rear of 52 Wickendon Street, where he died of pneumonia less than three months later.[88] She would have associated the Fox Point address, located near the intersection of Wickendon Street and South Main Street, with the loss of a child. In the Wickendon Street apartment, amid the clamor of nearby shops and houses, she might have heard this baby's cries much as unwed Narragansett mothers on the reservation would have heard the wailing of their babies who, according to tribal stories, were abandoned at a pile of ancient rocks ("Crying Rocks") on the edge of the Cedar Swamp because they were too sickly or had been fathered by non-Indians.[89]

Sarah Cone died of consumption two months after the death of her baby. She had lost other children: a one-month-old daughter, a stillborn son, and a nine-month-old son who died from hydrocephalus almost exactly a year before the death of her last-born child.[90] Whether 52 Wickenden Street became a place of an urban legend comparable to Crying Rocks is purely conjectural. The places where Cone's other children died—Riley Street in the Lippitt Hill homeland and Messer Street near Long Pond—would also have had memories of loss attached to them. Writing about the deaths of these children—four out of five or possibly six, born in less than ten years to a woman whose body was compromised and wasting away from tuberculosis—is difficult. She may have known that her babies might die prematurely, or she may have always harbored the hope that the next one would survive, especially the boy born in Fox Point as her own health declined. His death seemingly extinguished her future as well as his own, no matter how uncertain and grim the prospects might have been. Similar to stories embedded in visible places on ancestral lands, new place-based stories such as the one proposed here would have certainly come into being in Providence's Native homelands, given that "such constructions are everywhere to be found," as Keith Basso reminds us.[91] They provided Native people with reminders of the obstacles and disappointments they would face in life and moral guideposts for overcoming mounting resentments and bouts of self-loathing. Although these new place-based stories would have been constructed in any of the city's Native homelands, they might have been most prevalent at its gateways—places where Native people encountered more strangers than family and friends, and where the all too evident uncertainties of city life made unspeakable pain harder to bear.

Safe Havens: Conditional Security and Danger in a Waterfront Homeland

Closer to Fox Point's easterly shoreline, where Roger Williams crossed over the Seekonk River, Native sailors and dockworkers also paused and made their homes on land that was once theirs. Alexander Ammons was one of them. Born in Charlestown in 1848, he was the son of Gideon Ammons and Caroline Rodman, members of the Narragansett Tribe. He lived in Charlestown until about 1865 with his father, his father's second wife, Sarah Eleazer, a Shinnecock from Sag Harbor, New York, and his siblings and half-siblings.[92] Gideon, president of the tribal council from 1847 to 1878 and a former whaler, worked as a stonemason. His masonry skills helped build the Narragansett Indian Church on the reservation in 1859 that replaced an older wooden church; he was among the first congregants to attend services when it was completed.[93] In January 1865 Alexander enlisted in the Union Army from Providence for one year. Described as five and half feet tall with a mulatto complexion and black eyes and hair, he was mustered into the Seventh Regiment of U.S. Colored Troops as a private in Company K of the 118th Infantry.[94]

His name appears in records during the detribalization hearings, at which his father had a vocal role in testifying for and against many claiming membership. When Alexander's name was registered as a tribal member at the meeting on July 14, 1880, he was living in Providence. He had not visited the reservation for seven years, had married out of the tribe, and did not have children.[95] These slivers of information pertaining to his standing in the tribe suggest that he might have returned to Providence after the war, though records do not place him in the city again until the early 1880s, when he is listed in city directories in Upper South Providence at the same address where Eliza Hilton, the daughter of Ben Thomas, another prominent Narragansett tribal leader and council member, had lived in the late 1870s.[96] Alexander found work as a stevedore—an occupation that required both knowledge of equipment and techniques and organizational skills to coordinate the difficult and often dangerous work of loading and unloading ships' cargos. He later moved to Pitman Street near the Seekonk River, where today the ruins of bridges that once spanned the crossing and skeletons of boats that can be seen at low tide are eerie reminders of the nineteenth-century Fox Point homeland. India Point, the new name given to Tuncowoden for the merchant ships that sailed to the West Indies and East Asia, was a short walk along the river's shoreline from Pitman Street. It was where stevedores and gangs of longshoremen recruited from the neighborhood would have found work offloading raw materials from ships' holds and refilling them with manufactured goods.

Alexander Ammons and other dockworkers followed the Seekonk River down to India Point to work, making the trip daily for a more or less steady job or as dictated by the arrival of ships in the harbor. Sometimes the walk to work would have been only one way because of the dangers of dock work. With few safety checks to ensure dockworkers' protection, many were injured or killed by the occupation's inherent dangers.[97] Ammons, who drowned in the Providence River in 1885 under unknown circumstances, may be counted among the fatalities.[98] The river in which he lost his life had been dredged since the midcentury to accommodate larger and deeper vessels. It competed with India Point as a place on the city's waterfront where people of color went to find work that was at best episodic and low paying and at worst extremely risky.

Alexander Ammons's father Gideon went to sea on whaleboats out of Newport, Rhode Island, Westport, Massachusetts, New Bedford, Massachusetts, and Sag Harbor, New York, where some of the Northeast's most active whale fleets were based. He gained a reputation as one of the best boat-steerers in the whaling business. Gideon, or "Uncle Gid," as he was sometimes called in his later years, shipped out from Newport when he was twenty years old. He sailed on his first whaling voyage from Westport, left from New Bedford to hunt whales in the Indian Ocean, and was discharged at Maui in 1844 in the Pacific island chain of Hawai'i that Capt. James Cook named the Sandwich Islands.[99] On these voyages, he rounded Cape Horn at the tip of South America and visited ports in the larger indigenous world beyond southern New England and the North American continent.[100] He, like his son, was part of the diaspora from the region's reservations that brought Native people to locations near and far where they hoped to gain some financial stability and improve the quality of their lives.

Alexander did not travel halfway around the world, sail uncharted seas, or share in the excitement and traditions of the chase.[101] Although less sweeping in scope, his life experiences also crossed waters and cultures, and were more complicated and cosmopolitan than those generally attributed to indigenous people. Mostly undocumented by white record keepers, his experiences comment on his struggles to make a space for himself in the city much like other Native people whose lives were, and have remained, largely inconspicuous. Whereas Gideon (except for the approximately two decades when he was mostly away at sea) was a country person at heart who farmed and did stone work in his later years, Alexander spent more than half of his thirty-seven years in Providence.[102] Ironically, they died in watery places seemingly worlds apart—Gideon in a Charlestown swamp and Alexander in the Providence River not far from his home.[103] Coincidences aside, the differences in their life experiences provide insight into modes of creative survival in which they, like other Native people, lived within a community that was increasingly diverse and far-flung.

Other Native people involved in maritime industries also made Fox Point their temporary home. Christopher R. Champlin, a sailor, was living at Fremont Street near Governor Street during the mid-1860s.[104] He had been in Providence since the 1850s, first with his natal family, then as a single man, and later as a husband and father. Although he still worked as a mariner, by the late 1860s he had moved to Upper South Providence on the west side of the Providence River. After life as a seaman was no longer profitable or feasible, he worked as a laborer and would do so until his death in 1901.

By the time that Alexander Ammons and Christopher Champlin left Fox Point, the India Point waterfront had begun to decline. Despite fewer opportunities for maritime work and the influx of foreign immigrants vying for jobs on the wharves and on ships, Native people continued to live in Fox Point. Harry Rocker (Chappaquiddick Wampanoag) from

Edgartown on Martha's Vineyard, whose father was a mariner from Valparaiso, Chile and whose mother was Wampanoag, lived on South Main Street with his wife when he registered for the World War I draft.[105] Emily Rocker, another family member, lived with her children, listed as Spanish Indians, over on Gano Street, closer to the Seekonk River, in a multifamily house where one of the other families was identified as Indian.[106] Like many Wampanoags from Edgartown and nearby towns on the Vineyard, the Rockers had strong maritime ties. Young men usually went to sea so that they could accumulate enough money to build comfortable homes for themselves and their families in their ancestral homelands. Those who moved away to seek a better life frequently settled around New England's other shipping ports. Although there were no guarantees that they would secure maritime work, there was the assurance that other Native families from home and elsewhere would likely be their neighbors.

Nancy (Noka) Cheeves lived on Benevolent Street, north of the enclave of streets close to the city's waterfront, as early as the 1860s.[107] She was the daughter of Samuel and Alice Noka and the wife of George Cheves, "an African," whom she married in Providence in 1863.[108] Her father, elected to the Narragansett tribal council five times from 1850 to 1862, was among the first to worship at the newly rebuilt Narragansett Indian Church.[109] Although Nancy was not a whaling widow, and she had not gone to sea as a captain's wife or a servant, the experiences of her brother, Peter Noka, a mariner, would have made her aware of the perils of maritime work and its effects on families—many of whom lived in port towns and some close to the docks.

Peter, who was also preacher, lived during the 1830s and 1840s on the west side of the Providence River. He worked as a wood sawyer and whitewasher while waiting to go to sea on vessels that took him to Havana, Pictou in Nova Scotia, and beyond.[110] His name appears in a late nineteenth-century newspaper article about Squaw Hollow near Lippitt Hill as one of the three burly men who kept peace in the neighborhood by their imposing presence, if not their ability to achieve consensus through other means.[111] In tribal oral history, he is remembered as "a big and mighty man of much muscle," who "found it easier to pray away his difficulties, than to use his muscle," an assessment that suggests that he did not have to resort to strong-arm tactics to settle disputes among his neighbors or to deal with other difficult situations in life. An often-repeated story recounts that while he was on a schooner rounding Cape Horn on the way to San Francisco, he saved the ship and his shipmates during a treacherous gale by praying out loud before taking the helm. "Master, the tempest is raging! Speak to the winds and the waves, as you did on Galilee! Calm our troubled seamen, as you did the disciples of old, etc." The seas suddenly became calm and the battered ship sailed "into a lull." It arrived at its destination a few weeks later, where Peter was discharged after a disagreement with the captain, despite pleas from the crew not to leave him so far from his Native homeland. The "ship sailed on without him, but it *never* made port again." Years later, he "finally reached the Narragansett Country and lived to preach many more good sermons."[112] He had weathered this storm and, I suspect, weathered many others with the same spirit, moral courage, and presence of mind, throughout a story of survivance that spanned nearly eight decades.

It is not known how long Nancy Noka Cheeves—who was born in 1812, either a year before or two years after Peter—lived in Fox Point. By 1880, she and her husband had moved to the village of Arctic in Warwick.[113] According to testimony that Edward Cone, who knew her before she was married, gave at the detribalization hearings, she was connected to the Second Freewill Baptist Church (known as the Pond Street Church) in Upper South Providence.[114] She had lived on the reservation for two years at some point, had but not been to Charlestown in thirty years.[115] In 1879 she and Peter, who then lived in Westerly, and another brother, Edward, petitioned to the Rhode Island General Assembly to sell land that they owned on the reservation.[116] Despite her family name and its history, she, though not her two brothers, was left off of the 1881 tribal roll. She died in 1889, eight years after the list was finalized.[117] She was buried in Swan Point Cemetery on Providence's east side, where Edward, a veteran of the Civil War, had been buried two years earlier.[118] In 1863, about the time he enlisted in the Union Army, his address was 52 Benevolent Street, the same as hers.[119]

In addition to Anstriss Nichols, Amos Brewster, Maria Blunt, the Cones, Alexander Ammons, Christopher Champlin, the Nokas, and the Rockers, two Indians from South Dakota who drove wagons for a living lived in Fox Point, over on South Water Street near the Providence River. Frank Howard and Frances Rodman lived farther north on Thayer Street, a little bit outside of Fox Point proper. Howard, whose mother was the daughter of a Snoqualmie chief of the coastal Salish people in what is now Washington State, and whose adoptive African American family owned a hotel and restaurant in Olympia, moved to Providence in the early 1880s.[120] Rodman, a laundress, boarded with Amelia Wheeler, who like Frank Howard's wife was a dressmaker. The surname Rodman would have signaled kinship to Fox Point's Native people, as would some of the other names mentioned, though they might not have been recognized as indigenous by non-Native neighbors. The name Wheeler, too, might have struck a familiar cord. Amelia might have been the "A. A. Wheeler" whose name is handwritten on a note card announcing "the last meeting of the season" of the Canonicus Branch of Indians at Reformers Hall on June 3, 1925.[121] On the announcement, dated June 2, she identifies as the secretary of this Providence-based group of Narragansett descendants and family members affiliated with the Indian Council of New England, an intertribal organization. Mary Brewster, Amos Brewster's second wife and his widow, cosigned as president. James M. Stockett Jr., a Howard University–trained lawyer and "descendant of old lines of Narragansetts," who lived on East George Street from the 1920s to the 1940s, appears in photographs in the Indian Council's scrapbook in which other memorabilia related to his life are also preserved.[122] Whether inspired by his middle name, Metamora (a popular nineteenth-century pseudonym for Metacom, the seventeenth-century Pokanoket-Wampanog leader), or the struggles he faced over his Native identity, Stockett was an active participant in the Indian Council's public performances that raised Native visibility across New England's towns and cities in the early twentieth century.

Games of Skill and Rules of Movement:
Unexpected and Predicted Urban Passages

Even when it's not possible to hear Native people in New England's cities in their own voices, mining strands of evidence that are notoriously partial and ambiguous, toggling them together, and grounding them in particular localities on the urban landscape provide insights suggesting that these people were neither invisible nor entirely silenced. Their words that appear in written documents, however imperfectly transcribed or invented in acts of ventriloquism, reveal, directly or obliquely, what mattered in their lives. Even in the much criticized published accounts of the deliberations to determine tribal membership, the voices of Narragansett Indians who made Fox Point their urban homeland can be detected, shedding important light on their life experiences, the role that the neighborhood played in their adjustments to city living, and ties binding them to their ancestral homes. Anstriss Nichols's petitions to the Providence municipal court to keep her home and family intact give undisputable credence to the supposition that Native voices can be heard in city records. Inventories of material goods allow entry into her home and, remarkably, into the most private precincts of her living space. Census schedules, vital records, and city directories, all flawed with uneven information and confounding omissions that often make it exasperatingly difficult to trace what really happened in a Native person's life, sometimes divulge how these very same people whom federal, state, and municipal institutions codified and counted to advance strategic political agendas represented themselves. In these instances it is possible to detect glimmers that cast light on their lives in unexpected ways and hear more clearly the echoes of their silenced voices.

Clarence Herbert Freeman, who lived on Transit Street in Fox Point around the turn of the twentieth century, was a checkers player. It was an occupation that would have befuddled canvassers who logged where people lived and what they did for a living for the Providence directories, much as it did me as I searched through documents that listed laborer and teamster as the most common form of employment for Native men in nineteenth and early twentieth century New England cities. For Clarence Freeman, who held a series of jobs after moving to the city from Connecticut while in his teens, identifying as a checkers player made him stand out. But the information was neither incorrect nor a joke.

Clarence Freeman *was* a checkers player, and one who earned a reputation as the "Champion Beater" and the "Peerless Player of Providence." Described as a "full-blooded" Pequot Indian (and as a person of Indian and African descent), he was the son of Daniel Freeman and Ida Mary Proffitt.[123] In 1880 he was living with his mother, stepfather, and his mother's eight-year-old niece around Hoyle Square on the west side and had found work as a porter at the Hoyle Hotel, a stopover for travelers and revelers, where he sometimes boarded.[124] "Intelligent and modest in demeanor, and his only offense in appearance [being] a somewhat lavish display of jewelry," Clarence defeated opponents in Providence and Boston, among them some of the great checkers players of his era.[125] In 1876 he won first prize in the city checkers championship, and in the years that followed he won against world-class veterans, playing in state and national championships and nontitle matches. In the Championship of America in 1885, a checkers match running from April 11 to April 29 that is considered one of the longest and most stubbornly contested in the history of the game, he again emerged the winner; he lost his only high-stakes match a month later. In 1890 he had the winning score in another marathon match (fig. 4). But Clarence mostly preferred to play against members of the Checker and Chess Club on Westminster Street in the downtown business district, even the poorest of them, sometimes simultaneously and sometimes even blindfolded, regardless of the wager.

Understanding how Clarence Freeman reached the heights of fame and respect in the art of checkers and became one of the game's best strategists requires some guesswork. Biographical sketches suggest that he learned to play a game similar to checkers, using yellow and white kernels of corn or black and white beans as gaming pieces, as was "the custom among his people," when he was about seven years old and being raised by his maternal grandmother in Plainfield, Connecticut.[126] Roger Williams writes that the Narragansetts had a game "like unto English

Fig. 4. "The Great Checker Match" between Clarence Freeman (*seated right*) and Charles Barker of Boston (*seated left*) at the Providence Checker and Chess Club, where they met every afternoon and evening, except on Sundays, in a match that lasted from September 1 to 17, 1890. Online-Museum-of-Checkers-History.org.

cards; yet, in stead of Cards they play with strong Rushes" (*akèsuog*) and "a kinde of Dice which are plumb stones painted, which they cast in a Tray, with a might noyse and sweating" (*wunnaugonhómmin*).[127] Involving strategy, skill, and some luck, these games shared much in common with the game of checkers played by English settler colonists. More than pastimes, these games tested guile and fortitude, personal attributes that would have enabled Clarence Freeman's survivance. As the child of divorced parents whose marriage had ended on charges of intemperance and cruelty (or possibly adultery), he would have had to strategize ways to overcome insecurities and the dire prospects he faced coming from a broken and demoralized family and being Native American and poor in nineteenth-century New England.

Yet his grandmother, who continued to take care of him even after he was grown and "had traveled about a great deal," was a stabilizing force in his life. An article in *Narragansett Dawn*, a monthly magazine published by the tribe in the mid-1930s that covered tribal history and news, oral traditions, language, recipes, and more, reported that once when Clarence was gravely ill and hospitalized, and not expected to survive, his grandmother "performed wonders." She went into his hospital room, shut the door behind her, and worked on him with medicines that she had brought in "her little bag." When the nurse came to check on him, he was "packed in lard and breathing more freely.... He had had a concoction of Indian herbs and was decidedly better." The remedies that his grandmother ministered to him were apparently effective. Not only did his breathing improve but he lived for many more years and would go on to win many more checkers games. Among his friends, his feats as a checkers player would be rivaled only by his grandmother's skills as a curer.[128]

Massachusetts marriage records indicate Clarence married Seraphina Etolia Curry of Providence in Mansfield, Massachusetts in 1889. That same year, this unassuming, quiet man with a fondness for music and playing the violin, who a *New York Times* reporter guessed "must eat, drink, and sleep checkers" when not working as "a factotum and collector," simultaneously played with twenty of the strongest players said to have ever assembled at Providence's Checker and Chess Club and won a resounding victory.[129] The couple lived briefly near Clarence's relatives around Hoyle Square before settling in Fox Point in the 1890s. The house they rented on Transit Street was a step up from the former places where Clarence had lived. According to aficionados of the game, he did not play in any competitive checkers matches of note after 1890, but continued to play the game for its mental challenges and sheer enjoyment. He died at Rhode Island Hospital in 1909 after being hospitalized for six weeks for a bladder disorder and was buried in Providence's Grace Church Cemetery. During the last several months of his life his wife went to live with her sister and he moved in with his mother and grandmother in East Providence.[130]

Without the clues in city directories and in *Narragansett Dawn*, I might have never learned that checkers was more popular than baseball in the decade before the turn of the twentieth century, or might have dismissed the idea that playing checkers was Clarence Freeman's real occupation. He would have seemed as unremarkable as most Native people living at the margins of society for whom there were no expectations of fame or special recognition. Terse data in statistical records that provide a litany of jobs held by Native men are devoid of any commentary about work performance and individual accomplishments, except for what might be inferred from patterns of employment and residence, and from other evidence that gives insight into the reputations that some gained for their skill and diligence in certain fields. That checkers player was listed as Clarence's occupation in city directories (occasionally along with janitor) from the late 1880s to the late 1890s suggests that he chose to draw attention to himself and his talents as an accomplished player in this game of strategy when his greatest matches were behind him and he could reflect on his achievements. One could also read into this his self-awareness about how he and other Native people were expected to conform to categories of legibility as defined by the dominant society. Although he understood the rules of recognition, or what Homi Bhabha calls the texts of intelligibility, he opted to subvert them in ways that challenged municipal record-keeping by insisting on making his presence known by his expertise in a game of strategy played against whites and his survivance in the settler-colonial world.[131]

Besides destabilizing the numbing monotony of listings in city directories, Clarence Freeman might be considered as someone who in the context of his Fox Point neighborhood stood out as a public character, a term coined by Jane Jacobs in *The Death and Life of Great American Cities*.[132] The qualifications do not require any particular talents or wisdom, only an ability and willingness to have contact with and talk to different people, be visibly present, and have eyes directed toward the street.[133] Characterized as humble and unassertive, this skilled checkers strategist might not have had the disposition that normally signals the loquaciousness and sociability characteristic of a public character. Yet his engagement with other enthusiasts of the game, regardless of their standing, along with his years as a hotel porter, seem to imply that he was far from an introvert. With his reputation as a champion checkers player secure and his high-stakes-match games behind him, one could suppose that he had come to grips with his fame and enjoyed the modest financial rewards that it had brought him. His home on Transit Street would have been a venue where he recounted his stories of survivance, in which games of skill—played on both woven trays and checkerboards—had major roles.

The street where he lived in Fox Point had been named for a rare yet predictable astronomical phenomenon called the Transit of Venus that occurs when the planet is seen passing between the earth and the sun. It was a geographic imagining that did not refer to the mundane activities of people getting from the Providence River to the Seekonk side of Fox Point or to "the projects of elimination and replacement predicated on colonial occupation."[134] Rather, it commemorated a sighting in June 1769 observed by spectators and amateur scientists from a promontory near the southern end of Thayer Street and what became Transit Street. More than a street spectacle, it was an opportunity for local astronomers to participate in an international scientific enterprise aimed at measuring the distance from the sun at different latitudes and verifying Providence's exact latitude as part of an ongoing colonialist effort to make places legible.[135] Clarence Freeman probably did not know the derivation of the street's name or about the gathering that happened there in 1769. Few if any did, including other Native people who lived in the neighborhood. Yet for him, Transit Street was a place of possibilities not normally envisioned by Native people in the nineteenth century or by the crowd that witnessed Venus's passage through the sky at the same location more than a century earlier. His journey there had involved crossing homelands, rather than the sky, to make his presence known.

Close to Clarence Freeman's a two-and-a-half-story Federal-style house on Transit Street there is a narrow alley called Mohawk Lane. Its name, unlike that of Transit Street, is not recorded in city documents that keep track of street names and their changes or in anecdotal histories that are part of Providence's folklore. Native-themed street names are not uncommon, and are part of the practice of appropriating indigeneity.

Yet rather than invoking Native ghosts from Providence's creation story, the name is a reminder that Fox Point was, and is still, known to some as a Native place where narrow streets and even narrower alleyways evoked a sense of belonging. This is true despite the late-nineteenth-century urban renewal project that cleared nearly 400 acres for city expansion on the pretense of halting the spread of the cholera virus said to be festering in the pigpens and slaughterhouses of Fox Point's crowded waterfront, and recent efforts to address the neighborhood's rundown and poor conditions.[136] Many of the houses slated for demolition, such as the one where Clarence Freeman lived on Transit Street, were spared when historic preservation rather than slum clearance became the modus operandi because of public outcries about the loss of historic-period buildings, though not necessarily about the loss of the histories of all the people who lived in them. Preservationist ideology and its counterpart, gentrification, rescued much of Fox Point's surviving historic architecture and halted further physical decline, but wrenched many people of color from their moorings.[137] These acts of violence to the human geography were no less harmful than earlier colonial dispossessions that attempted to preclude Native settlement and land use in Fox Point and urban histories that fail to acknowledge the experiences of Native people during the nineteenth and early twentieth centuries. The stories of these experiences, hidden and overwritten, are as much about urban living as those typically told about Fox Point.

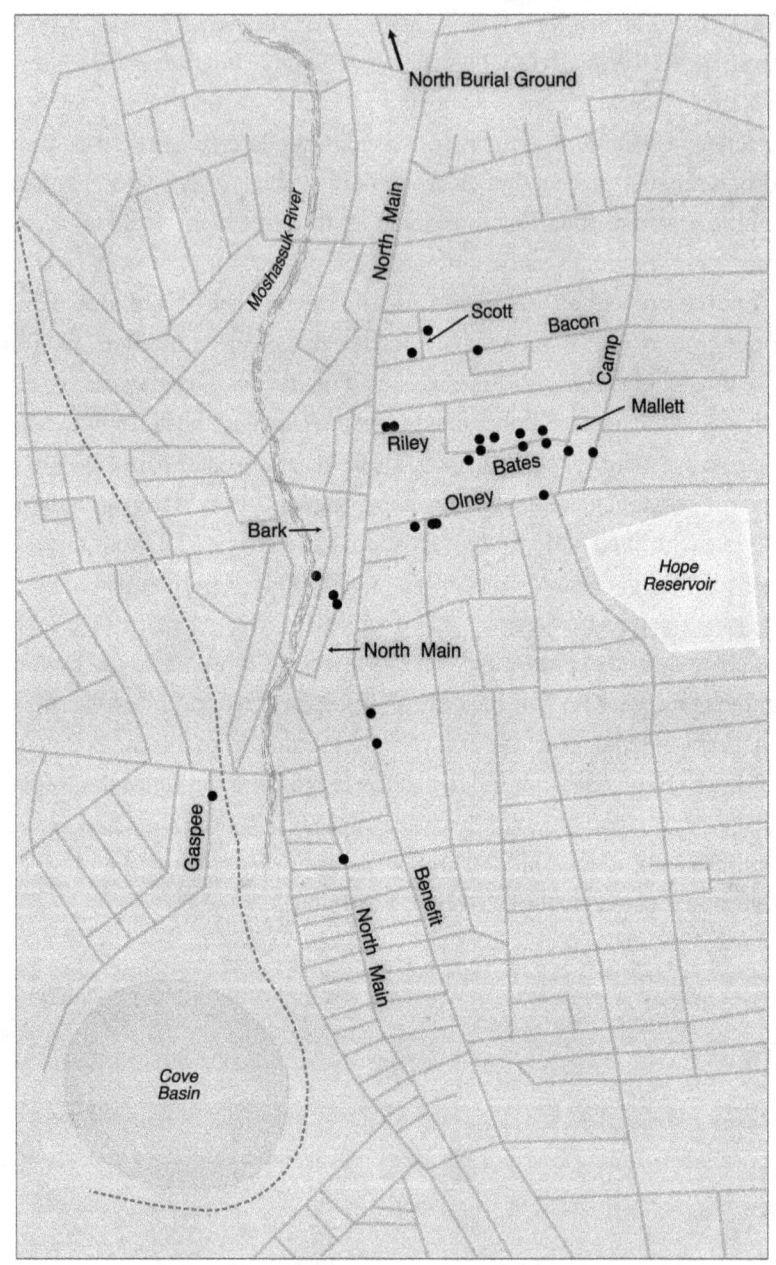

Fig. 5. Map of the Lippitt Hill homeland, showing the locations of selected Native households. Map by Lynn Carlson.

Lippitt Hill   2

Homelands of the Hill and Hollows,
Unholy Water, and Traditional Knowledge

The Lippitt Hill homeland is located to the northwest of Fox Point. At its southerly end, Olney Street demarcated a geographical as well as an economic and cultural borderland beyond the predominantly white enclave of College Hill and Fox Point farther to the south. Much like Providence's other Native homelands, Lippitt Hill's boundaries were permeable, with people of different ethnicities and economic means crossing over and intermingling for work and entertainment. In sections such as Addison's Hollow (nicknamed Hardscrabble) along the west bank of the Moshassuck River and the Olney Street area called Snowtown (considered to have been traditionally, if not strictly, African American) many residents were Native American—some with African American ancestry. As in Providence's other urban homelands, they would have bumped into, come across, and interconnected with each other.[1] Their shared experiences and bloodlines, along with labels such as "African Indians" and "Afro-Narragansetts," hardly begin to describe the complicated individual and collective histories of Lippitt Hill's Native residents, let alone shed light on the complexities of identity formation and ascription in nineteenth- and early twentieth-century New England.

Envisioning Lippitt Hill as a Native homeland challenges our imaginary. Its residences, many of them poorly constructed wooden structures that were tenements at best and shanties at worst, were repeatedly destroyed or threatened with destruction beginning in the nineteenth century. In 1824, dwelling houses were torn down or partly demolished in a race riot that erupted after a white mob assaulted a "dance hall" after months of mounting interracial tensions between white and Native and African laborers vying for occupation of the streets and the "Shingle Bridge" over the Moshassuck River at Smith Street where they congregated to find work.[2] The devastation that left Addison's Hollow, as the section of the Lippitt Hill homeland north of the bridge was then known, in ruins was judged to be beneficial to safeguarding public morality by ridding Providence of places considered to be nuisances, even if in a "somewhat improper manner."[3]

In 1831 Snowtown, south of the bridge at Smith Street, not far where the Rhode Island State House has stood since the early twentieth century, was the scene of more widespread destruction. It began with an altercation at a "cooky stand"—a nineteenth-century equivalent of a convenience store that sold fruit, vegetables, bread, cake, cookies, candy, rum, and beer—located in the basement of a brothel.[4] What started as disorderly conduct and a street fight in which a Swedish sailor was murdered by an African American man escalated into three nights of mob action popularly known as the Snowtown (or Olney's Lane) Riot, in which a dozen houses identified as brothels and unlicensed liquor establishments were leveled or gutted and other dwellings ravaged. Similar to the episode at Addison's Hollow, the Olney's Lane Riot was not just the kind of street brawl common in seaport towns, but an incident of racial and class unrest that eliminated many homes of Native Americans and African Americans. As a tactic of spatial and ethnic cleansing, it contributed to the erasure of the tangible presence of Native people from the urban landscape and from the pages of the city's history.

Industrialization also contributed to the neighborhood's physical erosion by placing a premium on residential land that could be developed to accommodate the city's expanding manufacturing base.[5] Land along the Moshassuck River, which furnished waterpower for mills starting with the settler colony's first grist mill in the seventeenth century, became one of the most industrialized areas of the city—and one of its most polluted, a condition that continues into the twenty-first century. Industries not only usurped residential and exterior space and contaminated the water, soil, and air, but they also transformed the most personal and protective of spaces, the home, into a place of potential illness and fear. For Native people, these effects could be felt in terms of their physical health, and in an ever-growing awareness of the impacts of loss and destruction on the future of their neighborhood.

This process of destruction continued after World War II, when Lippitt Hill, as well as other parts of Providence, became the focus of urban renewal, slum clearance, and redevelopment, the nomenclature of efforts aimed at reengineering America's cities on the grounds that particular neighborhoods were undesirable and posed social dangers.[6] In the late 1950s, the Providence Redevelopment Agency determined—from data compiled from the U.S. Census's 1940 and 1950 Censuses of Housing and from housing evaluation surveys done by the city—that the area bounded by Olney Street and Doyle Avenue on the south and north and Hope and North Main Streets to the east and west had a preponderance of buildings used or intended as living spaces with physical deficiencies. These conditions were conducive to ill health, disease transmission, juvenile delinquency, and crime that adversely affected the area and presented a menace to public safety and morals as well as community welfare.[7] Most of the houses inspected had at least one basic deficiency, such as irreparable structural deterioration, overcrowding, lack of dual egress, absence of sanitary facilities, and inadequate lighting and ventilation, and were slated for clearance.[8] The Providence Redevelopment Agency had the task of demolishing a large number of houses in this "slum blighted area," some filled with furniture and boxes of personal possessions, using a twenty-ton M19 surplus army tank and more conventional wrecking tools. Streets such as Bates, Clorane, Howell, Kirk, Lippitt, and Mallett, familiar to generations of people in the neighborhood, were eradicated and replaced with a shopping center and apartment complex, a school, and a church.[9] Many of the displaced moved to houses that were available nearby on Lippitt Hill as part of the redevelopment and rehabilitation plan. Some resettled to South Providence on the west side and other parts of the city.[10] In the pretense of urban renewal, a part of this Native homeland was obliterated, and its houses, yards, streets, and open lots were re-envisioned as a new matrix of housing, facilities, and external space intended to improve quality of life.

Lippitt Hill 73

This destruction, condoned by regulations of morality, class, and race, requires devising alternative pathways to exploring Lippitt Hill as an indigenous homeland. These physical erasures and the caricatures of neighborhood localities resonating in historical narratives and public perception do not mean that the experiences of the Native people who lived there are inaccessible. They exist in stories woven through both individual and community memories, documentary evidence, and archaeological traces. These evidentiary strands create interpretive bridges to the past regardless of the degree to which Lippitt Hill or other urban neighborhoods have been effaced by redlining for development, invaded by industry, ravaged by vandalism, or mythologized.[11]

Archaeological evidence indicating that Lippitt Hill was an indigenous place long before it was reconfigured by settler colonialism has been reported since the 1700s. According to several accounts, a laborer discovered an "Indian skull" about 1786 while digging at the foot of Bowen Street in a public improvement project aimed at facilitating ascent from North Main Street, close to where the seventeenth-century settler colonists laid out their house lots.[12] The skull was associated with the post-cranial bones of someone described as being arranged in a sitting posture with "a stone pipe near his mouth and the bail of kettles hanging on his right arm."[13] The kettle had rotted away, but other human remains and artifacts were found nearby in what was a relatively recent burial ground "unknown and unexpected" to Providence's Euro-Americans.[14] Arousing only mild curiosity, the pipe and kettle bail were taken to the Indian Tammany Society's "wigwam" (or headquarters) above Watson and Gladding's dry goods store on North Main Street, where the group's members delighted in all things Native American. The objects would have been used in their secret rites in which "playing Indian," to borrow Philip Deloria's words, was a way of imagining American identity amid the contradictions of newly won independence and modern capitalism.[15] These "Indian Relicks" are thought to have been "swept out with the rubbish" after the society moved from North Main Street and have never been found. To facilitate the movement of traffic and ease pedestrian ascent up the steep hillside to the tonier homes of College

Hill, the bones and dirt found on Bowen Street were removed, carted off to fill Zachariah Allen's wharf.[16] Allen, a successful textile manufacturer, mechanical inventor, and civic leader, is credited with spearheading these public improvements, from which he benefited collectively and as a private citizen. A tireless antiquarian, he spoke and wrote about the treatment of Native Americans on the bicentennial of the burning of Providence, and worked to ensure the visibility of places associated with settler colonialism's narratives of triumph such as "What Cheer" rock in Fox Point, the other name for Roger Williams's landing site. But he neglected to protect the Native burial ground beneath Bowen Street.[17]

The discovery of this sacred place (below an orchard where "a colored boy" was reported to have amused himself in an improvised game of ninepins by rolling small boulders in the direction of an old gravestone near the spot where Williams was buried) should not be surprising.[18] Nor should the existence of a large, well-preserved Native settlement that archaeologists found nearly two centuries later buried under six feet of fill at Gaspee Street at Carpenter's Point on the north shore of a former salt pond formed by the flow of rising tidewater and the confluence the Moshassuck and Woonasquatucket Rivers. The site's tools, cooking hearths, storage pits, and dense refuse, dating from around 900 to 1300 AD, attest to its importance as a place of habitation in Providence's long-term indigenous history.[19] The pond, which English settler colonists called the "Great Salt Cove" and later simply "the Cove," had natural and cultural qualities that were highly valued by Native people. By the late eighteenth century, wharves and factories had been constructed around its edges; and a century later, this watery landscape, which Thomas Doyle, Providence's long-term mayor, called "holy water," was completely filled to create additional space for railroads leading into the city. The fate of the settlement, excavated because of historical preservation laws that required archaeological recovery prior to the construction of a new train station in the 1980s, and the burial ground, unearthed during roadwork, are entwined with expansionist colonialism. Town- and city-making intruded into these indigenous spaces. Human and material remains were incorporated into landfill to expand Providence's commercial and industrial waterfront. Both places are potent reminders of settler-colonialist interventions into the indigenous past and of that past's disquieting effects on the separation of urban and indigenous histories.[20]

Native people might very well have been onlookers to the roadwork on North Main Street who had their own place-based stories to tell, though Henry Dorr writes that "no Indian was left to relate any tradition of their date or history."[21] Nancy Brown Garcia (Shawomet Narragansett), an expert beader and chief deputy historical preservation officer of the Narragansett Indian Historical Preservation Office, reported that her father, Max Brown, a crane operator in the Providence area for fifty years, kept a small, tattered notebook in which he secretly recorded thousands of sites with Indian remains uncovered during the construction of new roads and buildings.[22] Max Brown, who lived in Warwick, told her that his employers would typically look the other way, ignoring these remains rather than stopping to investigate them because delays could put building projects behind schedule and be expensive. When he called attention to the human bones, his concerns were disregarded because "the order of the day was to pave it over," as Brown Garcia recalled. After a series of personal misfortunes that he attributed to speaking up about the burials, and fearful for his life after his house was blown up, he never again spoke to coworkers about his encounters with the dead. I suspect that Max Brown's notebook contains accounts about what compelled him to follow through on his responsibilities to respect the ancestors' burials, not just hastily jotted notes about the locations where they were inadvertently dug into. The sites of these encounters were the wellsprings of ancestral voices that he might have heard or ancestral visions that he might have seen and of his own experiences, even though the landscape had become congested with strangers and filled with new construction.[23] Even as Native communities face increasing competition from their colonial dispossessors and move closer to the mainstream of U.S. society, place-based stories both old and new, as Keith Basso reminds us, are everywhere to be found.[24] The newer ones, like those that Max Brown told to his daughter, offer a pathway to understanding the experiences of indigenous people on the streets of Providence and on the roads they traveled to and from the city, to compensate for the untold stories about what happened at Bowen and North Main Streets.

Navigating Landscapes of Betrayal and Unholy Waters

William J. Brown wrote in his memoir that he moved from Fox Point to Olney Street on Lippitt Hill. His grandfather, Cudge Brown, had purchased two lots on Olney Street, one more than 100 feet wide that he bought from Moses Brown, his former enslaver, and an adjacent 30-foot parcel that he had purchased years before, where he dug a cellar hole and raised the frame for a house. A storm, followed by an illness, prevented him from finishing the house. But more significantly, Moses Brown's negligence in providing a deed caused the family to lose most of the land. After Cudge's death, Noah, William's father, was told that the deed could not be found and that Moses Brown had mistakenly resold the land. He took possession of the smaller lot, which had been secured by a deed, and was given a strip of land 10 feet wide from the parcel purchased from Moses Brown as compensation for the latter's betrayal and negligence. The resulting 40-foot-wide property, which Noah plowed and cultivated to provide food for his family, was William Brown's home for most of his adult life.[25] Other people of color also relocated to this north end neighborhood of Providence where land was cheap, though their life stories are not the subjects of firsthand accounts like William Brown's. Some bought land and built small houses in Addison's Hollow, the section of the Lippitt Hill homeland named for the builder responsible for constructing much of the inexpensive housing on the banks of the Moshassuck River that was torn down in the riot and who, according to Brown, rented to anyone who would give him his price.[26]

Brown's recounting of his family's attempts to secure land is important to understanding the often unjust and unscrupulous land deals that affected Providence's people of color, but also for the insights it offers about Lippitt Hill as a lived space. In relocating to Olney Street William Brown, like many of his contemporaries, moved to a part of the city that he had known. It was where his grandfather, a former slave, had started to build a new home and where his father, like his grandfather, had raised a vegetable garden. It was where he and his classmates made visits to Sullivan Dorr's orchard at Bowen and Benefit Street up the hill from North Main Street during school recess to steal fruit and engage in other pranks.[27] It was a section of Providence's east side where—except for a few thickly developed stretches of Camp, North Main, and Olney Streets—there were still unbuilt upon tracts to about 1900. Inflected with the experiences, subjectivities, and resistances of a person of color, Brown's sense of place is the kind rarely acknowledged in the city's narratives.

A city person born and bred, whose life was largely circumscribed by Providence's east side, William Brown is generally considered more African American than Native American. Yet his attachments to the extended Narragansett community of his maternal relatives and their cultural traditions were part of his upbringing and his experiences into adulthood. In 1842 when he was about twenty-eight years old and living on Olney Street, he went to his grandmother Chloe Prophet's funeral, held at "a meeting house in Cranston [Rhode Island], situated four miles from her residence and five miles from the city of Providence," where she was eulogized by a white minister. Including William, one hundred and five grandchildren, filling twenty-six carryalls and wagons and only accounting for a portion of her relations, were in attendance. He recalled that after the service her body was loaded onto "a nice, clean lead-colored farm wagon, partly filled with straw about half-past eleven o'clock for the old Indian burying ground." The funeral cortege "moved in a line, on a trot," and stopped along the way at "a house and shop," where "many got out to get something to drink" that he presumed was an "ancient practice" because he had never attended a country funeral. When the revelers had satisfied themselves, the procession continued to the burying ground where the mourners were met by "a tall Indian man," the manager of the meetinghouse, who had traveled there by foot. The coffin was lowered into the prepared grave, which was then filled and a large stone placed at its head to mark the spot so that Chloe Prophet's relatives would know where she was buried. The burial ground was "the most wild and lonesome place" he had ever seen, where "thousands of Indians had been buried." Situated about two hours from the meetinghouse, allowing for the stopover at the tavern and some "fast driving," the burial ground was either "the old Indian burying ground" on the Charlestown, Rhode Island, reservation or possibly one in the Providence-Cranston area.[28]

The ways of life of country people seemed strange to him, as he remarked in discussing his grandmother's funeral, but they were not entirely foreign. Stories that his grandmother, mother, and other maternal relatives told him were meant to teach lessons and provide a larger context for coping with life as an indigenous person, regardless of his mixed ancestry. One such story was about the Old Blood's Mine, a place belonging to the Narragansetts that his grandfather visited with Chloe's father, "a man of note and one of the chiefs," at his grandmother's request. According to Brown's retelling, the two men rode by horseback from Cranston for four hours on a road that "was filled with Indians all the way" to get to the spot. The account of what happened when they reached the destination "to dig for money" is reminiscent of tales in New England Native folklore that use motifs about hidden treasures to warn about disturbing or disclosing the locations of important sites of memory keeping.[29] William's grandfather, who was not a member of the tribe, went into the mine with Chloe's father (Grandfather Jeffrey), where the specter of "a large Indian with his head cut and the blood streaming from his wounds" so frightened him that he vowed never to go there again. The elder man, a Narragansett, neither saw nor heard anything as he dug for silver. The story was about the possession of cultural knowledge, rather than wealth, and about which individuals had the right to acquire this wisdom.

For William Brown, this place-based story and its teachings would have reverberated against presumptions about his race and any conflicts he might have harbored about his identity. He might have been reminded of the words of his maternal relatives and of his grandmother's funeral at services that he attended at the Congdon Street Baptist Church south of Olney Street or at meetings of the Young Men's Union Funds Society and other African American mutual aid organizations that he joined. That his genealogy was different from but most likely similar to those of many of the people standing next to him could have surfaced at other times and in other contexts that he chose not to mention. Although he says nothing more about his Native ancestry beyond the first few pages of his memoir and does not discuss Rhode Island's decision to abolish the Narragansett tribe, which occurred between the time that he wrote the preface in 1874 and when he completed the book in 1883, he was, as Joanne Pope Melish has argued, conscious of being an Indian.[30] He died of apoplexy in 1885 after having resided on Lippitt Hill for decades and knowing that many others like him, who were assumed to be African American, had core relations in and with tribal communities. Some opted to be "colored," as they might have been officially classified, while others staunchly held onto their Native identity or claimed both, either simultaneously or at different times during their lives, as they charted courses of survivance in Providence's urban homelands.

Alice Chace Northrup (Troy-Watuppa), who was from a small tribal reservation in the easterly part of Fall River, Massachusetts, about five miles from its business district, lived on Gaspee Street in the Lippitt Hill homeland in the 1860s. Called the Fall River Tribe in public documents or simply the Troy Indians, the Troy-Watuppas were described as Pocasset by geography, Wampanoag by political allegiance, and Algonkian by linguistic affiliation.[31] Alice's husband, Cato Northrup, born in East Greenwich, Rhode Island, was identified as a "colored foreigner" living in Providence with his Fall River Indian wife and their six children in John Milton Earle's report on Massachusetts Indians.[32] Providence directories place him at Cushing Street on the east side at the time of the city's incorporation in 1832, which suggests that the couple probably moved there soon after they married. Four years later the growing family was living on Planet Street in the same neighborhood. They then moved across to the Weybosset (west) side of Providence, where they lived near the city's downtown commercial area into the 1850s. Around the mid-1850s, the family returned to the Fall River reservation and stayed there until the end of the decade, when they moved to Gaspee Street in the Lippitt Hill homeland.

The conditions that drove the Northrups to leave Providence for the Troy-Watuppa reservation are unclear. Cato was a laborer who probably held a series of unsteady jobs to help support the family. The work was typically unspecialized and was considered to be the lowest rung on the occupational ladder, requiring almost as much effort to find as to do.[33] Two of the Northrups' sons, James and David, were also laborers and might have found jobs through Cato's connections. Their wages would have supplemented the family's income along with any earnings that Alice made from doing housework or laundry for other families. The family was reasonably comfortable, enough so that Cato's name appears in Providence land records. As treasurer of the Free Will Colored Church, one of many Protestant congregations in the city, he negotiated for the purchase of land near Pond Street in Upper South Providence that became the site of the Second Freewill Baptist Church, more commonly known both to Indians and African Americans as the Pond Street Church.[34] Cato was also a member of the African Grays, a fraternal organization and, according to William Brown, had enough spare cash to pull a five-dollar bill out of his pocket to ease over a minor incident that threatened to disrupt one of the group's public events at the city's Market Square.[35]

Despite these indices of reasonable economic stability in the family's life, people of color in the city as elsewhere struggled with the effects of prejudice. During the late 1840s and the 1850s a cholera virus struck the ramshackle tenements along the Moshassuck River (as well as residents of the Fox Point waterfront) particularly hard and threatened the rest of the city.[36] Although the Northrups did not live in the city's most vulnerable neighborhoods before they relocated to the Fall River reservation, the disease that hung over Providence would have been a recurring worry in their lives and in those of other city dwellers, especially those who crossed into these homelands to visit relations and friends during the summer months when cholera cases tended to be the highest. Conditions on the reservation, though not guaranteeing better economic opportunities, might have presented the attractiveness of a rural way of life unfettered by the city's everyday challenges. Benjamin S. Winslow, the tribe's appointed guardian, reports that the tribe's health in 1848 was good, and "with one or two exceptions, very good." The only illnesses stemmed from intemperance, as well as from smallpox that affected one family, which had recovered and was doing well. For Alice Northrup, who had raised her children in Providence apart from her ancestral community, there would have been other reasons to return to the reservation. Communal and family attachments to her homeland would have tugged at her despite the prediction that many of the tribe would never return.[37]

In 1857, there were only six families still living on the Fall River reservation, with three others living in the vicinity, though the community was described as better off than it had been. Houses were in "good repair" and a small portion of the land was cultivated.[38] Although Earle's report noted that only nine acres of land had been cleared in more than a half-century and that tillage was assessed to be very inferior, the move back to Fall River would have allowed Alice's family to live close to the land, where they could raise a small garden and some livestock, and find other ways to make a livelihood. More important, it was a place where she could rekindle her ties to the tribe and to places that were familiar to her and whose stories she would have shared with her children. This would also have been the case for other Wampanoags who moved back to the reservation after residing in New England's cities, however complicated and difficult these reverse migrations might have been. Zerviah Gould Mitchell, for example, attended public schools in the town of Abington in Plymouth County and a private school in Boston, where she taught briefly. She raised her children partly in Boston, but mostly in the North Abington section of Abington before moving back to the reservation in 1879.[39] She settled on land at Betty's Neck that she inherited through an unbroken chain of title dating from the seventeenth century with her two unmarried daughters, Charlotte (Wootonekanuske) and Melinda (Teweeleema). Educated and well accustomed to urban life, the Mitchell women, whose Native identity was steeped in traditional knowledge, made a successful transition to country living.[40] For Zerviah, an activist in the revival of Wampanoag cultural heritage during the latter half of the nineteenth century, the move was the culmination of a twenty-five-year battle to hold onto land that she rightfully claimed was hers. During the long-drawn-out legal struggle she and her "part Cherokee and part English" husband moved a house to a lot assigned to them by the tribe's guardian and worked to get it ready as a family home, only to see its windows broken and "other similar outrages committed" that were intended to discourage them from becoming full-time residents. In the wake of these events Earle thought that Mrs. Mitchell "would be better situated among her friends at her present home in Abington, where she has long resided, than among strangers, between whom and her unkind feelings prevail, on the plantation at Fall River."[41]

Despite Earle's views about where Zerviah should live and what would be best for her, she and her family had deep attachments to places in the Fall River homeland. Her son Thomas drowned while bathing in Elder's Pond in Lakeville, not far from Betty's Neck, on June 16, 1859, suggesting that family members traveled from North Abington to storied places that they had heard about to experience them firsthand.[42] Lying idle for years and encroached upon by squatters, the acreage at Betty's Neck had to be cleared and tilled, and a house, barn, and other outbuildings erected before it could become a suitable living space that the Mitchell women would eventually inscribe with their own experiences and memories. The process of possessing and dwelling in the land of their ancestors began modestly, if not tentatively, by taking steps toward country life as recounted in a diary that Charlotte kept during the winter of 1896.[43] Over the next few years, their small cabin with an all-purpose living and dining room and kitchen acquired a two-story extension that served as a separate sleeping quarters, their barns and poultry sheds were well stocked, their fields, gardens, and strawberry patch became lush, and they built several small camp sites along Assawompset Pond, where their lands were situated, that they rented out during the summer.[44]

The Northrups' move from the city to the Fall River reservation was short-lived compared to that of the Mitchells. They returned to Providence after about a year, apparently because they found the conditions too difficult.[45] Their new home on Gaspee Street was an extended household that included James and David, eight-year-old Mary J. Ellis (the only child of Alice and Cato's deceased daughter Mary), and a two-year-old grandson.[46] For the Northrups, the decade after their return to the city was no less trying than the time that they had spent on the Troy-Watuppa

Lippitt Hill 83

reservation. They had lost both a daughter and a son, and had assumed the responsibility of caring for their young grandchildren. The environs of Gaspee Street on the north shore of the Cove Basin had become increasingly compromised as a result of population growth and commercial and industrial development.[47] The low-lying water of the Blackstone Canal that flowed alongside the Moshassuck River skirting Lippitt Hill to the west was filled with sewage, decaying animal carcasses and vegetable matter, and industrial waste that was only partially carried out to sea by the tidal flow. The air was said to be saturated with "an unholy stench," and the area was beset with "black flies which were often so numerous as to cover the side of buildings and blacken the walls of rooms at some distance from the Cove."[48] It was here that Cato Northrup died of consumption in 1860, as did Edward Northrup, Alice and Cato's eldest son, who had been in and out of the Dexter Asylum for the last ten years of his life.[49] A year later, their daughter Mercy Ann and her son Benjamin, whom the Northrups had cared for, died, she of tuberculosis and the little boy of unknown causes.[50] Alice outlived Cato by five years. Her death was reported by Benjamin Winslow in his annual report of 1865 on the Fall River Indians, as was that of James, who died in 1864.[51] At the time of their deaths, both were living at the rear of 26 Spring Street in the city's Upper South Providence area, not far from the Pond Street Church. Alice Northrup's situation might be described as neither strictly urban nor rural, given that her life intersected both worlds. She was identified with the Troy-Watuppa community of her birth, as were her children, and was seemingly behind the family's decision to return to the reservation after being away for three decades. Despite the relocation, however brief, and other ways that she sustained ties with her tribal community, Alice and her family had become intricately woven into the emerging fabric of Native Providence.

Practicing Indigenous Knowledge in an "Unusually Spacious City"

Sarah Baxter, an Indian doctor, lived on Bark Street in the Addison's Hollow section near the Moshassuck River. Formerly called "the lane by the Mill Pond," Bark Street, which derived its name from a tannery where bark had been collected and stored for processing hides during the early settler-colonial period, continued to be one of the city's prime manufacturing areas into later centuries.[52] Sarah rented her home, a dwelling (or "laboratory") with an office and bedroom on the lower floor, two bedrooms, a parlor, and a sitting room above, and a separate kitchen house, from the American Screw Company, the nation's largest manufacturer of screws and rivets in the nineteenth century. It was where she consulted with clients, who, according to Zachariah Allen, sought her care "day and night" and on "all diseases," offering to cure them of the physical and emotional illnesses associated with urban life with her own brand of medicines. Allen claimed that Roger Williams had crossed the Moshassuck River more than a century and a half earlier from a spot near these "screw factories" (consolidated as the American Screw Company) to ascend the steep elevation west of Bark Street toward an Indian encampment opposite the colonists' grist mill, where he was intercepted by a sachem who told him to go back and that he would not be harmed.[53] In dispensing her medicinal knowledge Sarah Baxter made similar assurances to Providence's later settler colonists.

Little is known about her early life. Providence death records indicate that she was born in Nantucket, though her route to Providence, where she lived from about 1840 to her death in 1882, is untraceable.[54] Her date of birth, estimated to be around the late 1700s or early 1800s, suggests that she was born sometime after the "Indian Sickness," a deadly epidemic that struck Nantucket in the 1760s, and before pronouncements about its "last Indians."[55] J. Hector St. John Crèvecoeur, an astute observer of American life, wrote about that "strange fever" that afflicted the island's Native people, but not its settler colonists, stating that it foretold impending doom for the former, who were destined "to recede and disappear before the superior genius of the Europeans."[56] Yet neither Abram Quary nor Dorcas Honorable, the island's iconic "last Indians"—subjects of several paintings and an early daguerreotype photograph, who died in 1854 and 1855—would be the last.[57] Others less famous, who were also born after the epidemic, defied the dire forecasts by their presence. Sarah Baxter was one of them.

The names of her parents are unknown, though "Pendell" is written in her death record in the space for her mother's name.[58] Although the surname does not appear in lists of survivors of the Indian Sickness that I checked, I suspect that her mother was a Nantucket Wampanoag and that her father might have been African American or some other ethnicity. Intermarriage and cohabitation between Native Americans and African Americans were common on Nantucket, as in mainland cities and countryside, though the importance of seafaring on the island raised the possibilities for exogamous unions by employing men from "Nova Scotia to the Mississippi" and foreign ports.[59] Some Native people who survived the 1763 epidemic and their descendants amalgamated with the African American community known as New Guinea, where the Native American roots of residents were frequently logged into local marriage records and mentioned in public documents expressing anxieties over the education of children having appreciable Negro or Indian blood.[60] Whether Sarah Baxter was raised there or elsewhere on Nantucket, she was born into colonial circumstances in which her Native American ancestry, like that of other indigenous people, was a matter of consternation to European settler colonists. Accustomed to seeing women who ran households and shops while men were at sea, and inspired by stories of survivance, she had moral courage to go forward in life.[61] Yet precisely when and under what conditions she left the island, which John Winthrop once described as "full of Indians," remain unknown.[62]

Her name first appears as a resident of Providence in the 1850 U.S. Census, when she and her husband William, both listed as mulatto, were living at the city's north end. William, a retired merchant seaman, ran a "victualling cellar," or eating saloon, on Canal Street near Market Square's food and produce vendors.[63] His address is recorded as 23 Bark Street in the 1853 city directory, which suggests that this was the couple's home in 1850 and possibly as early as 1840.[64] The income from his business would have provided a reasonable measure of economic stability for the couple, as did Jimmy Axum's boarding house in Fox Point for him and his Narragansett wife.[65] Although these businesses offered the possibility of earning a better income than in other occupations open to people of color, they were subject to insinuations of moral impropriety that frequently led town officials to revoke their business licenses and made them the targets of random violence. Such outcomes, though not unexpected among people of color at Providence's economic and social margins, were not inevitable.[66] Whether for these or other reasons, William Baxter's "eating saloon" went out of business by 1854. He died a year later of typhoid fever at the age of forty-nine.[67] About a decade later, Sarah Baxter emerged in the urban labor market as an "Indian doctress."

Baxter was variously labeled Indian, mulatto, Black, and colored, but the tag "Indian doctress" remained relatively constant in references to her in public documents. The label combined a racial designation with the work that she performed—a common naming practice in identifying a Native person in New England since the eighteenth century that was later used for occupations considered to be quintessentially "Indian."[68] From the 1860s to the 1870s, Baxter's name was attached to a brand of remedies, most notably "Mrs. Baxter's Indian Healing Balm" and "Indian Bitters," that were marketed in Rhode Island and Massachusetts. Advertisements printed in Providence directories offer insights into how she participated in urban life from the home on Bark Street that she had lived in with her husband and a boarder, and later headed amid the din of large-scale industry that dominated this part of the Lippitt Hill homeland.

The earliest advertisement, printed in 1867, was for "Mrs. Baxter's Indian Healing Balm," an "Internal and External Remedy, for the cure of Asiatic Cholera, Rheumatism, Neuralgia, Sore Throat, or Dyptheria, and other Diseases," a liver syrup for both lungs and liver, and a cough or croup remedy. The copy claimed that all these medicines were purely vegetable and were prepared and sold only by Baxter. Not content to bank solely on statements about the products' effectiveness, the ads show a Native woman, partially dressed and with hair cascading down to her knees, holding a sprig of herbs in her left hand. The image, which is closely reminiscent of John White's sixteenth-century watercolors of Algonquian Indians, suggests that Mrs. Baxter's cures were prepared according to prescriptions derived from long-held cultural knowledge, rather than merely the result of experimentation and invention. As a marketing tool, the romanticized image connected Sarah Baxter and her remedies to generations of Native healers and deep stores of cultural knowledge. In acknowledging ancient wisdom, the advertisement sold tradition as an antidote to modernity and its afflictions in ways that would not have threatened the imaginative security of non-Indian consumers.[69]

In the 1870 Providence directory, a different image accompanies an advertisement for the same products. The brand's logo is a woman wearing a fringed dress embellished with Native American motifs, a beaded necklace decorated with what appear to be bear-claw pendants, bracelets, leggings, moccasins, and feather plumes at the back of her head. She holds a medicine bottle upright in her right hand, and her left hand, which is extended downward across her body, clutches a bunch of herbs. Except for minor variations, her manner of dress and quaint demeanor recall tropes of the Indian princess, a widely used image that in various iterations and distortions more closely fit the mainstream white imaginary about Native American women than did White's watercolors—or historical or contemporary reality.[70]

An 1874 ad introduced a new Baxter product called Indian Bitters "as a general Spring and Summer medicine" and remedy that could not be surpassed for headaches, dizziness, oppression of the chest, indigestion, darting pains all over the body, weak stomach, and bilious complaints. In this ad, the face of the brand defies stereotypes. Neither reminiscent of an "Indian Princess" nor John White's paintings, it is an image of a woman uncannily characteristic of Sarah Baxter herself, depicted in photographic realism (fig. 6).[71] She wears a dark-colored dress with a white ruffled collar and bow typical of widow's dress in the 1870s. From her hooded eyelids, her gaze is reassuring, exuding wisdom, reliability, and confidence. She represents herself as the person behind the brand—a "woman of color" of a certain age, strong and knowing, who would have no substitutes.

When the 1874 advertisement appeared, Euro-Americans were convinced that New England's Indians had become irreparably mixed because

Fig. 6. Sarah Baxter pictured in an advertisement for her Indian medicines in the 1874 *Providence City Directory*. Ink on paper, RHi X17 1702. Courtesy of the Rhode Island Historical Society.

of intermarriage and dismissed the validity of their Native heritage. Contrary to popular opinion, "real" Native women would not look like those in the earlier ads. With the Civil War ended and state governments in southern New England acting on ideas about Native American assimilation by abolishing local tribes, Sarah Baxter emerged from behind the guises of strategic essentialism to communicate directly to consumers.[72] Regardless of whether the brand's new face was a personal decision or a clever marketing strategy to differentiate her products from the glut of cures by impostors promising good health—or both—it underwrote her claims of authenticity and purity for Mrs. Baxter's remedies. It might not be a coincidence that the advertisement was printed at a time when expectations about what "authentic" and "pure" meant for Americans and their particular histories were being redefined as well as contested. Sarah Baxter stood behind her medicines by revealing herself as typical in appearance to many of the region's Native people as a result of historical conditions that contributed to intermarriages and to epistemic uncertainties among Euro-Americans that went far beyond the marketplace.

Lippitt Hill 89

After her husband's death Baxter, who was childless, continued to live on Bark Street. Although the need to support herself as a widow might have provided a practical reason for marketing her medical services and remedies, claims in the advertisements suggesting "years of experience" point to a seasoned and skilled practitioner whose doctoring attracted a following in Rhode Island and Massachusetts.[73] At a time when Indians were not supposed to be modern or urban, let alone entrepreneurial, she capitalized on her knowledge of traditional healing arts to navigate an increasingly urbanized, industrial, and alienating world. It provided her with the means for earning a livelihood, as it did for so many other Native men and women who came to rely on medicinal and divining wisdom to establish and maintain footholds in the region's towns and cities. As Indian medicine surged in popularity in the expanding nineteenth-century healthcare market, it not only competed with remedies prescribed by mainstream physicians and druggists, but attracted practitioners masquerading as Indian doctors, who sought entrée into urban communities. Sarah Baxter was neither a pretender nor merely a brand name. She was an actual person behind the medicines that bore her imprint, whose life experiences are testaments to the struggles over indigenous identity in nineteenth- and early twentieth-century New England. She died insolvent at the age of ninety, two years after her name and the tag "Indian doctress" were last recorded for 23 Bark Street in a Providence directory. After her death, Mrs. Baxter's medicines were no longer manufactured.

At the end of her life, the value of the contents of her house and kitchen was insufficient to satisfy what she owed to her debtors—her landlord, the American Screw Company, a physician who treated her in her "last sickness," a carpenter, and various individuals who provided medical services, supplies, and labor in her final years.[74] Both were razed along with the surrounding factory buildings and replaced with new construction, precluding any immediate possibility of recovering material and botanical evidence of her doctoring and medicine making. In adapting traditional healing practices to urban life, she might have purchased herbs from apothecaries or other providers, or possibly grew them herself.[75] Her post-mortem inventory indicates that she owed for unspecified "medical supplies." Although the entries are ambiguous, and were possibly related to charges for her own medical care instead of services and remedies she provided, they along with the ads suggest that she participated in the expanding and increasingly diversified network of medical practitioners and suppliers in nineteenth-century Providence, including the physicians who cared for her during her "last sickness." But as Providence was "an unusually spacious city," she would have found plants with medicinal properties that appear in Northeast Native pharmacopeia growing wild in vacant lots, along the banks of the Moshassuck River and the Cove, in swampy areas, in patches of land sheltered by buildings, and in cracks in sidewalks within a short walk of her Bark Street home.[76] Many of these plants, collected in Providence during the early nineteenth and early twentieth centuries, are in Brown University's Herbarium.[77]

Among them are yarrow (*Achillea millefolium*) and wild plum (*Prunus americana*), used by the Mohegans to treat liver and kidney disorders, that could have been ingredients for Baxter's liver syrup. Baxter might have incorporated maple (*Acer saacharum*), pigweed (*Amaranthus retroflexus*), jack-in-the-pulpit (*Arisaema triphyllum*), canker lettuce (*Pyrola elliptica*), spikenard (*Smilacina racemosa*), white clover (*Trifolium repens*), and the bark, roots, and leaves of American elm (*Ulmus Americana*), an effective treatment for sore throats, hoarseness, and coughs, into her "excellent remedy for cough, or croup." Her spring tonic, a cure-all calling for "as many as ten plants" or more in Mohegan recipes, might have been made by steeping wild cherry (*Prunus serotina*), sassafras (*Sassafras officinale*), sweet flag (*Acorus calamus*), boneset (*Eupatorium perfoliatum*), motherwort (*Leonurus cardiaca*), black birch (*Betula lenta*), and spikenard that were part of the city's flora when she was making her medicines.[78] So was the ubiquitous and widely used dandelion. Additionally, seeds of Jimson weed (*Datura stramonium*), a "powerful plant" in the Mohegan pharmacopeia, dock (*Rumex crispus*), a blood purifier, sorrel (*Rumex acetosella*), a stomach aid, grape (*Vitacea vitis* sp.), a pain reliever, and blackberry (*Rubus* sp.), a cure for dysentery, were recovered from nineteenth-century archaeological contexts associated with houses on Gaspee Street, a few blocks south of the narrow and mostly unpaved dirt road where Sarah Baxter lived and worked. This further suggests that plants with medicinal benefits were available to her within the Lippitt Hill homeland.[79]

Similar to other indigenous people who insinuated themselves into Euro-American society by nudging notions of indigeneity in directions they found useful, Sarah Baxter sometimes "played Indian" to appeal to the commonplace imaginings of non-Natives. At other times, she challenged these fantasies by overtly rejecting Indian-playing. Yet, rather than denigrating Native people, she used essentialized images of Indians as she maneuvered in the urban marketplace to reverse their negative political, social, and economic connotations in an attempt to appeal to and at the same time parody Euro-Americans' demands for authentic Indian remedies.[80] Much like inscriptions of her identity in official records, expressions of her identity in the ads were not static, but were refashioned amid continuing settler colonialism. From this perspective, art resembled life in the advertisements for her medicines—the life that she made for herself in Providence, where her knowledge and marketing of traditional healing practices were as much prescriptions for her own survival as they were for those who sought her care.

In an urban environment filled with all sorts of exploiters and imitators, Sarah Baxter exhibited the kind of resourcefulness and entrepreneurship that is rarely acknowledged for Native people, except for a few high-profile individuals. "Indian doctors" were epitomized as wandering practitioners who preferred desultory work and missed out on modernity. Sarah Baxter did not fit this archetype. Men and women seeking her care came to her home nestled among the factory buildings and shacks of Bark Street. Although there are no surviving records of the clients whom she treated or who purchased her medicines, her ads suggest that her reputation extended beyond her neighbors. Like her itinerant counterparts, she walked the unmarked trail between oppositional cultures, providing care for whites but presumably also ministering to people of color turned away by other doctors and seeking traditional cures.

On Street after Street: Unhidden Indians and Myths of Disappearance

In the maelstrom of nineteenth- and early twentieth-century urban life, other Native people made their homes in the heartland of Lippitt Hill east of Bark Street. Among them were Narragansetts with surnames such as Cone, Thomas, Creighton, and Nichols. Mary Jane Cone, whose family ties to Providence and the reservation ran deep, lived on Bates, North Main, and Olney Streets, all within a few blocks of each other, during the 1870s. Her name appears in the city's marriage books as early as 1866. The marriage was the second for her and for her husband, a blacksmith from Newport, Rhode Island, who was born on Block Island.[81] Sarah, her brother Edward's youngest daughter with his second wife, Frances Richmond, lived briefly on Bates Street. For Mary Jane, the other Cones, and the rest of the tribal members on the 1881 roll, the share that they received from the sale of the reservation would not have gone far, even judging by the economic standards of the late nineteenth century.[82] For those who accepted the payment—and not all did, according to tribal history handed down to John Brown and the late Ella Sekatau—it would have provided some cash for clothing and food or to help make the rent, and not much more.[83] When asked years later about what he did with the money, Charles Babcock, who was twelve years old when the shares were doled out, responded: "I did not see the money, but my father got me a new suit, the first store clothes I ever had. I also got a new overcoat and a new pair of shoes."[84] Whether they stayed in Charlestown or moved away, as some had previously done, tribal members could do as they wished with money. More than ready cash for families on the economic margins of society, a share in the money from the land sale brought with it confirmation of membership in the tribe that Rhode Island had declared extinct. It served as validation of a birthright that many Narragansetts who still called themselves by that name would be denied.

Frederick D. Thomas (son of Benjamin Thomas), who worked as a porter and coachman, lived on Bates Street near Mary Jane Cone and on Camp Street during the 1870s and 1880s (fig. 7). In an interview conducted in Charlestown during the summer of 1912, he told Harris Hawthorne Wilder, a forensic scientist from Smith College studying the effects of intermarriage with African Americans on Narragansett phenotypes, that he had been named after Frederick Douglass, who spoke in the village of Carolina on the outskirts of the reservation on the night that he was born.[85] No later than 1870, Frederick left the reservation with his mother and siblings and was living in Providence.[86] He had enlisted in the Eleventh U.S. Colored Heavy Artillery in 1865 from Providence, which would place him in the city a few years earlier.[87] He married Emma Slocum (Seekonk Wampanoag), who was from Pawtucket and whom Wilder described as having "Indian features and straight hair," at the Pond Street Church on May 25, 1871.[88] Their daughter, Annie, was born around 1875. Like his father, who described himself as "three quarters of everything but Indian" in a retort to arguments insisting that tribal membership should only be inherited by blood that was not mixed, Frederick Thomas was among the Narragansetts who would have been in "every part of the earth" and had even found "their way into Providence."[89] But he also would have been among those who, as recorded in the 1883 report on the Narragansett Tribe, went "in and out" of Charlestown, especially in August for the tribe's annual gathering when the place became "pretty thick" with Indians, many of them males over twenty-one who also lived away from their birthplace.[90]

Martha Creighton lived on Olney Street. Born in Charlestown or North Kingstown, Rhode Island, about 1824, she was living in the city with her husband, a non-Indian, by the 1850s.[91] In 1855, she and her siblings petitioned to sell about sixty acres of land on the reservation that they had inherited from their mother, Sarah Niles. Although Martha lived apart from and received little benefit from the land, she maintained her ties to the tribe by visiting occasionally, sometimes with her children.[92] Her son, Thomas H. Creighton (later known as Hamilton), who was born at the back of 407 North Main Street in 1857, stated in written testimony to the detribalization committee that he went with his mother when she visited her sister on the reservation, though he had never voted in tribal elections.[93] Martha Creighton was on the 1881 tribal roll, even though her

Fig. 7. Frederick Thomas lived at 51 Bates Street in the late 1870s. This photograph from December 9, 1959, shows the house after the Providence Redevelopment Agency took ownership of properties in the neighborhood for urban renewal. Courtesy of the Providence City Archives.

life as a Narragansett had long been centered on Lippitt Hill, where she lived for as many as thirty years. That was where most of her twelve children were born (at least most of those for whom there are birth records) and where some of them died.[94]

From the late 1800s to the early 1900s, Abigail (Abby) Smith, whose maiden name was Noka, lived on Bacon Street and, later, a few blocks south on Bates Street. Born around 1837 in Rocky Brook, a prosperous mill village in South Kingstown, Rhode Island, she was the daughter of John Noka, a master stonemason, and Esther Rodman, but was not included on the 1881 list despite having paternal and maternal surnames that linked her ancestry to the Narragansetts. As a child, she worked in the Hazard Mills, a textile factory in nearby Peacedale, where her family lived from when she was about seven years old. After she left the mills she attended the local school, and was later put out to work as a domestic servant for Samuel Rodman, a major landowner and manufacturer. While in the Rodman household, where she remained for fifteen years, she met Archibald Smith from Virginia. They married in 1874. By 1880 they were living with their two small sons on Lippitt Hill where, after decades of working for the Rodmans, Abby kept her own house and her husband was employed as a porter. The published transcripts of the detribalization proceedings indicate that she attended August Meetings regularly until the early 1870s and that she remembered having done so as recently as a year before the deliberations.[95] Abby died of pneumonia in 1907. Her obituary in the *Providence Journal* called her "A True Narragansett" with "high cheekbones and finely modelled features characteristic of her tribe," though her name was not listed on the 1881 roll. Aside from her appearance, she was described as having "few Indian traits," except for "a fondness for an out-of-door life more marked than is usual in a woman."[96]

According to the obituary, with Abby Smith's passing, "one more name was added to the death roll of the once proud and powerful tribe of the Narragansetts, whose remaining descendants are now so few that in a short time they will have vanished from off the face of the earth, and only the memory and the records of the part they played in the history of Rhode Island will remain to perpetuate the name and fame of the former lords of the forest primeval and the waters of the bay which bears their name."[97] This assessment was greatly exaggerated. Abby's sons remained in the neighborhood, where they continued to live in the family-owned home on Bates Street with their father. By 1910 her younger son, Roland, was the head of a household that included his wife and young daughters, his father, and his wife's mother. Her other son, Frederick, also stayed at the house on Bates Street, where he resided with his wife and Gideon Noka, his cousin, who was the son of his mother's brother Gideon and Gideon's wife, Abby Perry Noka of South Kingstown.[98]

Among the Narragansetts who lived on Lippitt Hill were those who were born and raised in Charlestown, those who had lived elsewhere, and those who had never lived anywhere other than Providence. This urban homeland was where those who were part of the diaspora from the reservation and their children found support among Native kindred with similar life experiences. The same was true for indigenous people from other tribal communities in the Northeast who moved to Lippitt Hill, such as Sarah Baxter, Alice Chace Northrup, and the Henrieses and Oling Jackson, Nipmucs with family ties to Worcester County in central Massachusetts. Winfred Henries, a teamster, and his wife Augenette, who were from the Webster/Dudley (Chaubunagungamaug) band, lived on Scott Street, an extension of Bacon Street, with their five children: Edith, Elizabeth, Edwin, Ethel, and Elsie.[99] Oling Jackson, a truck driver who delivered cake and other baked goods and who had lived in Providence since he was a young boy, was over on Mallett Street off of Olney Street with his wife, their son and daughter, and two foster children.[100] For the Native people of Lippitt Hill, their indigenous neighbors, regardless of their nativity and tribal affiliation, were the ones who would have been there for them during births, illnesses, and deaths, when jobs were scarce, when the day's or the week's pay was less than had been agreed upon, and when they could not make the rent. The Native people of Lippitt Hill supported each other when their invisibility in the eyes of most whites—on account of their skin color or hair texture or the perception that they were out of place—seemed almost too hard to bear. This Native homeland was more than a collection of closely-knit streets and houses where they lived. It was a place of a new colonial history inscribed with their subjectivities and moral lessons that existed within an evolving urban landscape that the descendants of the early settler colonists would continue to stamp with their own versions of Native history.

On September 21, 1883, Euro-Americans dedicated a monument to Canonicus, the seventeenth-century Narragansett sachem, at North Burial Ground. This former sand pile, deposited by the Moshassuck River and surrounded by swampland that had been set aside as the city's first public cemetery in 1700 and transformed in the nineteenth century into a garden-like, multipurpose space for the living and the dead, was a short walk away from the homes of Lippitt Hill's Native people.[101] The dedication was the culmination of efforts to honor the sachem that

Rev. Frederic Denison made more timely with his urgings a month earlier at the unveiling of a memorial rock at Fort Ninigret in Charlestown that symbolically marked the end of Rhode Island's detribalization of the Narragansetts.[102] His wish for "some massive, rugged rock" was answered when a stone meeting his criteria was discovered eight feet below ground during a sewer excavation on South Main Street about halfway between Fox Point and Lippitt Hill.[103] Its symmetrical shape, hinting of an original provenience near a stream bank long covered by urban fill, evoked themes of deep time, progress, and extinctions that in the rhetoric of detribalization made it seem particularly suitable for commemorating a dead sachem and a former tribe. The boulder, carved with the name "Canonicus" and "a rude bow and arrow," combined the name with Miantonomo's mark on the deed in which the sachems granted Providence lands to the seventeenth-century European settler colonists.[104] For Native people living nearby, North Burial Ground's curving roads, artificial ponds, ornamental plants, sculptured grave markers, and the Canonicus boulder—a landscape easily accessible from the heavily traveled North Main Street and its back streets or by crossing through neighbors' yards and vacant lots—was a space that was as inviting as it was foreboding.

The monument was unveiled by Moses B. Prophet (Narragansett), who lived and worked at Whatcheer Stables on Benefit Street on Providence's east side, south of Lippitt Hill. In his introductory remarks, Elisha Dyer, a past Rhode Island governor and chair of the dedication committee, said that Prophet "unite[d] with us in behalf of his people in this tribute of love and honor to the memory of this noble old chieftain."[105] Eight-year-old Annie Thomas, Fred and Emma Thomas's daughter, described only as "a little Narragansett Indian girl," presented the Hon. George Carmichael Jr. of the Indian Commission with a bouquet of flowers. Neither Prophet nor Annie Thomas is reported to have uttered a word. They were recruited as token Indians to attend this ceremony, which attracted as many as a thousand onlookers, including the mayor and other politicians, Rev. Denison and like-minded history enthusiasts, and about two hundred high school students from Providence who were

Fig. 8. The dedication of the Canonicus Monument, North Burial Ground, where as many as a thousand people watched its unveiling on September 12, 1883. Anonymous. Gelatin DOP photograph, RHi X3 7715. Courtesy of the Rhode Island Historical Society.

transported free of charge by the Union Railroad Company to sing at the event (fig. 8).

Although the voices of Moses Prophet and Annie Thomas were muted, their presence was evidence that detribalization had not done away with Narragansett people. Attendees who bothered to look around and listen closely, whether standing on the hillside or seated among the three hundred on the platform, might have seen or heard Native people from Lippitt Hill and the city's other homelands who were not merely shadowy figures of an indigenous past, but part of its present and future.[106] Their names might have been unknown and their faces unrecognizable, as well as difficult to make out in photographs, and a cursory inspection would have conveyed the distinct impression that those in attendance were overwhelmingly white.[107] Yet appearances can be deceiving. Moses Prophet, called Narragansett in the dedication program, was classified both as Indian and white in U.S. Censuses, though he was related to a long line of Prophets of Narragansett, Pequot, and African descent.[108] Putting aside the arbitrary nature of encoding racial identity in censuses, other Native people, not identified in the program, might also have gone unnoticed by Euro-Americans. They were not supposed be there, standing so close to the latter that the space separating them was reduced to zero, allowing their sleeves to brush against each other and their bodies to touch, intensifying racial anxiety.[109]

Not only were Providence Indians not supposed to be there, they were not expected to have their own attachments to and memories of North Burial Ground. Set against the Moshassuck River Valley, the burial ground's open space evoked a panorama familiar to generations of ancestors. But to Native people during the nineteenth century, the landscape also had characteristics of a park, one close to home that they might have visited at times other than when they buried the dead or celebrated them. Entering the space through the main gate off of North Main Street or climbing over or through its rail fence, they encountered a flat terrain relieved by a steep hillside created by a glacial esker, enhanced by ponds, trees, and shrubs. Here Native children from the neighborhood could roam and amuse themselves in games of hide-and-go-seek, concealing themselves behind tombstones, as children frequently do in urban graveyards, and older Native men and women could rue that the cemetery was on Providence lands that were once theirs. Notwithstanding the praise heaped on Canonicus by honoring him with a monument, even if belatedly in the opinion of some Euro-Americans, the romanticized views of settler colonialism invoked at the dedication ceremony would not have resonated with indigenous people. North Burial Ground may not have been a place that had special associations with the sachem for them based on stories they had learned from tribal elders. Yet one could guess that after listening to the speeches, poems, and patriotic songs, and seeing the horse-drawn carriages with local dignitaries and the U.S. flags and yucca planted around the monument, new memories were formed. North Burial Ground would have become a place with reminders of the politics of commemoration, of named Narragansett participants being relegated to nonspeaking roles, and of reiterations that the epitaph of the Narragansetts as a tribe had been written.[110]

For Moses Prophet, who must have driven along North Main Street to the north end many times, North Burial Ground would, after the ceremony, have seemed a more sinister and anxiety-inducing place in his road map of the city than it had previously. Even for Annie Thomas, who was too young to understand the meaning of the words spoken or why she was chosen to present flowers to the Indian Commissioner, the event must have left lasting memories that she could recall years later. With these recollections would come a deepening comprehension of that day and what had happened to the Narragansetts, along with an awareness that participation at public events such as dedications, pageants, and public anniversaries was a responsibility and a testing ground, especially for Native people like herself who lived in the region's towns and cities.[111]

Hamilton Creighton understood the importance of representing his Narragansett ancestors at these events, even though he was not on the final tribal roll and had never lived anywhere but Providence. His name appears in the scrapbook of the Indian Council of New England, whose members included Native people from Providence and other northeastern cities and towns. He attended its first meeting at the Pond Street Church on December 13, 1923, where he was a representative of the Narragansetts. At its meeting of October 14, 1925, held at the Masonic (Colored) Temple at the corner of Benefit and Cady Streets south of Lippitt Hill, he was named a "tribal chief, " a title given to officers of local "tepees" in the Indian Council's hierarchy.[112] As a member of the organization, Hamilton Creighton would have attended its biannual meetings, which combined business, lectures, and displays of Indian culture, and taken part in visits to historical sites where monuments to important sachems and events in the Narragansetts' early colonial past were dedicated. These outings offered opportunities to serve as a public ambassador for the region's indigenous people, to rediscover places known from oral narratives, and to socialize with individuals from other tribal communities. Traveling from Providence, he and other members would have retraced the routes of their ancestors as they made their way to storied places deep in Narragansett Country. Here, Hamilton Creighton might have temporarily suspended any resentment that he harbored about Rhode Island's treatment of the Narragansetts and felt a renewed sense of cultural pride. United by their individual and collective experiences of survivance, he and other Native people from Providence's homelands were at the forefront at these events. They stood shoulder to shoulder with non-Natives who might have been uneasy about these stirrings of activism and about the fact that Native people were not merely on the sidelines as invited guests, as Moses Prophet and Annie Thomas were when the Canonicus Monument was dedicated in North Burial Ground.[113]

News about the New England Indian Council's activities would have spread across Lippitt Hill from street corners where residents gathered, yards where they talked over fences, and kitchen tables where they shared meals, as would news about tribal and family matters, landlords, employers, tax collectors, and whoever was the city's mayor. It was a neighborhood where children often stayed into adulthood. Their families might have encouraged them to select a marriage partner from a family they knew, but, as Rob Welburn (Assateague, Cherokee, African American) suggests, extended kin's taken-for-granted "caveats, admonitions, and encouragements about who was acceptable for marriage" lacked the same stringencies in off-reservations and urban communities that they had on reservations.[114] These children, many of whom had intermarried, as had their parents, brought forth a new generation of Providence Indians who remained in the Lippitt Hill section and had connections to the city's other homelands where they had core relations and friends. They sustained the neighborhood by providing a sense of continuity that would attract other indigenous people and contribute to its viability as an Indian place despite relocations to other parts of Providence or to Charlestown and other ancestral reservations.

Other Narragansetts from Lippitt Hill also took active roles in awakening public consciousness about New England's Native people. Frank M. Nichols, known as Chief Gray Eagle, who lived on Mallett Street during the 1920s and 1930s and later two blocks over on Howell Street, was a member of the National Algonquin Indian Council, the organization that succeeded the New England Indian Council after 1925 and shared many of its goals. His uncle, Frank E. Nichols, whose name was on the Narragansett tribal roll along with the names of his children, lived on Bates Street around the turn of the century with his wife, Georgiana, and three of their children.[115] When she died, he remarried and relocated closer to Fox Point. Following his second wife's death, he moved in with his nephew on Mallett Street, who cared for him until he passed away in 1921.[116]

Modernity and Totems of Forefathers at Sunset Cottage

Edward Michael, known as Chief Sunset, also lived in the maze of streets that defined the Lippitt Hill homeland. He and his wife owned a house at 91 Bates Street in the 1920s and 1930s, and later moved to Olney Street between Kirk and Clorane Streets, where he resided at the time of his death in 1949. Born in Charlestown in the 1860s, he attended the Indian School, and was living on the reservation when his name was entered on the tribal list as "Edwin E. Michel." His father, Brister Michael, was a member of the Narragansett Indian Council during the detribalization process, and his mother was Mary Champlain. Like many Narragansetts, Edward Michael had knowledge of the proceedings from tribal elders—its outbursts of violence and behind-the-scenes strong-arm tactics—that did not match the public transcript.[117] Among the omissions in reports of the proceedings was that whites had lured his father, who was reluctant to sell the reservation, to Cross Mills, the site of the second of three public hearings to decide on abolishing the tribe, as a deliberate ploy to get him drunk and cloud his judgment. Edward Michael's life after the land sale is sketchy in official records.[118] His name appears as a servant in the household of a physician in Putnam, Connecticut around the turn of the century and a few years earlier, as a coachman in Providence.[119] After years of moving between Connecticut and Providence, he settled permanently on the east side of Providence by 1910 and worked as a chauffeur for a family "instead of ranging the woods" (in Earl J. Clausen's words) as his ancestors had done.[120]

As a public figure and member of the National Algonquin Indian Council active in revitalizing Native American culture in New England in the

1930s, Edward Michael did not go unnoticed.[121] Although his paternal grandfather, John Michael, was Irish and had married into the tribe and lived on the reservation, a Providence newspaper writer reported that he was one of the few surviving "pureblooded" Narragansetts with "all the attributes of the Indian—the tall wiry figure, lankiness, sharp, protuberant nose, sharp eye, coppery-red face and coarse back hair, with a clean-cut mouth."[122] When he dressed in full regalia, as he did at public events and at a drawing class at the Rhode Island School of Design where he modeled, Edward Michael was said to look very much like an American Indian whose "profile would be appropriate on a U.S. coin."[123] When he was dressed in this way while not at staged events or in a studio—as he was when the public relations chief for the Rhode Island Council of Defense encountered him on North Main Street on the morning of March 30, 1943—his presence could be disconcerting.[124] Native people whose appearances did not fulfill expectations of what it meant to be modern belonged in the past and not in cities.[125]

Yet Edward Michael was not merely "playing Indian" nor was he a ghost. His home on Bates Street among Lippitt Hill's mostly one- and two-family houses was a wood-framed one-family cottage close to Mallett Street.[126] I have not been able to find photographs of the house, which I confirmed on my drive-by is no longer standing, but a description of it, written by Princess Red Wing (Mary Congdon Glasko) (Narragansett-Pokanoket Wampanoag), editor of *Narragansett Dawn*, appeared in a 1935 issue. The detailed account is based on her two-hour visit to the Michael home, "snuggled in among the more officious buildings on the east side of Providence," with Chief Pine Tree (William Wilcox) and Princess Minnetonka (Marion Brown) during which Pine Tree asked Chief Sunset to sit in on meetings of the Narragansett Tribe of Indians, recently "retribalized" as a nonprofit corporation under Rhode Island law, because "every drop of Narragansett blood was needed." Red Wing wrote that a "little, old fashioned iron gate" led into the front yard of the home. Over its doorway that faced west toward the setting sun—"an old custom of the Indians, symbolic of the going out of life as easily as the going down of the sun"—hung the "signs and totems of his forefathers."

In the cozy sitting room, entered directly through the front door, Mary Michael served hot biscuits, homemade jam, and tea, while her husband brought out "old relics, books, newspaper clipping, pictures, etc." to show the visitors as he told stories of his childhood and the Narragansetts' past. A picture of Mollie Rodman, Edward Michael's grandmother, "a fine looking Indian lady of three generations ago, or more" whose features bore a striking resemblance to his, was displayed on one of the walls. As the guests lingered over tea, Chief Sunset talked about his grandmother and brought out more old family pictures. Another room in the cottage, described as a bedroom, had windows that faced east, "long the custom of many generations of Narragansetts," so that the rising sun could hear Chief Sunset's morning prayers.[127]

The picture of Mollie Rodman and objects of Indigenous culture in the home give the distinctive impression that its interior and exterior were marked in ways that expressed what it meant to be a Native while embracing modernity and not forgetting forebears.[128] Edward Michael's home was not a vestige of Indian life that persisted in the city from earlier times. It was neither a traditional *wetu* nor a tract house. Rather, this one-family cottage, like homes of his neighbors and others in the city's poorer neighborhoods, was constructed by small builders for small buyers looking for an investment, something tangible for their money, where they could establish a home.[129] It was a house that they could call their own among those of family and friends, Native or non-Native, and that they could furnish with family heirlooms and modern amenities as they saw fit and as their circumstances allowed. At 91 Bates Street Edward Michael seamlessly blended elements of modernity with mementos of his ancestors' struggles, his childhood and early adulthood in Charlestown and Connecticut, and his years in Providence. These were memories that he kept close as he drove through Providence, walked the streets of his Lippitt Hill neighborhood, traveled to Charlestown for the August Meeting and to Camp Ki-Yi, the Glaskos' Cranston farm, for Rhode Island's Tercentenary Celebration, and went to the Rhode Island State House in clear sight of Lippitt Hill in full regalia to watch Gov. Theodore Green be inaugurated in 1933 and sign the Fenelon Bill establishing an annual

Rhode Island "Indian Day" in 1936. These are memories that would have also accompanied him on his journey to Rhode Island Hospital where he died on June 12, 1949 after a long illness.[130] He was buried at North Burial Ground, as were Abby Smith, Martha Creighton, and William Brown, his Narragansett neighbors in the Lippitt Hill homeland, who predeceased him. His grave lies in the cemetery's Potter's Field, marked by a small stone monument undistinguished from others in the plot except for a number that identifies the interment as his.

Like Hamilton Creighton and Frank M. Nichols, Edward Michael broadcast his indigeneity in and beyond his Lippitt Hill neighborhood. His house and those of his neighbors on Bates and other nearby streets, such as Clorane, Kirk, and Mallett, no longer exist. Lippitt Hill's houses, stores, garages, and what the *Providence Journal* described as "other fixtures and bric-a-brac that make neighborhoods at once common and unique," were razed and built over by the redevelopment project that bears its name.[131] The project was conducted before historic preservation legislation would have mandated an archaeological study to evaluate its impacts. It buried the surviving traces of Native people's houses and the yards and alleyways that they shared with their neighbors beneath an apartment complex, parking lots, and a shopping center that is today almost entirely occupied by nationally-owned chains such as Whole Foods, Orangetheory Fitness, Mattress Firm, Sherwin-Williams, Staples, Starbucks, Petco, and McDonald's, along with a Santander Bank branch. Gone are the places of recent memory where, the *Providence Journal* wrote, even after houses were vacated pending demolition, the neighborhood's children played "cowboys and Indians and war games," hid among abandoned buildings instead of gravestones, and rummaged for stashed treasure.[132] Also vanished are the homes in Addison's or "Squaw" Hollow beyond the railroad tracks west of Bark Street, which could have easily been imagined as a "stronghold of brigand chiefs that flourish in dime novelettes" before it went up in flames seventy years after the riots of 1824, according to a *Providence Sunday Journal* reporter.[133]

The reporter wrote that among the ruins of the fire were the remains of small, poorly constructed houses, some partitioned into two-room tenement units that had ceilings so low that it "would be difficult to swing an Indian club" even in the largest room. Floors were thickly encrusted with dirt accumulated over generations and walls, relieved in places by bare laths, were mostly stained with smoke, tobacco juice, grime, and "what looked suspiciously as blood." The deserted home of an "old colored collector of rags and junk" was described as equally, if not more, miserable, though another apartment was "a little more pretentious." One of its rooms served as a kitchen, parlor, dining room, and bedroom; a spare bedroom was leased to help pay the rent; and the shelves of a small closet held an assortment of "fractured crockery ware." Another house, divided into three dwelling units, suggested that the disposition of the residents varied and not all could be accused of "filth and neglect." Some exhibited the outward signs of a "flickering ambition to live well." One had a room decorated with "cigarette pictures, old almanacs, and other cheap lithographs arranged tastefully around the walls, together with prints of President Lincoln and memorial to the year of Jubilee." The kettle and kitchen utensils were "bright and clean," though these examples of progressiveness in the domestic arts were contrasted to the built-up grease on the cook stove and the remains of bread, oil lamps, dirty rags, and tattered clothing. Broken-down wagons, boilers, and tin cans, and discarded furniture littered the neighborhood's roadways and back lots, where clotheslines flaunted wash that was testimony to the work of the neighborhood's laundresses. Traces of paint on the rotting and weathered wood of these simply constructed houses suggested that they had been painted yellow with green trim on the shutters and doors. The reporter advised that winter, when "snow snugly hides the rich hordes of junk that lie unguarded in the backyards and by-ways," would be the best time to visit, if at all.[134]

The transformed landscape of the Lippitt Hill homeland is a harsh reminder of the politics of inequality that have continuously altered its pre-urban and recent urban past almost beyond recognition. There is virtually nothing left to see of its many houses and streets, and the possibilities of uncovering archaeological evidence of its complicated histories of indigenous survivance are largely fortuitous. Yet Lippitt Hill was a place where Native people had substantial presence and significance, rather than being apparitions or disreputable characters. It was where a diversity of Native people established and maintained footholds in Providence while sustaining strong ties to their ancestral communities. They defied the caricatures, let alone claims of their absence, by making their presence known as they marketed indigenous knowledge, represented the region's Native culture in intertribal organizations and at public events, and conducted their everyday lives despite recurring condemnations of their living spaces, episodes of spatial erasure, and attempts to silence their voices.

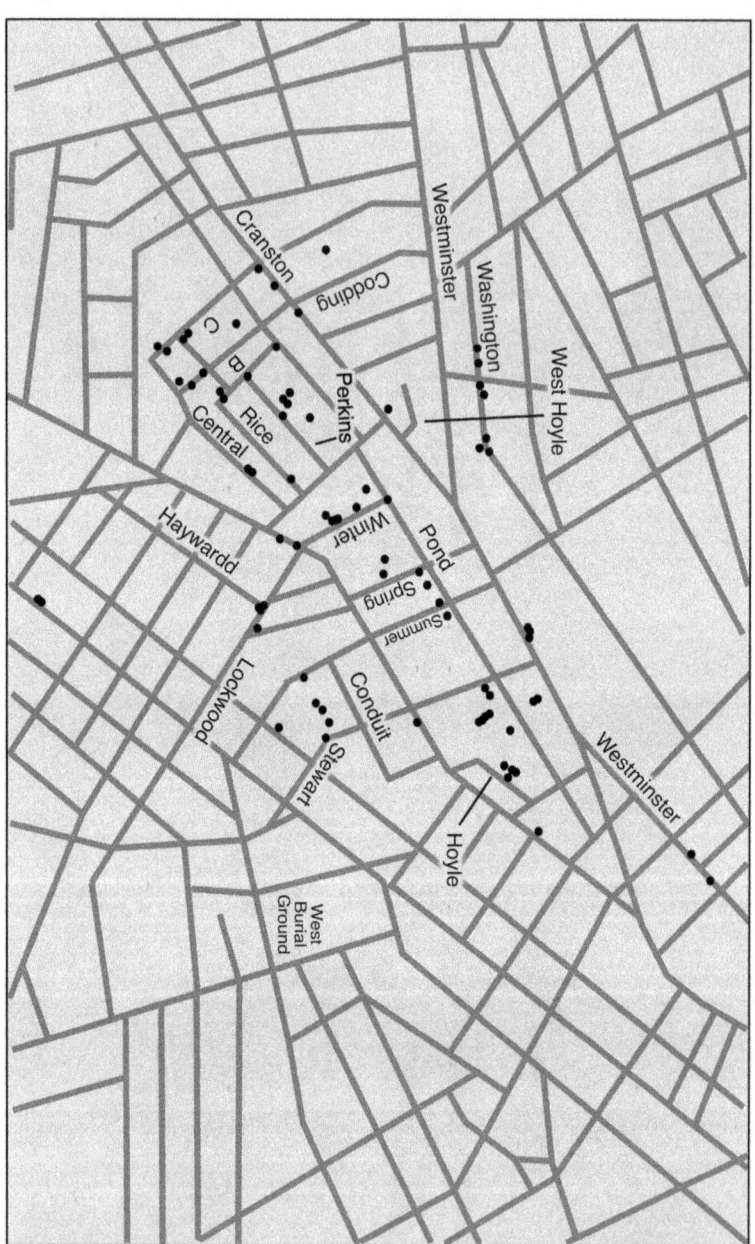

Fig. 9. Map of the Upper South Providence homeland around Hoyle Square, showing the locations of selected Native households. Map by Lynn Carlson.

Upper South Providence 3

*Homeland at the Crossroads, Churchgoing,
and Community Making*

Upper South Providence, the city's most densely populated Native homeland during the late nineteenth and early twentieth centuries, is on the west side of the Providence River in an area that early English settler colonists called Weybosset, a transliteration of Wapauysett, meaning "a fording place" where the river was narrow enough to be easily crossed. The shores above and below Weybosset Point were swampy. They provided lush meadows as pastureland convenient to Providence's easterly side, and later became place for shipyards, distilleries, slaughterhouses, tan yards, paper mills, and other noisome industries emitting reeking odors and putrid waste. As land was reclaimed from watery spaces, streets laid out, bridges built over the river, and a central railroad terminal constructed to link it to outlying areas, the Weybosset side, a landscape physically and socially apart from the original settler colony, emerged as the city's main civic and commercial center.[1]

Although settler colonists used its meadows as pasturage and relocated their businesses to the west side of the Providence River, Weybosset was an Indian place. What I am calling the Upper South Providence homeland was centered on Hoyle Square, a crossroad where well-trodden Native paths connecting Providence to the village of Mashapaug, Narragansett and Pequot homelands, and Neutaconkanut, the hilly, rugged borderland to the northwest, converged. Native people made their homes here at what later became the junction of Westminster Street and Cranston Street, a road laid down by the Town Council in the early eighteenth century along the course of the trail to Mashapaug, where passers-by saw more Indians than colonists a quarter-century after King Philip's War. Some relocated from Fox Point and Lippitt Hill and others from tribal reservations. They were concentrated on streets and in houses that anchored them to this homeland over successive generations, establishing an undeniable Native presence despite the city's historiography. Here they and Native people from Providence's other homelands gathered at the Pond Street Church. They had traveled by foot, horse-drawn carts, and later by trolleys to this homeland at the crossroads, and they would continue to remember the neighborhood as home even after urban renewal projects condemned their neighborhood, physically altered its landscape, and dislocated them from their individual homes.

The Accidental Homecoming of Canonicus Rock

The official name of Hoyle Square was Canonicus Square. This open, triangular space was given this name in 1899 to honor Canonicus, whose generosity to Roger Williams is credited in the city's origins tales with making Providence possible, though few residents of the city knew the square by his name. To most, it was Hoyle Square after the Hoyle Tavern. Built in 1739, the roadhouse was a stopping place for travelers, revelers, cattle drovers, and farmers who came to town to sell their products. It was where prominent citizens greeted General Lafayette when he came to Providence in 1824, where the Dorrites began their march through the city seeking voter rights for nonlandowners in the early 1840s, and where anyone could find a poker game. Here drivers would jostle with other drivers, wagons would be hitched, horse-drawn carriages would idle, thirsty and impatient horses would neigh, swoosh their tails, and stomp their hooves, and piles of manure and rotting produce would accumulate and their smells fill the air. During the late nineteenth century, trolley cars added to the comings and goings of the people and the miscellaneous vehicles frequenting the square. It was a place that was busy day and night, every day of the week, and especially on Sunday evenings, when, according to the *Providence Journal*, the clamor of "trolley cars, night lunch carts, fakers, loafers, and routine miscellaneous traffic" was replaced by outdoor religious services.[2] It was on these nights that Hoyle Square became a place where different values took hold temporarily and coexisted with alternative worldviews.[3] The sounds of preachers' exhortations, prayers recited in unison, music played by a succession of bands battling in sonic turf wars for possession of every inch of space, and jingling tambourines and jangling coins were said to be so loud that they could be heard on the streets beyond the western end of the square where the crowds gathered. These open-air performances were a means by which religious organizations in the neighborhood, among them the Salvation Army headquartered on Westminster Street, the Lighthouse Mission on Winter Street across from Cranston Street, and as many as half a dozen others, could lure followers to their indoor services, promising salvation. Apparently there was no shortage of people who flocked to this spot so thickly populated by religious denominations offering routes to redemption. The square's location at the intersection of heavily traveled thoroughfares and its open space free of vehicular traffic on Sunday nights made it an ideal place for street services, though none of the religious groups openly expressed the opinion that this neighborhood was any more in need of spiritual uplift than other parts of the city.[4]

The square's official designation in city records recalls still other stories of place. "Canonicus" was not an indigenous place-name for the land on which this wedge-shaped space was defined. Instead, it was the name of a notable sachem that Euro-Americans attached to a piece of urban real estate in what Natchee Blu Barnd calls a "disingenuous and ineffective 'reversal' of colonial impositions over Native geography and epistemology."[5] How the naming came about or what the Narragansetts and other northeastern Native Americans thought about it has not been recorded. Like other place-names transcribed or translated from sounds heard in Algonquian dialects, it was a gesture of "anti-conquest," a term that Mary Louise Pratt uses to describe a strategy of representation whereby European settler colonists seek to assert their innocence in the appropriation of Native lands.[6] Whether intended as forms of anti-conquest or symbols of respect, Indian-themed street names served to connect Euro-Americans to a deeper history in a rapidly changing and increasingly pluralistic society. Yet the use of Canonicus's name did more than evoke innocence and counter fears of displacement; it linked the sachem to a spot on the urban landscape that was significantly smaller than the expansive indigenous lands that became the city of Providence.

Some city residents only became aware that the place they called Hoyle Square was recorded in municipal records as Canonicus Square when a petition was made to rename it "Citizens Square" after Citizens Savings Bank, which had been built on the site of the old Hoyle Tavern in 1921. In lobbying for the name change at a public hearing at City Hall before the committee on street signs and numbers, the bank's spokesperson said that the request was made because the new building improved the character of the neighborhood. A representative of a rival bank that planned to build on the square questioned the use of a trade name, because it would give an unfair advantage to Citizens Savings Bank by raising brand awareness that would help to promote its products and services. "Canonicus was a good Indian, even while a live Indian," the Citizens Savings Bank lobbyist reasoned, and "his name should be perpetuated, but we have a boulder in the North Burial Ground named for him." He claimed that 20,000 to 25,000 backers had signed the petition for the name change.[7]

Among those opposed to the petition was Thomas Bicknell, who was instrumental in founding the Indian Council of New England. Declaring the proposal a "sign of the degeneracy of the times" and a symptom of "commercial barbarism," he argued for retaining the name, stating, "I want to make a plea for my old friend, Canonicus." Aside from the commemorative boulder in North Burial Ground, the sachem's advocate said, "this seems to be the only place he has left for a local habitation. But I suppose it is natural for a businessman to want to get as much as he can and then as much more as possible, but Canonicus has a right to be remembered in Providence because he owned it all first."[8] The city's Board of Aldermen voted five to three to accept the recommendation to retain the name Canonicus because of the other bank's concerns, older residents' sentimental attachments, and perhaps Bicknell's plea.[9] Still, one alderman felt that a name change was long overdue, given that in the more than twenty years that had passed since this public space was named Canonicus Square, there had been no change in popular usage.

Most who knew of this place at the crossroads, including the neighborhood's Native people, called it Hoyle Square.

During the 1980s, the name of the square would be revisited in reaction to the cumulative effects of urban renewal and highway construction. In 1961, the Official Redevelopment Plan for the Central-Classical Project targeted the area just south of Hoyle Square as what it termed a "slum blighted area" and relocated more people than any other single urban renewal project in Providence.[10] Within the project area, a sixty-seven-acre tract bordered by Broad, Westminster, and Winter Streets, and the north-south freeway (I-95), more than 300 families and approximately 400 "roomers," both white and nonwhite, were displaced.[11] Many local churches, among them the Pond Street Church, which had stood in the neighborhood for more than a century, were condemned.[12] The Central-Classical Redevelopment Project's transformations of the urban landscape were rapid and sweeping. Evacuation proceeded at such a fast pace that the city's relocation service agency questioned whether the process should be slowed down.[13] Even the disposal of the wreckage from the buildings to be torn down created a conundrum. The ordinances of nearby towns such as Cranston prohibited dumping nonlocal waste within their borders. The alternative, to burn the wood rubble at a site such as Fields Point in South Providence, would have inadvertently added to the accumulations of indigenous refuse in ancient shell middens as well as violating the city's air pollution regulations, though the wood from the buildings to be demolished was described as being "so old and dry" that a truckload would be rendered to ashes in fifteen minutes.[14]

In less than ten years, the square was virtually emptied of pedestrians. Monroe, Pond, Spring, and Summer Streets, where Native peoples had lived since the nineteenth century, existed mostly as memories. Family residences, most of them built before 1900, rooming houses, and shops had been leveled. Classical High School, whose academic reputation attracted students from other parts of the city, was razed to replace its outmoded and deteriorating building with a new facility (fig. 10). Central High School, an inner-city school located two blocks away at the corner of Pond and Summer Streets, was saved and connected to

Fig. 10. The Central-Classical Redevelopment Project's modernist Classical High School. The school is part of an educational campus that replaced the 1843 high school building and much of the neighborhood around Hoyle Square in Upper South Providence. Photograph by Patricia E. Rubertone.

the new Classical High School by a commons where students from the two schools could interact. The behemoth complex starkly contrasted with the school building it replaced and the one it subsumed, as well as with other buildings left standing in the neighborhood. Its high modernism, a statement of social engineering intended to revamp not only the schools, but also the surrounding neighborhood, overshadowed—if not obliterated—the once lively bustle of people and commerce at Hoyle Square. It was an absence that did not go unnoticed by those too resolute to leave their homes or abandon their businesses.

In an effort to reinvigorate the square, the neighborhood business association approached the city for new signage to direct the flow of traffic and pedestrians toward this once busy intersection. The city denied the request on the grounds that the name of the square was Canonicus, not Hoyle. Although members of the association vaguely knew the historical significance of the "Indian" street-name, they decided against petitioning to have the official name changed to Hoyle Square, because it might be perceived as offensive to the Native community. They had the Canonicus Boulder moved from North Burial Ground to the square in the late 1980s in a desperate marketing maneuver to forestall further decline of their businesses because of the displacements resulting from urban renewal, highway construction, a steady exodus of people from the inner city to the suburbs following World War II, and anxieties about redevelopment projects looming on the horizon.[15] No city records document how this three-thousand-pound rock, standing almost five feet high, was moved and by whom (fig. 11). At its new location it was set on a rectangular granite block with little fanfare, compared with the ceremony conducted at its original installation, and became the centerpiece for the neighborhood's hopes of economic recovery.[16]

Although the Canonicus Monument was relocated to an eponymous and visible spot on the colonized urban landscape, it did not fulfill business owners' expectations that it would draw shoppers to the square and revitalize the area's businesses. Instead it became a local landmark that neighborhood people referred to as "the potato," presumably because of its irregular and oblong shape.[17] Despite this familiar moniker, many who might not have known the official name of the square in city records recognized the name carved on the monument and knew something about the sachem it commemorated. Some were aware of the route that the boulder had traveled from the city's necropolis at North Burial Ground to Upper South Providence and of its meaning in relation Rhode Island's formal termination of tribal relations with the Narragansetts. Others might have wondered why it suddenly appeared in their neighborhood after many of their homes had been obliterated by urban renewal. Still more might not have paid much attention to it in walking to school, commuting to work, or going about other daily routines.

But for the Native people of Upper South Providence, the relocation of the Canonicus Monument was an unexpected homecoming symbolizing that their neighborhood was a Native place despite dispossessions and

Fig. 11. The Canonicus Monument at its new location at Canonicus (aka Hoyle) Square, 1996. Courtesy of Erik Gould, photographer, Rhode Island Photographic Survey, www.erikgouldprojects.com.

the incalculable losses inflicted by urban redevelopment. Precariously ensconced on a traffic triangle at the east end of the square, the monument became firmly rooted in place. Weeds grew in cracks in the concrete sidewalk. A street sign wavered overhead. To some, its condition was a disgrace.[18] To others, it reinforced the boulder's embeddedness in the urbanized Native landscape of Upper South Providence. Yet the Canonicus Monument remained at its new home only for a short time. It was uprooted sometime in the late 1990s. Its disappearance from the square remains a mystery, though many suspect that it was the victim of a traffic accident or foul play. My efforts and those by several municipal agencies to find the fallen monument and return it to Canonicus Square, if not its original field of memory, or to the Narragansett Tribe's reservation in Charlestown, Rhode Island, have been unsuccessful.[19]

Crossing Over: The Pond Street Church,
the Indian Council, and Community

Much like the Canonicus Boulder, Native people from urban homelands on the east side of the Providence River crossed over to Upper South Providence on the Weybosset side. Movement back and forth between the Lippitt Hill and Fox Point homelands and Upper South Providence to find work or to be closer to family and friends was not uncommon. Alexander Ammons lived on B Street briefly during the early 1880s before moving to Fox Point. Christopher Champlin, a former mariner, left Fox Point in the late 1860s for Upper South Providence, where he found steady work as a laborer and as a foreman, and by the turn of the century was employed as a curer of meat.[20] In 1895, he and his wife, Henrietta, who lived on Rice Street for about ten years before moving to nearby C and Booth Streets, filed a petition with the municipal court exercising probate jurisdiction to adopt the daughter of their late son, John, and his wife, Mary, who they claimed had willfully deserted the child and neglected to provide her with proper care and maintenance. The document indicated that Christopher, fifty-seven, and Henrietta, who was fifty-five and worked as a laundress, had the ability to raise the child, who was about seven or eight years old, and furnish her with "suitable nurture and education." Their request was granted because "of the degree and condition of her parents."[21] The Champlins continued to live at Booth Street until Christopher's death in 1901. Henrietta stayed in the neighborhood where she and her husband had lived for more than thirty years and where they had raised their two sons, one of whom died in childhood, and granddaughter.[22]

Amos Brewster also left Fox Point for Upper South Providence, as did his sister, Maria Blunt, and her husband, who had moved there a few years earlier. Amos and Mary, his second wife, both widowed when they married at the Pond Street Church in 1889, first lived on Pond Street and later on Codding Street. Amos, whose stride was impaired by the loss of three toes from a gunshot wound to his left foot during the Civil War, stopped driving teams and picked up work as a laborer. Mary supplemented the couple's income as a dressmaker, an occupation that offered the possibility of securing a more comfortable livelihood for them than he could provide. Ten years after they married, Amos died of endocarditis and paralysis to his right side.[23] After his death Mary Brewster stayed in the neighborhood. She moved in with her half-brother, William Hall, and his wife Annabelle, who was also a dressmaker, on Stewart Street in 1900.[24] She later relocated to 7 Angle Street, the home of James M. Stockett and his wife, Jessie, where she and Amos had lived at the time of his death. A few years later, she was living at Winter Street just off of Hoyle Square in a two-family residence that was also home to Rev. Zachariah Harrison, the pastor of the Pond Street Church. She is listed at other addresses on the same street into the 1920s.[25] In 1930 she left for Cranston, where she moved into her recently widowed brother's house. About a year later, she relocated to Transit Street in the Fox Point neighborhood, where she lived until her death in 1934 at the age of eighty-one.[26]

Mary Brewster's rootedness in the city and particularly in the Upper South Providence homeland might not seem worth mentioning. She was identified as colored, Black, and Negro in documents, but never as Indian.[27] Her place of birth on her marriage record to Amos was given as Sturbridge, Massachusetts, but when and under what circumstances she arrived in Providence and at Angle Street in Upper South Providence, where she lived for more than a decade before their wedding, are unclear.[28] As a woman of color and later as a widow, she would not have garnered much notice by historians. Official records that count, take notice, or inscribe, as Barry O'Connell, a scholar of Native American literature, writes, are notoriously problematic and often fail to report all "that actually happened" and "mattered" in the lives of New England's people of color.[29] Only an anonymous comment in a brief biography of Amos compiled by Brown University students on individuals buried in Providence's Grace Church Cemetery that describes Mary Brewster as a "humble seamstress who was known for her caring warmth and her kindness toward children" gives any insight into her character.[30] Attention to place, particularly to the many spaces where she lived in Providence, offers a keen sense of affective investments not easily grasped from vital records alone and of experiences she shared with—and as part of—the urban Native community.[31]

The Stocketts possessed a surname that frequently appears on the pages of *Narragansett Dawn* and also in other documents that have preserved the region's recent Native history. James M. Stockett was born in Norwich, Connecticut, about 1858. He married his wife, who was from Seekonk, Massachusetts, at the Pond Street Church in 1889, and lived at 7 Angle Street from the mid-1880s to his death in 1917.[32] He ran an eating house on South Main Street on the east side of the Providence River for a while, but worked mostly as a clerk, manager, and caterer in the food trades in Upper South Providence. By the early 1900s, he and his business partner, Howard E. Johnson, had a grocery that they had named Stockett and Johnson on Stewart Street. It was one of the many small stores around Hoyle Square.[33] His eldest son and namesake, James M. Jr., born in 1891, chose to study law instead of following his father's trade.[34] He was commissioned as a first lieutenant at Fort Des Moines, a training camp for Black officer candidates recruited during World War I from Howard University (from which James Jr. graduated in 1914) and Tuskegee, as well as from Harvard and Yale, and served in the 367th Infantry on the Meuse-Argonne front in France.[35] After the war, he moved to Fox Point, where he practiced law. In 1923 he was named one of the trustees of the Exeter Hill Monument, three boulders commemorating Miantonomo, his wife, Wawaloam, and Aspanuasuck, the place where they lived.[36] The monument, the first erected by the New England Indian Council, was unveiled in front of a large and mixed crowd that included Narragansetts and Native people with different tribal affiliations and ancestries who, like James Metamora Stockett Jr., had traveled from Providence.[37]

James Stockett Sr.'s sister, Wealthy, lived at 7 Angle Street in a separate household headed by their mother, Mary E. Stockett, a widow. Wealthy was a Hall by marriage.[38] In the early 1920s William Hall, a janitor at the Pond Street Church, rented the Cranston home that he shared with Mary Brewster after his wife's death to the pastor Rev. Zachariah Harrison. Connecting the dots between the Brewsters, Stocketts, and Halls and the places where they lived, and probing them more deeply, helps to reconstruct, at least partially, Mary Brewster's social network and makes it possible to derive inferences about what mattered in her life. What emerges from the silences in the records are not just people she bumped into, but family and friends who remained an integral part of her life through widowhood, advancing age, and residential relocations, as did the Pond Street Church.

Davis Leroy Jr., a historian, contends that Black churches such as the Pond Street Church were the "cultural womb" of African American life in Providence, but they also nurtured the city's Native American community.[39] For Mary Brewster, this wood-framed Gothic church at the corner of Pond and Angle Streets held special meaning. She married her husband there, and after his death continued to worship, catch up with friends, and find support at this site, built on land reclaimed from a glacial pond and purchased by the congregation from Cato Northrup for $422.[40] Although this area was once considered the outskirts of the city, urban engineering left "no quiet green stretches of pasture or meadow, no pond in which to swim in the summer or on which to skate in the winter, no pond into which slaughter houses [could] dump their refuse," as Florence Simister, a local historian and radio personality, remarked, "but in its place a crowded built up section of town."[41] Its houses, shops, schools, and a church would be where colonized people could contemplate an alternative future.

Besides Mary and Amos Brewster, the church had other members associated with the Providence Native community. Nancy (née Noka) Cheeves belonged to the congregation when she lived in Providence, as did other Narragansetts whose names appear on a church membership list from 1890 (Benjamin Gardiner/Gardner, Carrie and Hannah Hazard, Eliza Hilton, James M. Stockett, and Benjamin Thomas). Olivia (Olive) Henry, a Nichols by birth descended from Samuel Niles, an eighteenth-century spiritual leader of the Narragansetts who became an ordained Christian minister of the Narragansett Indian Church and an itinerant preacher, was also a congregant. Others listed had surnames that appeared on the 1881 tribal roll (e.g., Helm, Jackson, and Robinson). Like Mary Brewster, Alice Mosby, another church member, had been married to a Narragansett.

Some of these Narragansett descendants had not been born or raised on reservation land. They visited Charlestown to deal with family matters, vote in tribal elections, and attend the annual August Meeting before and after detribalization, as much as time, finances, and distance would permit. But after the reservation had been purchased, some might have felt that there were few practical reasons to participate.[42] Without a land base, sustaining the community would have become a more compelling priority and would have required even more work by those who still called themselves Narragansetts. Attending August Meetings, visiting family and friends living close to the former reservation and away from it, and finding gathering places within urban homelands where they could socialize and share stories would have been a critical part of a concerted and creative effort to maintain and build community. For the Native people of Upper South Providence and those from the city's other homelands, the Pond Street Church became this sort of gathering place by serving both the broader social needs of the community and the religious convictions and spiritual strivings of particular individuals.

Native oral history suggests that beginning in the 1880s, churchgoing for Providence Natives entailed more than attending Sunday services to listen to preachers' sermons or to profess their Christian faith. Narragansetts and Native people from other tribal communities as far away as Maine and Delaware also met informally in the city's churches to talk about issues that mattered to them, such as detribalization, land sales, language preservation, cultural traditions, and dealing with government agencies.[43] These meetings, called sachem's councils by a Narragansett informant, as Ann McMullen reports, would have been held at the Pond Street Church, much like those of the antislavery organizations of Free Baptist African Americans during the antebellum period that met at the churches to discuss pressing issues and to prepare members for social activism outside of church walls.[44] Although the topics that concerned antislavery organizations, namely abolition, fugitive slaves, and freedom, were different from those that concerned Natives, African Americans and Native Americans had similar doubts about what U.S. citizenship meant for peoples who had been dispossessed or enslaved.

At a philosophical level, they questioned how U.S. democracy, shaped by colonialism and enslavement, could be inclusive. At a practical level, they wondered how they, as the people whose ancestors provided the land and the labor upon which democratic society was built, could find ways to survive in their everyday lives.[45]

In the 1920s many activities of the sachem's councils that had met in local churches, which I assume included the Pond Street Church, were taken up by the Indian Council of New England, a change that helped bring to a more public stage what until that time had been private conversations about survivance within Native communities. The newspaper clippings, programs, and other ephemera preserved in a scrapbook assembled by Thomas Bicknell and curated by the Haffenreffer Museum of Anthropology illustrate the group's efforts to make Native people and their culture more visible and document its meetings at various venues in the city. Its first formal meeting and powwow was at the Pond Street Church in 1923 (fig. 12). The program for the event announced the day's activities that began with Bicknell, the "paleface honorary sachem," welcoming members of the tribes, and the chiefs smoking a peace pipe and invoking the Great Spirit. Elections were held to choose a sachem from each tribe and to fill other offices; these representatives would report to Bicknell, Gov. Nicholas Sockbeson, a Passamaquoddy identified as "a Penobscot from Old Town, Maine," the Native honorary sachem, and a chief sachem. Among those elected to leadership positions were Alfred C. A. Perry (Narragansett) of Cranston, who was chosen chief sachem, and Thomas Creighton (Narragansett), Leroy Perry (Wampanoag), and Ben Dailey (Pequot), all from Providence, who were named sachems. Other elected sachems included John Braxton (Nipmuc) from Roxbury, Massachusetts, Mary Chapelle (Massachusett) from Boston, and Chief Strong Horse (Abenaki) from Philadelphia, who studied with Frank Speck, an anthropologist at the University of Pennsylvania who was also a member of the council. Minnie Steele (Narragansett) from Pawtucket was chosen as secretary.[46]

Other items on the agenda were a formal plan for the Indian Council, a proposal to raise Indian memorials across southern New England to

Fig. 12. Members of the Indian Council of New England at the Pond Street Church, 1923, some of whom have been identified (*seated front, left to right*): Edward Michael (Narragansett) (*second from left*); Chief Joseph Strong Wolf (Chippewa); Susan Cisco Sullivan (Nipmuc); Mrs. Lone Wolf (Narragansett) and her adopted child; Charles D. Mitchell (Penobscot); Minnie Steele (Narragansett); Gladys Tantaquidgeon (Mohegan); and Occum Fielding (Mohegan); (*standing, second row*): Horace Cisco (Nipmuc) (*second from left*); Lemuel Cisco (Nipmuc) (*fifth from left*); Thomas Bicknell; Gov. Nicholas Sockbeson (Passamaquoddy) (*wearing headdress and Elders' coat with beaded lapels*); Lone Wolf (Narragansett); Mathias Spiess; Lone Bear (Narragansett); and Alfred A. C. Perry (Narragansett) (*wearing hat*); (*third row, far left*): John W. Braxton (Nipmuc) and Leroy C. Perry (Wampanoag) (*wearing bow tie*). Courtesy of the Haffenreffer Museum of Anthropology, Brown University.

honor sachems and events in Native history, Indian citizenship, and a powwow. Following the conclusion of formal business, there was a joint meeting with the Rhode Island Citizens Historical Society. Council members Cyrus Dallin, an artist known for his statues of Native Americans, Chief Occum (Lemuel Fielding) (Mohegan), Gov. Nicholas Sockbeson, Chief Nonsuch (Western Niantic), and James M. Stockett Jr. spoke, as did W. A. Heathman of the historical society. At the end of the day most left for home. Some may have stayed behind to visit friends or family in the Upper South Providence neighborhood or nearby. Joseph Neptune, another elected sachem, decided to stay in Providence for a while so that he and other Passamaquoddys who had traveled with him could try to sell some sweetgrass baskets and other handiwork before returning to their reservation five miles north of Eastport in Maine.[47]

In October 1924 the Indian Council met at the Roger Williams Park Museum in Providence. The yellow-brick, French Chateau–style building with classical and Gothic elements, originally planned as an art museum, became a repository for plant, animal, and geological specimens as well as Native artifacts collected by local antiquarians from the 1880s into the 1900s.[48] Beyond providing a pleasant setting for the meeting, the venue gave Native members of the council the opportunity to see this urban exhibition space and reconnect with objects from their past that had been removed from their homelands, mostly on the assumption that the things and places memorialized in colonial settler histories were the only remaining, if imperfect, evidence of Native people.[49] There is no record of how Native viewers interpreted the objects on display, or if they shared their thoughts amid the ceremonies, speeches, and business discussions, and the powwow that became standard practice after the inaugural meeting at the Pond Street Church. Nor is there any record of their impressions of historic places in "Narragansett Country, the area west of Narragansett Bay," that some council members visited the day before the June meeting, according to the *Indian Tepee*, the Official Speaking Leaf of the Algonquin Indian Council of New England. The *Indian Tepee* reported that the group including Chief Strong Horse, Chief Robert Clark (Nanticoke), and Frank Speck, were met at Union Station by Alfred Perry, Minnie Steele, Gladys Tantaquidgeon (Mohegan), and others, and proceeded "through the bustling streets of the city, through Elmwood" on Providence's west end, to Auburn in Cranston, through East Greenwich, and "down country roads to Wickford and Exeter."[50]

There, they stopped at Queen's Fort, Devil's Foot Rock, and Roger Williams's Trading House.[51] At Queen's Fort, a semicircular enclosure of Native-built walls and glacial boulders with bastions and a natural cavern (called the "Queen's bedroom"), they might have weighed against what they knew about this place from their tribal histories antiquarians' interpretations that the fortress was the last stronghold of Quiaipen, a Narragansett sachem, and her warriors, who had evaded capture after colonial troops killed or burned to death hundreds of Narragansetts along with Wampanoag refugees at the site of Great Swamp during King Philip's War.[52] At Devil's Foot Rock they would have seen marks in the stone that local legends purported to be footprints left by the devil, who traveled from Massachusetts in pursuit of Indian woman who tried to escape his clutches, as J. R. Cole writes in his *History of Washington and Kent Counties*, or from Conanicut Island in Narragansett Bay bound for Connecticut, as J. Earl Clauson, a columnist for the *Providence Evening Bulletin*, recounted.[53] They might have recalled from their elders that this ledge was instead a meeting place of the Narragansetts, where Canonicus sat with his councilors. At their last stop, the fabled Roger Williams Trading House, which had a reputation for having more ghosts than any other spot in Rhode Island, including the ghosts of Indians, they were met by Bicknell and a "host of visitors," according to Bourgaize.[54] I suspect that they would have been told about the wampum and beaver traded for brass kettles, iron hatchets, cloth, and glass beads. They might have also heard about the colonial troops who assembled at this trading house (which Richard Smith, its subsequent proprietor, turned into a blockhouse) before advancing to the Great Swamp, and about the forty soldiers who died in the attack or on the return march to Smith's blockhouse and were buried in one grave, but nothing about the desecration of a Native burial place on the property four decades before their visit.[55] For Narragansetts who had never lived anywhere except Providence or had moved away from the reservation and Rhode Island's South County decades ago, and for Native people from other homelands, the outing offered a chance to see places they might have known only from their elders' stories, or to rekindle memories they had forgotten and now could share. On their return to the city the group retraced its route through the streets of Elmwood and Upper South Providence filled with their own storied places.

The Indian Council's meeting at the Masonic (Colored) Temple at Benefit and Cady Streets in October of the following year, billed as an all day and evening event, was filled with the usual exercises. A two-dollar assessment on members was discussed to cover the expenses of renting venues for the meetings and the cost of stationary and stamps to keep in touch with and expand the membership.[56] Providence members used their social, work, and church connections to find meeting places where a rental fee could be waived or kept to a minimum. Leroy Perry, the head janitor at Hope High School on Providence's east side, noted in a letter that he had reserved the school's auditorium for an event on the evening of June 16, 1924, and, on the city's west end, "the hall at 310 Cranston Street, which [was] the Odd Fellows Hall, for Sunday afternoon, April 20, 1924 on the west side."[57] At Hope High School members watched a tableau of Indian life performed by a local Boy Scout troop and a dance by chiefs Edward Michael, Alfred Perry, Strong Wolf, Robert Clark, and Thomas Bicknell.[58] By attending meetings at these different venues, Indian Council members had another reason to cross into different urban homelands aside from when they visited family and friends or went to church or work. As they socialized and revitalized cultural practices, they would have traded new stories about their urban place worlds that they committed to memory. Like their ancestors, they would have expressed through their words that beyond the visibility of these localities was a moral reality that deeply influenced their sense of place as well as their unshakable sense of indigenous identity.[59]

The Indian Council's Executive and Finance Committee was reminded of the moral reality of place when they attended a meeting at the office of Herbert Sherwood, a former Rhode Island State Senator, on the fifteenth floor of the Turk's Head building in downtown Providence. Overlooking the historic Board of Trade building at Market Square across the Providence River, the office offered a vantage of the place where Native people had been sold into slavery in the seventeenth century. The *Indian Tepee* remarked that in this place "where Roger Williams found asylum, and rest and surcease from rebellion, it seemed fitting that, like an eagle in its aerie, we should look down on the scene of past despair and, guided by the all-pervading spirit of Gitche Manito, plan and pray and hope for a brighter dawning to the prospects of New England's much neglected and almost-despairing Algonquins."[60] Here they were reminded that their ancestors, more than two thousand of whom were taken captive at the end of King Philip's War, were unwillingly brought into the households of English settler colonists and into the Atlantic diaspora.[61] More than a space of dislocation, Market Square was where many Native people later found voluntary employment and, much like members of the Indian Council, would congregate to plot their futures.

The creation of local "Tepees" is a testament to the success of the Indian Council's efforts to identify and recruit people of Native descent in the Providence area and beyond as members. Although the organization promoted a broad sense of intertribal identity across the region, it also recognized particular tribal affiliations. Like congregants at the Pond Street Church, who when asked might have stood up at services and identified themselves as "Narragansett," "Coweset," "Pawtuxet," or "Lantern Hill," or as from any one of the region's homelands, the Native members of the Indian Council held onto their tribal identities.[62] Comments in Bicknell's scrapbook indicate that they did so while participating in the modern world as wage earners and pondering how their basket-making, woodworking, and beading skills could raise awareness about their knowledge of these cultural practices and create markets for their products. The tone in the Indian Council's correspondence was generally optimistic, but there were undercurrents of discontent that had less to do with being indigenous and modern than with issues of race. Some questioned whether Native people of mixed ancestry should be registered as Indian members. Others chose not to participate in events in which "mixed blood" members were included.⁶³ Despite the rumblings, the New England Indian Council recognized that mixed ancestry did not erase cultural heritage. Membership in the organization whose motto was "I still live!" was open to descendants of any New England tribe or any other tribe of the Algonquin Nation without reference to phenotype or blood as an index of cultural identity.

Diasporas, Reversals, and the Indigenous Urban Order

Frederick (Fred) D. Thomas and his wife lived near Hoyle Square in the 1870s when their children—Annie, a stillborn son, and another daughter who died in infancy—were born and would move back to the neighborhood in the early 1900s. The neighborhood was a familiar place where they had lived before at addresses within a few blocks of their new home. Except for the mention of his daughter Annie's participation in the dedication of the Canonicus Monument (see chapter 2), Fred Thomas's life did not attract the attention of white historians and newspaper reporters. For most of his adult life, he worked as a porter and teamster, much like many other Native men who had moved to Providence. One could suppose—and rightfully so—that like them and other Native people in New England, he struggled with what citizenship meant for him. His father, Benjamin Thomas Sr., understood that the terms of citizenship offered to the Narragansetts in exchange for their remaining reserved land would not make them equal partners in American democracy, given that it entailed giving up land that was rightfully theirs. This caveat made citizenship contingent on selling acreage that tribal members had inherited from their ancestors and that the Rhode Island legislature legally controlled under the terms of a 1709 quitclaim agreement.⁶⁴ In a statement that he made at a public meeting at the Indian Meeting house in Charlestown on July 30, 1879, one of three such meetings about abolishing tribal authority, the elder Thomas acknowledged that the tribe was "poor enough now." Yet he maintained that if the land, which had dwindled in size and depreciated in value, was sold, the tribe would "be still poorer."⁶⁵

His children, who opted for life off the reservation in the hope of securing better futures, faced conditions in Providence that were not significantly improved. If they had not yet experienced incidents that reinforced the dominant society's prevailing expectations for them as Narragansetts and as citizens, they would have been made aware of these contradictions as they congregated at loading docks, street corners, and stables seeking temporary or dependable employment. These harsh realities would have become evident as they knocked on doors with rental signs only be turned away and were forced to move in with friends or pitch their tents near railroad tracks on the edges of the city while searching for places to live that could call their own.[66] Fred Thomas found work in low-paying jobs that would cover the rent but not put home ownership within his reach. He moved from one rental property to another and from one neighborhood to another, but some of his closest ties were to Upper South Providence, where he had family and where he had been married at the Pond Street Church.[67] He would go back to Charlestown yearly for the August Meeting and at other times. During the first decade of the 1900s, he is listed in Providence records as a Baptist clergyman in nearby Westerly, where he worked as a gardener for a private family.[68]

By 1911 he relocated to Charlestown, his birthplace, with his wife and sister-in-law and farmed his own land.[69] It was during this time that he talked with Harris Hawthorne Wilder. Wilder's field notebook contains information that Thomas revealed about his family and about places on the reservation. Although portions of Wilder's field notes are difficult to decipher, a kinship diagram of the Thomas family indicates that Annie Thomas resided in Providence and was married "presumably [to a Negro]" and had four children. In the version of the Crying Rocks legend (see chapters 1 and 5) that Fred Thomas told to Wilder, Narragansett women hid their babies fathered by African American men at a cavernous rock formation where they could nurse them in secrecy to avoid the wrath of older Indians on the reservation. Annie might not have faced such harsh criticism in the city.[70]

Like other Narragansetts, Fred Thomas revealed his insider's knowledge about his father and other members of the Narragansett Indian Council being bribed by offers of a hundred dollars and alcohol to sign the agreement to sell tribal land.[71] He died in Charlestown on September 30, 1917, five years after Wilder interviewed him. He was an unlikely subject, given that Wilder was more interested in dead Indians than living ones. Unexpectedly, Wilder's field notes provide rare, firsthand insights into the experiences and cultural knowledge of a Narragansett who lived most of his life in Providence and was buried on his family's lot in Charlestown.[72]

The elder Ben Thomas's son Benjamin Franklin and his daughters Eliza Hilton and Hannah Hazard also lived in Upper South Providence. A younger daughter, Lydia Harris, who married in Providence in 1876, divorced, and died at 126 Codding Street at the age of forty-four, left a thin evidentiary trail compared to her older siblings.[73] Benjamin Franklin was living in the neighborhood in 1870 when he married Emma Spurlock, whose father, John Spurlock, was a deacon of the Pond Street Church.[74] He and Emma raised their children, Elizabeth (Lizzie), Cora (Carrie), William (Willie), Lorenzo (Early), Albert, and Rosebud (Rose), there and stayed until around the turn of the century.[75] The younger Ben Thomas was an occasional visitor to the reservation and had not voted in tribal elections before 1880, though his name was on the 1881 tribal roll as were those of his children except the two youngest, Albert and Rosebud, who were born after the list was finalized.[76] But he was active in the Pond Street Church, where he attended Sunday services and participated in community building events. A broadside in the collections of the John Hay Library indicates that he served on the reception committee for a banquet given by the Ladies of the Pond Street Baptist Church at Union Hall on Broad Street on November 23, 1871, with Dr. Samuel Rodman, an Indian.[77]

By 1900, he, his wife, and their two youngest children moved to South Kingstown, Rhode Island. With the change in residence came a change in occupation. After almost three decades as a teamster on the west side of the Providence River, Benjamin turned to stonemasonry. This skilled profession and honored tradition among the Narragansetts gave him the opportunity to work with his hands and reconnect to the land in ways that he could not as a teamster. Within the next ten years, his youngest daughter, Rosebud, who lived with her parents in South Kingstown, married and gave birth to a son. Her husband, Christian Mars, was also a stonemason. Benjamin continued to do masonry, a job that many Narragansett men preferred to factory labor, into his seventies. His wife worked as a laundress from their home to supplement their income. Their sons William and Albert, who lived nearby with their wives and children in a Thomas family enclave, followed in their father's and grandfather's footsteps as stonemasons.[78] Benjamin F. Thomas died in 1930 and was buried in Riverside Cemetery in Wakefield, Rhode Island.[79] Of the Thomas siblings who had relocated to Providence before the reservation was sold and lived in Upper South Providence, only he and his brother Frederick D. went back to the ancestral homeland where they had been born and raised after years of city living.

Eliza Hilton, the eldest of Ben Thomas's daughters, was thirty-two years old and a widow with a twelve-year-old son in 1880.[80] She had married Edward Burns Hilton in Providence in March 1875, was widowed by December, and never remarried.[81] From the ages of thirteen to twenty, her husband, who was born in Providence, was as a domestic servant in the household of a white jewelry manufacturer with his younger sister.[82] When he and Eliza married, he was a coachman for the same employer, and years later their son, Clarence, would be employed as a hostler for the same boss. After Edward's death Eliza lived on Livermore near B Street with her sister Hannah Hazard for several years and then moved to Warner's Lane and then to Hayward Street, where she and Hannah made their home from about the middle of the 1880s to the early 1890s.[83] Eliza moved to Cranston for a short time and lived in the Benedict Pond area off and on. Around the end of the first decade of the twentieth century, she was living at 54 Winter Street with her son Clarence, who had the Thomas surname, and his wife. It was the same address where Mary Brewster had lived a few years earlier. During the late 1910s to about 1920, "Lizzie Helton" (Eliza Hilton) stayed with her son and daughter-in-law and their one-year-old niece at a rented two-family house on Pond Street and did housework for a private family.[84] From the early 1920s to the 1930s, Providence directories place her in Fox Point.[85] Eliza, who supported herself (and her son before he reached adulthood) during her long years of widowhood as a domestic servant or laundress—occupations that would have become increasingly difficult to hold down because of advancing age and a chronic heart condition—died at the State Infirmary (formerly the State Almshouse) in Cranston in July 1932 and was buried at Providence's Locust Grove Cemetery. Before being admitted to the State Infirmary she lived with her son on Cranston Street in the Upper South Providence homeland.[86]

Eliza's younger sister, Hannah, married Walter G. Hazard, a teamster, in Providence in 1875 when she was twenty-three years old. The couple and their infant daughter lived with family on Federal Hill before moving to Hayward Street, where Hannah gave birth to another daughter. In 1895, when she was forty-three years old, she gave birth to twin boys in the family's new home in the Benedict Pond area who died a few days after their birth. The death of the infant named John Hazard was attributed to spina bifida and eclampsia. The other child, who survived for four days, one day longer than his brother, and was unnamed, succumbed from exhaustion.[87] Eclampsia is a condition that follows a serious complication in pregnancy known as preeclampsia that causes a woman to have high blood pressure, seizures, and other health problems. The current medical opinion is that the risks for the condition increase when a woman is thirty-five or older and when she is expecting twins, both of which were true for Hannah Hazard, though there are other contributing factors.

Hannah's pregnancy and delivery would have been difficult, and the condition's effects on the babies' well-being devastating. During the twenty-year period in which she had given birth to five children (Carrie, Grace, May, Bessie, and Edith), nothing would have compared to the complex biomedical, social, cultural, and personal circumstances surrounding the birth of her twin sons. Ethnohistorical and ethnographic texts that comment on childbirth among northeastern Native women and twin births in Native North American mythology provide some insights into cultural practices and concepts, but are woefully inadequate to account for Hannah's experience, let alone the birthing experiences of Native women more broadly in the nineteenth and early twentieth centuries.

Without Hannah's own narrative, it is impossible to know whether she carried the twins to full term or whether they came too soon, or what traditional medicines or other interventions were used to ease her pain during labor or facilitate the births. Nor do we know what emotional toll the delivery and death of the babies took on her, her husband, and those who stood by helplessly during the months she struggled with her health and the days she labored and waited with uncertainty about the fate of her sons. We can only guess what emotions she recalled even years later or what would have triggered them.[88]

The Hazard's home at Jessamine Street (renamed Benedict Street) would have been filled with these memories. It was a place where the babies' cries might have been heard, where glimpses of them might have been seen, and where locked closets may have held things intended for them. Their presence would have been palpable in the home they shared with the rest of the family and would have come into focus when summoned or perhaps unexpectedly. Life would go on for Hannah and her family. She presumably continued to attend services at the Pond Street Church where she and Carrie, her eldest daughter, were listed as members in 1890, and where she could find emotional support from members of the congregation. Five years after the twins' deaths, Carrie was no longer living at home, Grace and May were working as servants, and Bessie and Edith were at school. In 1910 Bessie, who had married and had a four-year-old son (Andrew Young), and Edith, a dressmaker, were still living at home with Hannah and Walter, who now worked as a gold refiner in a jewelry factory. After Walter died in 1913 Hannah continued to live in the house on Benedict Street with Bessie, Edith, and her grandson.[89] Around 1920, she moved to Dove Street in Fox Point, which was a few blocks from where Amos Brewster, Maria Blunt, Anstriss Nichols, and others had made their homes in the later nineteenth century. She died in 1925 and was buried in the same grave plot as her husband Walter at Locust Grove, where her name on the headstone reads "Hannah M. Thomas."

There were other Native people living in Upper South Providence. Some had also crossed the Providence River to get there, and others arrived via overland routes from their ancestral homes. Sometimes their pathways to the neighborhood were direct, and at other times detours took them in different directions before they eventually reached the city and Upper South Providence. Among them was Frank E. Nichols, who was born around the middle of the nineteenth century in the city's sixth ward, which at the time of his birth encompassed the Upper South Providence homeland. His father, David Nichols, was born in Wisconsin's Brothertown Indian community, and his mother, Hannah, was identified as "a sister to Ben. Thomas" in the 1881 *Report of the Commission on the Affairs of the Narragansett Indians*.[90] By 1860 the couple and four of their five children (George, Charles, Olive, and Frank) were living in Stonington, Connecticut, with Priscilla Nichols, Frank's paternal grandmother.

Within the next few years, the family was back in Providence. David, a former stonecutter, found work as a teamster, and died shortly after from a fall at the Neptune Steam Company wharf on the Providence waterfront.[91] Frank lived at the rear of 26 C Street in Upper South Providence with his mother, Olive, and his grandmother from 1870 to about 1876. His wife, Georgianna, whom he married in 1872, gave birth to their daughters, Georgianna and Mabel, in the extended household. The couple subsequently set up their own home, first on Booth Street near B Street, where their son Charles was born, then at Pond Street, and later at Monroe Court, all within the maze of streets within a short walk from Hoyle Square. In 1880, the year their daughter Grace was born, Frank, his wife, and their four children were registered as claimants for shares of the purchase money from the sale of the Narragansett reservation. Georgianna, who was born in Thompson, Connecticut, "had never been to the reservation before" the June 26, 1880 hearing at the Indian meeting house, according to the commission's report. Frank, who lived in Providence most of his life, had been there as recently as the previous March and had attended nearly every town meeting.[92] His name and those of his children were entered onto the 1881 tribal roll. In the early 1900s he relocated to Lippitt Hill with his family and held jobs as a janitor and a waiter.

Other Nicholses also lived in the neighborhood as part of an extended network of people related by blood, kinship, and common residence that defied characterizations of urban Indian life. From about the mid-1870s to the early 1880s, Hannah and Priscilla Nichols lived in a building at the rear of 19 Spring Street that was situated on a large property between Pond and Broad Streets. Hannah died there in 1883 at the age of seventy-one. Priscilla boarded with a laundress, another widow, and later shared an apartment at the same address with her sister and niece. Priscilla raised her children, worked as a domestic servant and as a seamstress to support herself as a widow, and stayed close to family members as part of their extended households. She died in 1885 at the age of eighty at Sarah E. Hazard's Vinton Street home on Federal Hill. Sarah was Hannah's daughter (and Frank's eldest sister), and Priscilla had lived with her twenty years earlier.

Olive Nichols is recorded as residing at 19 Spring Street the year before her marriage to James Henry in 1881. By the 1890s the couple was living on Summer Street, and by 1900 they were over on Codding Street. A year later, they moved to Livermore Street. That same year (1901) Olive filed an application for a share of the money appropriated to Brothertown Indians and approved by an act of Congress in 1900 for lands in Kansas that had been set apart for them as "New York Indians" in the Treaty of Buffalo Creek in 1838. She based her claim on descent from Narragansett and Brothertown Indians through James Niles, her great-grandfather, who emigrated from Charlestown to Brothertown, New York, with his wife, Hannah in 1796.[93] In her affidavit, witnessed by Georgianna Nichols and Thomas P. Wheeler, she made repeated references to James Niles having received two lots at Brothertown, and said that they were divided among his heirs in 1829. She also stated that her husband of fifty-two years, who was from Pawtucket, just over the Providence city line, had ties to the Brothertown and Narragansett communities. Although her claim to be a beneficiary was rejected, it illustrates arguments about the diverse and complicated routes that brought Native peoples to Upper South Providence and about the bonds of kinship that permeated the neighborhood's Native community and rooted them in place.

Individuals and families made decisions about where they would live to solve immediate needs, though their choices could result in patterns of long-term residence on a certain street or in a particular dwelling. These attachments are evident among renters as well as homeowners, which suggests that ownership does not necessarily make a home a more personal or protective space. A rented apartment could be a long-term family home, as 10 Booth Street was for Christopher Champlin. A tenement house was sometimes the home of relatives or of individuals connected through wider networks of kinship, church affiliation, or awareness of shared histories. Nineteen Spring Street, where members of the Nichols family lived, for example, was also the home of Benjamin G. Gardner, who was connected to the Narragansetts through his mother, Betsey Dyer, and his grandmother. Although he had never lived on the reservation, he, like many other Narragansetts, voted in tribal elections and had attended meetings.[94]

Benjamin Gardner's ties to Providence are documented in Civil War draft registration records for 1863, in which he is listed as subject to military duty as a resident of the city. He enrolled and served in the Fourteenth Heavy Artillery Colored Regiment of Rhode Island in Louisiana and was mustered out in October 1865.[95] He would have been part of the company trained at Dexter Field at the west end of the city and paraded through the streets of Providence on August 28, 1863 before being deployed. Although he was not mentioned by name in a *Providence Journal* article remarking on the novelty of seeing "three-hundred muskets in the hands of many sturdy, stalwart black men" marching in the city, Jeremiah Noka, another Narragansett, was. Standing nearly five feet eleven inches tall with black hair, brown-hazel eyes, and an Indian complexion, he was singled out not only as "a noteworthy specimen of a Rhode Islander," but also as "one of the purest examples which modern intermingling of African blood has left to us of the once powerful tribe of Narragansetts." Although Benjamin Gardner might not have had Noka's "fine shape" and his "decidedly Indian cast of features, his genial and winning smile, [and] his generous expression" that were said to recall "the memory of the lost Narragansetts," he and other Gardners shared with Noka a complicated and intertwined family history.[96]

Like Noka, who was a blacksmith when he enlisted, Benjamin Gardner worked with his hands.[97] He was a farmer or gardener, presumably self-employed, who had a fruit store before serving in the Union Army. This occupation was rare among Providence residents during the second half of the nineteenth century and among Upper South Providence's Native Americans, who were mostly teamsters or laborers. Although the cornfields observed at Mashapaug in the seventeenth century were a distant memory, garden plots of fruits, vegetables, and flowers could be still cultivated even in what John Ihlder called "the dingiest sections of the city."[98] The lot at 19 Spring Street where Gardner lived from the early 1870s was relatively spacious. It measured 11,569 square feet and had ample open space between the building fronting Spring Street and the two structures at the back of the property. Located within a stone's throw of these tenements, but distant enough so that shadows cast from the buildings would not completely shut out sunlight, the space would have been a decent spot for an urban garden that could sustain Benjamin Gardner's livelihood. For Native people and other inner-city residents, the available yard space would have been a coveted feature of any home, whether owned or rented. Such extra-mural areas compensated for cramped living quarters by expanding the space that could be used for gardens, waste disposal, animal pens, socializing, and sweat lodges.[99] These different uses might have conflicted at times, though each became integrated into the rhythm and routine of everyday life at 19 Spring Street in a process that made the urban space more familiar and increasingly storied to the Native people who lived there, such as Benjamin Gardner, Hannah and Priscilla Nichols, and others.

Urban stories of place, archived and passed on through knowledge, beliefs, practices, and experiences, may withstand the effects of civic-engineering projects that attempt to rewrite them by interrupting or seriously curtailing routines of everyday life and destroying their material manifestations. Sometime in the period from 1875 to 1882, the lot at 19 Spring Street was divided into two lots, one at the front (or Spring Street side) of the original property and the other at the rear. The finely drawn property boundary was part of the ever-tightening regime of spatial segregation in the colonized landscape that limited access to and effectively reduced the availability of open area between the front and back buildings. To what extent, if any, Benjamin Gardner might have assumed what Denis Byrne calls "a tactical, willful blindness" to the constraints imposed by the property division and the surveillance of property owners and neighbors and availed himself of yard space for raising a garden as he presumably had always done, is unknown.[100] By 1877, he had left Spring Street for Lilac Street in the Benedict Pond area, a section of the city that was urban yet countrified, where he continued to work as a gardener. He returned to Upper South Providence a few years later, where he lived at various addresses in the neighborhood such as 7 Angle Street and 1 Warner's Lane that were home to Narragansetts and other Native peoples, and found work as a laborer.[101]

Like many of their neighbors in Upper South Providence, Benjamin Gardner and his fourth wife, Sarah Ann Elizabeth Abrams, were members of the Pond Street Church, though their marriage was not officiated by a clergyman affiliated with the church.[102] Widowed three times before his marriage to Sarah Ann Elizabeth, Benjamin G. Gardner died at 55 Codding Street in 1901.[103] Thus, another Gardner, Stephen, called "the Last Narragansett" in his *New York Times* obituary from 1896, was neither the last Narragansett nor the last Gardner. Formerly of Providence, he moved to New York City around 1890 to be treated at the Eye Hospital, and after he recovered he remained in the city and worked as a butler for a woman on West Twenty-Eighth Street. His employer, who described this one-time church organist "as a most faithful servant," gentlemanly, educated, proud, and high-spirited, "having good taste in clothes," and delighting in relating the traditions of the Narragansett Tribe, said that he left no relatives except for an old aunt, "a half breed," living in Stonington, Connecticut.[104] Other than sharing a surname and Narragansett ancestry, Benjamin's life followed a different course than Stephen's. His death was not reported in an obituary that gave insights into his life and character. Instead, he was remembered in an inscription on his gravestone in North Burial Ground that read "Benj. G. Gardiner Co. A, 14th R.I. H.A. rt" and failed to mention that he was Narragansett, a son, a husband, a farmer, a gardener, and a laborer who had lived most of his adult life in the Upper South Providence homeland.

There were other Native people who had also migrated to Upper South Providence in search of urban opportunity and whose lives became intricately interwoven into its social fabric. Thomas Wheeler, who was born in Connecticut, and his wife Hannah, who was born in Warwick, Rhode Island, lived in Providence's sixth ward beginning in 1850. The city's birth records indicate that the Wheelers welcomed the birth of daughters in 1853 and 1856 and a son in 1858 at their home at 3 Angle Street.[105] Thomas Franklin, their son, died of hydrocephalus shortly after his first birthday; a daughter named Sarah died in 1856 when she was two years old and the other daughter when she was only a month old.[106] After the deaths of their children, the Wheelers moved to Cranston, where they lived with Benjamin Gardner and his first wife, Sarah. In the 1860s the family returned to Upper South Providence, where Hannah gave birth to two more sons, Edwin in 1861 and Thomas P. in 1867, and another daughter, Ann, in 1864. By 1870, they were back living on Angle Street. Their address—7 Angle Street—figured prominently in the residential histories of the Native individuals and families of Upper South Providence during the late nineteenth and early twentieth centuries. By the mid-1870s the family had moved to Winter Street, a few blocks away, where they lived in a three-family house that was also home to Benjamin Thomas, his wife Emma, and their daughters, Lizzie and Carrie. Thomas Wheeler, who had previously worked as coachman and as a sexton at the Stewart Street Baptist Church at Stewart and Pond Streets, found work as a porter, while Hannah kept house and their children attended the local public schools. The Wheelers stayed at Winter Street to about 1885. Except for the 1860 U.S. Census that places them in Cranston and Providence directories that list them at Jessamine and Halton Streets in the Benedict Pond area for a few years in the mid-1880s, the family was firmly rooted in Upper South Providence. Their lives were entwined with those of other Native families at a fine-grained spatial scale that involved coresidence at 7 Angle Street, a place of short-term and extended housing for Native peoples that would have been an important local landmark steeped in the experiences of urban living.

The Wheeler's youngest son, Thomas P., would continue to live in the neighborhood. At the turn of the century he was living at 149 Codding Street with his mother, wife, six-month-old daughter, and George Congdon.[107] He had married Carrie (Caroline Perry) a year earlier and was working as a day laborer.[108] Hannah, who headed the household, took on work as a laundress, and her brother-in-law, George Congdon, eleven years old, was enrolled in school. All were identified as Indians in the 1900 U.S. Census. Hannah died at Codding Street in 1909.[109] Thomas P. Wheeler and his family remained there for the next ten years. George Congdon, who was born in Rocky Brook, Rhode Island, relocated to Worcester County, where he worked as a hired hand. He later moved to Stamford, Connecticut, and worked as a chauffeur before enlisting in World War I. Thomas P., who held a series of menial jobs as a porter, janitor, and messenger, would be a lifelong resident of Upper South Providence. Identified as "full blood Narragansett" in the 1930 U.S. Census, he died in 1953 at his home on Saunders Street in Upper South Providence where he and Carrie had lived since the late 1930s.

The surnames of neighbors, such as Helm and Blunt, also resonate with those of Narragansett Indians and individuals related to tribal members through marriage. Some Helms were on the 1881 tribal list, but others were determined not eligible for tribal membership. Among them was Frank V. Helme (or Helm, as the surname appears on the 1881 Narragansett tribal roll), who resided in a three-family dwelling on Winter Street where Thomas Wheeler and Benjamin Thomas and their families also lived in the 1870s. Born in South Kingstown in 1841, Frank Helme had enlisted in U.S. Navy out of New Bedford, Massachusetts, in 1862. After the war he returned to South Kingstown and lived in a Helm family enclave at Narragansett Pier before moving to the Upper South Providence neighborhood. He would stay there for the next three decades working as a coachman before returning to South Kingstown in the early 1900s. Before moving to Winter Street in the middle of the 1870s, he had lived at 10 Graves Lane, an address that was also home to Benjamin Thomas. From Winter Street he later moved to addresses on Pond and B Streets. During the time that Frank Helme lived in Upper South Providence, he and his wife, Martha, daughter of a Noka on her father's side and of a Cone on her mother's, were members of the Pond Street Church, as were Benjamin Thomas and other Narragansetts.

There were certainly other Narragansetts in Upper South Providence as well as individuals and families from other tribal communities in southeastern New England. Willis A. R. Ownsley, born in Burrillville, Rhode Island, around 1814, had shipped out of the port of Providence in 1838.[110] His parents, Benjamin and Sarah (née Reeves), were Wampanoags. His father traced his descent to the Watuppa community, and his mother was probably from Nantucket, where they married in the late 1800s. His brother Samuel, whose given name was recorded as Judson (his middle name) and variously transcribed as Jephson and Jettson, lived at 10 Dodge Street in 1852 and worked as a tanner.[111] Willis's wife, Harriet Newell, born in Griswold, Connecticut, about 1824, was the daughter of Stephen and Henrietta (née Warmsley) Congdon.[112] She was thought to be Mohegan on her father's side and Narragansett on her mother's. In 1850 the couple was living in the town of Milford in Worcester County, Massachusetts, with their three daughters, ranging in age from three years to four months.[113] They resided in Milford for at least the next five years in an extended household that now included another daughter and Harriet's younger brother, Moses C. Congdon, who was a bootmaker, and her sister, Hannah Congdon.[114] In 1860 Harriet was still living in Milford, apparently as a single mother of four daughters, and working as a washerwoman. By 1870 Willis Ownsley, who was identified as an Indian in the U.S. Census, boarded at 116 Pond Street in Upper South Providence with another family and worked as a porter.[115]

Four years later the Ownsleys' daughter Phebe, nineteen, died of typhoid fever at Dahlia Street near Benedict Pond.[116] Her death came nearly twenty years after the Ownsleys lost a four-year-old daughter and their only son within three months of each other, the latter less than a month before of his first birthday. Having survived both infancy and childhood, Phebe's life expectancy would have seemed relatively good. She was not supposed to die at nineteen, an age when she should have been in prime health, though recurring typhoid outbreaks in the city posed a threat to all residents, not just the old and weak. The disease, common in U.S. cities during the nineteenth and early twentieth centuries, caused symptoms ranging from mild fatigue and loss of appetite to chills, coughing, nausea, diarrhea, nose bleeds, fever, and telltale rose-colored spots on the abdomen, to delirium and emaciation. It killed slowly and indirectly, and left survivors at risk for heart, kidney, and liver failure, and for respiratory and neurological problems.[117] Mortality statistics for Providence from 1885 to 1900 suggest that there were lower fatalities from the disease during the winter months than in September, when Phebe died.[118] Yet, neither the seasonal vigor of the germ nor the vitality of the victim adequately explains why some contracted and succumbed to the disease and others did not. That Phebe died in the Benedict Pond neighborhood on the city's western end seems to lend support to arguments by health professionals that crowded tenement areas were not necessarily hotbeds of the disease, but that water contamination from fecal matter and possibly industrial waste presented a potentially greater risk. Her physical condition—whether she was rundown or had some underlying health problem—along with exposure to contaminated water near her home and places she visited on the urban landscape would have heightened her risk for contracting the disease, as they did for other city-dwellers who fell victim to typhoid-like symptoms as their ability to move from place to place more easily and quickly increased.[119]

Willis, who outlived Phebe by four years, died at Potter's Avenue over by Long Pond in 1878.[120] Harriet, who had apparently lived apart from her husband since 1860, resided at Hayward Street near Lockwood Street in Upper South Providence following Phebe's death in 1874 and then moved to 10 West Hoyle Street in the same neighborhood.[121] She lived there from about 1879 to when she died in 1889. At the time of the 1880 U.S. Census she was recorded as living with her sister, Fannie Kendall, and Fannie's son, Stephen.[122] Fannie had moved from Federal Hill to the Upper South Providence neighborhood with her husband and children in the early 1860s and is listed as residing at the rear of 19 Spring Street during the 1870s. In the 1880 U.S. Census Fannie and Harriet, both laundresses, are recorded as Indians. Despite the inconsistencies of their reported identities in federal and state censuses, the sisters shared a common ancestry, followed parallel pathways to city living, and had similar life experiences as residents of Upper South Providence. They, like so many Native people who had migrated from their ancestral homelands to Providence, were never away from family.

Upon her death, Harriet Ownsley's life came full circle. Having left rural Connecticut for town and city life over forty years earlier, she was laid to rest in Evergreen Cemetery in Plainfield, where her parents and another sister, Mary Louise, had also been buried.[123] During Harriett's estrangement from her husband she, like her sister and so many other Native women who raised families on their own, continued to live in the city that she had come to call home. In Providence she could always find work doing laundry, an occupation that had sustained her as a single mother from her years in Worcester, and draw on the support of family members in the city.

Harriet Ownsley, Fannie Kendall, and many others who lived mostly in the Upper South Providence homeland had ancestral ties to Connecticut. The route of Benjamin West Dailey's family from Connecticut to Rhode Island is unknown, though records suggest that he was born in Warren, Rhode Island, around 1862. His given names call to mind other Benjamin Wests, such as the Pennsylvania-born artist (1738–1820) known especially for his painting *The Death of General Wolfe* (1770) and the Providence astronomer (1730–1813) who observed the Transit of Venus from a lookout in Fox Point in 1769. Whether Benjamin West Dailey's parents named their son after the brilliant astronomer or the artist, who in his rendering of the British general's death in the Battle of Quebec depicted a Native American figure as a historically situated protagonist reduced to the role of bystander, is pure conjecture.[124] Benjamin West Dailey had neither a plucked scalp nor a topknot with feathers. His body was not adorned with paint. He did not wear a blanket, animal skin, or beaded pouch, or carry a tomahawk or musket as part of his everyday dress and accessories. He neither conformed to the template of a generic Indian in the artistic and popular imaginary nor did he meet the broad expectation that Native people were mute and disengaged, judging by his participation in the Indian Council of New England.

By 1880 Dailey was living on Washington Street with his brother Charles, Charles's wife, Frances (or Fannie), and a boarder. The two brothers worked in a livery stable, where Ben was a footman and Charles a hostler. In 1884 Benjamin married Florence Jackson in a ceremony officiated by an AME pastor in Providence.[125] At the time of the marriage he lived on Rice Street near A Street in Upper South Providence, where the couple would reside for a few years.[126] Florence died of unknown causes in 1896.[127] After her death Benjamin mostly stayed in the neighborhood. In 1900, like so many other Native people who had previously been recklessly misidentified in decennial U.S. Censuses, he was enumerated as an "Indian." Widowed and working as a coal and wood dealer, hauling cargo that he would be paid for by the load, he boarded at a two-family house on Monroe Street in a household headed by a woman whose last name was Gardner.[128] He later moved to Graves Lane and married for the second time, in 1913, to a widow named Alice Smith (née Cooper) of Providence.[129] In 1925, a few years after he was elected "sachem" of the Pequots at the New England Indian Council's meeting at the Pond Street Church, the couple was living on Monroe Street.[130] By 1930 U.S. Census, Benjamin, now a second-time widower, and his third wife, Anna, a hairdresser, were on Washington Street near Winter Street on the other side of Westminster Street. After a series of different jobs he eventually found steady work as a church janitor, a position that he held for at least the next ten years, during which he continued to live in the neighborhood. Charles, who was a stableman for most of his working life, lived in the Upper South Providence homeland with his first wife, Fannie, into the early 1900s. Their home on Booth Street, a five-family tenement, was a few blocks from where Benjamin lived. The brothers had worked together and lived nearby through much of their lives. Benjamin was identified as the first of kin when Charles died at his home on Federal Hill in 1921.[131] Other than his ties to his brother, little is known about Charles's involvement in the Providence Indian community.

Perry Henries, a blacksmith, lived over on Lockwood Street. He was born Brimfield, Massachusetts, around 1864 and made his way to Providence from the Worcester area. His father was Lemuel Henries and his mother was Lydia Sprague Henries of the Nipmuc community in Webster, Massachusetts. John Milton Earle's 1861 *Report to the Governor and Council concerning the Indians of the Commonwealth under the Act of April 6, 1859* identifies Lemuel as a colored foreigner who married Lydia in 1857. Perry Henries lived in Webster with his parents and siblings into the 1880s.[132] He married in Brimfield in 1891 and by the turn of the century had moved to Providence, where he was the head of a single-person household. His name does not appear in any later Providence records. Living alone, he would have been hardly noticed by Euro-Americans who enumerated or wrote about the city's residents during the late nineteenth century. He left the city after a short tenure and returned to his natal homeland. Also known as Payne or Paine Henries, he died in Quinebaug, Connecticut, in 1936. Townspeople remembered Henries with epithets that identified him as the last Nipmuc. In 1933 the *Bartlett Chronicle*, the yearbook of Webster's Bartlett High School, featured a picture of him with the caption "The Last of the Nipmucks" and a speculative biography of this "lone survivor's" early years.[133] During the last part of his life, he lived in a shack on Whitin Pond near Thompson, Connecticut. Alice Kitka, a retired telephone installer, told the *Worcester Telegram and Gazette* that she remembered him from when she was "barely old enough to count." Her late aunt described him as "soft spoken, sprightly, lean, with mostly long black hair, but with some grey." A retired Webster police office said he was like most everyone else, except for his "mode of dress." After Henries collapsed from a heart attack on Webster's Main Street, the police took him to his brother's house in Quinebaug. He was later admitted to a hospital in Putnam, where he died two months later.[134] Perry Henries, who was survived by other family members, was not the last of the Nipmucs, nor was he the last of the Henrieses who lived in Providence and would be forever part of the history of its Native homelands.[135]

There are other Native people who made their homes in Upper South Providence during the nineteenth and early twentieth centuries whose urban experiences are difficult to trace because their lives failed to attract the attention of Euro-American observers or mostly went unnoticed by record keepers. They bear surnames that resonate in tribal genealogies and other records and are a persistent presence in the spaces where other Native people made their homes. Malbones, who shared a family name with Rhuahammer Malbone, a 108-year-old elder on the 1881 Narragansett tribal list, lived in Upper South Providence as early as the 1860s.[136] Caroline Malbone lived at the rear of 22 Spring Street in 1865, and 11-year-old Hannah, born in Providence, was at 5 West Hoyle and attended Public School Number 3.[137] Charles Malbone, who had been born in Pomfret, Connecticut, and moved to Providence in the 1860s with his wife, Priscilla Croud, lived over on Codding Street at the turn of the century, next door to James and Olive Henry.[138]

Nettie Cooper was also born in Connecticut. Her last name suggests Mohegan or Pequot ancestry and is also mentioned in association with Narragansett family histories. She lived at 12 Perkins Street in 1910, where Fred Thomas had lived more than twenty-five years earlier, and where Susan Holden, a widow identified as "Indian" in the 1910 U.S. Census, lived with her daughter, son-in-law, grandson, and son.[139] Susan had been born in Uxbridge, Massachusetts. Her son, Lloyd Garrison, who was born on Pond Street, was identified as an "Indian citizen" on his World War I draft registration card.[140] For Native individuals and families whose genealogies and diasporic pathways are difficult to trace, and others for whom there is more complete information, Upper South Providence had become a new homeland where personal and community histories were reproduced as well as redefined in shared spaces of the urban landscape.

Contentment and Discontents at the Crossroads: Identity, Place, and Resilience

Native people from near and distant places arrived at the crossroad where Cranston Street and Westminster Street intersected by the middle of the nineteenth century, if not earlier. Many had taken the same paths that their ancestors had followed when they had visited Providence centuries before. Some who made their homes along the streets that had been laid out near this gateway became long-term residents. They created an urban homeland where they engaged in city living, maintained family ties, and built new communities. Within this urban homeland, relatives and friends coming into the city from outlying areas could find short-term or extended housing and become conditionally acclimated to urban life. Some new arrivals made the decision to stay and became long-term residents in the hope that their cosmopolitan ambitions and dreams of making better lives for themselves and their families would be realized. City living sometimes fulfilled their expectations for a better future, but often it fell short. Many struggled economically by working at unsteady and low-paying jobs, though some held positions that provided stable employment and decent pay, enabling them to achieve their ambitions to greater or lesser degrees. Still, city life could be isolating. Close ties to family, neighborly living spaces and cohabitation, and membership in the Pond Street Church and the Indian Council of New England helped maintain and build community, though they did not always compensate for living apart from tribal reservations and for the frustrations associated with citizenship. Some, such as Benjamin and Frederick Thomas, who had lived in Providence for decades, and Perry Henries, who lived in the city only briefly, chose to return to their ancestral homelands where they resumed more rural lifeways.

Yet reservation or pastoral living did not define indigeneity. The rural versus urban binary cannot serve to determine who was Native or who was more so, nor can racial designations in censuses and vital records that both Native people and non-Native researchers agree are problematic. Native people were not chameleons who could change color at different times according to the circumstances; rather their inscribed racial identities were largely the products of historical contingencies and the subjectivities of official record keepers.[141] Racial labels and perceived phenotypes can be as deceptive as clothing, speech, and other external cultural signals. This is not to suggest that marriages among Native Americans, African Americans, and European settler colonists did not contribute to blurring the color line or that Native people were unaware of differences in skin color among individuals within their own and other tribal communities, and even within their families. Clearly, complexion was an issue that was discussed among the Narragansetts during the detribalization hearings and was later raised by some Native members of the Indian Council of New England who had concerns about interacting with individuals with mixed ancestry from Providence and other cities.[142] Frederick Thomas told Harris Hawthorne Wilder that one of his grandmothers hated "the Negroes, whites, and about everything," and that his Aunt Patience Stanton, described as a Block Island Indian who called herself a Negro, had "straight hair and a thin nose" and spoke "Indian," though she talked a "different lingo."[143]

Skin color or mixed ancestry should not casually be assumed to correlate with place, identity, or cultural knowledge. Like many Native people in cities, those who remained close to their tribal reservations did not necessarily fit stereotypical notions of a Native American phenotype. Both could be misidentified, though those living on or near reservations or in towns traditionally considered to have a Native presence would more likely have been recognized as tribal members than those residing in cities.[144] But as I argue, the ways in which Native individuals and families were interwoven in urban spaces, also provides a more accurate picture of "Indianness" than inconsistent and ambiguous racial labels in official records and broad assumptions about where Natives live (or should live). For the Native people of the Upper South Providence homeland, lineage and tribal identities were not severed as a consequence of their migration to the city. Certain streets and houses resonated with "Indianness." These were places where nuclear and extended families lived contemporaneously and often sequentially. From the detailed litany of the indigenous people living around Hoyle Square emerges a sense of place and rootedness that goes beyond a recounting of names and addresses. Certain houses and streets, let alone the Pond Street Church, fastened them to this homeland by intertwining placehood with what it meant to be Native in Providence.

At 7 Angle Street there were Brewsters, Stocketts, Wheelers, Champlins, a Gardner, and Mary Peckham, a widow from Griswold who was connected to the Narragansett Tribe through her grandmother, Hannah Harry.[145] On Pond Street, you could walk into the church at the corner with Angle Street through its gray double doors any Sunday and see a showing of hands of people from different urban and tribal homelands as attendance was taken. Cones, Helms, and Holdens, along with Amos Brewster, Eliza Hilton, Frank Nichols, Willis Wamsley, and Samuel Rodman, lived along the street, some as early as the 1860s and 1870s. Other Native residents were over on Winter Street, Spring Street, and Summer Street. At 19 Spring Street you might have spotted Benjamin Gardner out back, Hannah and Priscilla Nichols, Fannie Kendall and her children, Mercy Hazard (an elderly widow from Charlestown), or John E. Brown and his wife, Isabella (daughter of Hazard Champlin), both of whom were Narragansett and lived in the neighborhood for a few years.[146] You might have seen Amy Jackson (Narragansett), put out to work in Newport as a young girl, who now worked at the railroad depot in Providence, and Alice and James Northrup (Troy-Watuppas).[147] On Hoyle Street during the 1880s you could find some of the same people who at one time or another lived on Spring Street. Providence's former alphabet streets, such as A, B, and C Streets, had a strong Native presence, as did Booth, Hayward, Livermore, and Lockwood Streets, and Warner's Lane. On Codding Street, where a Brewster, a Croker, a Gardner, a Henry, a Reckling, a Rocker, and a Wheeler were neighbors, word might have spread about the death of Ben Thomas's daughter Lydia, forty-four and divorced from John Harris, her non-Native husband, at number 126.[148] To be indigenous in Providence—and particularly in Upper South Providence—meant living on these streets and in houses with familiar addresses and histories. These streets and houses were as much the exterior places of their lived experiences as they were the interior landscapes of mind and memory, what Keith Basso calls a landscape of the moral imagination.[149] The Native people of Upper South Providence knew that beyond these visible spaces was a moral reality that deeply influenced their sense of place and their sense of self. Cities then were no different than reservations or other places where Indians lived. In each new location, they made a place theirs and the place shaped them, suggesting that notions of placehood and selfhood contributed to the resiliency of urban Native life and indigenous culture in nineteenth- and early twentieth-century New England.

The Central-Classical Redevelopment Project of the 1960s cleared area just off Hoyle Square. The house at 7 Monroe Street, where Benjamin Dailey lived at the turn of the century, and the house at 8 Monroe, Frank Nichols's home two decades earlier, were razed. Number 12 Perkins, a vernacular, Federal-style building with a central entry at street level, where Fred Thomas and others lived, and 24 Saunders, the home of Thomas P. Wheeler and his wife from the late 1930s to about the mid-1940s, were also demolished.[150] Nearby, the Codding Court Project targeted a three-acre parcel of buildings bounded roughly by A, Dodge, Lester, and Booth Streets. Of the thirty-nine structures, not one dwelling met the minimum standard housing requirements. All were condemned, taken by eminent domain by the Providence Housing Authority in the early 1940s, and destroyed. Yet before wrecking balls could completely demolish what was considered "the center of the most extensive colored area in the city," abandoned houses and storefronts fell into further disrepair and became prime targets for rampant vandalism, making the Codding Street neighborhood look like an urban ghost town.[151] After ten years of delays owing to shifting housing policies and changes in national priorities during World War II, ground was finally broken at what appeared on the surface to be a vacant lot off Cranston Street. The 119-unit Codding Court housing project replaced 149 Codding Street, where the Wheelers had made their home for more than a dozen years in the early twentieth century, and homes on Booth Street where Christopher Champlin, Charles Dailey, and Frank Nichols had lived. This federally funded public housing complex was envisioned as being fully integrated, with Black families living next to white and Native American families, as they had before. But whatever similarities existed between the former enclave of homes occupied by Native people and Codding Court were superficial.[152] Urban renewal changed the face of the neighborhood, making it difficult for Native people to maintain connections to places where they and their ancestors had lived, worked, and socialized, and that had become layered with their experiences of city living. Like other tactics of erasure, the leveling and covering over of these storied places with new construction rendered their Native history invisible. Yet these flawed visions of modernity have not succeeded in obliterating memories of the Native people who made the neighborhood their home and the memories of those who still do today, as they struggle to be both Indian and modern.

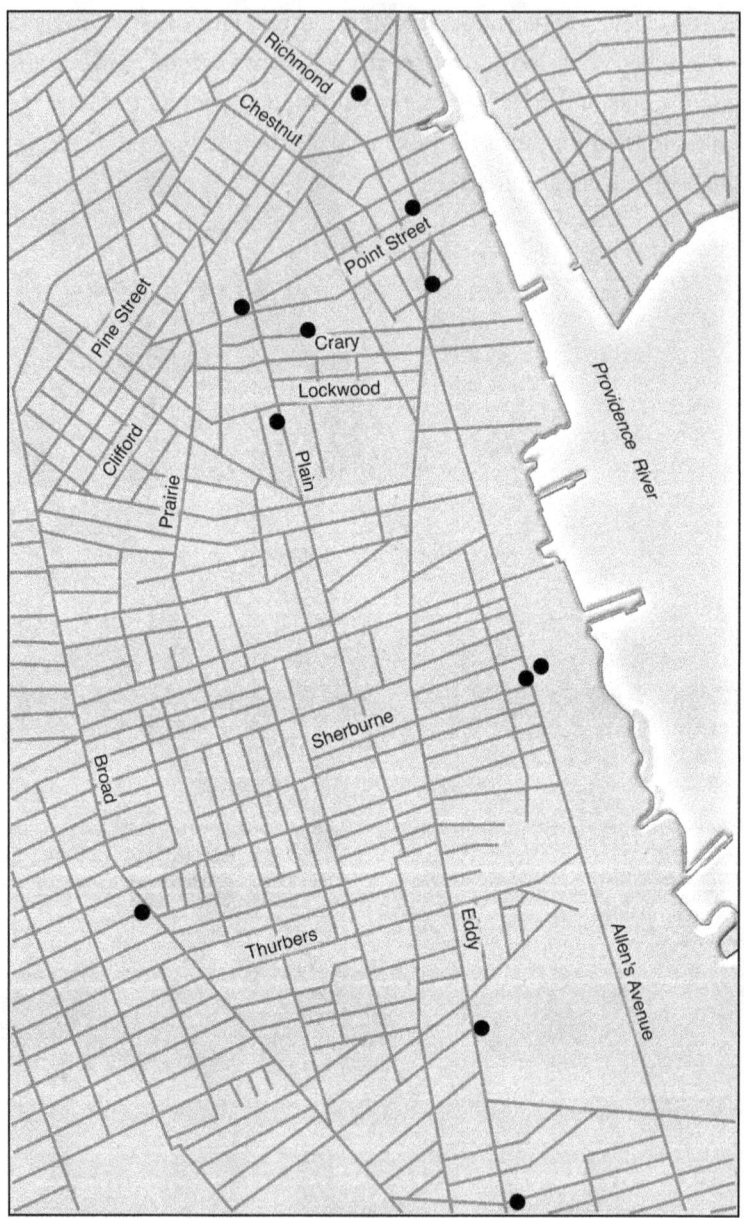

Fig. 13. Map of the Lower South Providence homeland, showing selected Native households. Map by Lynn Carlson.

Lower South Providence   4

*Habitations by the River and Bay, Mobility,
and the Urban Imaginary*

The section of South Providence bounded roughly by Allens Avenue and the Providence River waterfront to the east, Broad Street to the west, and Point Street and Thurbers Avenue to the north and south has been called "a local geographic area, a city neighborhood, and a state of mind" by Patrick Conley and Paul Campbell in their pictorial history of South Providence.[1] It is an urban area without precise borders that is considered apart from Hoyle Square in city planning documents and encompasses tracts referred to as "Upper, Upper South Providence" at its northerly edge and "Lower South Providence" in a more southerly direction.[2] As a Native homeland, it can be configured as an arc of settlement stretching from downtown Providence southward along the easterly waterfront that has a distinctive history compared to Upper South Providence and other Native neighborhoods. Until the early 1800s it was mostly undeveloped except for lands set aside for smallpox and yellow fever hospitals, a burial ground, an aqueduct system that brought pure drinking water to city residents, and a few small farms. In 1754 the sections farther south (which a 1978 historical preservation report described as "still wild and unpopulated") were ceded to Cranston, only to be reannexed by the city of Providence in 1868.[3] Decades before this political and geographical realignment was accomplished, industrialization and improvements in transportation laid the foundation for the area's growth.

In the central and largely rural section of South Providence, slaughterhouses provided jobs for unskilled laborers, many of them recent Irish immigrants who settled close to their workplaces at the near edges of the city's hinterland. Here sheep, hogs, and cattle bound for the stockyards and slaughterhouses arrived after being herded from downtown along a path later called Prairie Avenue, seemingly in a nod to the rolling and largely treeless terrain where settler colonialism in the nineteenth century expanded into indigenous territories farther to the west. Other local place-names also recall the dominance of the provisioning industry. Oxen (or Hog) Pond was named for a small pond, now filled in, where animals destined for slaughter bathed, splashed, bleated, and squealed before meeting their fate, and where boys from the neighborhood playing hooky from school would hide under the branches of willow trees that skimmed the pond's surface. Even "Dogtown," the common, if not pejorative, name of this part of South Providence, often associated with notorious street gangs that defended the community from outsiders, is derived from the packs of dogs that roamed the neighborhood scavenging on the offal and scraps at the slaughterhouses and snatching meat that consumers had purchased directly from purveyors.[4]

The completion of the Providence-Stonington line of the New York, New Haven, and Hartford railroad in 1837 spurred development in South Providence. The line approached Providence from the south following the Pawtuxet Turnpike along the present course of Eddy Street to Burgess Cove (or Broad Cove, as it was called during the eighteenth century).[5] Until then the Pawtuxet Turnpike that followed a Native trail was the principal artery leading to the city from the south. The opening of the railroad line provided an alternative and faster means of transportation that could more readily link together thinly populated rural towns and the densely populated urban community. Stops and housing multiplied around the terminal to accommodate travelers and employees. Yet as surely as the railroad contributed to the growth of a service community in South Providence, so did Native people traveling from Stonington, Connecticut, and Westerly, Rhode Island, who disembarked at Burgess Cove. At the Providence-Stonington railroad terminus, located less than two miles from the Weybosset Bridge that linked the city's east and west sides, they could take a ferry to the Boston-Providence depot at India Point in Fox Point. The trip from their ancestral homelands in the country could be filled with trepidation, not just because of the possibility of derailment and other technological mishaps, but also because of Native peoples' perceptions about how railroads might affect their communities. Their anxieties about the latter resonate in a story recalled by the Narragansetts in the twentieth century about where the railroad crossed over White Dog Swamp between Westerly and Bradford, Rhode Island. In the story as related by Lone Wolf (Lawrence W. Wilcox), an Indian was killed by the train when walking home with his dog via a shortcut made by the railroad. "Ever since on dark nights, the dog and the Indian have been seen there. The great white dog is seen coming down the track cut half in two while the Indian beside him has no head. The two go down the middle of the track as far as the brook and then disappear." The story and sightings of the ghosts are said to keep many away from the location on dark nights.[6] As much as the railroad crossing was foreboding, it did not deter some Native people from getting on the train to Providence at Stonington any Wednesday, Friday, or Sunday morning.[7]

Carried on trains that traveled along new tracks through rural villages and towns, and eventually along a causeway running parallel to present-day Allens Avenue at the foot of Lockwood Street in Lower South Providence, Native people either reluctantly or daringly crossed over the ominous swamp. Familiar places lay in the direction they had come from, but not necessarily where they were headed.[8] The crossroads and thoroughfares they passed through were crowded mostly with strangers and frequented by ghosts that might have guided them on their journey or warned them against departing from ancestral ways as they visited or migrated to new places.[9] Railroads were critical to their imaginings and engagement with modernity. They aided all sorts of movements common to Native people, as Jean O'Brien writes, from visiting, searching for wage labor, and marketing their manufactured goods to providing a means of widening the geographical range of places where they might encounter non Indians.[10] To imagine Indians on trains, like Geronimo at the wheel of a Cadillac, puts two different symbolic systems in dialogue with one another.[11] Trains played a role in transporting Native people to urban spaces at increasing frequencies, serving as tools of their cultural survival and challenging primitivist and essentialist discourses that positioned them as separate from and as victims of new technologies.[12]

Lower South Providence 157

Although Native people might be in the proverbial or actual driver's seat in cars, they were passengers on trains who took advantage of how the quick, efficient, but not necessarily reliable technology could bring them to new places where they could craft new lives. Trains allowed indigenous travelers to consider the possibilities of a world in which their mobility was not limited by foot, horse, or canoe, but was increasingly facilitated by streetcars and automobiles as well as trains.

Although railroads were not the only mean of transportation between rural and urban areas, or to South Providence specifically, they facilitated Native people's engagement with cities and modernity, contributing to the transformation of urban spaces and the creation of cosmopolitan communities. As elsewhere in the United States, Native people in Providence not only traveled the rails, they also found work with railroad companies. In the early 1900s Benjamin West Daily, who held a variety of jobs during his lifetime, was employed as a porter at Union Station, the passenger depot built on Exchange Place in the downtown commercial district in 1848 to accommodate railroads entering and leaving the city. Amy Jackson, who was born on the Narragansett reservation about 1817, by her own estimation "worked in the Providence depot fifteen years, and never came out of it."[13] More than a means of transportation or source of employment, railroads contributed to reconfiguring the social and geographical borders of indigenous New England. Stepping off at the Burgess Cove terminal of the Providence-Stonington line, Native people began the process of carving a place for themselves in South Providence's economically diverse and multicultural community, as had Euro-Americans whose businesses serviced travelers and railroad workers and Irish immigrants who worked in the slaughterhouses.

Yet long before Native people stepped off the Providence-Stonington railroad at Burgess Cove in the nineteenth century as new migrants, the area had been home to generations of ancestors. Their material traces, mostly stone tools recovered at inlets and prominent landforms along the waterfront such as Burgess Cove (formerly known as Old Maid's Cove and Bold Water Cove) and Field's Point, a promontory overlooking a mile-wide expanse of Narragansett Bay south of Thurbers Avenue, are from different time periods, varieties of raw materials, and stylistic traditions that have been identified by archaeologists.[14] The names given to the manufacturing traditions, such as Poplar Island, Brewerton, Squibnocket, and Wading River, do not recall Native place-names for Providence lands, but nonetheless speak to a history of place that is much deeper than, and independent of, what is documented in written records. Like Native people's later arrival in the city, the archaeological evidence does not provide an absolute starting point or suggest an unbroken trajectory of Native settlement in Lower South Providence. Rather, both preface an urban history that remains to be told.

Narrating Movement and Becoming Rooted in Place

Although Native Americans are not mentioned in discussions of South Providence's long history of ethnic diversity, at least not until the late twentieth century, they were living in the area by the early 1860s. Amy Jackson, who lived on Chapel Street, on the downtown fringe of South Providence not far from the railroad station where she worked, was among the invisible even after her retirement and up until her death in 1884.[15] Jackson, a long-time resident of Providence who came to the city after she had been "carried down to Narragansett" by her master and "brought up with Ben Hazard's daughter in Newport [Rhode Island]," made Chapel Street her home for more than twenty years.[16] Other Native people also lived in this section around this time, including the "Indian Physician" Samuel Rodman, who practiced medicine from his home on Pine Street in the late 1860s and early 1870s. The earliest recorded Native residents of this loosely configured modern urban homeland lived near West Burial Ground, a sprawling cemetery complex between Friendship and Plain Streets that grew by accretion and by the addition of private cemeteries on adjacent land purchased by the Beneficent and Benevolent Congregational churches for use as a burying ground in 1785.[17] Thomas Wheeler, who held a series of jobs working as a porter and coachman, lived at 20 Plane Street at the north end of the burial ground before moving to the Hoyle Street neighborhood. Alice and Cato Northrup were at the same address around the mid-nineteenth century. John F. Cone, Edward's father (see chapters 1, 2, and 5), also lived on Point Street in the late 1850s, and a Sarah Cone was listed at the corner of Point and Plane Streets near the southeastern corner of the cemetery in 1862.[18]

William Apess (Pequot), a noted activist, speaker, and writer, was a member the Second Methodist Meeting House at Chestnut and Clifford Streets to the north of West Burial Ground, where he was appointed to the ministerial position of class leader for two years in the mid-1820s. Apess, who was born in Colrain, Massachusetts, in 1798, began attending Methodist meetings in the New London–Groton area homelands of his Pequot relatives as a young man. Independent of any spiritual stirrings he, like many Native Americans and African Americans, would probably have been drawn to Methodism because of its emphasis on community-building through gatherings such as camp meetings and conferences and on performative aspects of worship involving the use of the body and voice.[19] He moved to Providence, where he had a sister, Mary Ann, in the winter of 1825, with his wife, Mary, a woman of Spanish/West Indian and white parentage and a devout Methodist.[20] The couple and their two young children settled at 221 North Main Street, a multifamily dwelling owned by James Thurber Sr., a justice of the peace, in an area consisting mostly of tenements and boardinghouses occupied by Native Americans and African Americans and some whites, located a short distance from the Hardscrabble Riot in Addison's Hollow a year before.[21] Apess found work to support his family in "trucking," a menial job of loading, unloading, and pushing carts of goods that Drew Lopenzina, a literary historian, suggests were books on Methodism.[22] After a few years, he left Providence for Mashpee and from there, moved to New York City.

It was from Providence that Apess embarked on the first legs of his journey as an itinerant preacher. This was a demanding life that, as Douglas Koskela, a theologian who writes about the religious culture of American Methodism, states, required "setting aside any ambitions of wealth, comfort, and deep roots in a particular locale."[23] As Apess recounts in *A Son of the Forest* (1829), the first autobiography published by a Native American, his excursions as a circuit rider would take him across the Northeast with stops at Newburyport, Massachusetts, Portland, Maine, Sag Harbor on Long Island, New York City, and Albany, New York, and back to his "abiding place at Providence, R.I."[24] Although the details are fuzzy, Apess, who had been given a verbal permission to preach, was denied a formal license to exhort either because he had not lived in Providence long enough or because he was an Indian, or both. In 1829 he split from the Methodist Episcopals, joined the Protestant Methodist Church, and set out on a career as a public intellectual in which he wrote five books, delivered speeches, and garnered notoriety in the press for his role in inciting the Mashpee Revolt of 1833 against the resident missionary and state-appointed guardianship.[25] In writing about the class dimensions of religious experiences in antebellum Rhode Island, Mark Schantz described Apess as "a Pequot among white New Englanders, a transient laborer among settled farmers and townspeople, a drinker among sober churchgoers." His early life experiences—poverty, family separations, beatings, and indentures—comment on his social and economic marginality, which Max Weber characterizes as an attribute of charismatic religious figures. These experiences and the racial prejudice he witnessed in Providence and in other colonized spaces where he worked among mixed groups of Native Americans and African Americans as an adult shaped his consciousness about the injustices in American democratic society.[26]

During the years that Apess was affiliated with the Second Methodist Meeting House (or the Chestnut Street Church, as it was frequently known), there was very little to distinguish the building from a barn, according to William McDonald's *History of Methodism in Providence, Rhode Island*. It had "no steeple, no bell to call people to the sacred altar, and no organ to make melody, or, as it ha[d] sometimes done, discord within. All was plain, simple, Methodistical."[27] Once could suppose that the church's architectural simplicity reiterated the denomination's interest in reaching out to all people regardless of class, race, or gender—a precept that had attracted Apess to Methodism. Yet the Chestnut Street church had 280 white members and only 35 members of color in 1822. By 1826-27, about the time when Apess was a class leader, the membership included 194 white individuals and only 25 persons of color (roughly 11 percent of the congregation).²⁸ Beginning in the 1830s, after Apess's tenure, the church building and the congregation changed. A steeple was added, galleries were enlarged, a parsonage was built, expanded, and moved from the backlot, the interior was frescoed, a new choir loft and stairway to the vestry were constructed, and the exterior and interior were refitted. These capital improvements that made the church "a most commodious and attractive house of worship" by the end of the nineteenth century created a substantial debt, which was allayed by appealing to a base of more affluent and white congregants than might have been expected, given Methodism's older ideals of social egalitarianism.²⁹

The Chestnut Street Church has not occupied the corner of Chestnut and Clifford Streets since the first decade of the twentieth century. Other Protestant churches and groups reoccupied the building in quick succession and continued to maintain a church presence at the location for a time. Today the building is no longer standing and the land it once sat upon is now poised for development (fig. 14). Probably few passersby know the spot's association with William Apess or, I suppose, are aware of his importance to the region's indigenous communities. There are no surviving transcripts of the words he spoke as a prayer leader at Methodist class meetings with church members "to support, encourage, and press" them, as well as himself, "on the way to salvation."³⁰

The modest meeting house of the 1820s was not the same kind of stage as the Odeon, Boston's famed lecture and concert hall, where Apess delivered his "Eulogy on King Philip," first on January 8, 1836, and in a shorter version on January 26, seemingly in response to the newspapers' criticisms of the earlier oration. One might presume that his critics expected to hear more about his views of the Christian mission than about Philip (Metacom) and early encounters between indigenous people and English settler colonists. It seems likely that some in the audience were shocked by his audacity in saying that Philip should be immortalized as much as George Washington in America's collective memory. But as Barry O'Connell has guessed, Apess gave the speech to observe the 160th anniversary of Philip's death and to honor him by insisting that the past treatment of New England Native Americans had contemporary resonance in the nineteenth century when Manifest Destiny and removal defined U.S. Indian policy. The lecture was as much an accounting of history as it was a call for change.[31]

In the second oration, Apess did not back off from political statements but may have been more emphatic about articulating his complicated and painful history as a Native person in nineteenth-century America, and in asserting that just because he was a Christian, he was no less Indian. At the end of the speech, he recited the Lord's Prayer in the Wampanoag language as it was translated by John Eliot, an English missionary, and John Sassamon, an indigenous interlocutor, in the seventeenth century. The recitation was an attempt to provide the audience with a specimen of words and intonations that Philip would have used and, I suspect, also to show that Christianity and indigeneity were not antithetical. As unintelligible as it was to Euro-American ears, his utterances of a language that had slowly fallen out of everyday discourse as its native speakers increasingly worked, lived, and were schooled in the dominant society made a powerful counterstatement about the disappearance of the region's Native people and their culture that was made even more potent by his denunciation of white culture and his prediction that its destructiveness would be reversed.

Although the Chestnut Street Church offered a different kind of platform than the Odeon, the camp meetings, and Mashpee, the audiences at these venues would have seen the same William Apess, whom U.S. Army enlistment records described in 1813 as five feet two inches tall with hazel eyes, black hair, and a dark complexion.[32] A lithograph produced by the engraving and printing firm Illman & Pilbrow in New York from a portrait by John Paradise (1783-1834), an American artist known for his paintings of Methodist diviners, and published as the frontispiece to the second edition of *A Son of the Forest* (1831), shows Apess about twenty years later.[33] His facial features, as best they can be read from the reproduced image, do not contradict the physical description of him inscribed in army enlistment records. He is clad in formal, dark-colored attire and wears a white cravat fashionably wrapped around his neck

Fig. 14. Site of the former Chestnut Street Methodist Church, at the corner of Chestnut and Clifford Streets, where William Apess presided over a small Native and African American congregation in the 1820s. Photograph by Patricia E. Rubertone.

and knotted in the front. Apess recognized that some who flocked to his hear his exhortations on the Northeast circuit or attended his class meetings in Providence and his speeches in Boston "to *see* the Indian, as he put it in his autobiography," would have been sorely disappointed.[34] Apess did not fulfill popular Euro-American expectations about what Indians should look like. Even at the Odeon, the site of his most public performances, he passed on the opportunity to commodify himself as an Indian in the American imagination. Hardly resembling Northeast Natives described by early colonial observers in the seventeenth century, Apess's manner of dress and speech and his complexion would have challenged most nineteenth-century Euro-American conceptions of "real" New England Indians. But for those who could look beyond his appearance, his very presence should have been evidence enough that New England Indians had not died out. They had acculturated and accommodated, as well as resisted, as Apess had, in order to persevere.

Born in the hills of northern Massachusetts "where [his father] pitched his tent in the woods," and having grown up in rural southeastern Connecticut, Apess was a country person who might very well have been considered a novelty in the city.[35] Yet his connection to Providence, his trips to Boston and other New England cities, and the time he spent in New York City suggest otherwise. He visited Manhattan in 1829 to deposit the copyright for the first edition of *A Son of the Forest*, and probably again in 1831 to sit for the portrait that appeared in the second edition, which was published there that same year along with his sermon "The Increase of the Kingdom of Christ." Years earlier he had run away from his indenture in New London to New York City, where he enlisted in the U.S. Army and was trained on Governor's Island. Sometime after his appearance at the Odeon and several lawsuits in Massachusetts for nonpayment of debts, he moved to New York, where he died on April 10, 1839. Obituaries that appeared in New York City newspapers and an inquest into the circumstances surrounding his untimely death indicate that Apess had been living with a wife named Elizabeth in a boardinghouse in lower Manhattan, a neighborhood of cart men, day laborers, and other transient workers not unlike the neighborhood where he had lived in Providence.

The coroner's report concluded that he died of apoplexy, a term used in the nineteenth century to describe a sudden death that neither verified nor identified the underlying disease processes contributing to the individual's death. These uncertainties, together with the unexpected timing of Apess's passing, have led scholars to speculate about its causes. Whether he was killed by "bad medicine" prescribed by a mainstream doctor the day after he became ill or by a remedy he was given the next day by a "botanical physician" whose cures would have been more familiar to (and trusted by) Apess, or whether his drinking caught up with him after he had struggled with alcohol for years, might not be knowable.[36] The last few months, or possibly last several years, of his life might have been ones in which he succumbed to the sense of victimhood that he had battled throughout his life. Surviving records, at least ones that are known, are silent about any connections he might have had during this period to a larger Methodist community through which he might have found a welcoming audience and support, about his ties to other Native people, and about his relationship to his first wife, Mary, and their children. But one thing is sure: William Apess was neither an urban novelty nor an anomaly. Two of his siblings, Elisha and Leonard, whalers, traveled widely and had life experiences as cosmopolitan as his. Elisha settled in New Zealand and Leonard, a ship master, earned bourgeois respectability and a mention in local history with the marriage of his daughter Lillias to Alfred E. Lamoreux, a Rhode Island pharmacist, businessman, and state senator.[37]

William Apess's brothers are more visible than the majority of Native people born on the margins of white society in nineteenth-century New England because of the efforts of Barry O'Connell and Nancy Shoemaker, a historian, to raise them from obscurity, though they are less visible than he because of the written accounts he gave about his life and the attention he attracted as a speaker. Still, he shares with them and other Native people who did not write about their lives or express their opinions on public stages experiences that were harsh, complicated, and alienating. Like so many of them, he also condemned social injustices in his everyday life, while making accommodations to the changing world order shaped but not determined by his detractors.

Defying Victimhood: Interlopers, Tricksters, and Voices of Experience

Born in Charlestown, Rhode Island, in 1811, Roxanna Dwight was sixty-nine years old and living at 211 Richmond Street when her name was registered as a claimant for a share of the proceeds from the sale of the Narragansett reservation at the third meeting of the Commission at Samoset Hall in the village of Carolina on July 25, 1880.[38] Her father was Frederick Bosemsdes, a Protestant immigrant and watchmaker from Switzerland who arrived in the United States in 1806.[39] Her mother was Fanny Daniels, who belonged to the Narragansett Tribe. Fanny's mother was named Sarah, and her father was John Daniels, an Indian from Charlestown who served as a private in the American Revolution.

An advertisement from the *Providence Gazette*, April 26, 1777, identifies him as a deserter "about 20 years of age, 5 feet 7 inches high, [with] long hair," who left his company in February with another young Narragansett soldier from Charlestown and a man about forty years old who formerly lived on Block Island.[40] Daniels, who died about 1781, shortly after Fanny was born, had been in the colonial army for eight years, according to a pension certificate filed posthumously.[41]

Frederick Bosemsdes, a part-time translator, deciphered documents and wrote letters for the Narragansetts.[42] Although how he came to live among them is unclear, he possibly may have been one of the many would-be missionaries who visited the community during the late 1700s and early 1800s. Putting aside his intentions, Bosemsdes was not the only white foreigner to have been accepted within a Native community in southern New England. Other outsiders, often described as runaways, deserters, vagabonds, or criminals, also found refuge, as did shipmates of returning Native mariners, who accompanied them to their home places and often wound up staying and marrying Native women.[43] Regardless of the circumstances under which Native or non-Native outsiders arrived, the influx of newcomers and the movement of tribal members in and out of ancestral homelands increasingly became matters of concern as Native groups struggled to maintain their communities and surviving land base and resist mounting challenges to their sovereignty by state governments.

Frederick Bosemsdes's presence on the reservation, where he lived with Fanny and Roxanna on land that Fanny had inherited and where he had built a house, barn, and corncrib and made an extension to an existing dwelling house and other improvements, was eventually contested.[44] In 1815, the Narragansett Indian Council brought a petition to the Rhode Island General Assembly asking that he be removed from tribal land. The reasons were that he was a "Swede and a white man" who did not belong to the tribe and that he had violated laws and regulations regarding marriages with outsiders. According to tribal customs, an outsider who married a woman from the tribe was expected to take his wife away unless "the council pleased to let them to stay in the town." Apparently Bosemsdes had not taken his wife away, nor had he been given formal permission to stay. He was also accused of being a "frightening fellow" who had threatened the lives of some his neighbors and fellow creatures "with a sword." The Narragansett Indian Council stated that it was "afraid he would do damage to some of the tribe" and would continue to disregard tribal laws and regulations and do as he pleased.[45] After reviewing the petition, the General Assembly denied the request to remove Bosemsdes from the reservation. The rationale was that he was connected "either by marriage or other ways" to Fanny Daniels, a female member of the tribe, who was the legal heir to some land in her possession.[46] Whether Bosemsdes stayed on the reservation after the decision was handed down and if so, for how long, is unclear.[47] Fanny Bosemsdes's name appears in records of the tribe concerning land matters into the 1850s and 1860s. She died of old age in 1865 and was buried in the "Bocemsdes" Lot in Charlestown across from the Indian Cedar Swamp. The marble gravestone marking her burial suggests that only her remains were interred in the grave.[48]

When Roxanna Bosemsdes left Charlestown for Providence is uncertain. The first known stop on the route that would eventually bring her to Providence may have been Newport, Rhode Island. She appears in the 1850 U.S. Census as Rosanna Melville, the wife of Andrew Melville, a victualler, and the mother of Harriet, twelve, Jane, six, and Jerome, four.[49] She married Joseph Dwight, a shoemaker who was born in Newport, in the small village of Teaticket in the town of Falmouth, Massachusetts, in 1855.[50] By 1860, and possibly before, they were living in Providence with her children Jane (or Jennie) and Jerome and their seven-year-old son Theodolphus, who was born in Fall River, Massachusetts.[51] Their home on the west side of Richmond Street was a wood-framed, multi-family dwelling located near the intersection with Point Street across from the Point Street Iron Works and the Barstow Stove Company, two of the many heavy-industry complexes along the portion of the Providence River that opened into Narragansett Bay. Compared with the large brick industrial buildings on the waterfront, the Dwights' block was dominated by wooden structures facing Richmond Street. In 1867 the 2,137-square-foot lot, the dwelling house, and other buildings were sold for one dollar to Roxanna's son, Jerome Melville, who was named the trustee and manager of the property for his mother. According to the agreement, she could continue to occupy the property and would be paid any rents or profits collected from the estate.[52] By 1870 the family had taken in two couples and a single woman as boarders. None was identified as a person of color. Five years later the family, which now included Jerome's wife and Theodolphus's second wife and infant daughter, was still living at the house on Richmond Street, which they shared with a woman described as a clairvoyant and her adult daughter.[53]

Like Joseph Dwight, Roxanna's sons worked in skilled or semi-skilled trades and might be considered artisan-entrepreneurs.[54] Jerome, who worked as a baker in addition to managing his mother's Richmond Street property, later moved to Brooklyn, New York, and became a stockbroker. Theodolphus was a jeweler when he first married in 1870 and a carpenter at the time of his second marriage in 1873; he was later was employed as a salesman. Her daughter Jennie married Thomas G. Glover, a butcher, in Providence in 1863.[55] These trades suggest that Roxanna Dwight's sons and son-in-law had relatively stable incomes from wages that would have been higher than those of day laborers. On September 19, 1871, the city's recorder of deeds certified that Jerome, who had real estate investments in other properties besides the family home on Richmond Street, received a payment of $175 for a half-interest in "one carpet, a safe, mirror, sideboard, stove, three tables, one lounge chair, and fifteen chairs" at No. 4 Westminster Street.[56] Although he and Theodolphus changed jobs, they did not shift from one low-paying job to another, as was often the case for Native men in nineteenth- and early twentieth-century New England cities. Rather, they moved up into positions in sales in which they could be persuasive in creating demand and bettering their lives.

Sales would have given the two brothers, especially the stock trader Jerome, opportunities for economic advancement into the ranks of America's burgeoning middle class of entrepreneurial artisan-shopkeepers and, increasingly, of manufacturers and white-collar workers.[57] Aside from Natives who marketed baskets and herbal medicines, or the occasional shopkeeper, such as James Stockett Sr. (see chapter 3), jobs in sales were rare among Native people in Providence and other New England cities in the late nineteenth and the early twentieth centuries and hardly mentioned by scholars who have written about them during these later times. Urban Indians, if they were employed at all, were expected to hold jobs as day laborers at livery stables, railroad stations, or coal yards, or to work in the building trade or as entertainers; they were not expected to be stockbrokers. For Jerome Melville, the potential benefits of the work were marred by a lawsuit in 1902 in which he was sued for fraud in a stock transaction and accused of heading a gambling establishment on West Thirty-First Street in New York City that ran a Ponzi-type scheme.[58]

Betwixt Native and white cultures by birth, and described as white in records (as was his mother and other members of his family), Jerome Melville evokes the image of a trickster in Native American mythology who had the intellect and seemingly the guile to disobey conventional rules of behavior. In defying expectations of Indians living in cities, his life offers insights into experiences that invoke irony, chance, and traditional logic. By privileging survivance over victimhood, he was not alone. Others of Narragansett descent made their way to New York City, where they lived seemingly unconventional lives. Chief Thundercloud was among them. Born around 1856, he left Rhode Island to work as traveling medicine man and possibly joined Buffalo Bill's Wild West Show before settling in Harlem, a neighborhood on New York City's northern end. Harlem, an open grassland during colonial times, was a crowded, urban landscape of apartment houses and tenements, where "thousands of African Americans are reported to have bought herb tonics and cure-alls" from Chief Thundercloud, whom they knew only as the "great medicine man" in the forty years that he lived there. Finding it "hard to be an Indian" as his medicine business declined and advancing age robbed him of the "fire and energy" for maintaining a profitable practice, he worked at a paint store in the Bronx until it went out of business. This six-foot-tall Indian with "a fine physique and the high cheekbones of Northeastern Indians," who still was an impressive figure in spite of his age and "shabby modern clothes and bad haircut," was later arraigned on charges on being a fagin who persuaded boys steal for him, an accusation that he vehemently denied. In 1934 his body was discovered by his friend "Uncle Jake" Wickham, an elderly African American man, who lived with him in a hut made from a packing crate in Coogan's Lot, a squatters colony on the banks of the Harlem River near the Polo Grounds, one of baseball's hallowed grounds.[59]

In his eighties or nineties and destitute, Chief Thundercloud would have been buried in New York's Potter's Field, an inglorious graveyard where William Apess was probably laid to rest almost a century earlier.[60] Although Thundercloud's death did not occur tragically early or seem suspicious enough to require a formal inquest, it was brought to the attention of the National Algonquin Indian Council, which investigated his ancestry and determined that he was eligible for burial in the Narragansett burial ground in Charlestown. Edward Michaels (Chief Sunset), a member of the organization, said that Thundercloud's name was Frank Wicks and that he had known the other man's mother, who had lived in the vicinity of the former reservation. Through the generosity of Dr. M. Sales Taylor, a radio personality known as "the Voice of Experience" whose own physical challenges made him sympathetic to the needs of those destined for Potter's Field, Thundercloud's body was brought back to Charlestown and buried with honor in the presence of more than two hundred Natives and some non-Natives, who stood in frigid temperatures and braved snow-packed roads to attend the service. The *Westerly Sun* reported that many of those gathered at the old Indian Meeting House to pay homage to this "forgotten man" of New York City's waterfront and "one of the last reigning chiefs of the Narragansett Indians" were members of the National Algonquin Indian Council and the American Indian Federation, an intertribal organization founded in 1931. Some had made the trip from Providence or other cities and towns across New England. Others had traveled from New York City and as far as Cristobel in the Panama Canal Zone. Most had stories of survival that could easily rival Chief Thundercloud's and had come to his funeral to make sure that he would not be forgotten."[61] An enigmatic figure with a hazy genealogy, Thundercloud, like Jerome Melville, was enterprising and resourceful. Both were modern-day tricksters, crafty and neither wicked nor treacherous, who had chosen a course of survivance over victimhood. Based on their skin color or dress, each man might have gone unnoticed on the crammed streets of New York City or along the flats of the Harlem River, which long before it became the site of a squatter compound of destitute and forgotten Native Americans and African Americans in the nineteenth and twentieth centuries was the northernmost and most populous Lenape Indian homeland.[62]

From threads of evidence about Roxanna Dwight's life in Providence, it is clear that hers too did not follow a conventional script. There is little documentation to suggest that either she or her children interacted with South Providence's Native community or with individuals and families in the city's other Native homelands, though she was staunchly Narragansett on her maternal side. Surviving records do not comment on whether she attended the August Meetings or participated in tribal elections each March in the years before detribalization; or whether she went to Charlestown to look after the land that she had inherited from her mother and grandmother, though her name was registered as a claimant during the detribalization hearings.[63] Predeceased by her husband Joseph, she died in 1887 at the age of sixty-nine.[64] In her will, written in 1867, she left Jerome, whom she named as the executor of her estate, the Richmond Street property, "consisting of a house and lot together with appurtenances thereunto belonging." Her "household furniture of every description" went to Jennie. Theodolphus, a minor, was to receive 400 dollars, which was to be kept for him in the Mechanic's Savings Bank until he came of age; if he died before her death, the money was to go to Jennie. Finally, she gave each child who would survive her an equal share in her "house and lot and about two hundred cords of standing wood in the town of Charlestown," which had been her patrimony, or tangible heritage. Jennie passed away on November 8, 1867, almost exactly one month after Roxanna named her as a beneficiary. In a codicil to her last will and testament dated October 29, 1883, Roxanna acknowledged that she had taken a mortgage on the property at 211 Richmond Street, and indicated that in the case of her death, Jerome would assume the deed.[65]

Roxanna, who had lived apart from the Narragansett Indian community in Charlestown for much of her life, was not buried on the Bocemsdes Lot with her mother, nor were her children. Her final resting place is the North Burial Ground, along with Jennie and her two sons, both of whom died in New York City, Theodolphus in 1910 and Jerome in 1919.[66]

Alternative Pathways: Migration, Lodging, and Residence

The northernmost part of South Providence was conveniently located within a comfortable walking distance of about a mile from Providence's downtown business district. It was more densely settled than blocks farther south well past the mid-nineteenth century. The southerly edge of this residential fringe of the city's commercial hub was home to some of Providence's Native people in late nineteenth and early twentieth centuries. Howard B. Hazard, the son of Sarah Hazard and John B. Hazard, and nephew of Sarah's sister Hannah (née Thomas) Nichols, was living at 111 Crary Street (roughly across from the Providence Gas Company's large, metal-domed, brick storage silo for coal gas) when he died in 1905 of cancer of the larynx at the age of forty-five.[67] The section of Lockwood Street between Plain Street on the west and Eddy Street on the east was home to Frederick Thomas in 1870.[68] Rachel Storms, the mother of Leroy Perry (see below), lived at 155 Lockwood Street from about 1930 to the time of her death in 1948, not far from where the terminus of the Providence-Stonington railroad had stood in the late 1830s.

Rachel, whose maiden name was Crank, a surname associated with the Fall River reservation on the east shore of the North Watuppa Pond, was born about 1856. Her father was Thomas Crank, a Fall River Indian, and her mother, Julia, was identified by John Milton Earle as a "mulatto" and a "foreigner," a term that he used to designate someone who was either not an Indian or not one of the kindred tribe by birth.[69] His survey of the reservation lists four children, two girls and two boys, though Julia gave birth to three more girls and another son by 1870.[70] Thomas, a farm laborer, owned a house and two acres of land that he cultivated. Conditions on the reservation were described as bleaker than those faced by families who had left for the Massachusetts towns of Fall River, New

Bedford, Abington, Middleborough, or Swansea, or for Providence, or ventured as far west as California in search of better lives. The six remaining reservation families existed at "the incipient or more advanced stage of pauperism," according to Earle, with the land they cultivated barely providing sustenance and their meager income from rents and the sale of wood scarcely contributing to expenditures subsidized by the state. Yet he reluctantly admitted that some of the *hardest cases* were among tribal members living off the reservation—especially in cities, where the existence of an "industrious, moral, and intelligent community" that could potentially have "a beneficent influence," did not offset "the prejudice of color and caste, and the social proscription to which colored people are subjected." In his judgment, these conditions had an unfavorable effect that detracted from Native people's self-respect, weakened their moral instincts, and threw them in with the more dissolute and degraded of other races where they were easy prey to immoral habits. Regardless of residence, some Native people were "worthy and respectable members of the community," who were able to rise above "the evil influences."[71] Aside from the values that the wider society used in rendering indictments of morality, Fall River Indians and other Native communities across the region faced indisputable obstacles resulting from misunderstandings of their Indianness, let alone being subjected to widespread prejudice directed against all people of color.

Whether the Crank family fell into the category of community members deemed worthy and respectable cannot be ascertained from Earle's report. Although there is no evidence to suggest otherwise, their struggles to make ends meet seem certain. Thomas's mother, Sarah Crank, was at age seventy among members of the tribal community who, because of their age and infirmity, received a large part of their support from the state.[72] By the age of fifteen Rachel was living out with a white family in Fall River, where she worked as a domestic servant.[73] In 1875 she married Commodore Perry, a hostler, in Fall River. He was the father of her twin sons, Leroy and Royal, born that year, and Theodore, who was born about three years later.[74] Prior to his marriage to Rachel, Perry, who was from North Carolina, had served as a private in the Fifty-Fifth Massachusetts Colored Infantry during the Civil War. He died in Fall River in 1893.[75] Rachel remarried in Providence on October 26, 1899, where she had been living since 1890.[76] Her new husband, George Storms, a Providence resident who was born in Boston, was an upholsterer at the time of their marriage.[77] Soon after, Rachel and George were living at a lodging house at 7 Calendar Street in downtown Providence's commercial district.[78]

The lodging house was run by a couple, identified as Black, as were the five lodgers, including the Storms. Around the turn of the century, lodging houses such as the one on Calendar Street became increasingly popular. Heads of households, whether they rented or owned a property, often would take in an occasional boarder to supplement their income, to obtain needed labor in exchange for a place to live, or to give a family member short-term or extended housing. For residents, lodging houses offered an alternative to tenement life and a more independent type of domestic arrangement than the communal living and dining typically found at boardinghouses such as the Dwights' on Richmond Street, and were another answer to city dwellers' housing dilemma.[79] Like most lodging houses that emerged in the later nineteenth century as residential destinations for unskilled workers migrating from New England towns and the countryside (and more distant places), the Calendar Street address in 1900 was home to male lodgers, one of whom was employed as a day laborer, one as a meat worker, and one as a porter at a saloon (George Storm), and two women, who worked as laundresses. Other than Rachel and George Storm and the couple managing the lodging house, the other lodgers, two of the men and a woman, were either married (and not living with their spouses) or widowed.

The Storms, like lodgers everywhere in America's cities aspiring to a better life in the nineteenth and early twentieth centuries, eventually left the lodging house. They moved to Noyes Street and later a few blocks away to Waldo Street, both in the Benedict Pond neighborhood. They lived on Waldo Street through most of the 1920s.[80] In the 1930 U.S. Census, Rachel, who was identified as an "Indian" (her parents were identified as "full-blood Wampanoags") was working as a domestic servant for a private family and living at the rear of 155 Lockwood Street, which would be her home for nearly two more decades.[81] Her son Leroy, who was active in the Indian Council of New England and served as the First Supreme Sachem of the Wampanoag Nation in 1928, moved from Fall River to Providence by the late 1890s. He is recorded in city directories for the first time in 1896, when he is listed on Lilac Street in the Benedict Pond area. He moved back to Fall River the following year and soon returned to Providence, settling near Long Pond north of Mashapaug Pond. Through the first two decades of the 1900s he worked as a laborer and as a clerk, and as a janitor at the Calhoun Avenue School near his home, and he later commuted to Hope High School on the east side, where he was promoted to chief building engineer. He is last listed in Providence directories in 1930 as a clergyman living with his wife, Susie, on the city's west end, in the homeland where he had resided for almost thirty years.[82]

Sometime in 1931 Leroy Perry moved to the Mount Hope area of Bristol, Rhode Island, where he lived on the grounds of Rudolph Haffenreffer's King Philip Museum and served as an on-site interpreter of its collection of North American Indian artifacts for school groups and other visitors. The relationship between the two men may have begun in Providence, where Perry's visibility in the Indian Council of New England of the 1920s might have caught Haffenreffer's attention. Quite possibly, their acquaintance was struck as early as 1914, when Haffenreffer was a member of the Watuppa Water Commission that conspired with the city of Fall River to take reservation land by eminent domain to protect the city's water supply, a maneuver that displaced the family of Fanny L. Perry, who was Leroy Perry's relative. Whatever resentment he might have felt about the incident was not apparent when Perry, who was also known by his Native name, Ousa Mekin (Yellow Feather), wrote a message to Haffenreffer in the museum's guest book on June 21, 1929, in which he addressed him with the Wampanoag phrase "Quai Nun Memaeu Netomp," meaning "Hello my loving friend."[83] In 1930 and possibly before his short residence at Mount Hope, he was interpreting objects from collections at Haffenreffer's museum and shipyard and from the town of Bristol exhibited at a bank in Providence to commemorate Bristol's 250th anniversary. There is no record of whether he was paid for the work, which, the *Fall River Herald News* reported, required him to be on hand to "explain the significance of the stones, weapons and other things used by his forefathers before the advent of the white man."[84]

Whether Leroy Perry camped in a traditional *wetu* while in residence at Mount Hope, following the archaeologist Warren K. Moorehead's suggestion to Haffenreffer that he should "secure a few real Indians anywhere in the region and have them set up an old-style wigwam or two and have them live there" during the summer, or lived in a wood-framed, Euro-American-style building there year-round is unknown.[85] Regardless of the living arrangements, the stopover was an important sojourn in his life's journey that allowed him to reconnect with a homeland of his Wampanoag ancestors and with the place where Philip was killed on August 12, 1676, in an act that effectively ended the southern New England war named after him. Perry was called to preach when he was living in Providence while in his twenties. The time that he spent at Mount Hope, a place of pilgrimage where the Wampanoags went to honor Philip's memory, would have offered quietude for reflecting on his mission as a preacher and Native activist. While there, he would have sought inspiration from Philip, whom William Apess called the "all-accomplished son of the forest" and a tragic martyr to the cause of the Wampanoags and all New England Indians.[86] Photographs of Leroy Perry at Mount Hope from about 1931 show him in Native regalia, complete with a Plains Indian–style feather headdress, examining the inscription on the boulder monument placed near the site of Philip's murder by the Rhode Island Historical Society to mark its 200th anniversary and sitting in "King Philip's Chair," a rock formation where the sachem is believed to have met with his councilors.[87] These images situate Leroy Perry at ancestral places steeped in indigenous memories that run much deeper than the moments caught in these staged photographs promoting the museum and its involvement with the region's living Native people.

From Mount Hope, Leroy Perry went Martha's Vineyard. In 1933 he was appointed pastor of the Baptist Church at Gay Head and led services for the Wampanoag communities of Aquinnah, Herring Pond, and Mashpee, where he preached at the Old Indian Church as William Apess had about a century before.[88] Yet he remained connected to Native Americans in Rhode Island who were his neighbors in Providence and those he met through the Indian Council of New England. He was also well known in Charlestown, where he had conducted services at the Narragansett Indian Church during the annual August Meeting beginning in 1923 (fig. 15). An article in *Narragansett Dawn* about the August Meeting of 1935 reported that "his beautiful messages of Sunday morning and afternoon will long be remembered by all races, who crowded the grounds to hear him. He has preached in many places all along our eastern seaboard, in pulpits filled by college men.... His hair is graying but his voice is clear and strong.... Great men and gracious ladies of all races, have paused to listen and been moved, as blessings fell from the lips of this little Indian minister, the Rev. LeRoy Perry."[89] The diminutive Ousa Mekin, who was described as "short" on his World War I draft registration card, also presided at a reenactment of a traditional marriage ceremony held during the August gathering.[90] On later occasions, he joined in the pageantry of the Narragansett Tribe of Indians' Tercentenary Celebration of the Coming of Roger Williams to the Lodge of Canonicus at Camp Ki-Yi, the farm of Princess Red Wing, in Oakland, Rhode Island, on July 4 and 5, 1936, and in the festivities of the First Rhode Island Indian Day on August 8 of that year.[91]

Leroy Perry also had family members in Providence who would have kept him connected to the city. His mother lived in Providence, and as did his twin, Royal, until his death in 1916.[92] The two brothers had moved to Providence about the same time. Royal (or Roy) first appears in the city directory in 1896, the same year that Leroy is also listed for the first time, but at a different address.[93] Royal, who initially found work as a bootblack and then as a teamster, was married in January 1896, and about a year later he was living on Salem Street a few houses away from where Leroy lived with his wife and two young children.[94] Like Leroy, Roy continued to reside in Native homelands in the Benedict and Long Pond areas and raised his children there. After Roy's death his widow, Hattie, moved to 155 Lockwood Street.[95] In 1930 Rachel Storms, her former mother-in-

Fig. 15. Unidentified Indians at the Narragansett Indian Church, August 9, 1925, where the Rev. Leroy Perry preached during Sunday services at the Narragansetts' annual August Meetings in the 1920s. Photograph by Avery Lord. Glass plate negative, RHi X17 3854. Courtesy of the Rhode Island Historical Society.

law, was living with her and her second husband, a naturalized American citizen from the Azores who worked on the docks as a coal heaver.

These known details outline only the broadest contours of the family's history that tied Leroy Perry to Providence. The day-to-day and year-to-year currents of his life and its tensions cannot be determined with certitude from the spatial and temporal patterns derived from documents, as suggestive as they might be. What is certain is that his life course was different than his twin's. Leroy Perry as Ousa Mekin assumed a public role that Roy, who died prior to the formation of the Indian Council of New England, did not live to see. Whether he too would have chosen to make bold statements about his Indianness, champion educational and economic opportunities for the region's Native people, question the benefits of the federal government's proposal to protect the multicolored amalgamation of clays that formed the much-storied, sacred Aquinnah Cliffs (Gay Head Cliffs) on Martha's Vineyard for the Wampanoags, or take a leadership role on other issues of concern to New England tribal communities in the 1930s, remains a moot point.[96] Despite the silences in written accounts, the Perry twins' mother, Rachel Crank Perry Storms, was the critical link that assured their identity as Wampanoags regardless of displacements and marriages to outsiders that might be perceived as diminishing their cultural values and their relationships as descendants. These family ties rooted both in Providence and in Wampanoag homelands tugged at Leroy Perry and pushed him away, as they did for many Wampanoags who made their homes in the city and others who might be characterized as cosmopolitan.

In 1880 Frank and Nancy Thomas and Louisa Morris, Indian basket makers from Nova Scotia, were living at the far southerly and largely undeveloped end of Eddy Street, a principle thoroughfare in Lower South Providence lined with shipyards and factories and traversed by roads and railroads. They might have settled in this section of the homeland because they knew that their basket-making skills were as important to the maritime industries on the docks as those of carpenters, joiners, caulkers, sailmakers, and riggers. The railroads that brought the Thomases and Louisa Morris to the city and facilitated the movement of people to and from work would also have provided them with transportation to other parts of the city. They embodied the experiences of their physical journey and their engagements with a modernizing settler-colonial world and were entangled in their sense of belonging to where they came from and where they stopped, almost as much as the baskets they had woven from trees.

In traveling to Providence to sell their baskets, the Thomases and Louisa Morris would not have been anomalies. Other Native people from Nova Scotia and Maine migrated to New England cities during the nineteenth and twentieth centuries to find markets for their baskets and medicines, perform as entertainers, and find work. The jobs that they found when they arrived were mostly unskilled or semi-skilled, such as washing dishes, doing low-end janitorial tasks, and working in factories and warehouses or in the construction trades. Jeanne Guillemin, an anthropologist who studied Mi'kmaq Indians in the Boston area during the late 1960s and early 1970s, noted that men assembled everything from door locks and curtain rods to the inner soles of sneakers and electronic equipment. Many moved back and forth between their homes in Mi'kma'ki, their homeland in the Canadian Maritimes, and Boston, and never became rooted in that city. Others established temporary homes in Boston's South End or became permanent residents of low-rent neighborhoods on the city's outskirts.[97]

Among those who traveled to the Northeast's cities in the nineteenth century was John W. Johnson. Taken captive at the age of three and raised by Wabanaki people in Nova Scotia, he wrote a memoir about traveling by foot, canoe, cart, steamer, and railroad to Northeastern cities to sell baskets during the 1840s and 1850s. The account provides glimpses of experiences that might have been similar to those of other itinerant basket makers who journeyed from different indigenous homelands and sometimes decided to make a home of short or long duration at one of their stops along the way. Johnson recounts that he spent a week in Providence during a trip that included a few days in New Bedford and stops in Fall River and New York, where he disposed of the balance of his stock.[98] After about two months on the road, he returned to Halifax to replenish his supply of baskets before heading back to New York accompanied by twenty Indians and "a great amount of fancy work." In New York City, he and his relatives rented a tenement. Leaving the children at home, "the older ones went out and sold baskets and boxes." They sold about a half of their stock, enough to buy four horses and two large wagons, and headed to Philadelphia. They camped along the way, and upon reaching their destination they set up cloth tents that served as their home for three months and made and sold more baskets. In Springfield, Massachusetts, they again pitched their tents, only this time they reinforced them with boards, built a shed for their horses, and settled in for the winter, making and selling many baskets before taking down their camp in the spring. Johnson recalled that from there they "went to Bristol, R.I., remaining there for two weeks, and then went to Newport, R.I. where we stopped all the summer." Their next stops were New Bedford, where they camped near the railroad depot; Roxbury, Massachusetts, where they pitched their tents behind a Catholic Church for two weeks; Boston, where they set up their tents on the Common; and Lowell, Massachusetts, where they camped at a place called Pine Hill. In the fall they returned to Boston and rented a house on Endicott Street in the city's North End, a neighborhood associated with the American Revolution and Victorian-era brothels, and stayed there for the winter.[99]

Johnson's account of his life "beyond the forest" defies stereotypes of basket makers as peddlers lacking any business acumen or as vestiges of an indigenous way of life estranged from cities and modernity. His story illustrates how other basket makers, while not foregoing the mobility that enabled their livelihood and survival and sustained and extended their social networks, lived in cities. Some, like the Thomases and Louisa Morris, eventually became rooted in urban landscapes for longer durations of time. As transients and newcomers perceived more as interlopers in cities than tolerated as curiosities, basket makers were not always welcomed. John Johnson reported that he and his group were harassed by Irish who surrounded their camp in Roxbury and troubled them so much that they could not eat or sleep, and that in Lowell Irish cut their tents and attempted to provoke them in other ways.[100] These experiences would have figured into decisions about whether to remain in a town or city, or whether to return the next year, as did other aspects of making and selling baskets. Business could be good, but basket making was also hard work that entailed collecting and processing raw materials as well as weaving. The smaller, intricately shaped fancy baskets made primarily for the non-Native market were especially labor intensive to produce.[101] Sales could be uneven and profits could be easily be diminished because of social obligations to relatives and friends, costs of living and transportation, and unexpected calamities. All would have been disincentives for continuing on the basket-selling trail or settling down in any distant place.

The extent to which the Thomases' and Louisa Morris's experiences mirrored Johnson's cannot be ascertained, though they might also have encountered the prejudice of different races and classes. They had gotten off the train both literally and figuratively, and like Johnson and so many other Native basket makers, rented a tenement. On the third day of June, 1880, a U.S. Census taker recorded their names, color, sex, age, relationship to the head of the family, occupation, and place of birth, and the birth places of each individual's parents. The census reports that Frank Thomas, the head of the household, and his wife, Nancy, were in their mid-twenties. They and their parents were born in Nova Scotia, as was their four-year-old son, Michael. Louisa Morris, a widow, fifty-eight, lived in a separate household at the same Eddy Street address with her nine-year-old grandson, Jacob Jandes. Both were born in Nova Scotia, as were their parents.[102] The Thomas surname, variously transcribed as Thom, Tom, and Tomah, appears in late nineteenth-century censuses of the Mi'kmaq in Nova Scotia. No one listed or recalled today by elders of the Confederacy of Mainland Mi'kmaq as one of the basket-making Thomases corresponds to Frank or Nancy Thomas on Eddy Street. The name Morris also appears in Mi'kmaq censuses, but none of the Morrises is named Louisa. Jacob Jandes's surname was probably Jadis, according to a Mi'kmaw elder, though his parents' names are not known.[103]

Except for the single reference in a U.S. Census schedule for Providence that rescues the Thomases, their son, Louisa Morris, and her grandson from exclusion in urban histories, they were unnoticed. Traveling from Mi'kma'ki to Providence, they were people on the move. While in transit, their short-term stops and encampments would not have garnered the attention of census takers. But in Providence, where they rented a small back building at 1162 Eddy Street, their presence on the urban landscape was recorded. They were the only Native people and the only basket makers on a block where the majority of residents were white. How long they stayed on Eddy Street or in Lower South Providence, or whether they moved to another Native homeland in the city, is as unknown as the material conditions of their lives. There is no available information about their household furnishings, the clothes they wore, personal items they might have brought with them as mementos, or their supply of baskets and basket-making equipment. One could suppose that like most people on the move and those with little interest in owning large amounts of property, they traveled light, with few material possessions except for necessities and some things that evoked connections to family and Mi'kma'ki. If basket sales were good, they might have bought new things during their travels or when they were in Providence. Otherwise they would have made do or improvised. Although they might have been "fabric-light," to borrow a term that Denis Byrne uses to describe the postcolonial material record of Australian Aborigines compared to white settler colonists, I suspect that the public perception of their Indianness was as noticeable on Eddy Street and on the wharves and sidewalks where they sold their baskets as it was to the census enumerator.[104] I have not been able to trace what became of the Thomas and Morris families when they left Eddy Street, their only recorded residence in Providence. They might have continued on their journey as transnational travelers and moved to some other Northeast city to sell their baskets. But they might have also returned to Mi'kma'ki with their stock of baskets reduced, but not their memories of the places they had visited and of Eddy Street, where they had seemingly lived briefly.

Other Native people lived off of Eddy Street. Earl Elderkin, whose parents were listed as "full blood Wampanoag" in the 1930 U.S. Census, as were his wife's, lived on Poe Street between Eddy Street and Allens Avenue, just north of Oxford Street and south of Potters Avenue in Lower South Providence, with his wife and their five children.[105] Their next-door neighbors on Poe Street were Isabella Busher, a laundress for a private family, who was an Elderkin by birth and widowed twice, and her two sons, described as Indians, and two daughters, labeled as white.[106] Earl Elderkin was an operating engineer at the Seaconnet Coal Company terminal of C. H. Sprague and Son on the pier off of Allens Avenue at Rhodes Street, where colliers (or coal-carrying ships) docked and were unloaded by steam-operated cranes.[107] The family had previously lived on Van Buren Street, also in the more southerly section of Lower South Providence. The Elderkin surname is common among the Seekonk (or Seaconke) Wampanoags, who lived and worked, mostly as farm laborers, in Bristol County, Massachusetts, in the nineteenth and early twentieth centuries. Like the majority of the surnames of the region's indigenous peoples, the name was Christian and speaks to a complicated history of enslavement, indentured servitude, and intermarriage with other ethnic groups during the late seventeenth century and eighteenth century. Elderkins appear prominently in rolls of the First Free Methodist Church, built in Seekonk in 1925, as church members and officers. According to the church's history, it was organized in Providence in 1911. After the church lost members and a pastor in the early 1920s, a new church leader, appointed in 1924, held meetings with the small congregation at his house in Rumford, Rhode Island, and at the home of a member in Providence until the new church was built.[108]

In writing about her family, Deborah Spears Moorehead of the Elderkin line recalled that her grandfather, William Elmer Smith, was one of many Wampanoag volunteers who helped build the church. While working on the church's roof with his son, he caught a cold that developed into pneumonia and died in 1929 before the church was completed. He left behind a hand-made wooden chest filled with old photographs, envelopes tied up with string containing carpenter's invoices and receipts, newspaper clippings, postcards, letters, invitations, and a leather-bound album. The album contained more photographs and newspaper clippings, and similar to a family bible, it was inscribed with the dates of family members' births and deaths and "a few lines" about these important events in the family's history, and held copies of official town certificates of these births and deaths. The chest and album constitute a rich trove on the Elderkins and their extended kin. For Deborah Spears Moorehead, the discovery of these documents sixty-four years after her grandfather's death rekindled memories of hearing her mother say to her, "Don't forget that you are an Elderkin" as well as a Wampanoag and a Narragansett.[109] Earl Elderkin also did not forget his Native ancestry, though record keepers sometimes disagreed. In the mid-1930s, after living in Providence for about twenty years, he returned to Seekonk, his birthplace, where he was a machinist for a retail oil company, bought his own home, and remained until his death decades later.[110]

Lower South Providence 185

Rethinking Indian Providence: Public Housing and Indigenous Imaginaries

In the 1940s the low-lying swampy area called Frog's Hollow in the part of South Providence bordered by Thurbers, Pavilion, and Prairie Avenues to the north, south, and west, respectively, and Rugby Street to the east became the site of the Roger Williams Homes, a public housing project planned to address the needs of the city's ill-housed. The 214-acre site that was home to South Providence's slaughterhouses and to Irish immigrants, Russian Jews, French Canadians, other foreign- and Native-born white settlers, African Americans, and people of Native descent had some of the city's most dilapidated houses, with the majority of the wood-framed dwellings determined to be substandard and overcrowded. Consequently, these homes were acquired by the Providence Housing Authority and demolished. This slum clearance project that targeted 125 buildings displaced more than 200 white families and about a dozen households identified as Black, some of whom had been living as neighbors for decades if not longer and had strong ties. The 744 new housing units that tripled the amount of residential space were contained in 28 three-story brick buildings that were designed to embody architectural ideals advocated by urban reformers since the nineteenth century to remedy the dirty, noisy, and crowded conditions endemic to industrialization and to cities. Accordingly, buildings were sited on higher ground at the edge of the hollow and oriented to maximize the beneficial effects of prevailing breezes to carry away air-borne pollution from local industries. Windows were built to ensure adequate light and ventilation, and brick construction reduced the fire hazard posed by the wood-framed former structures. Citing the Providence Housing Authority's 1941 report, Paul Campbell writes that the ample distance was created between buildings at the Roger Williams Homes to ensure that there were "no large angles or corners where the sun never shines."[111] Crowded, traffic-congested streets and narrow, dark back alleys considered prime breeding areas for crime and moral decay, especially for the youth, were eliminated. Streets were closed to vehi-

Fig. 16. The Roger Williams Homes in the 1940s, modeled on an idealized New England village landscape, with buildings arranged around a green space, had segregated blocks for Native people. Courtesy of the Providence Housing Authority.

cles, grounds were landscaped, and a large, enclosed open space built at the center of the housing complex for recreation.[112]

In concept and design, the Roger Williams Homes were meant to reflect the nostalgic ideal of a New England village, an imagined community of nineteenth-century industrial capitalism (fig. 16).[113] In reality, neither accurately represented the diversity of the region's social and cultural landscapes. The displacement brought about by the housing project came at a high cost, sometimes reducing and fracturing social networks and causing other trauma in people's lives. Residents experienced the loss of home and life in a place they had known and, as compensation, were given the option of public housing. Residents of the Roger Williams Homes were overwhelmingly white, Catholic, and blue-collar working poor, and the housing project was faulted for

Lower South Providence 187

not setting aside enough units for nonwhites.[114] Although the housing blocks were initially segregated, the hardships that families had experienced during the Great Depression, the war effort during the 1940s, and the availability of decent housing contributed to building a sense of community that may have tentatively crossed racial divides within the project and with neighbors on the outside. Patrick Conley, a former resident of South Providence who grew up on Byfield Street about 150 yards from the Roger Williams Homes in the early 1950s, recalled that most of his friends and classmates lived there rather than in the neighborhood's wood-framed one- and two-family houses and three-deckers. Conley, who frequently cut through the Roger Williams Homes on his walk to St. Michael's School, which he attended in South Providence, said that there was a great deal of interaction between people in the rest of the neighborhood and those in "the projects." Locals would gather at Conley's Ice Cream Parlor, which his uncle owned, at the corner of Thurbers Avenue and Rachel Street about a block from the Roger Williams Homes, and at Richardson Park, a recreation area with a ball field and concrete grandstand, swings, a basketball court, and a swimming pool. At the park, he met up with and developed close friendships with some "Blacks" from the segregated blocks at the Roger Williams Homes. They were Cape Verdean and African American and like Conley, they excelled at sports, as did Clifford Guy, who was also from the "colored" blocks of "the projects." Guy, a wrestling champion at Central High School, became a leader of the Pokanoket band of the Wampanoags known by his Indian name, "Lion Heart."[115] His parents, Clifford Sr. and Esther, had some personal setbacks in the winter of 1936, when Clifford was an infant. His father had fractured an ankle in a fall while employed as a kitchen helper at Rhode Island Hospital and was temporarily out of work.[116] Clifford Sr. eventually went back to his job, and Esther, who took care of both him and their son during his recuperation, became active in Native affairs. On April 25, 1936, she attended the signing of the bill that established an annual Indian Day in Rhode Island; in July, she participated in the Narragansett Tribe of Indians' Tercentenary pageant.[117]

One of Clifford Guy's neighbors in the housing project was his cousin, Everett G. Weeden Jr., who was of Wampanoag and Pequot descent. His family moved from 7 Rodney Court in Upper South Providence to the Roger Williams Homes about 1945, when he was eight or nine years old. His father, Everett Weeden, worked for the Rhode Island Department of Health, and was known for his athleticism on the playing fields of Central High School as well as for his dancing, for which he won several amateur prizes. He performed both in modern dance revues in Providence and at powwows, where he did traditional dances; and he had a role as an Indian youth in the Tercentenary pageant.[118] Everett Jr., who like Patrick Conley attended St. Michael's school, was only ten months apart in age from Clifford Guy. They were as close as brothers growing up.[119] The younger Weeden, known as "Tall Oak," the name given to him by Princess Red Wing when he was sixteen years old, eventually moved from public housing, as did Clifford Guy.

Although their families relocated to other parts of the city, the friendship they formed as boys in Lower South Providence remained strong and went beyond the obligations of kinship. As adults, their careers took different paths, and their residential trajectories led them to different places. Tall Oak trained as an artist at the Rhode Island School of Design, where he took art classes from sixth grade through high school. He was awarded a scholarship after graduating from Central High, became an activist, speaker, and performer, and moved to Rhode Island's South County.[120] His art is a visual statement about Native dispossession, enslavement, and survival in New England, informed by his family's history. He has carefully traced that history from Jamestown in the eighteenth century, where a distant relative, Toby Weeden, was an indentured "Indian servant," to Jewett City in southeastern Connecticut, where his grandfather was born, and to Providence and South County.[121] Clifford Guy moved to Jamestown RI.

By the 1960s, conditions at the Roger Williams Homes and the outlying area of Lower South Providence were in decline, crime was on the rise, and the sense of community that had crossed the racial chasm had given way to isolation, mounting tensions, and incidents of overt discrimination.

Buildings and grounds at the housing project fell into disrepair as a result of a cut in federal support for maintenance. By the end of the decade, all but one of the buildings was boarded up and abandoned, and soon all but two of the original buildings were demolished. In 1965 Conley's, the local ice cream parlor where children of all colors had congregated, fell prey to neighborhood vandals and closed its door for the last time.[122]

Decades after Frank and Nancy Thomas and Louisa Morris had settled on Eddy Street, people from other indigenous homelands in the Northeast would also call this street in Lower South Providence home. Alfred C. and Alice R. Sebastian's family, of Pequot and Cape Verdean ancestry, was among them. The family lived at 1060 Eddy Street, near Pavilion Avenue and Byfield Street, not far from the Roger Williams Homes. Their daughter Debra Sebastian Jones, a member of the Mashantucket Pequot tribe who was raised at 1060 Eddy Street in the 1960s and 1970s, remembered "a lot of tenement houses in the area and that it was a rough neighborhood" and that "people were pretty poor." She recalled, as others have, that the neighborhood's residents were of different nationalities, and that the section where she lived was mostly Black.[123] Debra and her siblings were descended from a Pequot line that, like so many others in New England tribal communities, had intermarried with whites, African Americans, and Cape Verdeans. Her skin color and that of her brother were lighter than those of their other siblings, whom she described as "brown skinned."[124] The perceived differences in the Sebastian family befuddled neighbors, who could not figure out how they could be brothers and sisters. Their ability to comprehend the diversity within the Sebastian family in the 1960s and 1970s was as imperfect as that of official record keepers charged with the task of distinguishing people by complexion, descent, or however racial determinations were made in the nineteenth and early twentieth centuries. Those in the neighborhood confounded by the different skin colors of the siblings failed to understand that intermarriage or other links between cultures did not create homogeneity, but rather an array of combinations that blurred commonly recognized identities and were often fraught with tensions within Native communities and families.

Debra Sebastian Jones's memories of her Lower South Providence neighborhood are not only about challenges to her identity; she also comments on changes in transportation technology and music during the time that she lived there. Cars had become a common means of getting from one place to another. They had made cities more accessible, extended opportunities for employment beyond a comfortable walking distance from home, and facilitated urbanizing Native people's movement back and forth to the communities and families they might have left behind.[125] Like trains, cars expanded horizons and increased the speed with which one could travel to new places, often in the company of others who shared the ride. Even more than trains, cars were about social aspirations. As Philip Deloria observes, high-end luxury cars like the Cadillac that Geronimo is shown driving in a 1904 photograph drew attention to the driver and riders.[126] They made a visual statement that the driver, especially if the driver were also the owner, had achieved a piece of the American Dream. But any car—old, dented, or malfunctioning—would do to take a "dream ride," Debra Sebastian Jones's term for her family's Sunday road trips. On those "long, long ride[s] in the country to get ice cream" with her mother, stepfather, and brothers, "they would go by houses, [thinking] 'I wish I had a house like that.'" They would pass "by vegetable stands and get fresh vegetables, stuff like that." After stopping for ice cream, they would go home to Eddy Street.[127]

These dream rides that reconnected them with rural areas beyond the tenements of Lower South Providence and put them closer, if only fleetingly, to a world of imagined possibilities were as much a part of the routine of everyday life as sitting on the stoop of the house on Eddy Street with friends. They were as common as the Portuguese food that her mother cooked—*manchupa* (a corn-based soup), rice and beans and pork chops, codfish cakes, and a Portuguese stuffing for a Christmas turkey—and the Motown and Doo Wop music that filled the house. Neither the food nor the music fit expectations about Native Americans in popular culture, not even the musical tropes of "Sam Cook and people like the Platters" with their soulful sounds and repetitive rock-and-roll beats that Debra remembered.[128] Crossing multiple expressive genres and cultures, the music of Debra Sebastian Jones's youth is about hybridity and the constant process of becoming in which she contended with the past and present, authenticity and modernity. But mostly, it was and still is about good memories of her childhood when everything seemed more innocent.

Her memories of coming of age in Lower South Providence offer real-life insights about living in the neighborhood in later decades of the twentieth century, when it was increasingly deteriorated, neglected, and impoverished.[129] Her reflections on the neighborhood and her home, racial and tribal identity, and growing up with an absentee father comment on experiences that were not unusual among Native people in Lower South Providence or in the city's other homelands during the nineteenth and early twentieth centuries. At times they might have reacted to these pressures with a condition that Anthony Wallace, an anthropologist, called "mazeway disintegration," a temporary paralytic response or shock in the face of the rupture of a shared way of life, similar to what their ancestors might have experienced when confronted with the impact of foreign diseases, the physical destruction wreaked by King Philip's War, and the loss of the Providence lands that once belonged to them.[130] But like their ancestors, the Native residents of Lower South Providence also found ways to survive within and against circumstances that could have easily triggered despair. They did so not just by reacting or waging all-out, unwavering campaigns, but through courage, hard work, and family ties, and by making survival a full-time, everyday job in which they persevered against racism, poverty, broken homes, alcohol, and displacement.

Trains and automobiles kept alive practices that challenged settler colonialism's determination to contain Native mobility. They contributed to the creation of new indigenous geographies and an urban imaginary filled with the sounds of whistles, chugging, hissing and screeching brakes, and horns, vrooms, and backfires that were part of the sensory experiences of place in New England cities. Along with streetcars and buses, they helped Native women, men, and children navigate the urban landscape by transporting them from their homes in the morning to work or school and back in later in the day, or to weekly church services along well-traveled routes where they could look out at pedestrians, houses, and storefront windows. Cars made it possible to take a Sunday drive to the country to restore emotional connections with the natural world and briefly escape city life. By car or train you could travel from Lower South Providence to Charlestown or some other ancestral homeland, where after steering through ruts in dirt roads or slogging by foot from the nearest depot, you could arrive at a meeting house, stomp ground, or home of relatives or friends. There are no surviving ticket stubs or gas receipts to document the mobility of the Native people of Lower South Providence. Nor is there any written evidence, as far as I know, about any discrimination they might have experienced using public transportation, such as being denied a seat or ejected, or having their station or stop bypassed. The role of new transportation technologies offers a way for thinking about Native people's mobility and aspirations, as well as the prejudices they faced as they moved to, from, and through urban space, and a counterpoint to ideas linking Manifest Destiny and progress with Euro-Americans' racialized expectations about modernity. In the context of Lower South Providence it also sheds light on the formation of an urban homeland that would become a refuge for many Native people who, like its residents, were displaced by urban renewal in the unfinished business of settler colonialism.

Fig. 17. Map of Mashapaug Pond and adjacent pond lands, showing selected Native households. Map by Lynn Carlson.

Mashapaug Pond 5

*The Pond Lands, from Planting Fields
to Industrial Transformations*

Mashapaug Pond, located two miles to the southwest of a crossing-over point from the east side of Providence, is today the city's largest body of fresh water, and its most toxic. Its name derives from an Indian town that defined the western boundary of lands granted to Roger Williams by Canonicus and Miantonomo in a deed dated March 24, 1638. Over the years the pond has been encroached upon by commercial and industrial development. Businesses fringe its northern and southern edges and an urban renewal project intended to remedy its unsightly and unsafe surroundings sits at its northwesterly corner. Warning signs in English, Spanish, and Cambodian inform passersby about the pond's risks to their health and well-being. Although these notices are factually accurate, they fail to communicate the vital role that Mashapaug Pond has long played in the lives of Native people who dwelled on its shores and those of nearby ponds. Much like these ponds, they have been ignored.

Mashapaug Pond is a place steeped in local Native history and memory. The records of the Colony of Rhode Island and Providence Plantations indicate that the "towne of Mashipawog" stood near an Indian planting field.[1] Its uninterrupted occupation can be traced back to the seventeenth century—and thousands of years before that, judging from artifacts discovered by local collectors. Those living around the pond have often found arrowheads when they cut their lawn or when they walked its fields after a freeze and noticed artifacts brought to the surface by frost heaves, an upward thrusting of frozen soil that can reveal hidden traces of the pond's deep indigenous past. Although the precise location is unknown, a settlement may have existed on the northern side of the pond, where, as William Simmons recalls, a stone woodworking tool called a gouge, "several thousand years old," was found.[2]

An Indian burial ground was opened in 1856 at the northern end of the pond, probably in the vicinity of icehouses shown on nineteenth-century maps. There is no description of a spoon and bottle that were recovered there, though similar objects reported from exhumations of other Native graves were often foreign imports made of metal or glass. If that was the case with the spoon and bottle that were found, the burial place at Mashapaug Pond was being used after European colonists had settled in Providence.[3] Its spatial extent and the number of interments made and over how long a period are not known. The existence of a communal burial area at the pond's edge—a metaphorically charged geographical location for burial places in Northeastern Native cosmology, in proximity to the populous Native village mentioned in the early annals of Providence and into the century following King Philip's War—suggests that Mashapaug Pond was a place that community identities were built around.[4] It was a place in which territorial identities continued to be grounded and remembered in local genealogies of people and stories. It was also where Native people would acknowledge their connections to a more encompassing social world that George Hamell describes as "comprised of grandmothers, grandfathers, aunts and uncles, and sisters and brothers of other-than-human kinds of man-beings" whom they could encounter through rituals of transformation.[5]

Arthur Fenner, who was born in Cranston not far from Mashapaug Pond in 1699, twenty-three years after King Philip's War ended, told John Howland, a former president of the Rhode Island Historical Society, that as a "young man, on travelling from the road from his father's house to town, it was usual to meet or pass more Indians than white people on the way."[6] According to a family story, an Indian woman who wandered into the colonists' garrison at the western edge of Providence during King Philip's War gave Dinah Fenner, Arthur's mother, a small basket woven of bark, wool, and possibly cornhusks in reciprocity for some milk. The basket, which is in the collections of the Rhode Island Historical Society, has miniscule fragments of wool fibers that under microscopic analysis appear finer than wool typically recovered from seventeenth-century archaeological contexts. Aside from American Indians' lactose intolerance, which casts doubt on the details of the story, the physical evidence makes it much less credible that the women encountered each other in the midst of the conflict than during the period of post-war reconstruction, when colonists and Indians engaged in uneasy accommodations toward an uncertain future.[7] It was during this interim between the war's end and the early decades of the eighteenth century, when local Indians were a liability as well as an asset in a labor-strapped town in the throes of rebuilding that Arthur Fenner traveled the well-worn path that led from the Indian town at Mashapaug to Providence. The route would have followed the present course of Plainfield Street or possibly Cranston Street crossing through the Mashapaug Pond area to Westminster Street where the presence of Indians could hardly have gone unnoticed.

Although Fenner rued the disappearance of "the villages, the warriors and the youth, the sachems, the tribes and their families," he observed that their graves were still there.[8] Through time, the repetitive actions of the colonists' plowshares would have intruded into these resting places of the ancestors as well as the locales where they lived, hunted, fished, and collected raw materials, just as surely as intentional exhumations revealed material traces that made Mashapaug Pond's indigenous history tangible for those who chose to notice or care. Its story as a Native place is not only about a village that disappeared long ago, romanticized by antiquarians and embraced by neighborhood residents who envisioned their own rootedness in the pond's environs as running almost as deep. Rather, it is about scores of Native men and women who continued to hold onto and carve their place into Providence's emerging urban landscape.

"Of Greater Magnitude": Dwelling on Urban Pond Lands

Roughly translated as "the place of still water," Mashapaug Pond presented Native Americans with a source of fresh water and an abundance of natural resources long before Euro-American settler colonists harvested its ice and sold it commercially. To Native people, pond land was "of more benefit" than upland or swampland. "They looked at ponds with greater

Fig. 18. Mashapaug Pond looking north-northeast. At a boat launch and picnic area at the southwestern end of the pond the signage prohibits swimming and warns that the fish are unsafe to eat. Photograph by Patricia E. Rubertone.

magnitude than they did at the [other] lands," remarked Gideon Ammons, president of the Narragansett Indian Council during the hearings to abolish the tribe in 1879.[9] Mashapaug Pond was no exception. It was a place of recreation that Native people explored and enjoyed long before they and their neighbors skated, played hockey, and raced horses across its frozen surface during the winter, or plunged into its cool waters in the summertime. It was a place of ceremony before the city's minority churches held baptisms by immersion in its waters, some as late as the 1940s. Not even reports of drowning, murdered bodies, dead horses, stolen and wrecked cars, old stoves, fifty-gallon oil drums, bottles, and construction debris found at its murky bottom, and rumors of hidden caves inhabited by ghosts of Indians and odd visitors, made the pond an ominous place. As one resident recalled, it was a multipurpose pond, where well into the nineteenth and twentieth centuries Native people continued to reside.[10]

Until recently, Mashapaug was an urban pond that was as good for catching bass, pickerel, and smaller fish as it had been at any point since precolonial times (fig. 18).[11] On the pond's edge you could find bulrushes and cattails that could be woven into mats, baskets, and belts using traditional Native finger weaving or braiding techniques. The mats would have covered the exteriors and the interiors of *wetus* at the Indian village on the pond's banks during the seventeenth-century. Native people still may have lived in *wetus*, perhaps with some structural modifications, into the eighteenth century. You could jump into a *mishoonémese*, the Narragansett word for a little canoe, and paddle across the pond's still waters to cool off, to search for better fishing spots at sunset, or to reach the thickets where blueberries and raspberries grew wild and in abundance, and still do today.[12] The pond and the brook that flowed from its southern end were also good places to find turtles, and their eggs in the late spring.

The pond was also where you might bathe after emerging from a hot house, called a *pésuponck*, typically built near a pond or stream, where heated stones caused profuse sweating. The sweat, as discussed in *Narragansett Dawn*, cleansed the body of impurities and "took away all aches and pains," contributing to the maintenance of physical, social, and spiritual well-being in the past and in more recent, urbanized times.[13] Indians, even in the coldest depths of winter, were immersed in baptism rituals at the pond that some considered a greater demonstration of faith than being sprinkled with water or dipped in a marble pool.[14] Mashapaug Pond, much like other ponds, would have had stories told about it. Narragansetts, for example, retell the story of Cocumpaug or Schoolhouse Pond. The legend, estimated to be about two hundred years old, tells of John Onion, the son of a white man with the same name and Deborah Onion, his Indian wife, who boasted that he could outskate other boys and even the devil. The young John Onion could not outskate the devil that chased his every move as he raced and twirled across the ice. This often-told story, whose details are rooted in colonial history, served as a warning to later Narragansett Indians not to venture too far beyond their peers, as would other versions of the story set at different localities, possibly even Mashapaug Pond, that emphasized community values.[15]

Threads of oral history suggest that Providence colonists attempted to remove the seventeenth-century inhabitants of the Indian town at Mashapaug, and enlisted a sachem known as Tom of Watchemoket (among other names) to help displace and relocate them, possibly to Cranston.[16] These efforts might have met limited success at best, given that Native people continued to dwell at the pond through the turbulent seventeenth century and into the eighteenth century. Written records indicate that by the nineteenth century, Wampanoags and Pequots were also living at Mashapaug and nearby pond lands.

Moses Dailey (Pequot) moved from Federal Hill to Public Street on Providence's west end, not far Mashapaug Pond, to be closer to his daughter, Nettie, and her family. The home was a wood-framed building owned by Nettie's husband, Abram Manchester, who rented out a floor to another family. Moses Dailey died there a few years later in 1915 at the age of ninety-four, while a typhoid epidemic raged through the city and attacks of German submarines on ships carrying American passengers inched the United States closer to involvement in World War I. His place of burial was not "the little Indian lot ... near the Tourtellot homestead, close by where the Danielson cars turn from Hartford Street upon the private right of way of the railroad company," where Dailey told the *Providence Journal* that his aunt Dorcas Dailey and "all the other Rhode Island Pequots, the originals and their few descendants" were buried.[17] Nor was it the ancestral burying ground at Mashapaug Pond that had become a storied place where spirits of ancestors dwelled and walked in the shadows. A dog pound and crematorium had been built on or close to this burial ground by a dogcatcher for Providence who had lived at the edge of the pond since the early 1900s.[18] Unlike the neighborhood's strays, Moses Dailey was a familiar figure on Public Street and before that on Courtland Street. He could hardly be considered a drifter. He was laid to rest in North Burial Ground, where many other Native people who had made Providence their home were buried.[19] Nettie, her husband, and their three children stayed in the house on Public Street until about 1930 when they moved to Los Angeles.

Other Native people would also be drawn to Mashapaug Pond or to nearby Long, Duck, and Benedict Ponds. The Rhode Island Historical Preservation Commission's 1979 report on the southwest corner of Providence that included the area surrounding Mashapaug Pond notes that Long Pond, situated to the northeast in "a shallow hollow north of Potter's Avenue through which Dexter and Bucklin Streets now pass and extending in a serpentine form from Cromwell Street south to Daboll [Street,]" was filled in around 1890.[20] It was sited between two hills. One of them ran parallel to Elmwood Avenue, and the other was near where Dexter Street continued south of Cromwell Street. "At its center were two points of land that reached out toward each other, where several churches held baptisms by immersion every summer." Swimming was safe at either of these points because the water was shallow and pond's bottom sandy. To the south of these promontories, where the pond was fed by cold springs, swimming could be hazardous. Several swimmers unable to reach the shore because of currents drowned. Besides being a decent swimming hole, if you knew to avoid certain spots, Long Pond was also great for fishing—large and small fish could be caught in ample numbers. In the winter it was a favorite place to skate that attracted people living on the east and west sides of the city because it was easier to reach than Mashapaug.

Despite crowds that gathered for swimming, fishing, ice-skating, and baptisms, Long Pond began to be filled about 1872 in a process that was characterized as "painfully slow." The procedure gradually transformed this pond land, a space that Native people highly valued, into "little more than a noisesome dump" that was a neighborhood nuisance. The city interceded and sped up the process by bringing in clean fill to cover up the old junk, refuse, and ash piles.[21] The filling was completed when sewers were installed on Dexter Street. Sometime after, the city graded the filled-in pond and constructed a playground with a baseball field, called Bucklin Park, behind the Gilbert Stuart Middle School.[22] The former pond's nearest neighboring pond, the much smaller Duck Pond, occupied the greater part of the block bounded by Potter's Avenue and Salem, Waldo, Dexter, and Sherry Streets. It was filled between 1882 and 1889.

Benedict Pond was slightly smaller than Long Pond. It lay in a hollow south of Union Street and west of Cranston Street near the railroad tracks, not far from the Providence-Cranston line. Mentioned in Providence records as early as 1659, the pond was fed by very cold springs that proved to be deadly for small boys unaware of the water's depth and how quickly the bottom dropped off, and for older boys and men attempting to swim through the strong currents near the surface that caused cramping. The fishing was considered good, but mostly, Benedict Pond was valued for the ice harvested there during the winter. On account of the distance that trash and cinder haulers from the city had to travel, the process of filling in the pond took over forty years. By 1922 it was three-quarters filled.[23] Long after the process was done, Benedict Pond looked "like it was an old sand and gravel pit," as William Simmons recalls.[24]

Native people continued to dwell in these pond lands even as some of their watery spaces were gradually disappearing. Leroy Perry lived around Mashapaug, Benedict, and Long Ponds from the late 1890s to about 1930 (fig. 19). His last recorded address in Providence directories was a house that he owned on Daboll Street at the south end of Long Pond and occupied with other families who rented apartments from him. When he first moved to Providence, he lived on Lilac Street (renamed Wadsworth Street) near Benedict Pond. He relocated to Salem Street, bordering Duck Pond, and then moved back to the Benedict Pond area, where he lived briefly prior to finding a place on Burrington Street at the northwestern end of Mashapaug Pond, and then on Benedict Street before returning to Long Pond. Despite the frequent changes in residence, he remained firmly rooted in the pond lands until moving to the grounds of the King Philip Museum and later to Gay Head.

Indians who had lived in other parts of the city relocated to the pond lands. Maria Blunt, who had lived on John Street in Fox Point during the 1880s and briefly in Upper South Providence, made her home on Plenty Street near Long Pond with her husband around 1900, and after he died in 1905 she continued to live there into the 1920s.[25] Her sister, Rosella

Fig. 19. Chief Leroy Perry in front of a brick commercial building in Providence, 1924. Photograph by Frank G. Speck. Courtesy of the National Museum of the American Indian, Smithsonian Institution, N12369.

Watson, a widow and a laundress for a private family, lived in the vicinity of Long Pond until her death in 1921.[26] She had moved there from 7 Angle Street near Hoyle Square about 1915 after leaving Narragansett Pier.[27] William Hall, Mary Brewster's half-brother (see chapter 3), also moved to Long Pond from Upper South Providence. Edward Cone (see chapters 1, 2, and 6), who had boarded at 70 John Street in Fox Point with his oldest son, Charles (see chapters 1 and 5), and at other indigenous enclaves in the city since arriving from Wakefield around the mid-nineteenth century, was on Wilson Street near Long Pond from 1869 into the early 1870s with his wife Frances, their children, and Caleb Rodman.[28] Charles lived on Lawrence Street east of Long Pond in 1869 and was over on Constitution Street to its north a few years later.

Ida F. Bent was born at 92 Sherburne Street in Lower South Providence in 1873, the same year that Benjamin and Frederick Thomas briefly

Mashapaug Pond 203

lived there. She was raised on Mawney Street, a block south of Daboll Street at the southern end of Long Pond in the 1880s, by her mother, Alice, a laundress and member of the Pond Street Church, and her stepfather, Isaac B. Mosby, who worked as a porter.[29] Her father, William Henry Bent, the son of Prince Bent and Nancy Stanton (Narragansett), an "Indian doctress," was born in Charlestown, Rhode Island. In 1870 he was living in Providence with John B. Hazard and John's wife Sarah (Narragansett), their daughters, and Sarah's sister, Hannah Thomas, on Federal Street. He worked as a teamster, as did many men from the tribe who had left the reservation for the city.[30] He married Alice (née Church), a non-Indian, at the Pond Street Free Baptist Church a year later.[31] Ida's relationship with her birth father is unclear, though he is recorded as living on Noyes Street on the north side of the New York, New Haven, and Hartford railroad tracks in the area between Benedict and Long Ponds in the early 1890s.[32] William, who married again in 1879 and was later widowed, died from "La Grippe " (influenza) and acute insanity in Bristol, Rhode Island, in 1898, where his sister, Betsey had made her home since about 1880.[33] He was buried in the Indian Church Burial Ground in Charlestown. Ida Bent, who was listed as Isaac Mosby's stepdaughter in the 1880 U.S. census, died on August 29, 1891, from "phthisis pulmonalis," a technical medical term for tuberculosis or pulmonary consumption, at 96 Mawney Street.[34] Providence death records give her name as Ida Florence Moseby. Other than these few, slim references, little else is known about her all-too-brief life, except that she and her father lived in the homeland around the ponds.

The extent to which the lingering illness that killed her affected her father's well-being cannot be ascertained from records. His probable estrangement from her and his feelings of powerlessness might have also been factors that led to his frustrations and gradual withdrawal from society. The life course he chose was different than that of his older brother Joseph (Joe) Bent, who chose to stay in Charlestown, and that of Betsey, who moved to Bristol. In an account of "Charlestown's Indians, the Last of their Shrines" printed in the *Providence Sunday Journal* in 1889, the reporter remarked that Joe Bent had a "fair farm, a son, a homemade hammock and a dog, but not much else." His house was in a hut made of slabs and shingles "scarcely four feet high, knocked together with great big cracks and cervices to afford plenty of ventilation." The home's furnishings—"a rusty stove in the corner, a frying pan, and a bunk with a dirty quilt on one side"—were meager compared to his "fine field of corn, a large crop of potatoes and several acres of mowing, which yielded several tons of hay" that attested to the time that he and his son spent outdoors tending to their crops. One dugout served as a root cellar and another, a "half-dug well," held buckets waiting to be refilled when Bent had the inclination to resume digging. The front yard was characterized as "an old wagon hospital" with a collection of parts that "would be the envy of any average country wheelwright." Out back and abutting the hut, there was a rocky bluff with "tuft grass and young oaks" where the elder Bent would take his repose "on a swinging board, suspended from the trees," smoke his pipe, and be "the lord of his own broad acres and waving crops around him."[35]

In terms of material possessions, Joe Bent was not affluent. Other Narragansetts who remained in Charlestown after detribalization had lives that were more or less comparable. They raised corn, vegetables, chickens, pigs, cows, turkeys, and sheep whose fleece they sold to nearby textile mills. Some supplemented farming by doing stonework.[36] Although city-dwelling Narragansetts might have had more material things than Joe or some of his non-Native neighbors, country life was not necessarily any more impoverished than city living. Cities were where Native people hoped to find work and build new lives for themselves. But cities could be places of unfulfilled ambitions, where prejudices and injustices were no less stinging than for those who opted to remain close to their ancestral homelands. William Bent's life story seems to fit this pattern. Ida's truncated life tells a very different tale. It was marked by separations and shortened by disease, but also by a mother and stepfather who created a home for her, saw that she went to school, and tended to her in her illness. Less than a decade after her death, the Mosbys had adopted a little girl who was listed as six years old and at school in 1900, as Ida had been twenty years earlier.[37]

In the 1930s, another family member, Jane Bent Hazard, Joseph Bent's daughter, wrote in *Narragansett Dawn* that the family bible, printed in Boston in 1822, was still in her possession after more than a century of being lovingly cared for, inscribed with "many names of births, deaths and marriage," and read from. Hazard described the treasured bible's dimensions, weight (seven and a half pounds), publication details, and engravings from the perspective of someone with intimate knowledge for whom the book was more than a "valuable relic" coveted by libraries.[38] For the family and the Narragansett community, the bible contains memories not often found in public records that go far back and link together those whose diaspora had taken them from the reservation in Charlestown to Providence, Bristol, and other places beyond their ancestral homeland. As a visible reminder of their struggles to survive, the Bent family bible is the key that provides written proof of the existence of their family line as they traveled from home to home, town to town, and city to city.

During the roughly twenty years that Long and Duck Ponds were being transformed to create more usable space for development, Native people continued to live nearby on streets such as Mawney, Daboll, Plenty, Lawrence, and others. As dumping intensified, the fishing might not have been as good, and swimming would have been increasingly restricted to locations where the water was shallow and where there was less of a chance of getting injured from unseen debris below the surface. The filling would have also affected edge areas, reducing the availability of cattails, bulrushes, wild berries, and other plants. Some Native residents would remain even after the city had completely filled these ponds. The ponds were where they had made their homes, before these watery places, which had increasingly become reservoirs for trash, were filled and leveled off for construction. As recorded in public documents, a Native presence at Long and Duck Ponds can be traced to the 1860s, though indigenous memories of the place known as Mashapaug extend back even farther.

The streets around Benedict Pond to the west of Long Pond were also filled with Indians. Frank E. Nichols (Narragansett) lived on Dahlia Street during the 1870s and 1880s. Thomas Wheeler was over at 9 Halton Street on the northeasterly side of the New York, New Haven, and Hartford railroad tracks. Edward Noka, who possessed a Narragansett surname that had not been changed to a Christian patronymic, lived across the street. In testimony read at the sixth meeting to the Commission on the Affairs of the Narragansett Indians, November 6, 1880, Noka said that he had "lived in Charlestown until he was about five or six years old, and his homestead was within a mile and a half of [the] Richmond switch."[39] He had been in Providence for about thirty or forty years before the Narragansett reservation was sold, and he moved to West Elmwood Street on the east side of Duck Pond after serving in the U.S. Colored Troops Eleventh Heavy Artillery Regiment in the Civil War.[40] Upon his return to civilian life, Noka, who had been promoted to a corporal in the Union Army, worked a laborer. Single and suffering from heart disease, the probable cause of his death, he died at his Halton Street address and was buried at Providence's Swan Point Cemetery.[41] His gravestone, much like the African American Civil War Memorial in Washington DC, records his military service and nothing about his Narragansett ancestry, his ties to "No Cakes" (as the name Noka was sometimes transcribed) who were among the first congregants to attend services at the Narragansett Indian Church in 1859, or his participation in tribal elections before the decision was made to sell the land.[42]

Halton Street was also the home of Walter Young from the mid-1880s to as late as 1910. Young, who held a series of jobs, had been raised in the Benedict Pond homeland.[43] He and his wife Georgianna, a Weeden by birth from Griswold, Connecticut, lived on Van Zandt Street near Mashapaug Pond for a few years after they married in 1898.[44] By 1910 the couple, their young daughter, and a niece were living at a two-family house at 11 Halton Street that they shared with Otis E. Weeden, Georgianna's brother, and his family.[45] Otis and Mary Jane Oliver, who were married in Cranston about 1894, moved to Wadsworth Street in the Benedict Pond area from Federal Hill around 1900 and then to Halton Street.[46] Walter Young left Halton Street sometime after Georgianna died of tuberculosis about a week before the 1910 census enumeration.[47] The Weedens stayed on for another ten years. They raised their children Otis Jr., James, George, Ruth, Clarence, and Esther on Halton Street, and their youngest, Everett, was born there before the family moved to Upper South Providence around 1920. Otis, who worked as a carpenter, as an egg candler (or inspector) in the wholesale-produce industry, and as a laboratory technician for the Rhode Island Board of Health, outlived his sister by twenty years.[48]

Frederick Thomas, who had lived in the homelands of Lippitt Hill and Upper and Lower South Providence (see chapters 2, 3, and 4), moved to Benedict Street about 1910. His sisters, Hannah Hazard and Eliza Hilton, lived on the same street. William Proffitt (Pequot and Narragansett), whose ancestry is tied to a long line of "Proffitts," a "name as old as the city of Providence," according to Tall Oak Weeden, also had a home on Benedict Street.[49] Born in Scituate, Rhode Island, about 1856, William was a farm laborer and gardener for most of his life. He moved to Block Island around the mid-1870s, where he lived with a white farm family, and then relocated to Warwick, Rhode Island, and eventually to Providence. His Providence addresses place him on the city's east side during the late nineteenth century and in Upper South Providence during roughly the first decade of the 1900s. By 1920 he was widowed, employed as a farm foreman, and boarding on Benefit Street with his only daughter, Nancy Elizabeth, his son-in-law, Francis Ford, and other roomers identified as Indians. He later moved to Benedict Pond, where he lived on Wadsworth, Waldo, and Homestead Streets, and then at 112 Benedict Street from the late 1930s to the early 1950s. Nancy Elizabeth Prophet, an internationally acclaimed sculptor who changed her surname from her married name back to Prophet (a spelling of her maiden name that she used professionally), was living in her father's house on Benedict Street in the early 1950s. She died there in 1960. Her road home—and to the pond lands—was unlike her father's or those of other Native people who called this locale their home place. Her journey can be traced from Warwick to Providence's east side, Paris's Left Bank, Newport's and Boston's art galleries, Atlanta's Spelman College, and finally to Mashapaug Pond.

Conflicted Urbanisms: Travel, Yearning, and Coming Home

Nancy Elizabeth Proffitt was born twelve miles from Providence in Arctic, a small mill village in Warwick, on March 19, 1890.[50] Besides the Proffitts, the village was home to other Indians, among them Nancy (Noka) Cheeves, formerly of Fox Point, who died less than a year before Nancy Elizabeth's birth. Little is known about Proffitt's early life before her marriage to Francis Ford in Providence on January 30, 1915.[51] By then, she had graduated from high school, worked as a domestic in private homes and as a stenographer in a law office, and had completed her second year at the Rhode Island School of Design, where she studied drawing and painting. Decades later, a white classmate at the art school remembered her as "the only colored girl there." Tall, slender, well-mannered, and fashionable, "she said she was Indian," according to the student, who added, "Yankees thought, oh yes, she's saying that because she doesn't want to say she's Negro."[52] After her graduation in 1918 she tried to make a living as a portrait artist, but finished only a few paintings and met little success in having them shown unless she agreed not to attend the opening and mingle socially with guests at previews, as Countee Cullen, a poet and W. E. B. Du Bois's son-in-law, wrote in short biographical sketch penned for *Opportunity, Journal of Negro Life* about this "slender, copper-colored" woman he had met in a Paris studio.[53] She withdrew her paintings from consideration and turned to domestic work in the hope that savings from her pay would allow her to finance a trip to Paris, where she could receive additional training and pursue her ambitions as an artist. Sailing alone on the ocean liner ss *La France*, she arrived in Paris on August 11, 1922 with little else than her "clothing, a few art supplies, an small cargo of treasured books, and $380 (fig. 20)." She rented an apartment in Montparnasse on the Left Bank and began keeping a diary. Her diary is composed of infrequent and often brief entries covering the years from 1922 to 1934.[54] In this telling narrative, she writes about her creative and day-to-day struggles as an artist that give insights into her personal relationships as well as sideways glances into the identity issues she grappled with as a person of Native American ancestry in the early twentieth century. Written in very readable longhand script and mostly in English, except for a spattering of French words, it is one of three diaries known to have been penned by a Native American woman from southern New England—the others are Charlotte Mitchell's and Fidelia Fielding's—and the only account about the experiences of an indigenous foreigner residing in a European metropolis.[55]

The diary begins with a lengthy entry dated August 11, 1922, in which she identifies herself as Nancy Elizabeth Prophet and reflects on her first few months through her first two years in France (quotations in this and the following two paragraphs are from the August 11 diary entry). There are no separate entries until November 11, 1925. She writes that Paris offered the opportunity to escape "the kind of work" she was obliged and disgusted to do in Providence. She had saved $1,000 from domestic work, but "loaned half of it to a worthless brother." After she paid for her travel and other expenses her "fortune" was reduced to $380, leaving her with much less money to live on than she had hoped. Bitter and hurt, she spent nearly two months in bed suffering from exhaustion and, in a moment of weakness, wrote to her husband asking him to come over, which she states was "a very stupid mistake" given that he was "a good man but completely helpless, without ambition, without hope, character, personality, and of a fearful nature." She worried that supporting "two people instead of one in a strange land . . . neither speaking the language" would add to her problems. When she regained her strength, she went to work on her first piece of sculpture "with a dogged determination to conquer" coupled "with a calm assurance and a savage pleasure of revenge." For days at a time she would survive more on sheer resolve than food, writing that this was "the first time in [her] life [she] was hungry." On one occasion she "stole a piece of meat and potatoe from the plate of [a] dog, who ate very well" that belonged to a woman whose Paris studio she shared, and "ate ravenously."

Comments about hunger, difficult living conditions, loneliness, and self-doubt fill the pages of the diary. The relationships she depicts with fellow artists, models who sat for her, members of the art world, landlords, other Americans in Paris, and sponsors in the United States comment

Fig. 20. Nancy Elizabeth Prophet on the deck of the ss *La France* en route from New York to La Havre, 1922. Courtesy of the Nancy Elizabeth Prophet Collection, John P. Adams Library, Rhode Island College.

on her interactions and practical dependencies with people of European and European-American, rather than Native American, backgrounds. She repeatedly refers to her husband, an African American, who she apparently did not live with in Paris (at least not regularly), though she mentions seeing him daily during her early years in the city. A female friend she lived with in Versailles tried to persuade her to leave him, which she claimed she was not yet ready to do. In 1923 she enrolled at the École nationale supérieure des Beaux-Arts to study with Victor Joseph Jean Ambroise Segoffin, an acclaimed sculptor. She moved into a new studio, where the landlord helped Francis find a job that brought in a "small wage" to help tide them over until the wooden bust she had been working on was finished.

The sculpture, accepted at the Salon d'Automme in 1924, brought her some artistic recognition but did not ease her travails. She continued to endure physical and emotional stress and survived on little food. By the summer of 1925 she had begun to make batik, hand-dyed cloth to earn some money, using a wax-resistant process popular in Europe in the 1920s. Prophet, who had moved for the third time, was now living in a little shack in a "filthy low section outside the walls of Paris," whose only attribute was "a garden about 600 metres square." There she raised summer and winter "vegetables for food, doing all the planting and cultivating." Physical work with her hands, whether with clay, wood, or stone in her studio, or with the earth in her garden, connected her to elements of life and nature that she was taught to value as a child, often in stories about how the first Narragansett man and woman were crafted from stone and then wood that might have still echoed in her cultural memory. Working with clay, wood, stone, and in the earth replenished her mind as well as her body, though even these activities occasionally failed to restore her wellness. An acquaintance arranged for her to go, "much against [her] will," to the American Hospital in Paris, where doctors suspected that she was a drug addict. Discharged after three weeks, she returned to her shack, where the "horror of its poverty struck." Unable to stay there any longer, she sublet another studio and began her first life-sized statue. She wrote that she was happy to begin work in the new studio, where "she came alone with an attempt to leave [her] husband."[56]

In the entry of November 11, 1925, she unleashes her loathing of having to be constantly on the move and living under all sorts of horrid conditions in places where there was no toilet, where water trickled down the walls and froze during the winter, and where it was so cold that she could not bathe regularly. She suffered from melancholy, fretted about money, and had to deal with the complexities of an unhappy marriage in a place far from home. On December 8 she writes, "The man I married coming to see me with a great bunch of roses. There he lies on the couch asleep. O god, o god. He came drunk." By December 22, she was "cutting stone," and remarks how she loved working alone where she could "feel so much in contact with [herself]." But on Christmas Eve, she was feeling terribly lonely. As spring approached, she looked forward to having a studio built that she could call her own. She continued to work at her art, though she was not always satisfied with the results. She smashed one of her pieces and later admonished herself that she "must not be guilty of doing with [her] work as [she had] formerly too often done with people." After a short trip to Normandy in May, she returned to her "small little apartment," waiting for the studio to be completed. On June 4 she wrote about her eagerness to escape the apartment "with its gas stove in the corner, coal stove against the wall and a squalid sink in the middle embellished by a faucet with a rubber end that seemed ready to squirt at any instant" and move into her new studio where she could work. Even the bedroom, the apartment's most intimate of spaces, "with a great mahogany wardrobe with a beautiful glass and walls lined with bedbugs," and "another little mirror in the kitchen" reflected "her work hungry self.... Otherwise the place suggest[ed] nothing, but to cook or clean and the poverty of [her] situation."[57]

By the end of June 1926 she was in her "beautiful new studio" that she repainted from yellow to a cool gray green, and she began to feel at home. Depression, sleepless nights, and starvation would continue to plague her, however, and were only temporarily alleviated over the next few years. On April 10, 1929, she wrote that her husband had left for America. She had helped to send him away with the proceeds from the sale of a piece of her art. Over the next few years her skills as an artist would gain increasing recognition. She would travel to the United States in October of 1929, and in April of that year her work was shown at a New York gallery and accepted by the Rhode Island School of Design Museum for its permanent collection. She returned to Paris with $500 in August. The following March she wrote that she was "penniless again." She traveled to United States for a second time in the spring of 1932. On her itinerary were stops in Newport, where she was welcomed into the Newport Art Association and entertained by local society; in Boston, where her work was exhibited; and in Providence, though there is no mention of her visiting with her family. As the winter of 1933-34 began, so did "the usual lacks and worry." She applied for a Guggenheim Fellowship, one of many grants for which she submitted applications while in Paris with the expectation of securing financial support for her work, and managed to make it through what she described as a "slow, difficult, anxious winter." Toward the end of "Févier" (February) 1934 she started to tear down the partitions that separated her work area from the space where she had "slept, eaten, and rested," because she had rented a small studio upstairs to use as her living quarters. In the entry of March 30, 1934, she reports that she did not receive the Guggenheim. She dealt with the disappointment by continuing to refurbish her studio, "putting two coats of paint on the walls from ceiling to floor and the ceiling." She saved and split the wood from the partitions for the winter. She was 10,000 francs in debt to her landlady, who continued to subsidize her so that she could pay her bills and install electricity and plumbing in her studio. In the last sentence of her diary, on July 19, 1934, she writes, "I feel well and calm."[58] Later that year, she moved back to the United States, where she accepted a faculty position at Spelman College, a historically Black women's liberal arts school in Atlanta.[59]

She resigned from Spelman in 1944 and returned to Providence. She rented a room at 82 Olney Street in the Lippitt Hill neighborhood, less than a half-mile north of where she had lived before she went to Paris. One of her biographers reports that she began looking for a studio in

New York and spent some time there in the late 1940s while taking odd jobs.⁶⁰ She moved to Benedict Street back in Providence about 1950. By that time her father's health was failing, as was hers. Her relationship with him is not discussed in her diary, though during the time that she lived in Paris she often inscribed "For Dad" on the backs of photos of her work.⁶¹ In 1945 the eighty-eight-year-old Proffitt took a break from his yard work at 112 Benedict Street to visit the main branch of the Providence Public Library on Washington Street, where two of his daughter's wooden busts had been installed in a glass case in the first-floor hallway as part of a temporary exhibition. "So," he said softly, "that's what they look like. First time I've ever seen them." The pieces were taken out of their cases, as was another head carved in white marble that was ensconced behind glass on the library's second floor, so that he could inspect them. Running his fingers over the wooden pieces, he said, "She made a mask of my face once. Looked just like me too."⁶² Described as a quiet man who was slight in stature and build and bewildered by his daughter's fame, he had accomplished what he had set out to do by going downtown to the library. He graciously declined the librarian's offer to show him around the building. He was anxious to get back to Benedict Street (fig. 21).

William Proffitt's pride in his daughter's achievements and his comments to a bystander at the exhibit that she "had been home all winter until about three weeks ago" hint at the relationship the two shared despite the geographical distance between them during the twelve years she was abroad. These sentiments, along with the dedications she wrote on the photographs of her work, and the fact that she had taken her widowed father to live with her on Benefit Street before she went to Paris and now, years later, had moved into his home at 112 Benedict Street, suggest that the bond between father and daughter was strong and had weathered tensions that have been alluded to over her choice of career. Theresa Leininger-Miller, citing the article "Can I Become a Sculptor? The Story of Elizabeth Prophet," writes that from William's and his wife's perspectives, occupations such as housekeeper or teacher "among her people" were more realistic choices for a young woman of color, even

Fig. 21. William H. Proffitt in his backyard on Benedict Street, 1940. His surname on the clipped photograph is Prophet. The note on the back is dated Father's Day and was apparently written by Nancy Elizabeth Prophet. The faded handwriting is difficult to decipher. Courtesy of the Nancy Elizabeth Prophet Collection, John P. Adams Library, Rhode Island College.

one with talent and big ambitions.⁶³ Although Nancy might have interpreted the Proffitts' advice as obstructionist, they were also attempting to protect her from the uncertainties associated with not having a regular job with steady wages, the disappointments and unforeseen ridicule she might encounter in the art world, and prejudices that were all too familiar to them. Despite her parents' reservations about her pursuit of art as a career, they instilled in her a strong work ethic and impressed upon her lessons about what it meant to be an Indian in New England.

Like many Native people in the Northeast and in Providence's indigenous homelands, Nancy Elizabeth Prophet confronted questions about her identity. She responded in ways that have been interpreted as expressing ambivalence, though most characterizations of her identity can be attributed to perceptions of outsiders who chose not to think of her as a Native person. Her mentor, W. E. B. Du Bois, who was apparently aware of her quandaries over racial categorization and circumspect about the words he used in his correspondence with her, opted for the vaguer and more inclusive term "colored," rather than "Negro" or "Indian."⁶⁴ Some of the most acclaimed sculptures she did in Paris were African figures. Others depicted Classical-looking or ambiguous images that she rendered in marble, bronze, and, most often, wood, as she did most of her extant work. Years later, when living on Benedict Street, she declined an invitation to be included in a book project by Cedric Dover, an anthropologist—*American Negro Art*—stating "an anthropologist must certainly know that I am not a Negro, and though I am of mixed blood the two races which I represent are quite different from that which you wish your publication to represent." Dover in response stated to readers that they would have to reconcile themselves to the loss and that he knew that she was not a Negro—"and a little more as well."⁶⁵

Despite any conflicts Nancy Elizabeth Prophet might have had over her identity and how it was perceived by outsiders and about how her art was racially categorized in artistic and intellectual circles, her behavior and words suggest self-awareness about her Native ancestry. Living on the edge of poverty in the squalor of the outskirts of Paris, she wrote about a garden she planted and cultivated for food. Perhaps more than a necessary means of survival, her urban gardening seems to simulate the activities of generations of Native American women who planted, cared for, and harvested corn, beans, and squash. It speaks to her knowledge of these practices. Presumably as these traditions were being adapted to urbanized conditions they were passed down by her father, who farmed before moving to Providence, worked as a gardener for the city's Parks Department, and tended his yard on Benedict Street, and by her mother, described as a "mixed negro." For Nancy Elizabeth Prophet, urban gardening, domestic work outside of the home, and needlework, which she did while briefly under psychiatric care at the Rhode Island State Hospital during the 1950s, represent ways that she wrestled with her aspirations and needs, with modernity and tradition, and with being an indigenous New Englander whose life experiences crossed waters.

She spent her final years on Benedict Street, sometimes commuting there on weekends while residing with a Providence family during the week in return for doing household chores. Described as embittered and dislocated, she continued to insist that she was of Indian heritage, as would Narragansett Indians who claimed her as strictly one of their own.[66] She died of a heart attack in 1960 at the age of fifty. Nearly penniless, she would have been buried in a pauper's grave if not for the intercession of the head of the family that had befriended her, who made sure that she received a proper funeral. She left behind a few possessions and the modest house on Benedict Street, which she had inherited from her father. Her things were supposedly still stored in the attic when the house was about to be torn down, but they were in such poor condition that they were considered not worth saving.[67]

Nancy Elizabeth Prophet's pathway to Benedict Pond had crossed rural and urban homelands and international borders. Like other Native people in the neighborhood, she was not rooted in the Mashapaug homeland during her entire lifetime. Unlike them, her life was played out on a large, cosmopolitan stage. Yet her experiences were not unique. Other Northeast Indians also became entangled in urbanisms at distant corners of the region's towns and cities. Among these was Molly "Spotted Elk" Nelson, a performing artist, who led a life almost parallel to Prophet's.

Born to a Penobscot father and a French-Malisset mother, she lived in Paris between the world wars and experienced poverty, illness, self-doubt, and prejudice, as well as success. She too traveled across the Atlantic several times before returning permanently to her family home, on Indian Island, Maine. In the interim she danced in cabarets, nightclubs, and recital halls in Paris and in cities across Europe and the United States as an Indian, or as she remarked, as a "universal Indian"—not as a Penobscot. To have success as an Indian entertainer, she was expected to perform in ways that appealed to non-Native audiences, rather than as an interpreter of the more subtle and expressive qualities of Penobscot traditional dances for those who wanted to learn about the culture. On her return to the United States she moved between Indian Island and New York looking for work as a dancer, but finding jobs as a waitress, factory worker, and mail clerk. After being institutionalized for a mental breakdown, she remained on Indian Island where she gardened, made baskets and dolls, and walked in the woods.[68] Despite differences in their professions and the particular details of their travel, the contours of these women's lives are uncannily similar. As conflicted cosmopolitans, they returned home, where they were not mere foreigners and could find comfort in family and familiar routines. For Nancy Elizabeth Prophet, this meant resuming her life in a city that had changed as much as she had, but where pieces of her past quickly fell into place.

William Proffitt and his daughter made their home at Benedict Pond after it had been filled, when grasses and other plants would no longer have grown at its edges, and fishing, swimming, and skating were no longer feasible. Varieties of sedges and rushes, St. John's Wort, plantain, and milkweed from Benedict Pond in Brown University's Herbarium provide a partial inventory of plants available to the Thomas, Weeden, and Wheeler families and others who lived there during the late nineteenth and early twentieth centuries. They could have harvested sedges and rushes for use in weaving mats and bags and collected plants valued for healing properties in the Native pharmacopeia. Even as it was reduced in size, Benedict Pond would have served as a setting for gatherings and maintaining time-honored practices, in addition to offering a diversity of plants and other resources to supplement store-bought food and remedies dispensed by pharmacists and physicians. The filling process, completed sometime after 1922, eliminated its watery space and dramatically altered its surrounding natural habitats. But it did not erase community histories and social memories. These would have continued to make this pond land a place that the Proffitts and other Native people would call home. The same would be true of Long and Duck Ponds.

Rural Urbanity, Indigenous Persistence, and Kinship Ties at Later "Mashipawog"

Mashapaug Pond escaped such a fate, though land on the road leading to the pond was drained and filled in the late 1800s to diminish the threat of malaria, which, according to a report by the Providence's Superintendent of Health, at one time had invaded "nearly every house."[69] By the middle of the twentieth century, the city proposed that the state of Rhode Island should study the advisability of acquiring all the land and water of Mashapaug Pond to eliminate water pollution caused by dumping.[70] State reports claimed that there were no signs of bacterial pollution after multiple tests, except for a single sample that showed a "slight condition" that would make the pond unfit for bathing. However, because of floating bottles and debris, a ban was issued on supervised swimming and recreation in July 1951.[71] Opinions about the conditions of the pond were mixed, with some charging that its waters were polluted and created a health menace.[72] The extent to which these reports affected the everyday realities of families that lived at the pond are unclear. Many who grew up there during the 1950s remember swimming in the pond and not thinking it was polluted, though they could not help noticing the debris in the water, as others probably had decades earlier. For generations of indigenous people, Mashapaug Pond was a semi-rural space in an urban environment. Its open fields, topography, watery spaces, and dirt roads, such as Hamburg and Jonathan Streets, unpaved as late as the mid-twentieth century, made it attractive. Many residents had gardens in the back lots of their houses. Some raised chickens. Beyond their house lots open fields were planted with vegetables and fruits. Here

Native families assumed traditional land use rights rooted in Mashapaug Pond's history as an Indian place rather than in legal ownership. It was not unusual to spot foxes, coyotes, and deer crossing over the railroad tracks on the other side of the Calhoun Bridge to the neighborhood.[73]

Clifford Guy Sr., who had lived on Calhoun Avenue at the corner of Van Zandt Street in the Mashapaug neighborhood before moving to Roger Williams Homes in Lower South Providence in the 1940s, eventually moved back to the pond land. By 1956 he and his family were living on Jonathan Street. He was employed as a longshoreman and his son, Clifford Jr., was in the U.S. Air Force.[74] Clifford Jr. later worked as a barber at the Quonset Naval Base and as a metal fitter at General Dynamics in New London, Connecticut, while raising his family in Jamestown on Conanicut Island, Rhode Island.[75] Everett "Tall Oak" Weeden remembers visiting the Guys' home on Jonathan Street to spend time with his cousin Clifford Jr., whose godmother was Princess Red Wing. Along with the family connections, Tall Oak was attracted by the pond's rural environment, which he said reminded him of his childhood home in North Providence. Mashapaug Pond was a place that he often visited as a teenager to socialize with boys and girls who shared similar life experiences and where Indians could maintain their traditions, perhaps more easily than in the city's other homelands.[76]

While living on Calhoun Street the Guy family (Clifford Sr., his wife, Esther, who was a Weeden by birth, and their son Clifford), would travel to Westerly, Rhode Island, to visit with friends and family at Christmas and in August when they attended the Narragansetts' green corn ceremony and annual gathering. In turn their Westerly hosts, Mr. and Mr. Lewis Wilcox, would make the trip to Providence to attend social events that reunited them with members of the Weeden family. One such event was the Modernistic Dance Studio Revue at the Providence Plantations Auditorium on Weybosset Street in January 1936. The revue featured Everett Weeden Sr., known as "the Yanidizze of the Narragansett." *Yanidizze* meant "great dancer," an honorific title bestowed on him by Princess Red Wing. Afterward the Wilcoxes and other guests went to the home of Mrs. Mary Weeden, Everett's mother, on Rodney

Court in Upper South Providence, where she held a social hour for the Narragansetts visiting from Westerly.[77] In May Lewis Wilcox, his wife, and other family members attended a fashion show at Infantry Hall on South Main Street on Providence's east side organized by the social committee of the Church of Our Saviour.[78]

These social interactions, reported in *Narragansett Dawn* from August 1935 to May 1936, provide glimpses into the connections between some of the families at Mashapaug Pond and Native people living in communities on ancestral lands in the Charlestown and Westerly areas. The town of Westerly, an urbanized Indian enclave formed as nearby reservation communities were dispossessed of their lands or detribalized, was also where the American Indian Federation, an intertribal organization, was based. Formed in 1931 by Chief Silver Star (Atwood I. Williams) (Pequot), John George (Pequot), and Chief Pine Tree (William L. Wilcox) (Narragansett), a medicine man, the group was composed mostly of Pequots and Narragansetts, as well as non-Natives in its early years. More than its precursor, the Indian Council of New England (known later as the National Algonquin Indian Council), the American Indian Federation made a concerted effort to include Narragansett and Pequot Indians with African American ancestry and non-Native spouses and in-laws as members, and to expand non-Native participation in public events.[79] In addition to William Wilcox, Lewis Wilcox's father, other family members were active in the organization, as were the Weedens.[80] Because of family ties, visits between these individuals' homes were frequent, probably more so than were logged in the social pages of *Narragansett Dawn*. Their membership in the American Indian Federation created additional opportunities for getting together, though a change in leadership from its Pequot and Narragansett founders to Natives from outside New England in the mid-1930s contributed to controversies over recruitment that discouraged some from attending the organization's events.[81] Yet Indians from Westerly could often be seen at public events in Providence and in Bristol, where they visited the King Philip Museum, as well as in Boston, where Chief Pine Tree and others watched the Narragansett runner Ellison ("Tarzan") Brown compete in the Patriot's Day

Marathon in 1936. On these occasions they were joined by Indians from Mashapaug Pond and Providence's other Native homelands.[82]

For many Native people who settled in the Mashapaug homeland, the Pond Street Baptist Church continued to be where they participated in religious services and gathered for other communal events, even after they moved from Upper South Providence or from elsewhere in the city. It was where Esther Weeden taught Sunday School and attended weekly services with other church-going Indians from Mashapaug. Clifford Guy Sr. was buried from the Pond Street Church in 1977, when the congregation was over on Chester Avenue in the West Elmwood section after the church at the corner of Pond and Angle Streets was torn down as part of the Central-Classical Redevelopment Project in the 1960s.[83] The church's name resonated among the Indians at Mashapaug and across the city, according to Rev. Harold Mars (Narragansett), who lived at Mashapaug Pond in the early 1940s with his wife, Laura, and their sons.[84] Its mere mention evoked a vital sense of placehood and community among Providence's Indians that transcended generations and the church's dislocation and that of its indigenous members from urban homelands.

Harold Mars was born in 1911 and raised mainly in South Kingstown, Rhode Island, though his family moved for a brief time to Westerly and to Gay Head on Martha's Vineyard. His father, Christian Mars, was born in Providence, as was his mother, Rosebud, the daughter of Benjamin F. Thomas and his wife Emma (see chapter 3). Early in their marriage, the young couple lived with her parents, who had moved to the village of Wakefield in South Kingstown around 1900 after spending more than thirty years in Providence. Christian and his father-in-law worked as stonemasons.[85] Harold graduated from South Kingstown High School in 1929 and later worked as a day laborer, mostly on odd jobs, and then did stonework, a trade that he was taught by his grandfather.[86] By 1940, he had married and started a family of his own. He moved to Providence with his wife and two young sons by 1942. They lived at 13 Tyler Street off Calhoun Avenue. The couple left Narragansett Country in southern Rhode Island, where they had been born and raised, so that Harold could be closer to Quonset Point, where he worked during World War II.

Although the Mars family lived at Mashapaug Pond for only a few years, they knew the names and addresses of other Native families who were their neighbors. During an interview in the early 1980s, Reverend Mars told William Simmons about "another Indian family, down about a block, by the name of Elderkins," who were "direct descendants of the Seekonk Indians." He also said, "There was the Weeden family who were Narragansett," and that "a number of them are still surviving." Laura Mars told Simmons that the Bourne family also lived in the neighborhood. "The Born [Bourne] children's mother was Hattie Cheeks [Cheats] from the Lantern Hill Indians [Eastern Pequot Nation] and she had married this man and she lived in that section. And the Cheeks [Cheats] were related to my mother." The Mars, Weeden, Elderkin, and Bourne families, and the Adamses, the cousins of Laura Mars, "were all living there at that time [in the early 1940s] in that same community."[87]

Of these families, Providence city directories list Marcus Aurelius Elderkin, his wife Mary, and sons Marcus, Earl, and Oscar at 6 Tyler Street from the late 1930s to about 1943.[88] That year, they moved to Faith Street, also in the Mashapaug Pond area, where Marcus's younger brother Earl Elderkin had lived since the 1930s. Faith Street was Mary's home when her death was registered in Providence in July 1943.[89] Marcus Elderkin was born to John and Martha Elderkin about 1885.[90] He lived in Seekonk into his twenties and worked as a truck farmer, as did other Seekonk Elderkins during the nineteenth and early twentieth centuries.[91] Sometime before 1918, he moved to Rhodes Street in Lower South Providence with his wife and two children.[92] Like his brother Earl, he worked for the Seaconnet Coal Company on Allens Avenue. The family of nine—five of their children were born in Providence—remained in Lower South Providence until 1930. The following year, they moved to Calhoun Avenue, a short distance away from their subsequent home on Tyler Street.[93] Marcus's World War II draft registration card, filed in 1942 when the family's address was Tyler Street, identifies his employer as the Curran & Burton Coal Company on Allens Avenue, which suggests that he worked for the coal companies on the Providence waterfront as a cable engineer and laborer for most of his adult life.[94]

A Bourne family is recorded as living on Pacific Avenue near Tyler Street in the 1940 federal census. The head of the family, Philip, was born in Maryland, and his wife Harriett (or Hattie) was from Rhode Island. They married in 1918 and moved to the Mashapaug Pond neighborhood around 1924, when they are listed at 6 Tyler Street and on Pacific Avenue from the late 1920s.[95] Philip worked as chauffeur for a private family and later as a truck driver in the government's Works Progress Program, which provided some of the unemployed with jobs in public projects during the Great Depression. Hattie raised their nine children, some of whom were of age and holding jobs in 1940 and living at home. Her maiden name, Cheats, appears in the records of southeastern Connecticut's Windham County as "Cheets" and was attached to individuals that are identified as Indian.[96]

Harold and Laura Mars stayed at Mashapaug Pond only for two years (1942–1943) or possibly three, according to Laura, and cherished fond memories of the neighborhood. They would move to Rochester, New York, where Harold is listed as a pastor in the 1960 census.[97] After about ten years, they moved back to their home in the woods of the former Narragansett reservation in Charlestown. Harold, whose lineage included a line of renowned Indian preachers going back to Samuel Niles (see chapter 3), had close ties to the Narragansett Indian Church, where he delivered sermons and Laura sang on occasion in the late 1930s and the 1940s.[98] He led Sunday services at the tribe's annual August Meeting, an event he attended regularly regardless of where he lived, and preached at the Old Indian Church in Mashpee.[99] He was well versed in Narragansett oral narratives of place that he had been taught by his elders, and as a young man growing up in Wakefield he had experienced personal encounters with the supernatural. He recounted the more two-hundred-year-old Narragansett story of Crying Rocks (see chapters 1 and 3), a large stone formation located "a little less than a mile from the church going in a westerly direction . . . and right on the edge of the cedar swamp," where the cries of children could be heard in the middle of the night. In his version, babies left at Crying Rocks had been born with physical deformities and were put to death "with proper ceremony." Other Narragansett people gave slightly different accounts in which illegitimacy or a mother's concern about the welfare of a child fathered by a non-Native man made abandonment seem a less grim alternative than indentureship or a lifetime of prejudice from some within their own community, their Euro-American neighbors, and town officials ready to pounce on any sign they could construe as evidence of a loss of Indianness.[100]

Reverend Mars told other stories, such as one about Indian Run, a small brook in Peacedale, Rhode Island, where the screams of an Indian man, murdered and thrown into the stream (possibly by one of the Hazards, a white family with extensive land holdings and textile mills) kept Narragansett people away. He also told a story about Sugarloaf Hill in Wakefield, where the roar of trains passing through the Kingston station muffled the voices of the ghosts of those whose bodies had been buried in the hill.[101] Among the stories that Reverend Mars repeated, these in particular comment on the experiences of the Narragansetts in European settler-colonial society. They evoke feelings of land loss, agreements gone terribly awry, and the impacts of railroad and industrial expansion on their sacred places. Like the Crying Rocks legend that reminded the Narragansetts about life's challenges, these stories told about their struggles in a world that had become increasingly inhospitable to them.

Although associated with tragic events, these storied places also speak to resistance. The Indian Run story comments on Narragansetts trespassing on colonized lands that were once theirs, acknowledging what the consequences of such bold actions might be. Crying Rocks tells about the decisions that Native women sometimes made out of moral courage and natural reason to renounce dominance. The stories that Laura Mars had heard from her mother, such as the ones about John Onion or the strange light that lured children into dangerous swamps and quicksand, reminded Native people of the traditional values and connections to family and community that they needed to hold onto however far away they moved from their ancestral home places.[102] The lessons these stories told were as important to Native people living on reservations as they were for those who had moved to Providence and other cities and towns. Whether Harold and Laura Mars shared the stories they had learned from their elders with their neighbors at Mashapaug is not known, though I surmise that they did. Other Natives who lived on the pond lands also had stories that they carried with them and new ones associated with their experiences of dwelling there. These stories would have been especially prevalent at places where events of pervasive moral significance occurred, as Basso suggests. Among them were stories of whispering spirits and ancestors walking in the shadows that Narragansetts still recall today.[103]

There were stories about caves where Indians once lived on the east side of Mashapaug Pond near the Gorham Manufacturing Company that stood there from the last decade of the nineteenth century to when it was demolished in the late 1990s, and about an elderly African American woman in a white dress from Providence who would walk around the pond, though no one dared to ask why she was there and what she was doing. There were stories of drowning that heightened warnings to avoid swimming in certain areas of the pond because of cold springs and sudden drop offs. Stories about skating and horse racing on the frozen pond, which the owner of the Providence Ice Company at the south end of the pond allowed after his ice harvest, were memorable and might have rekindled for some Native people the legend of John Onion attempting to outrun the devil. Residents also talked about turning over the ground in their gardens in back lots off of Jonathan Street every spring to clear rocks. They said that they talked about rocks coming back in their gardens, knowing that there would always be more. In vacant spaces of the neighborhood where Native people did not have proprietary rights and where their access was constrained by the rule of the colonizers, they planted anyway, because they still considered themselves to be the rightful owners of the lands around Mashapaug. Some interlocutors remembered how, as children, they raided orchards on private property or plucked peaches and plums growing from trees in empty lots. If there were repercussions from orchard raiding or fence jumping, they were not mentioned.

These stories from everyday practices tell how the Native peoples of Mashapaug Pond lived in a space that had become colonized and how they navigated the numerous strictures imposed on their movement. Their maps of the lands of Mashapaug Pond were not drawn or published, as was typical of many indigenous maps of colonized landscapes that no longer belonged to their original owners. These maps, as David Byrne has argued, do not simply take "the form of an overlay (or underlay)," but map spaces lying in and around white spaces that are brought into being by spatial routines that do not necessarily have a separate place of their own.[104] In urban homelands such as Mashapaug Pond, these spaces were not only constituted by poaching on white space via orchard raiding or planting in open plots of land. Native people were not merely prior occupants of the pond who availed themselves of its resources in the late nineteenth and twentieth centuries. They lived there in single- and two-family homes that had mostly been built by 1919, which they rented or sometimes owned, and they did not follow an older pattern of living off the land.[105] They worked for wages as longshoremen and crane operators on the docks of the Providence waterfront, as carpenters, as gardeners, as laborers, and as domestics, as did many Native people living on pond lands on the west end and in the city's other homelands. They and other pond residents were employed in industry, in private homes, and by the city and the state. Their use of the pond and its surrounding lands for fishing, collecting, gardening, and raiding orchards helped to sustain rather than detract from their footholds in urban homelands. Melding modernity and tradition, they reinforced their enduring claims to Mashapaug Pond, not merely as shadowy figures reminiscent of an ancient past, but as a persistent presence with their own more recent place-based stories.

Poisoning the Pond: Industrial Transformations and Indigenous Dislocations

Mashapaug Pond remained the city's hidden oasis, even as nearby ponds—Long, Duck, and Benedict—disappeared from the landscape. It withstood the construction of the Gorham Manufacturing Company's complex that occupied over thirty-seven acres on its northeastern shore and would be an ever-present fixture of the pond's landscape and local memories even after its demolition in 1997, a decade after its operations ceased. The company, Rhode Island's largest and leading metal-working firm, was widely known for its silverware and bronzes. Its "Narragansett" pattern for silver flatware and hollowware, embellished with shells, barnacles, seaweed, bulrushes, and other forms of life in local waters and introduced in 1884, was praised as a masterpiece of naturalism that celebrated the eponymous bay that retained its tribal designation. It resonated with an earlier time when Native people launched a *mishoòn* to paddle down the Providence River to where it opened into this inland ocean and when freshwater ponds such as Mashapaug had not yet been polluted.

In the early twentieth century Gorham was selected by the Rhode Island Historical Society's Committee for Marking Historical Sites to manufacture bronze tablets to designate places of historic interest. The committee's decision to accept the foundry's bid was a prudent choice given the $1,500 budget appropriated by the Rhode Island General Assembly and the company's accessibility and reliability.[106] The tablets, measuring roughly twenty by twenty-four inches, were mostly fitted onto boulder monuments. They each contained about forty words, brought attention to a site, and served as a pivotal step in a commemorative process leading toward a path of veneration.[107] Although the bronze tablets were sometimes stolen, the Gorham Manufacturing Company's tablets begat other tablets—sometimes even before the whereabouts of the original were discovered. Gorham continued to make tablets for the approximately thirty sites that were marked by the end of the second decade of the nineteenth century.[108] This suggests that it not only reshaped the Mashapaug Pond homeland, but also created a storied landscape inscribed with tangible reminders of violent cross-cultural encounters and other events whose words omitted Native participation in a shared past.

The company also collaborated with many well-known sculptors to produce large- and small-scale bronze castings of their works that could be widely marketed. Among these artists was Cyrus Dallin (1861–1944), a member of the Indian Council of New England. Born and raised in Springville, Utah, a town sparsely settled by Euro-American homesteaders, where, according to an 1899 article on Dallin, the "Piute [Paiute] and Ute Indians were numerous," his artistic imagination was sparked by the beauty of their beading, basketry, and pottery.[109] With the financial backing of admirers who recognized his talent, he went to Boston to study sculpture. He worked at different studios in and around the city making statues and busts before moving to Paris, where some of his models were visiting Indians in William F. Cody's Wild West troupe encamped in the Bois de Boulogne for the Universal Exposition of 1889. These sessions resulted in *A Signal of Peace*, the first in a series of equestrian statues called the "Epic of the Indian" that depict what the dominant society considered a trajectory of colonialism that began with overtures of friendship to European colonists and led to suspicions of the invaders (*The Medicine Man*), warfare (*The Protest*), and eventual defeat in a contest over land and autonomy that had a preordained outcome (*Appeal to the Great Spirit*).[110]

Dallin returned to Massachusetts in 1899 and settled in Arlington, a suburb of Boston, where he bought a house from the sale *The Medicine Man*. Situated on one of greater Boston's highest points, the Dallin home had a commanding view of the harbor eight miles off to the east, its islands, the long peninsula known by its Indian name, Nahant, that jutted into the bay, and the ocean beyond. His bird's-eye view from this hilltop allowed him to imagine as Native space the surrounding landscape, colonial by design and the scene of dramatic urban transformations at the turn of the century. During the next three decades he produced other works of art depicting Native Americans, among them a figure of an Indian hunter that was purchased by Arlington's civic association in 1912 and placed on a hillside in the town center. In 1911 Boston's Metropolitan Improvement League and a group of leading artists initiated a campaign to purchase a larger-than-life-size bronze (*Appeal to the Great Spirit*), which they had acquired on loan and placed in front of the Museum of Fine Arts as a public monument for the city. According to a biography of Dallin, many questioned whether a statue of a Native American should be in such a visible location and suggested that a more remote spot would be "much more harmonious and keeping with the natural habitat of the Indian as well as the spirit of the work of sculpture."[111] After a year-long struggle during which fundraising languished and other U.S. cities competed for the work, a donor offered to contribute the balance needed to buy the statue, on the condition that it remained in the area fronting the museum and became part of its permanent collection. Probably few passersby today know the backstory of this statue, which has been a Boston landmark, a rendezvous point, and a subject of practical jokes for more than a hundred years. For most who pay any attention to what the statue represents in Native American colonial history, it remains as reminder "of an ethnic type since merging in our own and of an environment which since has passed away," as described in the Registry of Local Art section of the museum's 1913 Bulletin.[112]

Although the towering statue in Boston was cast in a Paris foundry, the Gorham Manufacturing Company's bronze division produced smaller-scale versions of it, along with some of Dallin's other sculptures. His contract with the company for bronze reproductions of *Appeal*, finalized in 1916, specified that the replicas were to be made in three sizes. One hundred and nine copies—standing nine and three-fourths, twenty-one and three-fourths, and thirty-six inches high—were cast and finished in a brown patine.[113] The company's 1928 exhibit catalogue of *Famous Small Bronzes* promoted the statuettes, marketed at $100, $350, and $1,300 each, respectively, as a "good example of the tendency of an American sculptor to go to purely American sources for inspiration." The face of the warrior in *Appeal* was described as having "for once lost the passivity usually considered essential in portrayals of the red man" and to be "alight with faith," making it "an usually fine and inspiring piece of work." Scaled-down copies of Dallin's *Scout*, which were also marketed in the catalog, were called authentic representations of Native Americans, given that the artist had spent "many years in the West among them, learning much of their life, their customs, and their philosophy." Gorham promoted its castings as "suited to adorn American homes in which elegance and dignity combine with comfort and convenience of appointments to create an atmosphere" resulting in a charming domestic space. Possession of these works should bring "pleasure and satisfaction to [the] owner in contemplation of not only [the] artistic conception, but [also the] patience, care and skill attendant upon [its] production." In addition to displaying one's "culture and advanced taste," ownership of a small bronze replica allowed one to experience the statue at home, without having to travel to Boston or Kansas City to view *Appeal* or *Scout* as public art.[114]

The Gorham Manufacturing Company's castings of diminutive versions of Dallin's equestrian Indian statues followed the logic of miniaturization that permitted an ease of vision that enabled the viewer to see effortlessly all around objects that otherwise could only be seen from a single viewing point and at a distance. Small-scale versions of public art seemed qualitatively simplified, fostering understandings that were both pleasurable and empowering. Compared with the monumental original statues, and despite the pathos of *Appeal*, the smaller bronzes made Indians seem less threatening. No longer enemies or rivals in real life, they were figures to be put in the parlor, where they drew attention to Dallin's artistic mastery and the Gorham bronze foundry's especially fine casting. They carried into the domestic realm messages of progress and technological achievement, as well as a sense of the world beyond the borders of Providence where indigenous people were also subjected to the settler colonialism's inevitabilities. In bourgeois homes, the company's small castings of Dallin's sculptures not only disseminated stereotypical messages about the demise of Native Americans, but they also signaled an owner's cosmopolitanism and awareness of ongoing agendas of settler colonialism. By ornamenting interior spaces, and more broadly by traveling, these objects that seemingly had been permanently fixed on the urban commemorative landscape came to have different economic, cultural, and social meanings.[115]

One of the Gorham Manufacturing Company's reproductions of *Appeal to the Great Spirit* was purchased by Rudolf Haffenreffer in the early 1930s for his King Philip Museum. At the time the museum was not only an exhibition space for Haffenreffer's Indian artifact collections but also a personal space where he spent many leisurely hours on weekends in a comfortable setting with a fireplace, books, leather sofas, reading tables, and "ready access to a wine cellar and a humidor."[116] The space was analogous to a Victorian men's smoking room, and its female counterpart, the Victorian parlor, in which women mixed consumer goods, Native decorative art, and visual depictions of Native Americans such as cigar-store Indians, Edward Curtis's orotones, or the Gorham bronze Indians to create an environment that was both a refuge from the outside world of business and competition and a product of it. Other institutions also acquired the Gorham reproductions of Dallin's sculptures and displayed them in more formal settings. At the U.S. Department of State *Appeal* is in the Walter Thurston Gentleman's Lounge, a diplomatic reception room—along with an engraved silver peace medal, a token of goodwill given to tribes; Benjamin West's painting of William Penn's meeting with the Lenape in 1682, a visual allegory of political harmony; and other art of the American West—where it serves as a poignant reminder of the consequences of failed diplomacy, war, and colonialist policies for indigenous people.

I suspect that Native people living around Mashapaug Pond and its nearby ponds did not buy the statuettes. The cost was prohibitively expensive for working people like them; and the statuettes' subjects, Euro-American stereotypes of Indians as soundly defeated warriors frozen in time, would have been perceived as offensive. The statues' "patina of nobility," as Carol Clark writes, was a way of signaling antiquity that suggested that "real Indians" existed only in the past or in Wild West shows, and failed to dignify actual Native people living in Providence or in other American cities who made their presence known through their everyday lives.[117]

One has to wonder if any Native people in the Mashapaug homeland worked at the Gorham Manufacturing Company when its bronze foundry was casting the reproductions and if so, what they thought. Did they consider the small bronzes a symbol of the victory of American "civilization" or an overdue acknowledgment of settler colonialism's effects on American Indians? Did the statuettes represent the possibility that they too could enter into middle-class America? Their opinions of the bronzes are unknown, as are the responses of most Native people to Cyrus Dallin's sculptures. Francis LaFlesche (Omaha), an ethnologist who spoke at the unveiling of *The Medicine Man* in Philadelphia's East Fairmount Park in 1903, remarked, "This statue at once brings back vividly to my mind the scenes of my early youth, scenes that I shall never again see in their reality."[118] Although he credited the artist with reopening the past for him, the voices of four Native American men photographed in front of *The Appeal* at the Museum of Fine Arts in spring 1922 were not recorded. Mounted on horseback and dressed in Plains Indians attire with feather headdresses, two look at the camera, one diverts his eyes straight ahead, and the fourth, in the far left of the picture, fixes his gaze on the sculpted figure depicted with an elaborate war bonnet not unlike his. The visiting Indians, who were in Boston for a Wild West show staged by the Ringling Brothers Circus, were photographed at the statue to promote the event. Later that year, the photo appeared in a brochure from P. P. Caproni and Brother, a firm based in Boston that also made replicas of Dallin's sculptures and was selling small plaster casts of *Appeal to the Great Spirit*. Caproni, like Gorham, touted its statuettes as suitable for homes and educational institutions, but advertised them using the photograph of "real" living Indians posed at the monumental bronze.[119] With the institution that owned the large sculpture in the background lending symbolic civic authority, the image of Indians "playing Indians" served as a silent endorsement of Caproni products. Although their faces seem to register curiosity, seriousness, disdain, and amusement that might not accurately reveal their innermost thoughts, they offer a graphic commentary on the jumble of conflicting opinions held by Native people about the practice of representation, whether by Dallin, the Gorham Manufacturing Company, or those like them who made a living by representing Indians.

While practices of representation were being carried out and mulled over, milling, forging, heat treating, plating, lacquering, polishing, and degreasing activities at Gorham Manufacturing Company continued to produce replicas of Dallin's Indian statues, other bronzes, and highly prized silverware. As the work proceeded, waste from the manufacturing process was dumped into Mashapaug Pond, which, like other urban ponds, offered a convenient disposal site. In the nearly hundred years that the foundry was in operation, heavy metals, chlorinated solvents, corrosive stripping agents, and other chemicals containing trichloroethylene, perchloroethylene, lead, zinc, and other pollutants were discharged into the pond and then leached into the groundwater and surrounding soil.[120] During the years that small bronze Indians were being cast and Leroy Perry, the Guys, Harold Mars, the Elderkins, and other Native families of the pond lands called Mashapaug home, no one knew about environmental contamination or how it might affect their health. Unlike the unwanted oil drums, broken machine parts, old cars and tires, and construction debris that cluttered the pond's sandy bottom and shoreline, the chemical castoffs from industrialization poisoning the pond were almost as invisible as the Native families who had continued to dwell at Mashapaug Pond; like the families, the pollutants were a constant presence only recently noticed by non-Native outsiders. Yet to Native people of the pond lands, the pollution's toxic effects would have become noticeable in fish that were dying, turtles washing up on shore, lilies that shriveled, sweetflag that blackened, and cattails that were reduced to ragged sticks, as Cheryl Savageau, an Abenaki-French poet, writes in "Poison in the Pond," in which she chronicles settler colonialism's effects on Native American space.[121] They would have smelled foul odors, seen the pond water turn brackish, and experienced burning arms and lips, itchy eyes, difficulty swallowing, sore throats, body aches, and a fatigue that they could not explain.

Although compromised, Mashapaug Pond has endured. Cleanup efforts spurred by the activism of the Urban Pond Procession, an arts-based organization educating the community about the pond's current heath and contamination issues, and the Environmental Justice League of Rhode Island are continuing.[122] However, the neighborhood enclave that was nestled on its northwesterly shore opposite the Gorham factory has not survived. As early as 1946, when the Providence City Planning Commission adopted a master plan for the city's future, it was classified as an arrested district because of its low density and low value structures, tax delinquency, inadequate water and sewer services, improper subdivision of lots and streets, and inadequate housing.[123] In planning reports into the 1950s Mashapaug Pond would continue to be classified as a "blighted area," a catchphrase in the parlance of city officials for undesirable physical conditions and residents. Platted in 1856 and again in 1900, the area, excluding its streets and a railroad right-of-way, was described as less than 50 percent developed as late as 1960, with vacant land distributed throughout the neighborhood.

Streets in the neighborhood were described as short; some were unpaved or had dead ends. Many house lots were too small and did not meet the city zoning minimum of 5,000 square feet for a single-family house or 3,000 square feet per family for two- and three-family dwellings. More than a third of the housing was estimated to be substandard, with a small fraction lacking toilets or baths, about 25 percent without inside piped water, and almost 50 percent without central heating. Additionally, concerns were expressed about children having to cross the New York, New Haven, and Hartford railroad tracks to get to school, and about the shrinking buffer zone between homes and industry. However, these issues seemed less important than the overall assessment that the neighborhood was a place with "many vacant lots filled with trash and overgrown with weeds, unkempt yards, often used for junk piles, [and] dirt streets in poor condition" that gave it the appearance of a "run down, semi-rural area."[124]

The neighborhood fell victim to the Huntington Expressway Industrial Park, an urban redevelopment project, in the 1960s. The redevelopment plan for Mashapaug Pond was approved in December 1960, despite outcries from residents that the city had exaggerated the statistics used to demonstrate that the area met the criteria as a blighted, arrested district to qualify for funding as a Federal Urban Renewal Project. In what the *Providence Evening Bulletin* called "vigorous, though unorganized, protests," they voiced their disapproval about being uprooted and their homes demolished to make way for industrial development.[125] Human values, which they demanded that the city council consider, did not outweigh economic progress. As a result, this neighborhood that had persisted as a Native homeland from the seventeenth century to Gorham Manufacturing Company's tenure as an uneasy neighbor was removed from the urban landscape in an act that was as much about spatial cleansing as it was about ethnic erasure.

Today, streets such as Burrington, Tyler, Hamburg, Faith, Jonathan, Van Zandt, and others no longer exist. For more than fifty years, they have lingered in the memories of former residents, who still fondly reminisce about living in the neighborhood and share remarkably similar stories about Mashapaug Pond. None of these are more poignant than those of Native residents for whom the pond offered an opportunity to hold onto a community-in-place that attracted Native people of the diasporas from Narragansett Pequot, Wampanoag, and other ancestral homelands and where elements of a traditional lifestyle of planting, collecting, trapping, and hunting could be maintained far longer than at nearby ponds or in the city's other neighborhoods. The stories of their lives and their pathways to Mashapaug Pond constitute new narratives about this indigenous place and the Indians who continued to belong there. They persist just as surely as the toxic effects of the silver and bronze industry have lingered and caused harm to all forms of life in this urban pond land.[126]

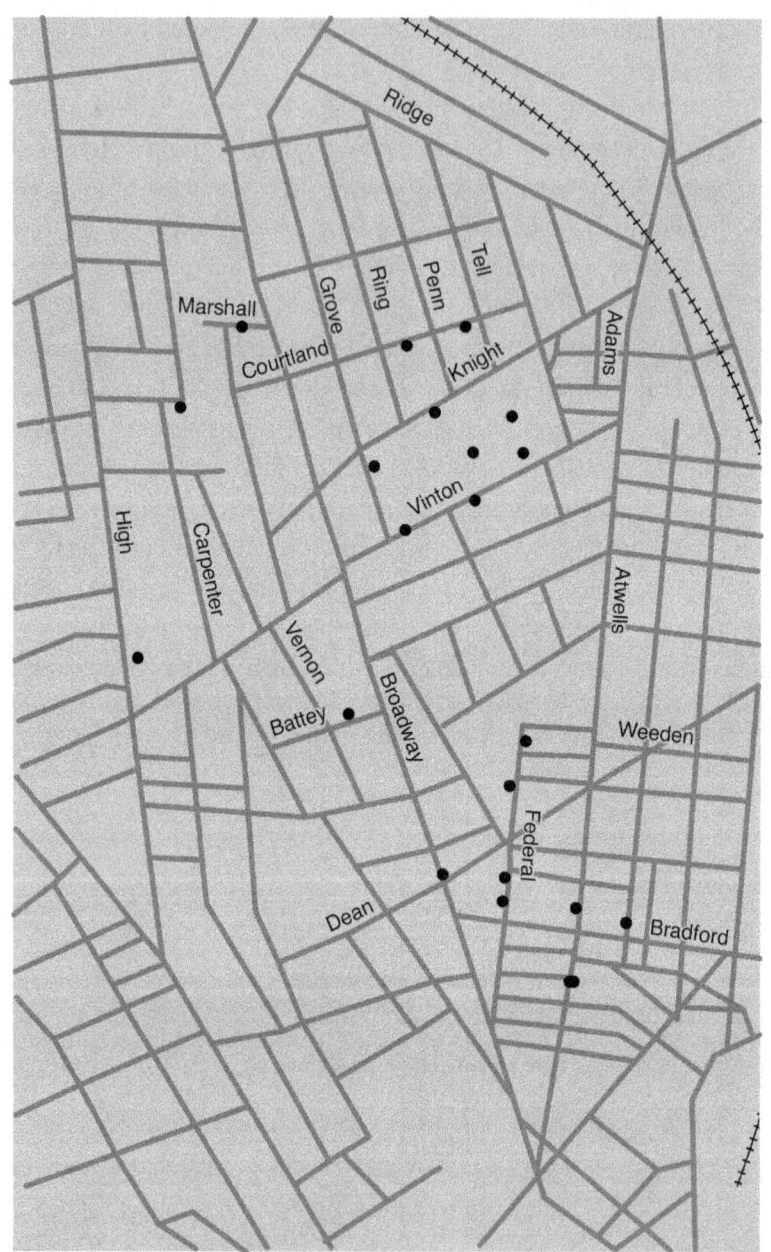

Fig. 22. Map of the Federal Hill homeland, showing selected Native households. Map by Lynn Carlson.

Federal Hill 6

*Homeland above the River at the Town's Doorstep,
Commonplace Streets, and Uncommon Labor*

Woonasquatucket is the name attached to one of two fresh rivers that defined the bounds of the lands and meadows that Canonicus and Miantonomo granted to Roger Williams in 1638 for his use.[1] Flowing southeasterly toward Providence from headwaters in North Smithfield at a fluid borderlands space of several tribal groups during and before the seventeenth century, the Woonasquatucket provided a north-south river route for the region's Native people that connected to the "Great River" (Providence River) and Narragansett Bay.[2] The "hill above the river" or "place between the ancient waters," called Nocabulabet, offered a vantage for viewing the lands, meadows, and well-traveled trails along this waterway and the Moshassuck River to the east. Known today as Federal Hill, or Providence's Little Italy, the location had long been a place where Narragansetts, Wampanoags, Nipmucs, and other Native people gathered to trade, socialize, and conduct ceremonies. In the nineteenth and early twentieth centuries they lived among recent immigrants and descendants of earlier European settler colonists.

Compared to Providence's east side, downtown, and Hoyle Square neighborhoods, Federal Hill was considered a more suburban place that was out in the country well into the 1870s. Many localities on the *colletto*, or "little hill," had place-names not identified on the street grid that had been coined by Irish immigrants who preceded Italians in successive projects of colonization and settlement on indigenous lands. Jones's Hill was at the intersection of Brayton and Dean Streets. Mollie Flynn's Hill was around Tefft Street. Tenement houses, known as blocks, also invoked Irish surnames. Nixon's Blocks were at Dean and Spruce Streets, McAleer's over on Spruce Street, McNally's at Acorn and Spruce Streets,

James McVicar's at Trainor and Aborn, McAloon's at Sutton and Atwells, and Biddy Savin's on a hill of the same name. Other familiar off-the-grid places were the large pine grove at Ridge Street, the sand bank on West Exchange Street, and the meadows or swamps along Harris Avenue that would have recalled particular sets of spatial relationships in the indigenous homeland long before the nineteenth century. So would have the sandy beaches known as the Turfs, where the Woonasquatucket River's waters ran along Promenade Street.[3] Today it is difficult to imagine the texture of this landscape. Jones's Hill was cut down in the late 1880s and used to fill Cove Basin to create space for a new transportation hub in the city's downtown. The Woonasquatucket hardly has the appeal of a popular swimming hole where children might have skinny-dipped and fishers might have cast a line, despite the U.S. Environmental Protection Agency's claims that it is a "river on the rebound" after decades of failing to meet water quality standards because of contamination from industrial and human waste.[4] The tenement blocks have mostly been pulled down, and Shoo Fly Village, a row of working-class cottages with small backyards near the railroad tracks at Federal Hill's westernmost edge, was a thing of the past by the early 1900s.[5]

The Lasting Pequots

Some recollections of Federal Hill as an Irish and then an Italian neighborhood homogenize its ethnic diversity and overlook that the bluff is still often referred to as Indian Hill. They are at odds with the presence of Native people who made the neighborhood their home during the nineteenth and early twentieth centuries. Moses P. Dailey, described as the "Last of the Pequots," in a *Providence Sunday Journal* interview in 1913, was a familiar figure on Federal Hill's Courtland Street for years as well as one of Providence's best-known Indians during the last half of the nineteenth century (fig. 23).[6] He lived in the neighborhood for about fifty years before moving to Public Street near the pond lands shortly before his death in 1915. In the interview he said that his grandfather's family migrated to Providence with his father, who was only three years old at the time, and two other families from Norwich, Connecticut, around 1800 to

Fig. 23. Moses P. Dailey, a professional nurse and longtime resident of Federal Hill, 1913. This photograph was reprinted in his obituary two years later. Microfilm reproduction from the *Providence Journal*.

escape the corrupting influences of European settler colonialism. Their route followed the "old trail," known as the Pequot Path, into Providence. They crossed the town to "a clump of bushes and trees" on the banks of the Seekonk River and pitched their tents at a spot with an excellent spring and fishing. The locale they chose, known today as Blackstone Park, had long been attractive to Native people, who had left behind at campsites, estimated to be between 5,000 and 3,000 years old, quartz points and small stone flakes for toolmaking and repairs that archaeologists say were "swept together, placed in a small depression, and then buried perhaps to keep the living area clean and free from sharp-edged stone debris."[7] Besides this cache and the remains of *wetus*, preserved as circular patterns of postholes, other artifacts have been found, often by accident, along the Providence side of the Seekonk River from roughly from this same time period and later.[8]

From the shores of the Seekonk, Moses Dailey's family and other Pequots went over to the west side of the Providence River and made their encampment next to a cart path that years later became Broadway.

The *Providence Sunday Journal* interview noted that the campsite was "at a point opposite the later site of the Harris Homestead and about where St. James Episcopal Church was erected."[9] Extrapolating from these clues, it was probably near Weybosset Point given that the Harris lot was located more or less opposite this landform on the early map of Providence home lots (1636-1650), as was King's Church (later known St. James Episcopal).[10] At the time when Dailey's grandfather arrived in Providence, according to the Dailey interview, the area of the Weybosset Plain "west of the top of Westminster Street was virtually covered with forestry." At the intersection of Jackson and Westminster Streets, there "was a thick grove, through which a narrow path led southeasterly, over this the Pequots were wont to travel as they went to the shore of Narragansett bay for fishing purposes."[11]

The group left Providence and moved to Warwick, Rhode Island, settling at a section called Norwood, where Moses, his brothers, Joseph and Jeremiah, a sister named Angeline, and two other siblings who died of tuberculosis when they were barely out of infancy were born. Moses's date of birth is given as August 11, 1825. He recalled that his father, Benjamin West Dailey, had been taught to read and write by Moses Brown (1738-1836), a scion of Providence's Brown family, a patron of education, a leading figure in the Industrial Revolution, and an abolitionist, who had taken "a kindly interest in him." The particular circumstances surrounding the relationship are unspecified, although, according to the younger Dailey, it instilled industrious habits in his father and provided him with the opportunity to observe other "modes of living." Although Benjamin West Dailey may have been exposed to more "civilized," urban, and modern ways of life, this did not prevent him from taking his son, who shared the first name of his mentor, to fish, skate, and ice fish on Narragansett Bay off of Rocky Point, to the south of Providence. As Moses recalled, "If night chanced to overtake them, they went ashore and slept in a cave in which they built a fire."[12] Such a cave would have been one of many at Rocky Point, a location that Joseph Banvard describes in a popular booklet published in 1858 as known for "its numerous trees, its uneven ground, its wild and massive rocks, piled up in a most grotesque confusion, forming caves and subterranean passages of singular character." [13] For most of the nineteenth century, this was one of Rhode Island's most popular resort areas and it drew visitors, many of them arriving on steamboats that left from the Dyer Street wharf in Providence, hoping to enjoy the scenery, ocean breezes, and amusements. By the late 1880s this popular destination for day excursions hosted Wild West and minstrel shows and the Providence Grays, a baseball team with African American, Native American, and Cape Verdean players that held games there on Sundays to evade Providence's blue laws.[14] Overnight visitors would have lodged in the seaside resort's hotels, rather than in the caves that Moses Dailey and his father, like generations of Native people before them, used when they went to Rocky Point to fish and continued to use even as the area evolved into an amusement park. Undeterred by the carnival atmosphere, Moses Dailey continued to visit Rocky Point's caves frequently well into his eighties.

Moses, who had worked as farm laborer in Warwick, was living in Providence in 1860. He is listed in the 1860 U.S. Census as a servant in the home of David Heaton in the city's seventh ward, which encompassed Federal Hill, and as a coachman at 163 Broadway in the city directory that same year. By 1865 Heaton owned a jewelry shop at 51 Westminster Street, and he and his wife had taken in additional boarders. Moses worked for Heaton as his coachman and boarded with the family and other lodgers into the 1860s and the 1870s. A childhood friend of Walter Heaton, David's son, recalled playing in the barn where Moses, who was then about forty years old, would amuse the two boys with his stories.[15] On March 28, 1878, when he was fifty-two years old, he married Maria Madelena Dickson of Providence, a woman less than half his age who was born on Olney Street in the Lippitt Hill neighborhood.[16] Lena, as she was known, gave birth to Jeanette (Nettie), their only child, at 130 Knight Street on Federal Hill on June 7, 1882.[17] Moses had moved to the Knight Street address a few years before their marriage, about when he left the Heatons to become a professional nurse. By his own admission, he turned to nursing because of the knowledge of the healing powers of plants that he had learned from his elders. Not only did traditional medicinal knowledge guide his career choice, but he also believed that it had helped save him, his brothers, and his sister from the bout of tuberculosis that had taken the lives of his younger siblings. Although Joseph, Jeremiah, and Angeline would survive childhood and live well into adulthood, they eventually succumbed to the chronic effects of the disease. Moses, who said in the 1913 interview that he "never knew the taste of liquor and [had] never used tobacco" on account of his grandfather's plan to bring up his family "as total abstainers," believed that the health of his siblings and other Indians "who had come from the Norwich camp" declined when "the tent was abandoned for life within four walls." [18] Given that tuberculosis a contagious infection that is spread by sharing close quarters with carriers showing symptoms, Moses's assessment of the conditions contributing to his family's illness is more in line with modern understandings of its etiology than with folk beliefs of Euro-Americans in nineteenth-century New England. Their beliefs attributed outbreaks of the disease to vampires—reanimated victims that Alan Dundes, a folklorist, called "bloodthirsty revenants"—who rose from their graves at night to suck the blood of living people, thus causing the emaciation, suffering, and death associated with tuberculosis.[19]

Moses Dailey continued to live on Knight Street into the 1880s. He and his wife later moved a few blocks away to Courtland Street. Characterized as "a most genial and kind-hearted soul" by the young man who knew him when he worked as a coachman for David Heaton, he lived at 151 Courtland Street for about twenty years.[20] His daughter, Nettie, who married in Providence in 1901, lived at the same address with her husband, Abram Manchester.[21] Moses and Lena moved in with Nettie and her family at 635 Public Street on the city's west end about 1913 (see chapter 5). "Tall and erect, with all of the racial features clearly in evidence" even as an octogenarian, according to the *Providence Sunday Journal* article, his presence would have not gone unnoticed on Federal Hill, nor would his daughter's. Although she was "not a full-blooded Pequot," the newspaper stated, "white blood" had not "effaced the attractiveness which counts largely from the Indian strain." Resembling him, she possessed the physical characteristics that most whites typically associated with Indians.

Despite claiming to be a "full-blooded" Pequot and being called the last of his tribe (as were so many others), Moses Dailey's identity was often mislabeled in official records, where he was recorded variously as Black, mulatto, colored, and white, as well as Indian. His claims of racial purity drew the ire of Sidney Rider, a local historian with a penchant for muckraking that filled the pages of his *Book Notes*, a weekly newsletter of literary gossip, criticisms of books, and local historical matters connected to Rhode Island, published from 1883 to 1916. In the August 28, 1915 issue, he responded to the account of Moses Dailey's life story that was reprinted in his obituary a week earlier. He questioned how Dailey could be a Pequot Indian, since "the Pequots were destroyed as a tribe nearly two hundred years before 'Moses' was born" in the assault of 1637, known as the Pequot War, "never to exist again," according to Rider. He did, however, acknowledge that a few had escaped and fled to the Niantics in the southwestern corner of Rhode Island, and that even fewer lived among the Narragansetts. He went on to state that Dailey had showed no knowledge of the six generations that "covered his descent" from seventeenth-century Pequots and that he did not have even the "slightest knowledge of his relatives back of his father." There were no family records kept (at least no conventional written genealogies), and marriages in those times, Rider argued, were constant between "negro slaves" and Indians. And besides, "Indians did not have three names, a first, a middle, and a family name" as Moses Perry Dailey did.[22]

Rider's indictments continued in the September 25, 1915, issue of *Book Notes*, where he persisted in ridiculing Dailey's Pequot ancestry and questioning his long-term ties to Providence and his claim that he had been a "nurse in the city for sixty years." Rider searched directories to track Moses Dailey's name and occupations. He observed, correctly, that Dailey was identified as colored in Providence marriage records, and that he and his wife (also colored) had a daughter listed as colored in city birth records. His parents, Benjamin West and Harriet, lived in Warwick and had "all American names," which, for Rider, raised further doubts about

Dailey's ancestry: "Is a Pequot Indian, whose mother is named 'Harriet,' a 'pure blood' after his Tribe had been wiped out of existence two hundred years, and born in Warwick?" If the name Harriet was American, then certainly the first and middle names of Moses Dailey's father were even more so, though Rider did not comment on them. Just why he singled out Dailey for vilification is unclear. Rider apparently knew David Heaton well and had patronized the jewelry store on Westminster Street where Heaton worked and that he later owned. To his knowledge, Heaton never had a "coach." Rider's suspicions touched on not only Moses Dailey's Pequot ancestry and employment history but his abilities as a nurse as well. Apparently, his concerns about Dailey's credibility, if not prejudice against him, ran deep. He reported that when Moses Dailey called on his ill mother, "she did not employ him."[23]

Whatever personal grudge Rider held against Moses Dailey may be incidental to his scathing criticisms about Dailey's Pequot ancestry. His remarks about marriages between Native Americans and African Americans, Christian names, multiple racial labels in documentary records, and about living in towns and cities reflect the criteria by which Euro-Americans in the nineteenth and early twentieth centuries evaluated tribal identity, and often enough still do today. The different labels used to describe Moses Dailey's racial identity should not be surprising, given that classifications used by U.S. Census takers varied greatly during the nineteenth and twentieth centuries. The decennial U.S. Census, as Nancy Shoemaker and others have noted, exposes shifts in the rise and fall of "mulattoes," a category that was dropped entirely by 1920.[24] The term "colored," used in federal and some state censuses as early as 1850, in birth, death, and marriage records, and colloquially to report an individual's race, generally lumped together all people of color, glossing over whether the person was African American, Native American, or both, or belonged to some other nonwhite racial category. Compounding the problem is that census enumerators and other official record keepers charged with the task of assigning an individual to a racial category often made subjective and hasty judgments, and those asked to identify themselves by race often made claims that were tempered by the political climate of the times or their perceptions of the particular logic of the moment. Enumerators often missed dwellings, households, and individuals. Adding to the confusion is that public records were sometimes edited by overwriting or by comments in the margins. In Nettie Dailey's original birth record, for example, her first name was not given and her race, as previously mentioned, was identified as colored. The name Jeanette was written in the blank space in a different hand and ink color "to agree with Family Records" on May 17, 1946. A few years later, on March 31, 1948, the term "colored" was crossed out under the category of race and "white" was added "to agree with Baptismal Record."[25]

That Rider did not "see" Moses Dailey's name in every city directory that he checked or find the word "nurse" consistently identifying his occupation over a sixty-year period were not adequate reasons for dismissing his account of his life in Providence, let alone his Pequot ancestry. Much like other Native people living in the city in the nineteenth and early twentieth centuries, Moses Dailey was not expected to be there and to share in modernity. To be urban and modern were conditions that Euro-Americans claimed solely as their own, to the exclusion of Indians. Yet, Moses Dailey was Native—a Pequot—and urban. That he was registered in listings of nurses in Providence directories suggests that the services he provided were widely available to all people of the city, regardless of the extent to which he incorporated his knowledge of the Native pharmacopeia into his healing practices.

Moses's aunt, Dorcas Dailey, whom he mentioned in his biographical account, also had ties to Providence. Born in Rhode Island about 1804, she lived in the Apponaug section of Warwick with other Daileys in a household she headed while working as a washerwoman.[26] She moved to Newport, Rhode Island, with her daughter Mercy and her daughter's husband, a sailor, in the 1870s and stayed there before returning to Warwick around the middle of the 1880s.[27] While living at Scott's Wharf, she was described as "one of the picturesque fixtures of Newport, as the maker and seller of Indian baskets," an occupation that official record keepers failed to mention. Both at Newport and at Narragansett Pier, another seaside resort that she might have frequented to sell her baskets, she would have been among the mostly anonymous Native people who participated in the summer tourist trade during the late nineteenth century.[28] She would have learned the techniques of basket construction and decoration from Pequot elders who brought this knowledge with them to Providence and Warwick, and who would also have instructed Moses about medicine. Her baskets, presumably woven in a decidedly Pequot style, would have had squared bases, wide wefts, monochromatic black design chains filled in with color and fringed with short lines, and other culturally distinctive traits.[29] She would have continued to make baskets that conformed to this style and imprint them with her own individuality, perhaps with some accommodations to labor- and time-saving devices and commercial tastes, and market them on Newport's wharves or at Narragansett Pier. Possessing knowledge of traditional Native practices—basketry and healing, respectively—Dorcas and Moses Dailey were able to adapt these skills as means of income without sacrificing either their indigeneity or their modernity.

As one of the basket makers whose presence was commonplace at some of Rhode Island's resort towns, Dorcas Dailey fulfilled Euro-American tourists' understandings of where Indians might be found, aside from on reservations or in Wild West shows. But Moses Dailey, who except for his visits to Rocky Point stayed close to his home on Federal Hill, where he was a recognizable and well-known figure, was an Indian who was out of place, despite his having resided there for about a half century. He had lived in the neighborhood for long enough that he would have known about the pine grove near Ridge Street; about the Woonasquatucket's clear water, sandy beaches, and good fishing; and about the dangerous railroad crossing near Dale Street that locals recalled as one of the worst in the city. Moses might even have caught a performance of P. T. Barnum's traveling Hippodrome show at Hazard's Lots, the open space off of Vinton, Asia, and America Streets, or watched local baseball and football teams play for championships and neighborhood bragging rights. But as a longtime resident of Federal Hill, Dailey would have also known that the meadows and swamps along Harris Avenue, where local boys settled their differences with bare fists, might be a place to avoid, or that he would not have been welcome at the San Souci Gardens between Atwells Avenue and Broadway, where the city's elites were entertained by Gilbert and Sullivan operettas on summer nights. He had other place-based stories to tell, some of which he chose to share with outsiders.

Other Pequots had also made their way from southeastern Connecticut to Federal Hill. Frederick H. Weeden (Pequot-Wampanoag) and his family lived on Courtland between Penn and Ring Streets during the first decade of the 1900s. Born in Griswold about 1869 to George and Susan (née Simons), he had moved to Providence from Cranston, Rhode Island soon after he married Mary F. Loquer in 1894.[30] By the turn of the century, he was renting a home at 54 Courtland Street that the couple shared with their two young children, Gladys and Frederick Jr.[31] His younger brother, Otis, who lived in a one-and-a-half-story, end-gable, clapboard cottage on Marshall Street a few blocks away, before relocating to Benedict Pond, arrived in the city about the same time.[32] That house is still standing today, which is remarkable given that such modest, single-family dwellings were readily torn down when the personal and familial experiences that—to use a cliché—"made a house a home" were overridden by interests of capital and market value. Although cottages were considered a poorer investment than two-family houses because, as John Ihlder noted in his 1916 study of Providence housing, the "initial costs of land, foundations, and roofs were nearly as great" and a nonresident owner would lose income if the tenant moved out, they were still the preferred type of housing.[33] Otis and Fred Weeden's brother Frank, who stayed in Cranston and worked for the New York, New Haven, and Hartford Railroad, had taken a mortgage on a single-family cottage by 1920. He lived in that house with his family for more than thirty years.[34]

Although Fred Weeden's house did not survive, an undated photograph of him has. It appears in a collage of Weeden family history made by Everett "Tall Oak" Weeden Jr., his grandnephew, in which Fred is shown wearing a suit coat and white shirt (fig. 24). His hair and mustache are neatly trimmed, and his dark eyes gaze into the distance. Although he is hatless, his manner of dress is similar to that of Moses Dailey in the photograph of him printed in the *Providence Daily Journal* in 1913, which suggests that the picture of Fred might date to around the time that he lived on Courtland Street. If so, he would have been between thirty and forty years old and working as a carpenter when it was taken. Soon after, the family left Courtland Street for East Providence, where Fred Weeden died fourteen years later. His obituary reports that the family Bible identified him as a fifth-generation descendant of Simeon Simon, George Washington's bodyguard, and as a grandson of King Philip. It also mentions that he was active in the affairs of the Narragansett Tribe and intertribal organizations, and served as a treasurer of the National Algonquin Indian Council.[35]

"Guardian of Their Persons and Estate": Indian Families on Mundane Streets

Hannah M. Hazard, one of Ben Thomas's daughters (chapters 3 and 5), who spent most of her life in Providence among people connected to her through blood and marriage, lived at the rear of 78 Vinton Street with her husband, Walter G. Hazard, a teamster, and their baby daughter in 1875. The couple had lived there from around the time that John P. Hazard, Walter's father, purchased the house and lot in the late 1860s. Hannah, who was born in Charlestown, Rhode Island, in 1852 and was married to man who was not an Indian, had visited the reservation occasionally before it was sold and was listed on the 1881 tribal roll.[36] Sarah E. Hazard (née Nichols), another tribal member, was married to Walter's older brother, John B. Hazard, and lived at the Vinton Street address from 1872 to the early 1890s.

Sarah and John, then a servant, had married in New Bedford, Massachusetts, in 1857 and were living in Providence with their infant son, Howard, on Federal Street by 1860.[37] Sarah's sister Olive, who was twelve years old, lived with John P. Hazard, his third wife, Abby, their nine-month old son, Leonard, and Walter, who was fifteen, at the same Federal Street address in 1860. Five years later, Priscilla Nichols, age fifty-seven, a Narragansett on the 1881 tribal roll, moved in with Sarah, John, and their son. In 1868 Sarah gave birth to a daughter named Min-

Fig. 24. Collage of Weeden family photographs and graphite drawing showing Frederick H. Weeden, taken from a larger work entitled *The Torch Still Burns*. Courtesy of the artist Tall Oak (Everett G. Weeden), Pequot-Wampanoag, Frederick Weeden's grandnephew.

nie. The elder Hazard, a teamster like his son Walter, died in 1871 at the age of sixty-eight, leaving the Vinton Street property and its contents to his youngest sons (John and Walter's half-brothers) Leonard and Rowland Hazard. In his will he named his eldest son, John B., the guardian of "their persons and estate." John B. and Sarah raised Leonard, who was the same age as their son Howard, and Rowland, who was a year younger, along with Minnie, in a household of extended kin that in 1875 included Hannah (Congdon) Nichols, Sarah's mother. Sarah and John continued to live at the Vinton Street address for about the next twenty years. After her husband died in 1899 Sarah and her children, by then adults, left Vinton Street, but not Federal Hill. They moved to 9 Tell Street closer to the pine grove over near Ridge Street, where they lived for a few years before moving to Cranston Street.[38] Hannah and Walter Hazard and their two children, both recognized as Narragansetts on the 1881 tribal roll (as was Hannah), moved from Vinton Street to the Upper South Providence homeland by the late 1870s, back to Vinton Street briefly, and later to the Benedict Pond neighborhood.

The family dynamics that led to one son's being appointed as guardian of his half-brothers and their estate and to another's move from the family compound are unknown. Despite unanswered questions, the inventory of John P. Hazard's estate provides a glimpse into the interior of the two-family, wood-framed house during the early 1870s and the material possessions that he had accumulated after years of driving wagons on the streets of the city's west side. Among them were a clock, a large chair, two bedsteads, two feather beds, a sea chest (a storage trunk for sailors that hints that he had been a mariner), four comforters, three blankets, forty-six yards of rag carpeting (made from old pieces of cloth that had been cut into strips, woven or braided, and then coiled and sewn together), six common chairs, two bureaus, and one wardrobe. There was also a refrigerator, a parlor table and a kitchen table, a cookstove, two rocking chairs, two small stands, a dozen plates, five platters, a glass dish, five goblets, six flat irons, nine looking glasses, a mortar and pestle, two pans and a measure, and a picture of the Lincoln family.[39] The inventory suggests that the Hazard home was a modest yet comfortable two-room living space. The first room was a sleeping and sitting area furnished with bedsteads covered with bedding, bureaus, chairs, a clock, and other furniture. The second was a kitchen equipped with some modern conveniences of late-nineteenth-century life such as the cookstove and refrigerator, as well as a kitchen table, cooking tools, dishes, and flatirons. Compared with Anstriss Nichols's home in Providence's Fox Point, the Hazards had little tableware, and they had no teaware or special accoutrements for entertaining guests. Nor was any of the furniture in the inventory described as mahogany. The furniture, however, regardless of what type of wood it was made from, defined the space thematically and would have been among the family's most cherished possessions. The refrigerator, cookstove, and the picture of the Lincolns, along with the clock and the looking glasses (mirrors)—symbols of time and self-awareness—comment on the embrace of modern consumerism and the elder John Hazard's stake in the American dream, though it cannot be assumed that all these items held the same meanings when they were purchased and when they were inventoried. Even without knowing how the looking glasses and the picture of President Lincoln's family were arranged, or the special histories attached to other household furnishings, these particular objects reflected identity more than others in the home. The photograph preserved a memory, but looking glasses provided onlookers with an image of their physical appearance and a glance of how they might look to others, as Rebecca Shrum notes.[40] Looking glasses that were permanent fixtures on the walls of a home, as they might have been at the Hazards, offered the members of this household of Native Americans and African Americans a sense of individual identity capable of eliciting an emotive experience that might not have been about racial difference, but about family connections and shared stories of complicated pasts. These glances of their own mirrored selves would have defied the simple categorization of the Hazards' identities found in public records, revealing resemblances that other observers might not have seen, but also providing clarity about a future secured through home ownership.

In addition to Hannah and Sarah Hazard, their children, and their relatives, there were other Narragansetts on Federal Hill. Charles H. Cone, Edward Cone's son (see chapters 1 and 5), lived at 31 Grove Street between Knight and Vinton Streets from the late 1860s to the mid-1880s, though his ties to the neighborhood can be traced back at least a decade before the late 1860s. Born in Providence in 1848, Charles, a teamster like his father, married Ann Elizabeth Banks, whose family had migrated to Providence from Wilmington, Delaware.[41] Their children were born on Grove Street—a daughter, Henrietta Francis, in December 1869, and a son, Frederick Henry, in June 1871—and were raised there.[42] Their names were recorded next to their father's on the 1881 Narragansett tribal list, as were those of Charles's sisters, Sarah and Mary, and other members of the Cone family who had been born in Providence and continued to lived there while maintaining connections to Narragansetts in Charlestown.[43]

Edward Noka lived on Federal Hill for many years before he enlisted in the Eleventh United States Colored Heavy Artillery in 1863. He is listed as "Edward Nokay" of Federal Hill in the separate section for colored persons in the 1844 city directory.[44] A decade and a half later, he was living at Weeden Street in the same neighborhood.[45] Described in military records as standing five feet ten inches tall with black hair and eyes and a mulatto complexion, he was mustered out of the Union Army in 1865 at the rank of corporal after serving in Louisiana and resumed civilian life in the neighborhood of Benedict and Duck Ponds, where he stayed until his death in 1887. Ida Bent, whose father was a Narragansett, as was she, lived with her mother and stepfather on Battey Street, also in the heart of Federal Hill, for a short time before the family moved to Mawney Street over near Long and Duck Ponds.[46]

Willis A. K. Ownsley (Wampanoag), whose ties to Providence extend to the late 1830s, was living in the home of Joseph Knowles, a printer by trade and an owner of the *Providence Daily Journal* and the publishing firm of Knowles & Anthony, at 43 Bradford Street on Federal Hill in 1865 and was employed as his coachman.[47] His wife Harriet's sister, Fannie Kendall, who was born in Griswold, Connecticut, in 1830, made her way to Federal Hill via Worcester and Fall River, Massachusetts, where she gave birth to her eldest children, Louisa and Franklin Edison (fig. 25). Her daughter, Albertina, was born on Atwells Avenue on November 12, 1859, about a year and a half after eighteen-month-old Franklin died of chronic bronchitis at 80 Knight Street.[48] A little over a year later, Fannie and her husband, William B. Kendall Jr., a barber from New York City, welcomed another daughter on Adams Street, a narrow lane between Vinton and Knight off of the south side of Atwells Avenue that seemingly ran nowhere.[49] The family later moved to Conduit Street near Broadway in Upper South Providence. Their son Stephen, named after Fannie's father, Stephen Congdon, was born there in December 1862.[50] William, who died from consumption in November at Spring Street, never got to see his second-born son, nor did the son have a chance to know his father.[51] Widowed when she was about thirty years old, Fannie stayed at the Conduit Street address with Louisa, Albertina, and Stephen at least until 1865.[52] She remained in Upper South Providence, raising her children as a single, working mother on Spring Street in the 1870s. When her daughters were nearly grown, she and Stephen, a sixteen-year-old coachman, moved in on West Hoyle with Harriet Ownsley, whose responsibilities in raising and supporting a family and heading a household were remarkably similar to Fannie's.[53]

Uncommon Labor: Hair Doctresses and Ladies' Hairdressers on "Indian Hill"

Susan Fenner, identified as Indian and as a "doctress" in the 1880 U.S. Census, specialized in hair restoration. She was born in Newport about 1815, and little is known about her Native ancestry, the circumstances that brought her to Providence, or the preparations she used for treating hair loss except for a passing mention that they were vegetable products. Susan was married to Manuel Fenner, a West Indian, who is listed in city directories as early 1838, when his name appears in the section for "colored persons."[54] From their home at 66 Atwells Avenue, where Manuel stabled horses and worked as a hostler and a farrier, styling himself as a veterinary surgeon, Susan sold her hair restoratives, scalp treatments,

Fig. 25. Fannie Kendall shown in an 1871 advertisement for a Spicers & Peckham Electra Cook stove. A copy of the image (without the water damage seen here), published by the Rhode Island Black Heritage Society in *Creative Survival* (1985), identifies her as Mrs. Kandell, a domestic who worked for a prominent white family in Providence. That original photograph, from the Rider Collection at the John Hay Library, Brown University, could not be located. Albumen print. Courtesy of the Rhode Island Historical Society.

and an ointment for treating piles.[55] Widowed in 1865, Susan stayed in business on Atwells Avenue, Federal Hill's bustling commercial strip, and then on Federal and Carpenter Streets into the late 1880s. Despite her advancing age and the challenges of remaining relevant and competitive in the marketplace, she lived and worked independently until February 8, 1893, when she entered Dexter Asylum.[56] She was hospitalized during her stay there, and she died three months later, at the age of eighty, from complications related to chronic suppuration owing to extensive damage to her knee joint resulting from an infection or possibly gangrene.[57] For much of her adult life, Susan Fenner engaged in a type of work that was generally considered unexpected for a Native American woman. As a specialization within the beauty industry, hair restoration allowed her to carve a niche in one of Providence's urban homelands by catering to the tonsorial needs and desires of her clients, and to introduce them to alternative treatments and hybrid concepts of beauty.[58]

The contours of Susan Fenner's life evoke those of Christiana Carteaux Bannister, née Babcock, a "hair doctress" known as Madame Carteaux, who was born about 1819 to an African American and Narragansett couple in the southwesterly corner of North Kingstown, Rhode Island, a section known locally as Dark Corners that everyone knew was Narragansett tribal land.[59] Christiana's genealogy is difficult to trace, similar to that of others with racially mixed ancestries who might have been more Native American than African American. There are no documents recording her birth or her parent's marriage that identify the names of her relatives on her mother's side. Yet her birth name, which appears in various reports, petitions, and other official records pertaining to the Narragansetts during the nineteenth century, and is frequently mentioned in *Narragansett Dawn*, points to a Native ancestry that is often overlooked. Other than the circumstances of her birth, nothing is known about her early life.

By her twenties Christiana was living in Boston, married to an older African American clothes dealer, and working as a milliner. By her thirties, she was running a hair salon in Boston and marketing her own line of hair- and skin-care products. She remarried in 1857. Her second husband, Edward M. Bannister, an African American from Canada, worked briefly for her as a hairdresser before devoting himself full-time to painting with her financial support.[60] While living in Boston, the couple was active in the abolitionist movement and the Histrionic Club, an African American theater group that rehearsed in a room above her hair salon. In an 1858 performance Christiana was cast as an American Indian "princess," one of many Indian roles that she would play in the club's shows.[61] In 1869 she moved to Providence, where she opened a hairdressing business a year later while still operating her Boston salon.

Federal Hill

Christiana Bannister and Susan Fenner, creators and purveyors of hair-treatment products, were entrepreneurial women of color who achieved different degrees of financial success. Fenner mostly made her living among the produce markets, pushcarts, and shops on Atwells Avenue, at an address she shared with her husband and the horses he looked after. Bannister's Providence salon was located in the city's upscale shopping district downtown, where it would have been patronized by fashionable women, many of them white, who would have flocked to her beauty shop for her treatments to improve the condition of their hair and complexion, and by men with concerns about hair loss.[62] Bannister and Fenner's businesses gave them an economic independence that many women were denied, though that independence did not sustain them as elderly widows.

After years of prosperity thanks to earnings from Christiana's business and Edward's success as a painter, the Bannisters were able to move from B Street in Upper South Providence to Cushing Street and then to Benevolent Street on Providence's east side, but they struggled financially as the end of the century approached. Christiana, the "stately figure who wore a purple dress walking on Benefit Street," went back to Boston, only to return again to Providence, where she and Edward settled on Wilson Street near Long Pond.[63] He died of heart failure during a service at the Elmwood Free Baptist Church at the west end of the city in 1901.[64] A year and a half later Christiana was admitted to the Home for Aged Colored Women on Transit Street in Fox Point, where impoverished women of color, most of whom had spent their lives working as domestic servants in white households, could be cared for during their later years. Ironically, Christiana had been a prominent donor and fund-raiser for the home and a member of its corporation. Lancaster writes that the secretary of the Home reported that Christiana "was in an excited, though exhausted state when she arrived, and in a few days became violently insane so that it was necessary to remove her."[65] She was transferred to the State Hospital for the Insane in Cranston, where she died three months later. A wake was held at the home of her niece, Melvenia Babcock, on Hope Street in Fox Point, and the funeral service was held at the church where her husband died. She was interred next to him in North Burial Ground, although, unlike her husband, she had no memorial to honor her accomplishments until a century later, when a bronze bust, modeled after a portrait of her painted by Edward, was placed in the Capitol Rotunda of the Rhode Island State House in 2002.[66] In the interim her nieces, Melvenia and Estelle, honored her life's work by continuing in the family trade.

Identified as Indian in the 1910 U.S. Census, Melvenia and Estelle Babcock worked as ladies' hairdressers on Knight Street at the southernmost end of Federal Hill. Their ties to Providence can be traced to 1850 (some years earlier than their ages in 1910 would suggest) when they were living with their father, John, a laborer and Christiana's brother, and their mother, Cornelia. In 1870 Estelle was living with Christiana and Edward in an extended household of Babcocks and Bannisters in Providence's eighth ward and did the housekeeping.[67] Melvenia is recorded as a resident of Nantucket in 1865 and 1880, when she is listed in the household of James and Rachel Williams (Rachel was her maternal aunt).[68] By the turn of the century, Melvenia, a coat maker, had taken up hairdressing in the tradition of a generation of Babcocks. A 1906 entry in the city directory gives her residence as 91 Hope Street and accounts of Christiana's funeral refer to that address, but Melvenia mostly lived at 381 Knight Street with Estelle in a house that they owned.[69] Estelle died in 1921, predeceasing her older sister by fifteen years.[70] She left Melvenia her savings accounts, spread among banks in Providence and the Boston area, and a little more than sixteen thousand dollars in cash.[71] Both single, they had shared the house on Knight Street and worked together since their fifties. They were buried in the same lot at Locust Grove Cemetery. As ladies' hairdressers running a small salon in the space of their home, their business did not attract well-off, stylish patrons, as Madame Carteaux's salon had, and it might not have been as lucrative. It was a local business and their clients would have been their neighbors on Federal Hill, much like Susan Fenner's probably were. The Babcock sisters provided a service that helped women of color to feel beautiful by boosting their self-esteem in a society in which they were often thought of as unattractive and worthless.⁷² Well into their later years—Estelle in her sixties or early seventies and Melvenia in her late eighties—they did the hair of the neighborhood's women. The profession and their entrepreneurship brought them financial independence and the means of home ownership. They allowed Melvenia, who lived her final years during the nadir of the Great Depression, to have an income and to hold onto the house on Knight Street when many of her neighbors were out of work and lost houses to foreclosure, and when local shopkeepers' storefronts were shuttered.

A Tent House at Pine Grove: Basket Makers at the Edge of Town

At the westerly edge of Federal Hill, the Providence, Hartford, and New Haven Railroad paralleled the Woonasquatucket's course, facilitating Native people's movement to and from the city much like the river long had. On either side of the railroad tracks and the river there were still vacant spaces even by the middle of the nineteenth century. Native people traveling to Providence, whether by rail, by canoe, on foot, on horseback, or by some combination of means, might have camped in these places before venturing into the inner city or to the waterfront to search for work or possibly a new home. Neither divided into lots nor crossed by streets laid out by town and, later, city ordinances, the open space along the railroad tracks and Woonasquatucket River was neutral territory right on the city's doorstep, where Native people entering the town might go unnoticed.⁷³ Although they could not be considered homeless, since they had come from somewhere and often had intentions of returning, their lack of conventional housing did not make them completely invisible to the city's white residents. Rather than being unseen, Indians' encampments and activities along a bend in the river or railroad tracks would have stood out on a colonized and increasingly urbanized landscape where their presence was not welcomed and played on the fears of whites.

The pine grove on Federal Hill might have been this sort of place. The Lowlings, a family of basket makers from Maine, are listed as living there in the 1865 Rhode Island Census (which refers to the neighborhood itself as Pine Grove), though no street number is given and the location does not appear on any maps. The names of nearby streets that recall natural features of the landscape, such as Grove Street, which ran west from Vinton Street toward the Providence, Hartford, and New Haven Railroad tracks, Valley Street, which followed the Woonasquatucket's sinuous course, and Ridge Street provide clues to its more precise location, as do descriptions in written sources and transcribed oral history. Annual reports of the Rhode Island Children's Friend Society and a memoir of Harriet Ware, its founder, indicate that the society occupied a building at the head of Ring Street, as does the 1865 Rhode Island Census. Located near the westerly end of Grove Street in the 1860s, the society's home was sited to take advantage of the location's natural amenities. The elevated setting gave children coming from extreme poverty and wretched conditions a place to live with full exposure to sunlight and a prospect of almost the whole city. Its spacious and fenced-in grounds provided ample space for recreation. What Ware called the "beautiful grove at Valley Falls," where the neighborhood's Irish boys and girls held parties on summer nights, as Federal Hill's residents later reminisced, offered a nearby place where the children could gather with their caretakers on summer days.[74] This pine grove was as appealing to the Lowlings as it was to the children at the home and neighborhood youth. The scents of the pines and the sounds of running water would have triggered memories of the Wabanaki homeland where they lived before moving to Providence and provided a semblance of home.[75]

It was here that they camped when they arrived in Providence about 1860, and where a Joseph "Loren," a basket maker, pitched a tent house that he shared with Francis, an Indian physician, Sarah, a basket maker, and two widows, Nancy and Sarah.[76] Unlike Wabanaki basket makers who pitched their tents at summer resorts along the Maine coast into the 1920s in an attempt to meet Euro-American tourists' stereotypical expectations that all Indians lived in "tepees," the Lorens might not have needed to make such a deliberate statement about their identity.[77] Their mode of housing, though temporary, would have been expedient and familiar. It was a part of a cultural understanding of home among Wabanaki people that Micah Pawling states was "not confined to a single place or bounded by walls or lines on a map" that they brought with them to Providence.[78]

The Lowlings at Pine Grove in the 1865 Rhode Island Census were Nancy, fifty-six; Frank N., forty; Newell, eighteen; Joseph, twenty-two; Sarah, thirty-three; Mary, nineteen; Susan Marley, three; and a one-year old whose surname was also Marley. All of them were born in Maine except Susan, who was born in Providence. But she was not the first member of the family to born in the city. An Elizabeth Loring had been born in Olneyville, located to the southwest of Pine Grove in the city's seventh ward, on April 4, 1860 to a Frank Loring and his wife, Mary. Frank, whose occupation is given as "Indian," was born in Portland, Maine, and his wife in Eastport, Maine.[79] The infant, identified as colored in the city's birth records, died of pneumonia at a location near Broadway in Olneyville on February 1, 1861, less than a year later. Similar to the inscription of her birth, her death record classifies her race as colored and her parentage as Indian.[80] The fact that her birth and death were noted at all in official records is unusual, given that migrant Native basket makers were the kinds of people who typically went unnoticed by municipal record keepers and history writers.

Members of the family sharing the surname continued to live in the vicinity of Federal Hill's Pine Grove through the 1860s. Nancy Lowling, a widow, who first appears in a Providence directory in 1860, resided at Tell near Courtland Street (later 27 Tell Street on city maps) from 1868 to 1875. William and Joseph Loren, basket makers, are recorded as living with her in the late 1860s to about 1870, though their relationship to her is not specified. On February 9, 1868 at the rear of 17 Penn Street, Andrew (a basket maker) and Sarah Loring, who were born in Perry, Maine, welcomed a baby girl they named Maria.[81] Besides these Lorings, other Native people from Maine's Wabanaki homeland traveled to Rhode Island in the nineteenth and early twentieth centuries. Some were also basket makers who came to find work in Providence or on its outskirts. Others picked potatoes and did farm work on the more rural edges of the city as they had done in Maine until small farms went out of business and their labor was no longer needed.[82] Daniel Steadman, a South Kingstown, Rhode Island, farmer and shoemaker, wrote in his diary on May 11, 1842 "that some Indians from Penabscot, the State of Main, pitched there [sic] tents in M. Chappell, Esqr.'s Lot and acted there [sic] Manuvers."[83] In 1860, a Penobscot troupe on a tour of Northeast towns and cities stopped in Warren on the west side of Narragansett Bay. Hardly considered an important urban hub, the area held special significance for Native people tracing connections to Wampanoags who had sought refuge in Wabanaki Country after King Philip's War. The visiting Penobscot camped on vacant lots on Franklin Street, just east of the railroad tracks, near the neck of land called Mount Hope. Mount Hope was the site of Sowams, the seventeenth-century ancestral village of the sachem Massasoit and his son Metacom. During their stay they sold bows and arrows, baskets, and other stereotypically Indian things from their tents during the daytime, and in the evening they entertained large audiences at the town's Armory Hall with their songs, dances, stories, and various other demonstrations of Indian customs.[84]

Among the Penobscots visiting Warren was Frank Loring, who may not have been a close relative of the Providence Lorings. Later known as Chief Big Thunder, he was from Old Town on Indian Island in Maine and claimed Wampanoag descent. According to Frank Speck, Frank Loring's father was of mixed Wampanoag-Portuguese ancestry and had married into the Penobscot tribe in the early nineteenth century.[85] His mother practiced traditional medicine in Boston and Portland.[86] After their deaths, Frank and his older sisters made and sold baskets to support themselves. But Big Thunder, whom Virginia Baker, a Rhode Island antiquarian, described in 1894 "as a man of considerable intelligence and a splendid specimen of his race, colossal in stature, of commanding presence and possessing features of statuesque beauty," was better known as a consummate showman than as a basket maker.[87] While still in his teens, he worked for P. T. Barnum, and later he put together a group of Penobscots who entertained and sold medicines and other Native-made products in towns and cities across the Northeast.[88] As a temporary sojourner in the Pokanoket homelands of Wampanoag Country, he visited ancestral places that he had learned about from Penobscot oral histories and from a rude chart of Sowams of unknown origins, given to him by the tribe but destroyed in a fire years before his visit.[89] Although his inability to produce the map cast a specter of doubt on his claims, the Wabanakis did make birchbark maps called *awikhiganak*. These maps were filled with pictographic messages about Native places and routes of travel along regional waterways and through a network of relations that communicated information about Native spaces. Conveying knowledge from one person or place to another, *awikhiganak* provided instructions about whatever place on the landscape a Wabanaki person might happen to be.[90]

Frank Loring's knowledge of storied places in Wampanoag Country that have become as much lore as fact should not be surprising, since even today many stories held dear by the residents of Indian Island, the Penobscot reservation, are about places beyond their immediate geography.[91] Those who continued to move across their traditional lands or who traveled farther took these stories with them as Frank Loring did. It was his knowledge of storied places that allowed him to connect with sites in a complicated ancestral history that until then he might have only heard about. Yet this place-based knowledge that gave him practical wisdom for navigating colonized indigenous spaces, guided him on a pathway of survivance, and offered a moral compass also failed sometimes to predict the locations of ancestral sites in Warren. Although some locations of storied places recorded in Penobscot narratives were not meant to be shared with outsiders, Frank Loring's missteps led some local antiquarians to question his credibility, as did later non-Native scholars who accused him of duplicity and being an impostor.[92]

Accounts of Frank Loring's visit to Warren have become part of town legend and have added to his reputation. Traveling widely and entertaining on numerous public stages in town after town, city after city, he made his imprint on the cultural space that Euro-Americans in the nineteenth century carved for Indians in their imaginations. He understood the importance of his Native identity and engaged in representational acts to earn a livelihood in ways that did not overtly imply a path of assimilation. He parlayed his Indianness to survive when the erosion of the Penobscots' land base and incursions by white-owned timber companies changed the ecology in ways that made it increasingly difficult to sustain their traditional way of life.

Loring's off-stage behavior when he was on the traveling circuit remains elusive. There is no written information that provides insights into how he might have renewed his ties with Wampanoags who might have visited his encampment near the railroad tracks. Nor is there a record of what this gifted story-teller might have shared with them about Indian Island, his family's struggles, or his travels, and in turn, what stories they would have told him. Their tales might not have been as entertaining—though they too might not have been above hyperbole. They were, after all, family. More significantly, they shared a survivor mentality that allowed them to creatively hold onto their indigenous heritage despite any cultural differences and pressures they faced in nineteenth-century New England. Records are silent about whether Frank Loring returned to Mount Hope after his visit in the summer of 1860. According to most accounts, he resumed life on the road where he continued entertaining and selling Indian crafts until he permanently resettled on Indian Island in 1889.

The Providence Lorings, though not anonymous, did not have the celebrity of Frank Loring. Their names might not have had the same historical resonance as his among Wabanaki and Wampanoag people or whites who had met him, heard about him, or attended his performances. They shared a surname and the urgency of individual and cultural survival, but they had different life courses. Theirs are more difficult to write about because they did not tell their stories to local history writers and, like the majority of Native people, they did not pen their own biographies. Their names appear only sporadically in censuses, vital statistics, city directories, judicial documents, and military records. Documentary evidence of births, deaths, and marriages does not exist for all family members with the surname in its various spellings known to have been in Providence in the 1860s. Information about where they lived while in Providence or before moving to the city is even scantier, and where they sold their baskets or found work is unknown. They were "the kinds of people who rarely appear in written history, except, and occasionally, as statistics," as O'Connell writes, and whose lives for the most part went unnoticed, uncounted, and undervalued in urban histories.[93]

Whether Providence was the Lorings' intended destination or a convenient stop in an itinerant family's journey is uncertain. Regardless of the route that they took or the means by which they traveled, they opted to stay at least temporarily. Here they made their homes, some of them for about a decade and a half, and had children. Basket making provided them a means of survival that came with assurances from their parents and grandparents that if they could weave, they would never go hungry.[94] If they could not find wage-paying jobs to feed themselves and their children, then they could always make baskets for their livelihood. In preparing for their economic venture, the Lorings would have made a supply of baskets to bring with them and would have carried these baskets on their backs like so many other basket vendors who trudged from town to town in the hope of finding buyers. If business was good, they might have had to replenish their stock by making more baskets at stops along the way from supplies that they had packed or collected en route, or on return trips to Maine, before resuming their journey to a new home that could be anywhere on the landscape where Wabanaki families camped, gathered, and departed—even far from their reservations and traditional homelands.[95] At their new home in Providence, the Lorings might have continued to make baskets using practices that were an expression of both their identity and their sense of what constituted home, possibly from materials gathered from different locales around city or that visiting relatives brought to them.[96]

Among Wabanakis and other Northeast Native people, making baskets was a household endeavor that involved men, women, and children. For woodsplint baskets, men cut down trees, preferably black or brown ash, and split them into logs and then strips that were pounded into the splints that basket makers, mostly women, wove into inexpensive and lightweight containers suitable for use in farming, fishing, and shipping.[97] But by the 1860s the Lorings, like other Wabanaki basket makers, may have also been weaving smaller, decorated woodsplint baskets to accommodate Euro-American tastes for baskets that could be used in their homes.[98] Some Wabanakis also made and marketed baskets from sweetgrass that they collected from saltwater marshes, where it grew in abundance, or incorporated its fibers into their ash-splint basketry. Deriving its common name from the distinctive scent that lingers long after the hanks have been harvested, combed, and trimmed, sweetgrass figures prominently in the Passamaquoddy legends "repeated through countless generations as sentimental fingers move gracefully on baskets," according to Joseph A. Nicholas, a tribal elder and basket maker.[99] These stories, as well as the texture, scent, and gentle sound of sweetgrass baskets, even those sold to non-Native tourists, brought forth memories of home and belonging, wherever home might be and whatever season it was.

When the Lorings appeared in Providence records, the opportunities for securing much-needed income from selling baskets might have not lived up to expectations they had harbored when they embarked on their travels. Sweetgrass (*Hierchloe odorata*) was available in swampy areas in and around the city from the 1860s to the early 1900s, as indicated by specimens in the Brown University Herbarium.[100] Yet though sweetgrass was apparently abundant, Trudie Lamb Richmond, a Schaghticoke elder, writes that the availability of ash in her western Connecticut homeland had declined by the mid-eighteenth century because Euro-American settler colonists had cut the forests for timber and firewood, forcing her ancestors to travel farther from their settlements to obtain those raw materials for their basket making or substitute other species of wood.[101] Although it is unlikely that the Lorings harvested ash or other trees in Providence when their stores of ash-splint baskets or splints had dwindled and returning to their Wabanaki homeland to replenish supplies was not a convenient option, they might have heeded their ancestors' advice and applied their woodworking skills to mending baskets, making brooms or scrubs, and bottoming chairs for income. They had after all become adept at holding onto parts of their cultural heritage that would enable them to survive while confronting the ongoing demands and challenges of settler colonialism.

Stereotypical "Indian work" such as basket making, other wood-weaving crafts, and medicine were not the only ways that the Lorings could eke out a living. On May 28, 1864 Newell "Loring," a Providence resident, appears among the Rhode Islanders who registered as volunteers for the Union Army during the Civil War. Other Native Americans also helped fight the war on either side, on sea or as "grunts" in the trenches or as commissioned and noncommissioned officers.[102] Their numbers are difficult to ascertain, especially for the Northeast, where many lived in smaller, off-reservation communities or among rural and urban white neighbors. Estimates are assumed to be especially unreliable for Native people who had migrated to cities, since they were considered transient and undocumented. Their motivations for enlisting are difficult to assess because they rarely left dairies or letters, except for those few who were literate and wrote down their thoughts about their service. Arguably, they might have been caught up in the surge of patriotism that swept through New England after the fall of Fort Sumter in 1861, generally recognized as the war's first battle, or have been following in the footsteps of family members and neighbors. Some might have seen wartime service as a way to gain income from the enlistment bounties offered by towns, states, and the federal government to fill their quotas; from individuals who sought to pay substitutes to fight for them; or from regular soldiers' pay and pensions.[103] Yet their reasons for going to war might have been as simple and as complicated as wanting to break away from the everyday routines of their lives. Not least, the anguish and loss they felt in being told that the land was no longer theirs would have been motivation enough for asserting that they too were Americans, the first and lasting ones, to paraphrase Jean O'Brien, despite official records and popular discourse questioning and ignoring their identity as "Indian," let alone as members of particular tribal communities.[104]

Newell "Lowling" was not one of the undocumented Native American migrants who came to Providence or other New England towns and cities to find work or sell baskets, though there is much about his life that is left unsaid in public records. He appears in the register of Rhode Island volunteers for the Civil War as having enlisted in Company M of

Rhode Island's Third Cavalry Regiment on May 28, 1864 at the rank of private. He deserted on August 13, 1865 in Homer, Louisiana. That he was in the cavalry, rather than the Fourteenth Rhode Island Heavy Artillery Regiment for Black and "colored" volunteers, suggests that he passed as white.[105] This perception of his racial identity differs from how he and other Lowlings were racially classified in the 1865 Rhode Island Census and in Providence records. The long history of marriages between Wabanaki people, and particularly those with the Loring surname, and Europeans of French and Irish descent that Frank Speck comments on in his Penobscot ethnography could explain why Newell Loren, whose given name is a family name of Malecite extraction, did not appear to be indigenous.[106] Yet aside from a history of intermarriage, his racial identification in the military should not be surprising, given it was made apart from his family members, whom house-to-house census takers typically lumped together in the same racial category even if they did not have the same skin color.[107] Regardless of how his race was labeled, Newell "Lorren" left Louisiana several months after the war ended and presumably made his way back to Wabanaki Country—though surviving records are silent about whether his homeward journey went through Providence.[108]

Thomas Loring, the son of Joseph and Nancy Loring, was born in Eastport, Maine, about 1849. He enlisted in the Union Army at Providence as a private in Company G of the Rhode Island Second Regiment of volunteers on December 15, 1864, and was mustered out on January 3, 1865. In July 1865 he was discharged for disability after spending three months in a general hospital.[109] He returned to Providence, where he would face tragedies that would prove to be even more difficult than those he had encountered during his service. He found work as a laborer, but his health, along with the uncertainty and short-term nature the work, limited the prospects for job security. In October 1868 he was convicted of burglary for having broken into and entered the home of William S. Johnson at Carpenter Street on Federal Hill at about eleven o'clock on the evening of the previous March 11 with the intention of stealing "goods and chattels," according to court records. The stolen items were five silver tablespoons, valued at thirty dollars; six silver teaspoons (eighteen dollars); a dozen silver tea knives (ten dollars); four silver forks (twenty dollars); and a silver butter knife worth three dollars. Besides the silverware, he was also accused of taking several pieces of jewelry: a gold watch, a pair of sleeve buttons, and a breast pin, valued at fifty, twenty-five, and twelve dollars, respectively. The account of the case in the Rhode Island Supreme Court records states that Thomas Loring was armed when he forcibly entered the house. He pleaded not guilty before the Court of Common Pleas, but because of the nature of the crime the case was referred to the state's Supreme Court.[110] A burglary committed at night was considered a capital offense under Rhode Island law until 1844, when the General Assembly abolished the death penalty for all crimes except murder and arson. Having survived the war and escaped execution for the crime charged against him in the indictment, Thomas Loring was sentenced to the Rhode Island State Prison for a term of five years. As fate would have it, his life as a veteran and a convict would be short-lived. Described as colored, single, and a basket maker, he died of consumption in the state prison in Providence on October 19, 1869, less than a year after being sentenced.[111] He was only twenty years old.

From what is known about Thomas Loring's life from documents, one could suppose that his troubles with the law were mostly the result of limited economic opportunities, transiency, and prejudice. But to suggest that his short life-course was invariably scripted or that the prospects for other basket makers from Wabanaki or other indigenous communities who migrated to New England's cities were for the most part predictable would be misleading. Such expectations are constitutive of opinions about the marginality of Native basket makers and the disorderliness of their households in nineteenth century Euro-American society. They are created by malice and prejudice that deny Native people their individuality both as human beings *and* as basket makers with different abilities, technological vocabularies, and personal styles and that serve to reproduce asymmetrical social, economic, political, and legal relations. Military service interrupted Thomas Loring's basket making. After being discharged he might have tried his hand at it again or done other "Indian work," but might have also taken whatever jobs he could find and was capable of doing. Why he burglarized William Johnson's home, the felony he was accused, tried, and found guilty of, can only be guessed. It might have been a random act spurred by sheer desperation or by mounting frustration over begging for work and haggling with consumers over and then transferring ownership of baskets that had more than mere economic value.

Johnson's middle-class affluence made him a likely target. He was the son of Oliver Johnson, who opened a successful drug company on Weybosset Street in Providence's downtown business district with a partner in 1833. As with most businesses of its kind, Oliver Johnson & Company sold a broad range of goods from prepared medicines to chemicals and supplies used by chemists and manufacturers. Two partners and less than ten years later, the elder Johnson went out on his own and moved his business to Market Street and then Exchange Street, where it occupied two buildings. William joined the firm in 1852. By 1865, the business expanded into manufacturing and distributing its own brand of colored and white lead-based paints. The new venture that capitalized on the company's reputation as one of Providence's leading businesses was so successful that a five-story factory building was constructed to accommodate production.[112] With three large stores, each having four floors and a basement, Oliver Johnson & Company operated at a far different scale and with different profit margins than the business of Wabanaki basket makers. Both responded to the demands of the capitalist economy, but their enterprises could not have been any more different.

The same was true of their life experiences. When Joseph Loring pitched a tent house near the Woonasquatucket River for himself and his family, William Johnson was living in a large three-story, gable-roofed Greek Revival-style building at 40 Broadway, at the opposite end of Federal Hill, with his wife and children, parents, and a servant.[113] He later moved to Carpenter Street, taking his wife, daughter, son, and servant with him. The Lorings moved from their tent at Pine Grove to a home on Tell Street that did not have a street number. The Tell Street home would not have been as comfortable as the wood-framed dwelling where William

Johnson lived, and it was not equipped with silver tableware for serving family dinners and hosting teas. Unlike William Johnson, Thomas Loring did not own a gold watch, sleeve buttons worth twenty-five dollars, or a twelve-dollar breast pin. Although Loring's motives were unspoken and whether he had any prior contact with Johnson is unknown, the possibility of unpaid wages, the loss of a job, or even a broken promise for an order of baskets or scrubs for the Johnson's What Cheer Paint Works and Drug Depot might have been the immediate cause of the burglary. If the allegations that Loring denied were true, he might have stolen these items not because of any personal desire to possess refined material goods, but for the necessities that they could buy.

Ironically, the name attached to the Johnson's paint business, "What Cheer," was the informal English greeting that Narragansett Indians allegedly used in greeting Roger Williams and his companions when they arrived in Providence in 1636. The phrase, the equivalent of asking how they were or what news their "*netop*" or friend brought, is the city's motto and has been attached to myriad local businesses, streets, and a Masonic lodge, as well as a town in Iowa and a California historical landmark. Repeated many times in naming practices, this iconic greeting from Providence's story of its settler colonial origins was not in all likelihood the one that the Lorings heard when they arrived at Pine Grove or when they encountered passersby on the city's streets as they peddled their baskets or looked for work. Nor was it the message that would have echoed in Thomas Loring's ears when the judge announced his sentence of five years of hard labor.

Nancy Loring would outlive her son. She would continue reside on Tell Street near Pine Grove where the family had settled in the early 1860s. Their Tell Street addresses, initially described in relation to the nearest cross street, would eventually be numbered as more buildings were constructed on Federal Hill. Consecutive numbering made buildings more spatially legible, enabling census takers, city planners, tax collectors, constables, and police officers to find people more easily. Nancy Loring's last address of record in a Providence directory was 27 Tell Street.[114] What became of her and other members of the family after 1875 is uncertain.

They might have left Providence for another northeastern city or they might have moved back to Maine. There is no archival trace of them in city records or federal censuses other than what I have been able to find and piece together.

Uncertainties about their continuing ties to Providence also surround their baskets and the axes, clamps, knives, gauges, blocks (or molds), and unused splints that Nancy might have stored for safekeeping in the house on Tell Street. Unfortunately, many Indian baskets that wind up in local museums have only vague documentation of their provenience. Some might be attributed to a tribal community or linked to a collector. Only rarely is a maker identified. Tools used in the various stages of production are hardly ever saved or collected. Notable exceptions are basket blocks incised with the names and initials of their owners. Yet for the Wabanakis, their baskets, as well as the plants and tools used in their production, were not merely part of an object record; they had deeper cultural significance that embodied sacred traditions, home, and family and personal histories. Designs sometimes carved into the handles of gauges evoked traditional ecological knowledge, such as the images of sweetgrass on gauges that Frank Speck collected from Old Town in the early 1900s, now at the Peabody Essex Museum in Salem, Massachusetts. Dyes used to decorate fancy baskets were derived from plants also used for healing and in other dimensions of Wabanaki life. The initials and names sometimes etched onto wooden blocks and gauges comment on how closely makers identified with their baskets at all steps in the manufacturing process, not just on ownership, while other markings on gauge handles might record a basket maker's accomplishments.[115]

In *Where Lightning Strikes*, Peter Nabokov, an anthropologist who lived on Indian Island for three months in the 1970s, mentions that some homes had storerooms from earlier times, "when skilled hands left an earthy sort of sanctity behind them." The garret of the 100-year-old house in which he rented a room had one of these storerooms, which his landlord said was off-limits. But on an afternoon when he was alone in the house, he pushed on the door of the closed-off room and when "the swollen frame gave way," he entered a space filled with the "scatter of detritus and implements" left by his landlord's grandmother, a master basket maker. From his description, the room still "smelled cool and woody," and the floor was "padded with curled shavings." There were clamps for holding ash withes, the makings of an ash-splint pack basket, hand gauges, balls of the inner bark of basswood, rolls of white birch bark, strips of lightweight brown ash, and sections of white ash for making basket rims and the frames of snowshoes. In the room's dark corners there were dried roots and berries for painting baskets, pieces of wood for their handles, and needlework paraphernalia. It was a rare, illicit glimpse into a space within an ordinary two-story wood-frame house in which the sacred and the vernacular were not distinguishable. Nabokov retraced his steps and closed the door, and he writes nothing further about the incident—other than reporting that he did not touch anything while in the room. He continued to live in the house, seemingly without reprimand. But when he returned home one day, toward the end of his stay, his landlord advised him to remain in his room for his own good. On his morning rounds the next day with a respected teacher, he visited an elder who told him that the "Little People" of Penobscot legend had "come out from them trees" at the edge of the ball field. They had emerged from the shadows of the landscape that they shared with the Penobscots, rattling the nerves of those in the community who saw, heard, or tried to approach them, and eliciting cries and drumming, which had awakened Nabokov in the night. For reasons unknown, these spirit-beings, "beckoned from their leafy bower" by tobacco offerings, had decided to pay a visit.[116]

What, if any, basket-making "detritus and implements" Nancy Loring might have put away for safekeeping in a room, closet, or cubbyhole at her Tell Street address can only be guessed. Unlike the Penobscot woman's materials, Loring's baskets and tools and those of other family members might not have been left behind as ghostly reminders of their skills and time-honored traditions. There were no Lorings in Providence after 1875 to take on the role of caretaker to safeguard the spirit of their basket making. When they disappeared from municipal records, they took along their stories of how basket making helped them survive. When they presumably returned to their ancestral Passamaquoddy homeland, the material evidence of their basket making might possibly have been enshrined in the home of a family member as a testament to them and their baskets, to the hardships they endured in their quest for opportunity, and most of all to their survivance.

Few Euro-Americans who referred to Federal Hill as Indian Hill were aware that Native people were still living on this "the hill above the river" between the ancient waters during the nineteenth and early twentieth centuries. It was not a specific "Indian" place-name. Rather, the term only vaguely acknowledged an indigenous presence thought to have once existed in this part of Providence. In a city filled with enduring Native place-names such as Mashapaug, Weybosset, and Woonasquatucket, the absence of Nocabulabet in Providence's geographical lexicon is a glaring omission that makes it difficult to imagine this locale as a Native landscape long before urban development. Although the persistence of an Indian place-name derived from transcriptions of local Algonquian words does not guarantee the possibility of comprehending indigenous geographies, the indistinct name "Indian Hill" relegates the Native people who lived there long ago to a hazy history in which their lives and experiences are undervalued, much like those of Native people who continued to inhabit this "hill above the river" in later centuries.

Native residents migrated to Federal Hill from Narragansett, Pequot, Wampanoag, and Wabanaki homelands to find work and build better lives for themselves and their families, many decades before new waves of European immigrants arrived in Providence around the turn of the twentieth century. Native men worked mostly as teamsters or private coachmen. Fred Weeden was a self-employed carpenter and Moses Dailey was a practical nurse. Native women typically stayed at home and kept house. Yet Susan Fenner and the Babcock sisters engaged in what was considered uncommon labor for women of color and owned businesses. And the Lorings hoped to find buyers for their baskets among people visiting the pine grove, among passersby on Providence's bustling sidewalks, or at market spaces along Atwells Avenue or Valley Street

Federal Hill   275

lined with the pushcarts of all sorts of vendors and small shops with goods overflowing onto the street.

On an urban landscape increasing crowded with Irish and then with Italian immigrants, Native Americans living on Federal Hill, like those in Providence's other neighborhoods, were identified as colored, Black, mulatto, white, and sometimes even Indian, though hardly ever by their tribal name—at least not in censuses and other city records. Frequently misidentified in public documents and unrecognized in the neighborhood, they lived on streets that became tightly packed with three-deckers and tenements constructed at the backs of undersized lots. Frontage offered open space that compensated for cramped one- or two-room living quarters, even though it typically had to be shared with ash bins, fifty-gallon drums filled with trash, uncontained litter, privies with tottering shelters and overflowing vaults, and rats.[117]

Nocabulabet had become an urban homeland that had been progressively encroached and built upon. Native people who were born or had lived there from their youth would have seen their children and family members die or move away and next-door houses and adjacent flats pass into the hands of new and ethnically diverse neighbors. The multifamily tenement at 31 Grove Street where Charles Cone lived in 1880 was also where Cesare Facchini, an Italian tailor, his wife, Isabelle, and their two young daughters shared an apartment with Thomas and Catherine Prophet and a boarder.[118] The Prophets, Isabelle's parents, were Narragansetts and related to the Prophets of Warwick (and presumably to others in Providence with that surname), and like her, they were classified as "Black" by the U.S. Census taker. Over on Tell Street, not far from where the Lorings set up their tent house, most of Sarah Hazard's neighbors in 1900 were born in Ireland or were first-generation Irish Americans.

Federal Hill's Native people would have noticed that stacking houses two deep on lots reduced the light between buildings and the extramural area available to their residents. As space on individual houses' lots became more limited because of overbuilding, undaunted Italian immigrants carved out gardens for their vegetables and flowers on the steep hillside where Ridge Street dropped off toward the Providence-Hartford-

New Haven railroad tracks and the Woonasquatucket River Valley. These were the very same terraces where Native women would have planted fields of corn, squash, and beans generations ago. They would have also noticed that some houses in the neighborhood had for-rent signs or were deserted, as Shoo Fly Village was by the early 1900s. Such abandoned houses might have become shelters for the homeless or hangouts for neighborhood youth. But for Native families in the neighborhood, who sometimes struggled to afford everyday necessities after their rent was due, the derelict structures might also have been a source of firewood or of recyclable materials for their own home repairs or for sale or barter, rather than the eyesores and public nuisances that reformers saw and wanted to tear down and replace with new construction.[119]

Native people on the Hill also would have known that the philanthropic organizations established in the early twentieth century to provide services for the neighborhood's immigrants were not concerned with addressing their adjustments to urban life. The Federal Hill House on Atwells Avenue and, before that, the Sprague House, were where Italians, not Indians, were taught good citizenship and middle-class American ways of life.[120] These lessons, intended to eradicate poverty and moral degradation, had been preached to and imposed upon Native people before the turn of century. As early as the seventeenth century, they had been taught what to wear, what to plant, what kinds of houses to build, and how to pray in order to become "civilized" in praying towns established by Puritan missionaries. Similar to Italian immigrant women at settlement houses, Native girls in residential schools were taught how to sew, mend, darn, scrub, and keep house, about what to cook, how to fold napkins and arrange cutlery, and about personal hygiene such as brushing their teeth to improve themselves. The majority of Native people resented programs that taught their women middle-class domesticity and their men work habits designed to eliminate idleness and keep them off the streets and out of trouble, and intended to mold both into ideal American citizens. But they did not completely reject the lessons of their white instructors. They took what could be useful as they adjusted to modernity and city life, while holding onto their cultural practices and tucking parts away for safekeeping. Yet for New England's Native people who had lost their land base or saw it rapidly dwindling in front of their eyes, resistance was complicated. It did not necessarily mean a steadfast commitment to return to or stay near remaining ancestral lands, given that retreat was not always feasible. Rather, it could entail becoming rooted in an urban landscape and reconciling their cultural heritage with the challenges of city living.

However wary of the city they might have become, they knew that they could depend on family and other Native people, not Federal Hill's settlement houses, to get through rough times. This would have been the case for many Native people in Northeast cities around the turn of the century living in small pockets within neighborhoods of the working poor typically characterized as ethnically homogenous Irish or Italian. Other Natives, often equally poor, if not poorer, would have provided assistance to those who needed it. They would have lent a hand as the self-employed waited for business to pick up, the unemployed searched for jobs, and veterans and their widows tried to hold on as their pension applications were being processed through yards of bureaucratic red tape. Caring for the poor was expected within Native communities and would have been reciprocated in kind or in turn. Existing records do not comment about whether the Lorings' baskets, Moses Dailey's nursing skills, Susan Fenner's cures for thinning hair and piles, or the Babcocks hairdressing services might have been provided to other Native people in the neighborhood as gifts in exchange for kindness shown or as gestures of goodwill. Nor have I been able to find evidence that other Native people on Federal Hill routinely incorporated traditional skills into their daily lives to make baskets, remedies, or beadwork for family and friends when their household chores or work outside their homes was done. They would have probably agreed with an elderly Mohawk or Iroquois woman living in a tenement on New York's lower west side who told Jacob Riis, a social reformer and journalist that "it is no disgrace to be poor, but it is sometimes a great inconvenience" when he photographed her weaving mats in her attic room with scarcely any food and an empty tobacco pouch on Christmas Day, 1897. Widowed and far from her natal home, she had recently brought a bundle elaborately wrapped in a blue cheese-cloth containing "a lot of little garments which she had made out of the remnants of blankets and cloth of her own from a younger and better day" to a friend who Riis guessed had helped her over a difficult spot or even paid her rent. Yet she only said that the gift was "for those who are poorer than myself."[121]

Few of the houses where Cones, Hazards, and others once lived on Federal Hill are still standing. Walking down Grove, Vinton, Courtland, Knight, Battey, and other streets north of Broadway to Atwells Avenue or to the south, stories about how the neighborhood has changed—how the Italians have fled, the pushcarts have disappeared, and tenements have morphed into empty lots—resonate loudly with me.[122] None of these stories express regret for the Native people who left "the Hill" or for most of their houses having been torn down. The houses that still remain often have been altered, sometimes beyond recognition, making streetscapes of the late nineteenth and early twentieth centuries difficult to envision. Yet the house at 118 Vinton, a two-and-a-half-story mansard-roofed double house with gable dormers, paired windows, and bracketed trim over the double entry probably looks much like it did during the 1880s when the Hazards lived there, except for the asphalt shingles. South of Broadway, the exterior of Otis Weeden's cottage at 9 Marshall Street has a modern hood over the entry, a storm door, and a wrought-iron banister and fence of recent vintage, yet it seems to be relatively well preserved. Moses Dailey's two-and-a-half-story Greek Revival residence at 163 Broadway, where he lived during the 1860s, is camouflaged by aluminum siding and a projecting one-story brick storefront. What the house looked like when he lived there can only be discerned with a critical eye willing to look past these alterations.

    The houses where Native people lived on Federal Hill do not have plaques identifying them as sites of indigenous history. Even the structures on Federal Hill that are on the National Register of Historic Places are listed only by their addresses and not the people who lived there, though the criteria for eligibility state that a property may qualify not only because of its architecture, but also because of its associations with a significant person or an important event in national, regional, or local history. The absence of signage recognizing that Native places persisted on Federal Hill into the nineteenth and early twentieth centuries reflects the larger problem of separating Native history and urban history. This separation is as much a function of the creation of historic districts as it is of the politics of representation shaping the official records of urban dwellers, the selectivity of memories of place filling popular history, and transformations to the built environment that target the homes of the marginalized. Comprehending the presence of Native people on Nocabulabet requires more than unearthing archaeological evidence about where they hunted, fished, collected, planted their cornfields, and gathered for trade and ceremony in the deep past. As important as these taskscapes and memory-making and memory-keeping places are for understanding Nocabulabet and its environs as a socially and culturally constructed landscape unimagined by Euro-Americans, they only tell an abridged version of its story. How its spaces were "dispossessed, expropriated, and transformed" represents yet another chapter, as Coll Thrush remarks in reference to Seattle, whose own urban story displaced indigenous people, territories, and histories.[123] Equally valuable and much less known are the stories of the Native people of Nocabulabet during the recent past. Drawn into Providence's orbit, they witnessed, resisted, and contributed to the transformation of this Native place that they might have known only as Federal Hill—unaware of or unconvinced by urban reformers who called the neighborhood one of the worst in the city.[124]

Fig. 26. Hipses Rock, the fabled marker of Providence lands, located off Morgan Avenue, ca. 1890. Courtesy of the Johnston Historical Society.

Johnston   7

Homeland at the Borderlands, Powwows, and Urban Mythscapes

Johnston and its natural landforms have long been intricately tied to Providence's history, as have its Native people. On the town's eastern side, Neutaconkanut Hill was identified in written records in 1637 as the northwesterly boundary of lands that Canonicus and Miantonomo granted to Roger Williams for use shortly after he arrived. Later transactions aimed at defining the extent of Providence's geography less ambiguously refer to Hipses Rock, a large isolated boulder at the westernmost foot of the hill, as the topographic marker of its northwestern border. In 1759 Rhode Island's General Assembly approved a petition by the residents of the borderland to be incorporated as a separate administrative entity from Providence because many did not want to travel that far to attend town meetings.[1] But not all the inhabitants considered travel to the city an inconvenience. Native people had been making the journey to the head of Narragansett Bay long before European settler colonists had taken possession of the land, farmed, and established mill villages. The Woonasquatucket River that fixes the town's eastern edge, meandering a southerly course past Federal Hill and through downtown Providence, was a well-traveled route—much like turnpikes, railroads, and trolley-car lines during the nineteenth century. Johnston's Native people and places are woven into its ancient and early colonial geographies as well as its continuing spatial and social order, and they are part of the conversation about its urban homelands.

Rock Stories of an Urban Borderland

Neutaconkanut Hill, the terminus of a pre-glacial hilly upland dividing the Woonasquatucket and Pocasset River Valleys, commands a magnificent panorama of Providence and its environs. Its rock formations have been compared to sentinels watching over the Native homelands that extend as far as Narragansett Bay.[2] Its topography is rugged and irregular with deep ravines, outcrops, and natural springs near its peak that feed brooks and swampy wetlands. Around the turn of the twentieth century, Frank L. Thornton, an enterprising townsperson, praised the purity of the springs' water, claiming that it was more healthful than the water from Providence's watersheds. Citing public health officials' warnings that the Pawtuxet River that provided the city with drinking water was a receptacle of the same kinds of pollutants — "chemicals, dye-stuffs, mineral and vegetable poisons, night-soil, and refuse filth"—found in the Cove Basin and linked to cholera and typhoid outbreaks, he pitched the water from Neutaconkanut Hill's springs as "palatable, wholesome, free from objections, and better than any now offered the public." Marketed under the brand name "Highland Spring," Thornton promised to deliver the water in bottles, jugs, or barrels, or in bulk to meet the weekly or daily demands of a limited number of consumers.[3]

For Native people, Neutaconkanut Hill is more than a place associated with settler colonists' land claims and business ventures or a hideaway for stolen cars, unwanted tires, and illicit activities. At the urging of a neighborhood group known as the Neutaconkanut Hill Conservancy, an effort has been under way since 2005 to discourage misuse and restore the trails created by the WPA in the 1930s. With a $50,000 Rhode Island Department of Environmental Management grant, in 2006 the Providence Parks Department hired a small crew and, with hundreds of volunteers, cleared the debris left by human hands and decades of unchecked vegetation to make the summit more accessible. But long before it became an urban park, this imposing pinnacle would have given Native people an unblocked view of ancestral homelands reaching as far as Narragansett Bay. From this vantage point, they could have spotted other people traveling along the Woonasquatucket River by canoe or on foot during the day and witnessed major celestial events at night. Additionally, the quartz- and mica-flecked rocks on Neutaconkanut Hill, having crystalline and reflective qualities that Northeast Native people value for their physical and spiritual healing powers, would have contained messages to guide generation after generation of those who lived there and visited the hill.[4]

Although no systematic archaeological excavations have been done at Neutaconkanut Hill, the Rhode Island Historical Preservation and Heritage Commission's site files mention that its natural features and "Indian" stones, uprights (standing stones) dotted with crystal-like properties, and curious stone rows and caverns are suggestive of precolonial Native American habitation. Many local children are reported to have found artifacts at the site.[5] Within recent memory, the Neutaconkanut Hill Conservancy claims, all "treasured their little box of arrowheads."[6] Howard M. Chapin, a former librarian at the Rhode Island Historical Society (RIHS), writes about a seated human figure carved from graphite, "three and a half inches tall," discovered at Neutaconkanut Hill.[7] Compared with mica and quartz, graphite is neither reflective nor milky white, but opaque and black. Its dark color had symbolic associations in Native cosmology that would have added a layer of meaning to the image. Yet like most portable carvings found in New England by relic hunters and avocational archaeologists, the figure lacks precise provenience and contextual data other than its place of discovery. Its collector, Samuel W. King (1786–1851), was "an energetic and public-spirited citizen of the town" and a four-term governor of Rhode Island, whose family owned land on Neutaconkanut Hill from the late seventeenth to the early twentieth centuries.[8] His artifact collection, less well known than his family's land, contained another human effigy, a face carved in soapstone, found near Warwick Pond in the early 1900s.[9] Chapin admitted that he did not initially believe that the effigies were authentically indigenous, but he was convinced by King's sincerity and honesty and by another collector who had made a similar find at Warwick Pond. That the effigies were made from raw materials available locally also swayed his opinion in favor of attributing the anthropomorphic carvings to Native people.

Although they had "a certain Indian cast," according to Chapin, he mused that they had possibly been made during the early colonial period by Native artisans "who had come into contact with European civilization and had seen figures made in Europe."[10] Yet the figures exhibit an economy of detail typical of human faces depicted by Northeast Indians, rather than in Europeans' figural sculptures. Styled with flatly carved eyes and noses defined much more than mouths, the images resemble human faces carved onto the castellations of ceramic bowls recovered from seventeenth-century archaeological contexts in southern New England and found on an ash burl bowl from the same period in a private collection.[11] The reasons for depicting human and other animal beings were variable and bore some relationship to the form of the object. Animal effigies likely represented clan symbols that connected people of common descent in a network of relations across multiple homelands. Visible on large stone pestles that were communal as well as ceremonial objects and on head ornaments made to be seen from a distance, these figures marked identity and ties to a deep past when the social worlds of Northeast Native people and their distinctive cultural practices were developing. Anthropomorphic effigies coveted by collectors are more puzzling. Archaeologists have interpreted them as having roles in shamanistic or healing rituals involving transformations in states of being, in intertribal communication, and in revitalization or resistance movements. More than "unusual Indian implements," effigies like the one that Samuel King found at Neutaconkanut Hill are crucial to decolonizing and expanding understandings of this landscape and discerning the contours of settler colonial violence.[12]

Much like the statuette, Hipses Rock at the base of the rock-strewn landform is also engulfed in questions of authenticity and meaning (see fig. 26). According to a local legend, it was named for a Native woman, a doctor whom early settler colonists called "Hipsie," short for Hipsabeth or Elizabeth, who lived in a lean-to or hovel abutting the rock.[13] Although the rock's association with a skilled Indian "woman doctor" trusted by Europeans is plausible, the reference evokes the practice of using Indianness, here cast in terms of hybridity, to mark the spatial extent of colonial possession and what discursively and demographically became a white space.[14] Still another story refers to Hipses Rock simply as "Indian Rock," a more generic name that makes no pretense of being grounded in a particular historical moment. Rather, the rock's physical configuration in the settler colonial imagination conjures an Indian sitting in "a deep musing position." The face and open mouth detected in the rock's craggy features are thought to be looking upon the onlooker's face anxiously, as if trying to be understood. Putting aside the accuracy of the resemblance and rueful ideas about resistance and reconciliation, the imagery suggests an unspoken conversation and the desire of Native voices to be heard and comprehended as their tribal survival was denied that are absent in the rock's other name.[15]

Other rocks on Neutaconkanut Hill also have stories attached to them. A nearly spherical boulder of monster proportions (estimated to be twenty feet in diameter and seventeen feet high) that was once perched precariously on the brow of the hill invites comparisons to balancing rocks in teetering positions that have figured in the memoryscapes of European settler colonists and Natives in New England. Called tipping, rolling, pulpit, and drum rocks, they often served as signaling devices in communication networks in the Native Northeast because of the booming sounds that could be heard from far away when they were rocked.[16] This perched boulder that was anchored by a large oak was apparently stable enough to be called "Football Rock" in a nod to the games played there by local boys known to strike poses from its top when they scored. Older residents mostly knew the stone as "Balanced Rock," preferring a toponym that described its position on the landscape in relation to ancient and larger-scale processes. After Hurricane Carol (1954), one of the most powerful storms to hit southern New England, uprooted the tree, the stability of the boulder and the safety risks it posed to people, property, and travel in the Johnston-Providence borderland became a concern. As a result, the untethered boulder was dynamited. A chunk of the rubble was brought to the Geology Department at Brown University, where it was identified as an interloper—a glacial erratic or "foreigner" deposited by diluvial agency from a distant location—as had been suspected as early as 1840.[17] Compared to this boulder, Hipses Rock defied destruction. Regardless of its name, the viewing angle, how it is photographed as geological and historical evidence, or how its temporal and spatial scales are understood in human terms, this borderland landmark is an intensely storied locale.[18] Although European settler colonialism inflected it with other meanings, it was an important location in Native placemaking not only because "once upon a time an Indian lived" there, as James N. Arnold writes, but also because many other Native people continued to live there in the nineteenth and twentieth centuries.[19]

Powwows in the Shadow of Hipses Rock

Located near the intersection of Morgan and Borden Avenues, Hipses Rock was the backdrop for powwows in the 1930s held on property owned by Col. Frank W. Tillinghast, a cotton-goods manufacturer, attorney, civic leader, and gentleman farmer since 1898 (fig. 27). The powwows were sponsored by the National Algonquin Indian Council (NAIC), which met on the third Tuesday of each month at the Swedish Hall at the corner of Pine and Chestnut Streets in downtown Providence to continue the activities of the Indian Council of New England after Thomas Bicknell's death in 1925.[20] At the powwows, held annually on the first Monday of September from 1931 to 1933 and again in 1935, members of the Onsley family figured prominently, as did Indians from other towns and cities in the region (fig. 28). Narragansetts such as Frank M. Nichols (Chief Gray Eagle) and Edward Michael (Chief Sunset) came from Providence, Minnie Steele came from Pawtucket, Rhode Island, and Alfred C. A. Perry, the chief sachem, his wife, Eunice, and their daughter Mrs. Annie Farrow (Natiesha), came from Cranston, Rhode Island. Philip H. Peckham (Chief Night Hawk), the elected leader of the Narragansett Tribe of Indians following its reconstitution as a nonprofit organization under Rhode Island law in 1934, his wife, Clara (Nokomis), their children Harry (Yellow Feather), Mary (Sweet Grass), and Clara (Sweetheart, or Teppekathitha), and Marian W. Brown (Minnetonka) traveled from Charlestown, Rhode Island. Rev. Leroy Perry (Ousa Mekin) made the trip from Baltimore for the 1932 powwow and from Gay Head to deliver the invocations in 1933 and 1935. Other Wampanoags in attendance were Margaret R. Lee (Wooseeit) of Providence, a "full blood Wampanoag," whose father was a "full blood Blue Ridge Indian" and mother a "full blood Wampanoag" in the 1930 U.S. Census, and members of the

Fig. 27. Col. Frank W. Tillinghast's farm, site of the National Algonquin Indian Council powwows in the 1930s. The view is eastward toward Neutaconkanut Hill. Courtesy of the Johnston Historical Society.

extended Taylor family of the Pocasset band.[21] Atwood I. Williams, Sr. (Chief Silver Star) (Pequot), who was living in Westerly, Rhode Island, attended as did Native people from tribes as far away as West Virginia and Oklahoma.[22] Non-Native politicians and members of civic associations typically turned out in force. Colonel Tillinghast, who was made an honorary sachem and presented with a feather headdress by Ousa Mekin at the 1933 powwow, routinely welcomed Natives and non-Natives for the powwows, occasions when his estate became a stomp ground.[23]

Powwows such as those held on Morgan Avenue were local, small-scale events of a few hundred people at most; some powwows today on the national circuit have many more Native and non-Native spectators.[24] Regardless of their scale, powwows cut across tribal boundaries to unite indigenous people in a wider urban, regional, or national network.[25]

Fig. 28. Indians at a Johnston powwow, date unknown. Ernest Onsley, Frank M. Nichols, Edward Michael, Alfred A. C. Perry, and Leroy Perry are kneeling in the foreground; standing behind them are Nellie Onsley, an unidentified man, and Ethel Steppo. The women on the far right are unidentified. Courtesy of the Johnston Historical Society.

Beginning in the early twentieth century, powwows in southern New England incorporated pan-Indian symbols such as elements of Great Plains regalia. These were substitutes for northeastern Natives' own cultural practices, which were not necessarily lost or forgotten. Instead they had evolved to meet the expectations of Euro-Americans observers and the changing circumstances of modern and often urban Native people who sang, danced, told fortunes, displayed traditional skills of beadwork, basketry, and archery, reenacted customs, lighted Council Fires, and smoked peace pipes. But powwows in the Native Northeast did not simply promote generic or ethnic Indianness. The Narragansetts' annual August powwow, which, beginning in the nineteenth century, incorporated church services and secular activities such as athletic contests and cock and dog fights, had religious affinities with traditional green corn thanksgivings.[26] In Narragansett Country and elsewhere, powwows were social reunions that created and enhanced connections within and across Native communities. They were intertribal in the sense that tribal affiliations and traditions were recognized rather than submerged, while people from different tribes and dispersed localities were allowed to express a shared colonial history and common concerns in the modern era. Participation in powwows was—and is today—considered "the discharge of an obligation, if not a pleasure," as Ethel Boissevain writes, which ranks highly as an index of involvement in a Native community.[27] Such participation rippled across rural communities and urban homelands in southern New England at a time when the number of Native people was growing (because of an increase in birth rates or an awareness of Native identities or both) and the revitalization of their cultures confounded predictions about their disappearance. In the years following detribalization, critics were unrelenting in questioning the authenticity of public claims of Indianness by powwow-going Natives. Those who lived in cities and had mixed ancestry seem to have been especially singled out for scorn or parodied in unflattering caricatures.[28] Yet they contributed mightily to Native survivance and resurgence, as did urban powwows. As critically important contact zones for gathering and exchanging ideas about indigeneity, powwows provide exceptions to narratives emphasizing cities as strictly places of European settler colonialism's dispossessions and alienations of Native people.[29]

Although distance might not be a deterrent from attending powwows, those held off of Morgan Avenue were more convenient to Providence's Native people than those that were farther away. The train that had run through the Woonasquatucket River Valley since the early 1870s and skirted Johnston's eastern border would have provided transportation for a leg of the journey, as would trolley cars. Those with cars would have given rides to their neighbors and relatives. Although often compared to ethnic festivals and parades, church or town fairs, and Buffalo Bill Cody's Wild West shows, powwows aligned with older cultural ideals of visitation and gathering among Native people.[30] The events on Morgan Avenue, which typically lasted a few days, allowed them to spend time with other Native families, friends, and acquaintances, visiting back and forth between tepees set up around the field, regardless of whether they had a role in the pageantry or were spectators.[31] At one of these powwows they could learn a few new dance steps, hear familiar melodies that were part of their heritage, pick up some advice about craftwork from skilled artists, and expose their children to cultural traditions shared not only within their family but with Native people across southern New England. These powwows also provided an arena where Native men and women could speak for themselves to those who were willing to listen about issues that concerned them.

Among the Onsleys participating in the NAIC powwows on Morgan Avenue were Benjamin Franklin (Chief Great Owl), his son, Ernest P. (Chief Rainbow), Ernest's wife, Nellie (Princess Flaming Arrow), Mrs. Ethel Steppo (Princess Corn Blossom), and her son, Melvin Steppo. The family had moved to Johnston about 1870. They were neighbors of Colonel Tillinghast and lived across from the powwow ground. In a 1997 interview Mabel Sprague, a long-time resident of Morgan Avenue, said, "Chief Onsley [Benjamin] was a chauffeur for a couple of years for the Tillinghasts."[32] As relatively new residents of the town, the Onsleys shared this ancestral homeland with generations of Native people who had lived there before them and with whom they established a connection based on shared experiences of place. Regardless of any cultural, biological, or linguistic differences, knowing that ancestors—mothers, fathers, sisters, brothers, aunts, uncles, nieces, and nephews who were not necessarily their lineal kin and whose names were unknown to them—resided in this land helped shape their sense of belonging. To honor those who had dwelled here before them and to protect the memory of Johnston as an Indian place, particularly the historical significance of Hipses Rock as a symbol of colonial land losses, they assumed the responsibility of acting as the indigenous hosts at these events.

Benjamin Franklin Onsley, born in Olneyville in 1863, was the grandson of Samuel Judson Onsley and Dolly Eaton Onsley of Johnston. Samuel, the son of Benjamin Wamsley, whose ancestry had deep Wampanoag roots, and Sarah Reeves, was born in Burrillville, Rhode Island, around 1814. He married Dolly Eaton Smith of Plainfield, Connecticut, in Uxbridge, Massachusetts, in 1842.[33] By 1850 the couple had moved to Providence's sixth ward with their daughters, Louisa, age six, and Josephine, age four.[34] Samuel Onsley (a.k.a. Warmsly, Warmsley, or some other variant) lived in Upper South Providence in the early 1850s, where his closest neighbors were other people of Native descent. His brother Willis, who had lived in Providence as early as the 1830s, resided on South Main Street in the Fox Point area in the 1860s before moving to Upper South Providence and then to Potter's Avenue, not far from Long Pond, where he died in 1878.[35] Willis's daughter Phebe, who predeceased him by four years, died at Dahlia Street in the area around Benedict Pond. His wife, Harriett, a Congdon, remained in Upper South Providence until her death in 1889 at the age of sixty-five (see chapter 3).

Samuel relocated to the city's northern outskirts by 1860, where he found work as a farmer and tanner.[36] Dolly gave birth to at least seven more children after the couple moved, bringing the number of babies she had to fourteen or fifteen by some estimates, and by her own calculations to an even dozen. Samuel died in 1879 at the age of sixty-six, leaving her with several children who were minors.[37] Dolly (or "Aunt Dolly," as she was affectionately called by some of her neighbors), who said that she had been born a slave, did laundry for Mabel Sprague's family, the Atwoods (fig. 29).[38] She lived down the street with her grandson, Benjamin (Ben), and his family, and went to the Atwoods' house every Monday to do their whole load of wash "in a kettle at the wash house" for 50 cents, according to Sprague. After the wash was done she would smoke her corncob pipe and have dinner with the Atwoods.[39] She died of tuberculosis at the Onsleys' house on the corner of Morgan and Borden Avenues in 1911 when she was probably in her late seventies. The home, built by Benjamin in 1905 after the family's older house burned down, was described by Mabel as "a show place and very pretty inside," where Benjamin and his wife, Annie, "entertained a lot" (fig. 30).[40]

As a young boy, Benjamin lived with his grandparents, his mother, Louisa, and her siblings, and he remained with the elder Onsleys through his teens, working on their farm.[41] He married in 1884 and had two children, Ernest P. and Ethel G., with Annie.[42] Both children were born in Johnston, Ernest in the Hughesdale neighborhood, not too far from Mor-

Fig. 29. Dolly Onsley, photographed at the Atwoods' home, where she worked as a laundress around the turn of the twentieth century. Courtesy of the Johnston Historical Society.

Fig. 30. The Onsley home at the intersection of Morgan and Borden Avenues, date unknown. Courtesy of the Johnston Historical Society.

gan Avenue.⁴³ Living in the city's near hinterland, Ben, like his grandfather, was a farmer who lived a rural life, yet he was part of the social network that linked Native people living in the city's distant and inner urban homelands. He had lived for a short time around Hoyle Square in Upper South Providence, as had other family members. As a resident of Johnston, he maintained ties to Native peoples in the city's other homelands through his participation in the NAIC and in the social gatherings and public events that the organization sponsored. His name is inscribed along with those of other members of the NAIC in the King Philip Museum's visitors' book as having visited sometime in June–August 1932.

Like his father and grandfather, Ernest Onsley lived and worked in the city of Providence proper and in outlying Johnston and traveled between them. He married Nellie M. Hall (a.k.a. Eldridge) of Warwick, Rhode Island in Johnston in 1906.⁴⁴ He continued working as a teamer after his marriage, driving teams of horses in Johnston and on Westminster Street in Providence, and he briefly held a job as a clerk.⁴⁵ In 1915 the couple was recorded as lodging at a boarding house on Pond Street, where Nellie was a servant. Ernest worked as a "chauffeur" at a public market, where he delivered produce from the family farm to sell in the city. By 1925 they had moved back to the Onsley family property on Morgan Avenue and were living in the house next door to his father's.⁴⁶ Like his father, Ernest farmed and was a "vault cleaner," someone who removed human excrement and waste from privies and cesspools. These noxious loads were not the only ones carted on Onsley's wagon. A neighbor on Morgan Avenue in the 1930s remembered decades later that an American Indian, presumably Ernest (or possibly Benjamin) Onsley, whose tribal affiliation was unknown to her, "knew a thing or two about growing gardens.... Each spring before the planting season approached, he would hitch up his horse and wagon and set out for the waterfront in Providence. There he would pick up the most odious load of trash fish." When he returned to Johnston, he would "proceed to dig small holes and place a dead fish in each one of them, then drop in the seed."⁴⁷ Chief Onsley's use of his aromatic cargo of fish to fertilize his garden suggests familiarity with farming techniques of generations of Wampanoag ancestors, but also offers an unexpected insight into the family's ties to Providence.[48] The flow of "trash fish" and market crops to and from their Johnston garden was part of a network of social, informational, and material exchanges that entwined them in the city's Native homelands. The odorous fish in the spring and the aromas of foods mingling with the wood smoke at the Labor Day powwows were scents of place that connected the Onsleys to their surroundings in profound ways and evoked memories of them, especially of the eagerly anticipated "summer spectaculars," as Myra Chapman, a neighbor, recalls.[49]

Ernest Onsley represented the Algonquin Council at other public events in Rhode Island besides the Johnston powwows. Among them was the powwow at Allentown, Rhode Island in July 1935 of the American Indian Federation, an intertribal organization based in Westerly. An article in *Narragansett Dawn* reports that Chief Rainbow and Princess Red Wing had "quite a discourse on the benefits of tribal organizations" at the powwow. Although the full contents of what was discussed are not given, Red Wing's printed remarks hint that there was "some unrest" about the implications of the U.S. government's Indian Reorganization Act of 1934 and the Narragansetts' retribalization as a nonprofit corporation under Rhode Island law for intertribal groups and other tribal communities in the region. Although this shift in government policy establishing procedures for federal recognition of tribal sovereignty and the incorporation of the Narragansett Tribe of Indians heralded a new era for the region's Native people, who lived with the stigma of having been called extinct, intertribal organizations had played an important role in their lives since the 1920s. They were not easily replaceable—at least not at this point in Northeast Native history. As organizations with dual goals of raising cultural pride and improving material and political conditions, they mediated between the conventional binaries of modernity and tradition. For Chief Rainbow and Princess Red Wing, and I imagine for others, these organizations' purpose was, in Red Wing's words, to teach "[our] children not to laugh at old rituals, ideals, and principles of their forefathers, but to live by them."[50]

Trepidations aside, Ernest Onsley participated the Narragansett powwow at Shannock in August 1935.[51] In October he was at the Narragansett Indian Church, where he delivered the greetings and asked for blessings on the harvest at a two-day Festival of the Harvest Moon that drew Native people from Rhode Island, Massachusetts, Connecticut, and New York.[52] He was also one of the speakers at Rhode Island's first Indian Day celebration at Goddard Park in Warwick on August 8, 1936, which marked the official opening of a replica of an Indian village constructed as a WPA project.[53] At the age of fifty-five, he registered for the draft in World War II, as he had done twenty-five years earlier for the war that was supposed to end all wars.[54] When he enlisted, he had been working as a butler on Providence's East Side. His employer, William A. Todd, was the former president of the Pocasset Worsted Company Mill, the leading employer in Thornton, the section of Johnston where many of the NAIC powwows were held, until it closed in the mid-1930s. Ernest Onsley returned to Johnston, where he farmed for nearly twenty years, retiring just a few years before his death.[55]

His World War I draft registration card, on which he is identified as an Indian, provides an evidential thread about his indigeneity, as do some other documents often taken as proof of his Native American identity. Along with other Native people, Ernest Onsley was not an Indian only when Euro-Americans decided that he was. Like Onsleys before him, he defied understandings of what it meant to be Indian and modern, rural and urban, and he deftly navigated the geographical terrain and intricate social worlds of Providence's innermost and outermost spaces. His life was played out across the city and its borderland, crossing them in ways that trace a more complicated scenario than suggested by binaries that separate rural from urban and Native history from urban history.

The Onsleys' family history crossed ethnicities, nativities, and geographies, and its ties to Johnston and Providence spanned generations. Samuel and Dolly's children were born in Uxbridge, North Providence, Providence, and Johnston. The mother of Ben Onsley's wife was English. His daughter Ethel's son was "half Polish and half Indian," as a census taker jotted down in the margins of Johnston's 1925 Rhode Island census schedule. In 1978 old-time Johnston residents remembered Ernest's widow, Nellie Onsley "as she drove her horse cart down Plainfield Street, with her hair in braids and paint on her cheeks" when she was "at least ninety."[56] Born about forty years before Johnston's powwows, her braids and face paint might not have been regalia that she would have worn at these gatherings. At the age of ten and while a public-school student, Ernest and Nellie's son, Chester Benjamin Martin Onsley, petitioned to have his given name changed to Eldridge Chester Onsley because he wanted to have the same name as a much-loved elderly and childless paternal uncle. Complying with his uncle's wishes, he wanted to perpetuate his name. Nellie consented to her son's request without contest and Ernest signed the decree granting the name change in July 1919.[57] Eldridge C., Ernest and Nellie's only child, was later given an Indian honorific, Trailing the Moon, which might have been conferred in a naming ritual conducted at a powwow.[58] Members of the Onsley family, whether through birth or marriage, had encountered and forged bonds with people of different ancestries who were part of their history. Theirs was a history divorced from a tribal land base, but redefined by their ties to Johnston and to their farm and the houses where they lived in the shadow of Hipses Rock, where they made their presence and voices heard.

There were other Walmsleys in Providence going back to the 1830s who are listed in the section of the city's directory reserved for persons of color. Sarah Walmsley, a widow, is recorded as residing near the "Tanyard" in 1832 at the city's north end.[59] Another widow, Patience, lived on the north shore of the Cove in the 1830s and 1840s, as did Thomas, a laborer, in the 1840s. Other Walmsleys were on Olney and Bark Streets in the Lippitt Hill neighborhood. George Walmsley, a laborer, who lived on Olney Street in 1838, moved to "near Pond Street" by 1844.[60] A Betsey Walmsley was at 66 Benefit Street, the same address where Nancy Elizabeth Proffitt lived with her father William and her husband as a newlywed before leaving for Paris. Others with the same surname were in the records of birth, death, and marriage that I skimmed in the city archives. Among them were babies who died all too soon of cholera, which struck the neighborhoods of people of color especially hard in the 1840s and 1850s, or from respiratory diseases, bowel disorders (infant diarrhea), and undisclosed illnesses.[61] One infant suffocated in bed on Prairie Avenue in Upper South Providence, the victim of what today would surely have been diagnosed as SIDS (sudden infant death syndrome); another was stillborn in an aborted delivery that also took her mother's life.[62] The four-year-old son of Louisa Walmsley of Bark Street in the Lippitt Hill neighborhood died of convulsions in 1854.[63]

The deaths of these Walmsley children are among the most heart wrenching to read about even in matter-of-fact public documents, as are those of other children consigned to an early grave. The deaths of adults, regardless of how old, glaringly recall the lived realities of nineteenth-century city life and the illnesses that caused suffering, loss of income, and death. After surviving infancy and childhood, people died of consumption, cancer, bacterial infections, enteritis, bleeding, and simply old age, and they were not immune to the outbreaks of typhoid that, along with cholera, plagued the city periodically during the course of the century. Aside from mortality, vital records indicate that some individuals with the Walmsley surname were born in the city of Providence and others in Smithfield and Burrillville at the county's most northerly reaches. Many of Willis and Harriet's children and a daughter of Samuel Judson and Dolly were born in Worcester County, Massachusetts. All were part of an extended kinship network of people who shared a surname that in its various spellings comment on separations and connections in a complicated colonial history.

Geographies of Colonial Justice

Amasa Walmsley was born in Burrillville, the same town as Samuel Judson Onsley, on August 24, 1806. According to his biography, he acknowledged that he was the son of Thomas Walmsley, "a half-breed Indian of the Narragansett Tribe," and Nancy Pike, a "native of Rhode Island," who later remarried and moved to near Jewett City, Connecticut.[64] Like Samuel, Willis, Ernest, and Benjamin Onsley, his name is entwined with the history of Providence. Yet the reasons could not have been more different. Convicted of a double murder in Burrillville in 1831, he was one of the last people to be publicly executed in Rhode Island before the practice was abolished in 1833. Accounts of the murder have been retold many times over and in many different versions. According to a town legend passed down for more than a century, the ghost of the Indian woman Hannah Frank, one of the victims, was said to haunt the woods in search of justice and a necklace that had been given to her by her betrothed, John Burke, the other victim in this homicide.[65] Legal scholars and social historians intent on understanding the colonial justice system, and particularly how race, class, and gender were imbricated in the ways that justice was dispensed, have been fascinated by the case.[66] Almost everyone from townspeople to later scholars have had an opinion, including Amasa Walmsley. His jailhouse confession was formulaic and probably heavily edited, as gallows confessions often were, but the transcriber did not completely appropriate Walmsley's utterances to further the transcriber's own agenda. This account, demanded and recorded by his jailer, offers a narrative of a life that most would consider obscure and unremarkable, except for the double murder for which he was convicted and which he denied committing right up to his death by hanging in Providence on June 1, 1832.[67]

In the brief biographical sketch in Walmsley's *Life and Confession*, written down by Stephen Wilmarth, Esq., of Providence, Walmsley recounts living on the social, economic, and geographical margins of the newly incorporated city. One of six siblings, he was placed out at a young age to work and lodge with Asel Albe, a farmer in Charlton, Massachusetts. After less than two years he "became discontented and absconded, alleging as a reason for [his] conduct, that he had been unjustly and severely treated." By his own admission, he was unworthy of pursuing; he was allowed to remain away, and he found work on Daniel Burlingame's farm in Glocester, Rhode Island. The new arrangement was strained, however, by frequent arguments with Burlingame's son, a person whom Amasa described as having a "severe and irritable temperament." After a year, he left and went to live with Joseph Paine of Smithfield, where he stayed for three years. At the end of his term of service, George Chace and William Buffum bought his indenture from Burlingame. He stayed with Chace for about a year and a half and then, because of "bad usage," he ran away again. He returned to the home of Joseph Paine and stayed there for an unspecified amount of time.[68]

Even a rough estimate of his indenture suggests that he was placed out for at least seven and a half years, during which he repeatedly ran away. Whatever modicum of security or bonds of good feeling he might have felt did not compensate for the poor treatment he experienced at the hands of some of his employers and their families or for his mounting dislike of steady employment, if indenture can be described as such, and his desire to rove. In many ways his early life echoes the experiences of the young William Apess, who lived apart from his family during his childhood and by the age of eleven and a half had run away from multiple indentures. Frequent moves from place to place, struggles with alcohol, and early deaths also invite similarities, but literacy and crime do not. Walmsley's *Life and Confession*, a first-person statement given under duress and liberally transcribed by Wilmarth, his interlocutor, a week before his execution and signed by him with an "X," a Native signature of assent, offers insights into the kind of life that is rarely written about. In this sense it is vaguely reminiscent of Apess's *A Son of the Forest*, though the authorship of Apess's biography has never been in doubt. Although different in scope and emphasis, Walmsley's *Life and Confession* sheds light on the complexities of Native life in nineteenth-century New England but is also meant to serve as a moral lesson about the dangers of intemperance.

Crime and punishment are entirely other matters. Amasa Walmsley, identified as an Indian and common laborer, and his younger brother, Thomas, also a laborer, were accused of assaulting John Burke, an Irishman, and Hannah Frank (Nipmuc), and causing their deaths. Burke, a peddler from Vermont, was considered a foreigner in Burrillville who, according to local stories, had a relationship with Hannah. In Walmsley's *Life and Confession* she is described as a mulatto woman and distant relative who had been staying at the house of an uncle, though she and Burke usually cohabited in the woods. Regardless of the couple's domestic arrangement, the incident occurred after Amasa and Thomas returned to Thomas's home from a local tavern to find Burke, Hannah, and another woman, who had also been drinking. What transpired next is murky. The group allegedly drank, sang, and danced well into the night. Burke and Hannah left at some point. Amasa and Thomas pursued them—either at the instigation of the other woman, Fidelia Smith, who claimed that Hannah had stolen some of her clothing, or because they did not approve of Hannah's relationship with Burke.

Court records report that Amasa struck Burke "with a certain stick of no value ... upon his head, breast, back and belly, sides and other parts of his body ... and then cast and [threw] the said John Burke down and into the ground with great force and violence ... beating, striking, and kicking him with the hands and feet ... and applying several mortal strokes, wounds, and bruises." The records state that he left his victim languishing from his wounds, yet still alive, but Amasa was accused of returning the next day to deliver the fatal blow, a cut four inches long and three inches deep to Burke's throat, made with an "axe of the value of 50 cents." Thomas, who was present at the time of the assault, was accused of "aiding, abetting, comforting, assisting, and maintaining the said Amasa E. Walmsley in felony and murder."[69] Amasa is also reported to have struck Hannah on the head with a stick of no value and caused her death by a mortal wound two inches long and a quarter inch deep near her right eye. Amasa's recollection of the incident in his *Life and Confession* tells a different story. In his account Fidelia attacked Hannah with a stone, and Hannah and Burke, though beaten, were still alive and lying about four or five feet from each other when the brothers left the scene. But he stated that when the couple was found about two weeks later in a state of putrefaction, Hannah's body was about "eighty rods" from Burke's.[70]

In the intervening fortnight few noticed the couple was missing, or if they did it failed to arouse any suspicions given that they "had some months, lived in the habits of criminal intimacy, in the forest of Burrillville, subsisting on the avails of occasional labor, and the results of predatory excursions on the farms of the neighborhood." People like them who lived on the edges of New England towns were devalued and not accounted for, though some were more unwelcome than others. Amasa, who professed a preference for an unfettered and roving life in which he could be "the master and director of [his] own affairs," was not concerned about Burke and Hannah and gave them little thought until Thomas told him that their bodies had been found. The brothers went to the site of the gruesome discovery and mingled among the "vast multiple of people" who had gathered to see the bodies, which by then had been placed in coffins. A few days later, Amasa Walmsley was arrested and charged with murder, then released because of insufficient evidence. A week or two later, he and Thomas were arrested for a second time and sent to prison to await trial before the Supreme Judicial Court of Rhode Island. Between the arrests, Fidelia Smith was questioned and furnished details that town officials decided warranted the Walmsleys' second arrest. Amasa was confined to the Providence jail from October to March. When the case was heard before the court at its March term, one of the witnesses who testified was Asel Alger (or "Albe"), Amasa's former indenturer, whom he had run away from because of unfair treatment. In sworn testimony Alger claimed that he had seen the prisoner on September 20, two days after the murder, wearing a shirt with a bloody sleeve. The guilty verdict, as Amasa Walmsley recalled, "fell like a thunderbolt" on his soul. Convicted of felony and murder, he was sentenced to death.[71]

Walmsley was taken back to the prison north of where Meeting Street (formerly called Gaol Lane) intersected North Main and Water Streets.[72] From there, according to his sentence, he was to be brought to the place of the execution on the morning of Friday June 1, 1832, "between the hours of nine & twelve of the clock in the afternoon," where he would be hanged by the neck until he was dead. With his petition for a postponement rejected by the Rhode Island legislature and all hope of a pardon extinguished, he gave the aforementioned account of his life and confession to his jailer, who certified that the condemned man approved the narrative as "true and correct." About two weeks before his execution, Amasa received a letter from his mother, Nancy Brayton (née Pike), of

Griswold, Connecticut, that is printed in typescript in his *Life and Confession*. She writes that she is unable to visit because of poor health but sends her love, as do his sisters, who cannot see him one more time because they are in such a state. She tells him about how "*truly awful and heart-rendering*" his situation is, and how much pain he has caused her "by yielding to the evils and temptations of the wicked one," and she implores him to pray for forgiveness and prepare himself for a Christian death. In the postscript under her signature, an X-mark between her first and last names, she adds, "I must tell you, my son, that I have not seen any comfort since I came home from Smithfield, last fall. Once more, Farewell." Her parting words imply that she had visited Amasa, a resident of that town, at about the time that his troubles with the law began.[73]

He was taken from prison at a little after half past nine on the morning of June 1 and placed in a hackney coach that carried him, the sheriff and his deputies, and the Reverends Crocker and Pattison to the execution site. The spot that was selected by the sheriff was about two miles from the center of Providence. Some accounts locate the site at the junction of Cranston and Pawtuxet Streets, a location known as Squaw Hollow, where legend says that an Indian woman had murdered and buried her child fifty years earlier.[74]

According to an 1882 guidebook to the city, a Squaw Hollow was between Orms and Martin Streets (now Chalkstone Avenue) adjacent to Bulldog Hill and north of the state prison, an area "inhabited almost wholly by negroes and a low class of white people."[75] During the 1840s, Peter and Joe Nocake and J. M. Brown, Narragansett men aspiring to the unofficial title of "mayor," often assisted the police in settling disagreements in this notorious part of the city. According to one police officer, more often than not "the lithe, strong Indian" Joe Nocake, whose "whims were given more than ordinary attention," obtained the upper hand in the dispensation of justice.[76]

The "Squaw Hollow" at Cranston and Pawtuxet Streets is closer to Field's Point, a bluff on the east side of the Providence River mentioned in a book about fortifications in the War of 1812, according to Florence Simister. She states that a woman who was a lifelong resident of Providence, writing her reminiscences, claimed that the place-name was derived from the early days of the town when "there were still Indians around." In her story, an old Native woman, thought to be too feeble to accompany members of the tribe on a long journey, was left behind alongside a small brook in a little hollow, with a large bowl filled with succotash. "Ever since, on certain nights—especially when it's dark or and windy—the old squaw has been heard to scream, 'Come bury me up! Come bury me up!'" As if her voice were not enough to reprimand the living, this urban legend also reports that her ghost has been sighted at the spot, seemingly to add authority to the seriousness of her words. In the tale Euro-Americans pass judgment on Native people, whose circumstances might have prevented them from carrying through on their family commitments.[77]

It is tempting to read into this account sympathy for victims of crimes and injustices who might not necessarily have had the last word as they clung to life. Here Hannah Frank and John Burke come to mind, but so does Amasa Walmsley, who met his own tragic end at a place called Squaw Hollow. The "solemn and awful scene" that awaited him for his crime, as it was described in the *Rhode Island American*, most likely took place at the Squaw Hollow at the intersection of Cranston Street and the road to Pawtuxet.[78] The location was where the Field family owned large tracts of land on "the western side of the salt water" opposite the point that has borne their name since the seventeenth century. Many listed in the 1832 Providence Directory with this surname lived in this area. Yet Ellen Field, who received a payment of $8.20 for the damages to her fence by the crowd assembled to witness the execution on her land, is not among them.[79]

Although the exact location of the execution is not known with certainty, Amasa Walmsley arrived in full health and strength, dressed in a white muslin gown spotted with black, white stockings, and black slippers. The sheriff read the warrant for his execution and a minister offered a prayer for mercy. Walmsley expressed his desire to address the immense crowd of spectators yet the *Providence Daily Journal* reported that the fortitude he displayed in wanting to have his last words heard failed him.[80]

His voice was near silent, or at least it was inaudible to the spectators, even those standing close to the gallows. After the final preparations had been completed, the sheriff informed him that the time for the execution of the law had come and instructed him to drop a handkerchief to signal his readiness. At a quarter to eleven the sheriff cut the rope and Amasa Walmsley was suspended in the air. He died with scarcely a struggle, still maintaining his innocence. Forty minutes later, his lifeless body was taken down and handed over to his friends for burial, though rumors circulated that it was delivered to several respectable surgeons for "galvanic experiments," with Amasa's prior consent in return for rum.[81] The overwhelming consensus was that Walmsley's conduct to the end was marked with "great firmness and resignation," and that he, in the words of one reporter, "met his fate like a true son of the forest." The sheriff was commended for "the complete and perfect arrangements" for this "most unpleasant and disagreeable duty." The hanging had gone according to plan—without any accidents and "with utmost propriety."[82]

The newspaper reports spare readers the horrific details of Amasa Walmsley's death by hanging. There is no mention of the thrashing, twitching, and bloodcurdling groans that typically occurred as a condemned person dangled from the hangman's rope before becoming still. His death by strangulation took around forty minutes—possibly more, given that the process could take as long as an hour. From the time that Walmsley arrived at his execution site to when his body was taken down from the gallows, the crowd looked on. His punishment was a public street spectacle in a part of the city that then had few streets. It was a performance not to be missed, given that it had been thirty years since the last hanging for someone convicted of a capital crime in Rhode Island. Ostensibly, the rarity of such an event might have been a selling point for the curious, who turned out ten to fifteen thousand strong, a sizable showing for a city of almost seventeen thousand, according to the 1830 federal census. Although there is no way of knowing if the onlookers were residents of the newly chartered city or had traveled from its hinterlands or other towns in southern New England, the hanging was an urban event of unprecedented magnitude. Despite the size of the crowd, no disorderliness was reported, and no town watchmen were on hand to keep order in case of mob action aimed at disrupting the dispensation of justice. The majority of the crowd had come to see justice served. As witnesses to a violent street spectacle, they could be assured that punishment was carried out for the murder of John Burke and Hannah Frank, and that their rights as citizens were protected. The general silence of the spectators indicated that they sensed the solemnity of the occasion and were convinced that justice had been done.[83] Yet the silence might have been misconstrued.

In the arena of public opinion, there was "nothing of instruction" in the life of Amasa Walmsley (as the *Providence Daily Journal* put it) and "in his death nothing worthy of notice but ignominy."[84] His *Life and Confession* was printed in the year after his execution so that it could instruct present and future generations to avoid his errors and sins. Of these, intemperance, "the curse of the world, that prince of all vices; that great generator and promoter of all outrages that disgrace the age," was cited as the fault to which he had succumbed.[85] It was under the influence of alcohol that he had engaged in the beatings of John Burke and Hannah Frank that led to their deaths as determined by the court and the jury. His hanging served as a warning of the dangers of alcohol, heralded by Providence's temperance movement, which began in earnest in the late 1820s as the city rapidly grew in population and wealth. Over the next two decades, thousands of Rhode Islanders would take the pledge of temperance.[86] The role that the Amasa Walmsley case played in moderating townspeople's consumption of alcohol and restoring morality is not known and is beyond the scope of the history of the Providence's Native homelands. Yet the exhortations in his *Life and Confession* provided a resounding admonishment about the potential dangers of intoxication for those who read it.

For those who did not or could not read the narrative, Walmsley's public execution served as a visible reminder of someone who had been, as he described in *Life and Confession*, "shut out by [my] complexion and the ignominy which the world has cast upon the tribe to which [I] belong[ed], and from which [I was] lineally descended."[87] Spectators came to see a hanging of a Native person, a sometime wall layer who had been bound out in his youth. Deprived of "all the benefits of education, and from all the opportunities for moral improvement—degraded, neglected and abandoned to all the snares of vice at [his] very birth," Walmsley experienced circumstances that were not uncommon among those who, because of their identity as Native Americans, are hardly written about and typically were subjects of public contempt.[88] The prospects for him were slim, despite temporary bondage that in theory was supposed to prepare him for a more upstanding life. His hanging might have somewhat quieted the uneasiness about people of color still lingering over the city following the 1831 riots in Snowtown in the Lippitt Hill section.[89] Its timing might also have been seen as confirmation of the 1831 report to the Rhode Island General Assembly by Dan King, a state representative from Charlestown, that racially denigrated the Narragansetts, chastised them for not properly caring for their poor, and recommended that sale of most of their tribal land as a solution to mounting debts to the town supposedly caused by their ineptitude.[90] In King's terminology, Amasa Walmsley would have been one of the many "mixed remnants" of the tribe. Like them, he rejected such accusations while remaining cognizant of the harsh realities of the life scripted for him on account of his lineage and class. Of the three individuals convicted of a capital offense and sentenced to death by hanging in Rhode Island in the thirty years prior to his execution, he was the only one who was not granted pardon, though he was not the only person of color among the condemned.[91] His hanging was meant not only to be a lesson about the dangers of imbibing too much rum, but a demonstration of the risks posed to mainstream society by Native men, mostly young, uneducated, and seemingly feckless, who drifted from job to job and town to town in search of work and respect.

Walmsley's behavior while under the influence of alcohol on the night of September 18, 1831, is not to be condoned or excused, nor was it by the jury that convicted him despite the lack of credibility of some witnesses for the prosecution. Although reading the pulse of popular opinion is difficult, not everyone approved of public hangings, preferring instead that they take place privately, perhaps within the walls of a prison, or not at all.[92] After Amasa Walmsley's body was taken down from the gallows, it was given to his friends, rather than to surgeons as rumormongers speculated.[93] A notice to subscribers in his *Life and Confession* states that, as "the last legacy he c[ould] give his friends," he wanted his body to be handed over to his brother Uriah so that it could rest "beside the ashes of his family." His last wish, "to be entitled to that repose which the grave affords" and to be "permitted to enjoy the rights and quiet of the tomb," may very well have been granted.[94] The accounts of the Rhode Island General Treasurer indicate that John Hopkins was billed for the coffin and cash was paid to Thomas Stone from the account of H. G. Mumford for conveying the body and burial.[95]

None of this guaranteed that his wishes would be respected, and I have not been able to confirm his burial place in public records. But the Walmsley burial lot is said to be on the east side of Broad Street opposite the entrance to Providence's Roger Williams Park and "within a few feet of the Harbor Junction cut of the New Haven railroad line." During steam-shovel excavations in 1912 for a roadbed for new tracks running west from Eddy Street, seven skulls and other bones were accidently exhumed, along with a gravestone inscribed "In memory of Patience Wamsley, widow of Stephen Wamsley, who died July 26, 1857, aged 80 years. Be thou faithful unto death, and I will give thee the crown of life." The name and age on the gravestone correspond to a Patience Walmsley in Providence death records, and the date of death differs by less than two days. Her name appeared in the list of colored persons in Providence directories in the 1830s and 1840s as a resident of the north shore of the Cove and of Gaspee Street, where she died.[96] Rather than regarding the human remains as all in a day's work and ignoring them, as construction crews frequently did to avoid costly delays, the workers paused to collect them as they were being scooped up until the steam shovel reached the sidewalk at Broad Street and stopped. Neither the construction company nor the Southern New England Railroad Company were aware of the burying ground's existence until then. Yet the inscription identifying a person by name buried there as recently as fifty-five years earlier provided unambiguous evidence that a historic period cemetery containing the graves of people who probably still had next of kin living in the city had been disturbed. I inquired at an auto parts store in the vicinity about its location and was directed to the railroad tracks below. From my vantage, I could not see the probable spot, hidden behind a wire fence and camouflaged by brush that an informant said her children had often cleaned up as community service.

The "Wamsley" lot (as the name is spelled on the gravestone) was a family burying ground. Until fifteen or twenty years before some of the graves were unearthed by the steam shovel, an apparatus that was a major boon to railroad expansion and urban growth, the burial plot's entrance of Broad Street was marked by a wooden arch with signage that read "Walmsley Burying Ground," according to Anna F. Taylor, a resident of Hamburg Street in the Mashapaug neighborhood and a relative of the Wamsleys. She said that the family sold the property adjacent to the burying ground, but continued to hold rights to the burial place. The new owners covered over the graves with grass and surrounded them with a hedge, then sold the property, including the hidden burial ground, to the railroad company. Mrs. Taylor said that besides Patience, the last Wamsley buried in the cemetery, there were other family interments and those of Narragansett Indians "from the earliest of times." Among the Wamsleys were Patience's husband, Stephen, and Thomas and Sarah Wamsley, Mrs. Taylor's great grandfather and great grandmother. She claimed that Amasa Walmsley was a member of another branch of the family and was not buried there. Local tradition has it that he was and that the place of his execution was chosen because of its proximity to the burying ground. If his bones were disinterred from the Wamsley plot, they along with those of about six other people in his extended kin network were "gathered up and placed in small boxes beneath the white house on the corner" next to the lawn where the excavations occurred; the Grand Trunk Railroad Company planned to remove the house.[97]

What happened to the bones next opens another chapter in Amasa Walmsley's Providence story. Florence Parker Simister reports that the Wamsley bones were taken from the house in a sack and deposited in the receiving vault at North Burial Ground. A later investigation into the identities of the deceased suggested that they had been "negro" and might have been slaves, because the bones seemed old, though further research confirmed that they were members "of a Negro family named Warmsley." Simister is convinced that Amasa Walmsley was "most certainly dug up by the railroad excavators in 1912" and refers to a report that implies that he, like many Native people in the region, would be easy to mistake for an African American, whether in the first half of the nineteenth century or a century later. She remarks that when the family heard that the bones had been unearthed, they stepped forward and demanded money from the railroad company to pay for a proper reburial and as compensation for its desecration of the burying ground. The railroad gave them $400, but Simister says that years later North Burial Ground still had "the sack of bones" and was trying to collect what amounted to a thirteen-year storage fee.[98]

Florence Simister's stories about particular localities on the urban landscape give a strong sense of place. Because they were supposed to be heard rather than read, their transcriptions do not have citations, as is often true of stories transmitted orally. Her claims that the Wamsleys' bones had been moved to North Burial Ground are correct, but only a partial account of what became of them. The cemetery's records show that five boxes containing remains of the Wamsley family removed from a burying ground on Broad Street were delivered on October 22, 1912, and placed in "two catacombs" in the receiving vault at a monthly fee of three dollars.[99] The vault's inventory indicates that they remained there until October 13, 1979, when they were reinterred in North Burial Ground's free ground section. If Simister is correct, Amasa Walmsley's bones were among them. He had traveled from town to town in Providence's northerly borderlands and through city streets that became places of his inglorious death and burial and unceremonious exhumation and reinternment.

Thomas Walmsley went on trial in September 1832. He was convicted of aiding and abetting in the murders of Hannah Frank and John Burke and condemned to death, but his sentence was commuted. Although he did not garner the same degree of infamy as Amasa, whose public hanging occurred three days before the new city government went into effect and the city's first mayor, aldermen, and common council took their oaths of office, his story was also played out against the backdrop of the fledgling city. Providence's new municipal government was intended to rectify inadequacies in its institutional structure to deal with population growth, increasing crime, and intemperance. Drinking, a behavior associated with wealth and fashion as well as with poverty and vice, was seen as worrisome, especially among workers and servants whose intemperance was perceived as a reason for idleness, tardiness, or worse. The riots at Providence's north end also added to concerns among many townspeople about the effectiveness of the existing system of governance. Yet the city charter did not automatically stop the violence, ensure the restoration of the social order, or ease ethnic and racial tensions any more than the measures taken to make Native Americans and African Americans legible and different by segregating their names in the "Colored Persons" section at the back of the city directory.[100]

The notoriety of the Walmsley brothers, especially Amasa, attests to this. Their convictions, and Amasa's execution, sent a message that reverberated through Providence that heinous crimes would be prosecuted and that culprits would receive sentences commensurate with their offenses. Amasa Walmsley in particular exemplified both the physical and moral risks to society presented by impermanence and intemperance. Living on the outskirts of the emerging urban core, his life was tied to Providence through myriad exchanges of labor, material, and goods that linked the young city and the countryside. Because of his crime and the perceived threat that he posed because of his ancestry, he was removed from the environs that had been his home since birth and brought to the city proper, where he warranted public attention—a hanging in front of urban dwellers and other townspeople. The attention was as unwelcomed, as he and other Native Americans often were in Providence despite their ties to the city. Displaced and undesirable, he became integral to the place-story of the city in which Native people did not have a role and vice was not tolerated. Equating the two overlooked that many Native people, whether they had deep attachments or had recently set down roots, lived in Providence's homelands as family members and employees and were part of its urban fabric.

Urban Mythscapes of Ochee Springs

The Ochee Springs Soapstone Quarry sits at the back of a commercial property on Hartford Avenue separated from a parking area by a chain-link fence. Juxtaposed between the parking area to the south and Route 6 to the north, the ledge seems anomalous, a vestige of geological history both overwritten by and intruding on modernity. More than a natural formation, it was a cultural space mined by Native people thousands of years ago for its soft, workable, talc-like stone that they carved into bowls and dishes. Here the sounds of their hammers and chisels that have been silenced by time and the din of traffic along Hartford Avenue and Route 6 are hardly detectable in the imaginary. Ochee Springs is another place of urban legend in which Johnston's Native people were pushed to the background and relegated to a symbolic landscape appropriated by Euro-American settler colonists, whose place-story had little room for modern Native people.

Euro-Americans discovered the soapstone quarry in the 1870s. A local tradition passed down by Arthur P. Angell, whose family owned the property, recounted that his father, Horatio N. Angell, suffered from an undisclosed ailment that physicians were unable to diagnose or cure. Turning to alternative medicine, he sought the advice of a Boston clairvoyant, Dr. H. C. Lull, who told him, "Right on your own property, a tract of land in Johnston, Rhode Island, there is a subterranean spring, the water of which will remedy your condition." That Horatio Angell sought a cure from a medical intuitive was not at all uncommon in the nineteenth century. Some practitioners, such as Dr. Lull, adhered to a water-cure philosophy that might entail taking the waters of hot springs at a luxury resort, or bathing at public bathhouses or at home using a variety of methods from wet sheets to sitz baths that usurped the need for drug and evacuative therapies.[101] Following the consultation, the two men traveled to Johnston, where the clairvoyant directed Angell to a spot on his farm and told him to dig "two graves deep." At this depth, he predicted that there would be " a soapstone ledge from which bubbles clear crystal water with medicinal properties." He informed Angell that he could also locate other things of interest on the property, including "a ledge from which Indians made dishes and pottery from stone," and "an underground well, a talc bed, a sulphur spring containing iron, an underground cave filled with Indian implements and curios, and a chair cut in the rock on which the chief of the tribe sat." He identified the Indian chief who once occupied the seat as Ochee.[102]

The predictions about the landscapes hidden beneath Angell's Johnston farm were not entirely figments of the psychic's imagination. The spring was uncovered and its healing waters that Horatio Angell was said to drink frequently, rather than bath in, cured him of his illness. The spring's miracle waters are credited for giving him robust health that he enjoyed until his death at the ripe age of seventy-four in 1896, twenty-odd years after the discovery. So convinced was Angell of the medicinal benefits of the spring's water that he decided to sell it, much like other local entrepreneurs would aspire to market water from Johnston's Neutaconkanut Hill. Until 1892, the Ochee Spring Bottling Company sold the mineral water mainly on the recommendation of Providence's leading physicians, who believed that bad air and water, inadequate light, and improper food could cause diseases. Their endorsement gained added weight after the city was struck by a typhoid epidemic in the spring of that year that was blamed on the condition of its water supply.[103] Claims about the benefits of Ochee Water might not have been exaggerated, though the Horatio Angell story might have been. If taken regularly, the water acted as a mild cathartic and diuretic; and it was considered a reliable supplementary treatment for kidney, liver, and stomach troubles.[104] In addition to being widely known for its health-giving properties and purity among the people of Providence, Ochee Water was also promoted as agreeable to the taste. Pumped directly from the bubbling spring into glass bottles sealed with corks that, unlike patent stoppers with reusable bales, did not require rewiring the cork with each refilling, the sparkling bottled water was delivered under the proprietors' supervision to consumers' homes.

Stating that corks were not reused and that recycled bottles were machine-washed and sanitized only in Ochee Water, the company guaranteed consumers the purity of the commoditized water from spring to table.

Horatio's son, Arthur, whose company office was in downtown Providence, extended an open invitation to anyone interested in visiting the site, a half-hour's ride from the city by trolley cars leaving Market Square at a quarter before and a quarter after the hour, and offered to show them the spring that was "never dry" and the bottling facilities.[105] Many took up the invitation and rode the trolleys to the city's northeasterly borderlands to visit Ochee Spring, where they received a free bottle of water as a parting gift. The location, a convenient destination for a day excursion from the city, attracted many visitors in pleasant weather. It is doubtful if any were aware that Native Americans also had used natural springs for healing and wellness, though the spring's Indian-sounding name and a growing fascination with mythologized places on the Native landscape might have drawn them to the site as much as Arthur Angell's offer of a free bottle of water. For Native people, springs were where they could give thanks and communicate with ancestral and spirit beings. Springs could purify and strengthen, bring good luck to those having the right to visit these places, and, as Gary Varner writes in *Sacred Wells: A Study of the History, Meaning and Mythology of Holy Wells and Water*, "were of great importance to shamans, hunters, warriors, gamblers, and specific craftsmen."[106] Rather than simply ecological phenomena whose waters could be bottled and sold for economic gain, these watery places were often imbued with cultural and historical meanings that made them sacred. The Onsleys and other Native people might have heard oral traditions about this place buried "two graves" deep (about twelve feet below ground, based on the six-foot standard for nineteenth-century graves) beneath a landscape farmed by Euro-Americans, and about cultural practices conducted there in the ancient past and possibly into later centuries, but they did not, as far as I know, speak about them. Long concealed from view, any healing or other ritual powers derived from the spring and ledge had been pushed to the sides of Native historical and geographical consciousness.

The quarry was uncovered in 1878, four years after the clairvoyant's vision. The location of the cave that he said was on Angell's property and extended under the adjoining farm was never verified. Nor was the existence of Chief Ochee and his chair ascertained. Similar to the face perceived in the rugged features of Hipses Rock, Chief Ochee's "chair" was a romanticized musing about New England's Native American past. At best it was a hollow in the soapstone ledge created by the removal of bowl preforms. Two of the largest bowl impressions would have been big enough to accommodate a seated adult and if not used by the fictive Chief Ochee, might possibly have been used by Native craftspeople as expedient seating as they worked to transform the pre-shaped chunks of soapstone that they had detached from the ledge into bowls.[107]

Soon after the quarry was discovered, Professor J. W. P. Jenks, director of Brown University's former Museum of Natural History, arranged for Frederick Ward Putnam, an archaeologist and curator at Harvard's Peabody Museum of Archaeology and Ethnology, to tour the site with him and Horatio Angell, who allowed Putnam "to take such specimens as [he] desired" for the Peabody. Putnam reported that the seam of soapstone, of which about ninety feet had been exposed at the time of his visit, had been completely covered by soil that accumulated over "the ancient chippings." In clearing the soil, workers had removed more than three hundred cartloads of manufacturing debris, leaving behind "fragments of pots and a large number of roughly pointed stones that were lying about and bearing evidence of having been used." Putnam estimated that at least two thousand of these chisel-like tools—uniform in size, with a blunted point at one end and the other end rounded "to fit in the hand"—had been found on the ledge or in its immediate vicinity. Some of them had been deposited a few hundred yards away to help fill in a low-lying piece of land, and others had been thrown in a pile on the ledge. After conducting a brief experiment he surmised that the chisels, if used with patience and muscle, were very effective for pecking away at the soapstone. Other stones, round in shape and weighing from twenty-five to one hundred pounds or more, were thought to be hammers that were used to break off pieces of the steatite. The most revealing evidence of quarrying and manufacturing was chisel marks and oval and round impressions on the ledge, several hundred roughly chiseled bowl preforms (or "blanks"), and fragments of pots broken during manufacturing. From the number of impressions in an exposed cross section of the ledge that showed where preformed vessels had been removed from the rock, Putnam guessed that three to four hundred pots had been made in this spot alone, and several thousand in the entire outcrop.[108] Measurements of the impressions on the ledge, made more than a century after Putnam's study, indicate that round and oval shapes were the most common bowl forms made by Native carvers. The impressions are clustered at discrete locations, suggesting specialization by families or individuals who may have lived near the outcrop or camped and worked there for short periods of time.[109]

The quarry's bowls were tied to identity. The pot, as Lisa Brooks writes, is a metaphorical image invoked in daily life and in ceremony among Native peoples of the Northeast that comments on sharing, a practice necessary to their survival.[110] Manufactured from hollowed-out places that were both deeply social and ecological, steatite bowls could carry or hold food and tolerate heat and water, making them an ideal medium for transforming the plant and animal parts that they contained into nourishment that could sustain families. Their open shape facilitated sharing between natural and social beings and within families as well as across Native communities. Bowls from three and four thousand years ago with material and manufacturing attributes similar to those from the Ochee Springs Quarry have been found on Conanicut Island in Narragansett Bay, furnishing compelling evidence of the pot's role in networks of relationships.[111] The notion of sharing in the concept of the pot relied on maintaining a balance between give and take. The failure to share food and other resources, to nurture and renew relationships by giving, or to acknowledge dependence on nonhuman beings through rituals of thanksgiving could rupture the network of relations and have serious repercussions for an individual's and a community's well-being. The ethics of the pot, and the importance of the hollowed-out places they were carved from to the ongoing Native history of Johnston, were not recognized by the institutions and individuals who acquired bowls removed from the quarry in the 1870s and mostly valued them for their form and function.

Among these institutions were "the Smithsonian Institution, the Permanent Exhibition at Philadelphia, the Museum at Brown University, the Peabody Museum at Cambridge, the Boston Society of Natural History, and the Franklin Society of Providence," as recorded in the RIHS proceedings.[112] The Franklin Society added "portions of soapstone bowls from the Great Elm Farm, Johnston by Mr. Angell in February 1879" to its eclectic collection of philosophical and scientific specimens, which included a hippopotamus skull, a "tattooed New Zealander's head... twin infants united at the abdomen from Mexico," minerals, bark cloth, petrified wood, plants, insects, historical memorabilia, and Indian artifacts.[113] Other steatite pots from the excavations on Angell's property—known for an elm tree of prodigious proportions said to be the largest in the state owing to its peculiar situation near the spring and ledge—became part of "the very valuable private Indian Cabinet of Mr. Charles Gorton of Providence," according to RIHS records. Gorton, a member of the RIHS interested in local history and Native antiquities, was responsible for bringing the discovery of the "soapstone pottery manufacturing establishment belonging to the period of aboriginal occupation of this country" to the attention of the society.[114] Putnam announced in his report to the Peabody Museum's board of trustees that the museum came to possess "a mass of ledge showing the remains of one of the pot-forms," some stone chisels, and a few fragments of pots broken during production that illustrated techniques of manufacture, but did not comment on the deeper meaning of the quarry and relationships that were nurtured there.

Given the interest in Johnston's Ochee Spring Quarry and the realization that Indian relics were eagerly coveted by major museums often willing to pay large sums for them, the RIHS formed a committee to explore the feasibility of preserving what was left of the quarry and how best to protect it. After consulting with various parties and weighing the evidence and opinions, the committee recommended cutting a section of the ledge measuring about twelve feet in length, nine feet in width, and seven feet in depth and moving it to Roger Williams Park in Providence, provided that the citizens of Rhode Island and the city were willing to contribute about six hundred dollars for the project through voluntary subscriptions. The committee proposed asking the city to grant a designated spot in the park for the relocated piece of what it called the "Old Indian Steatite Quarry and Pottery." The place that the committee had in mind was "on a slope within sight, at least, of the statue of the founder of the State."[115] At a meeting held on December 4, 1879, the committee's report was presented by Rev. Frederick Denison, one of its members. Zachariah Allen, who was also on the committee, gave an address on the domestic life of Indians and their treatment by the first settlers, and Charles Gorton displayed artifacts from his collection on a table, wall, and shelves. All in attendance strongly endorsed the plan.[116] By May of the following year, the funds had not been raised and the committee abandoned its plan to move a chunk of Johnston's Ochee Spring Quarry closer to the city.[117]

Antiquarians' interest in the quarry waned in the years following its discovery. They never regarded this hollowed-out space as a way of thinking about relationships that wove Johnston's Native inhabitants together and with a larger network of other beings. Nor did they consider that steatite pots, like dishes carved from wood and shaped from local or foreign clay, were invoked by Native people in their everyday lives and ceremonies as a metaphor for the shared spaces and experiences of their stories of survivance. Rather, Euro-American settler colonists preferred the mythic story of Chief Ochee that was spun to promote the eponymous bottling company. Nearly thirty years later, the Committee on Marking Sites in Rhode Island placed a bronze tablet on the outcrop. At the dedication on October 17, 1908, David W. Hoyt, who delivered the address, noted that in the time that had passed since Reverend Denison, Zachariah Allen, and William G. R. Mowry of the RIHS visited the site, Putnam published his account, Jenks took photographs, and the best of the handiwork of the Indians was carried away to museums and private collections, "much stone has been taken from the ledge and put to various practical uses, some of it having been ground to powder." In his speech Hoyt recounted procedures in the manufacturing process that Putnam had outlined in his report and stated that, although somewhat similar ledges and quarries, or "crockery-shops," had been found in southern New England and elsewhere in Native North America, none was as superior in value as the Johnston "pot-quarry" that the committee commemorated on that October day. "The Indians had made the most suitable choice of location and material for their purposes" because the place offered routes of communication and trade to the east and west, and to the north. "In this respect, this ledge is typical of the manufactures of our own day which have grown up in the vicinity." At the end of the speech, Hoyt said that he hoped "that whatever now remains, that is plainly the work of the Indian race, may be allowed to remain here, undefaced, just where the work was done."[118]

Despite Hoyt's and the committee's good intentions, however belated and misplaced, vandalism, highway construction, and later industrial development have rendered the site nearly invisible. The fields and fences on Horatio Angell's Big Elm Farm that can be seen in Professor Jenks's photographs of the quarry are long gone, as is the stately elm made famous by Oliver Wendell Holmes in "The Autocrat of the Breakfast Table" and by other writers who marveled at its girth, the size of its branches, and its vigor for a tree of such age. The Ochee Spring Water Company went out of business in 1923, and the epic story of its founding became a faded, if not tarnished, urban legend that some dismissed as a deceptive ploy to disguise the fact that Angell had the site dynamited in a futile search for gold.[119] In 1978, a hundred years after it was unearthed, the "Ochee Spring Quarry" was listed on the National Register of Historical Places. The designation did not put an end to its neglect, unfortunately, nor has it prevented visitors from defacing and chipping away at the ledge for souvenirs. Partially obscured by a chain-link fence and weeds and situated in a most unlikely location, the quarry seems out of place. Yet the presence of this urban anomaly is a reminder that Johnston endures as an Indian place.

Questions of authenticity that surround Johnston's "Indian"-named places cast a shadow on the lives of Native people in past centuries who occupied this Providence borderland. Hipses, the name attached to the territorial marker defining the limits of colonial possession, might be an inaccurate translation of an English name. Ochee is more lyrical and "Indian-sounding." Although seemingly preferable to the nonspecific but complicated term "Indian," it is most closely linked to lower Creek or Muscogee place-names in the Southeast rather than to those of Algonkian-speakers in the Northeast.[120] Considered as transferrable and generic as the label "Indian," it was attached to Johnston's mineral spring and steatite quarry in an urban legend created through a dual process of romanticization and commodification. Even Neutaconkanut, as Sidney Rider points out, has forty-two different spellings in the early records of Providence.[121] Aside from inconsistent and flawed orthography, place-names have implications for how Johnston's Native peoples were represented. The only room for them was in the past, where they were shadowy if not fictive figures in the Euro-American imaginary.

In contrast to Euro-Americans' stories about the varied meanings of Johnston's Indian-named places, the experiences of the Native men and women who lived there tell other stories. These are not tales about picturesque and quaint Indians of urban legend and localities defined by the movable boundaries of expanding settler-colonial possession. Rather, they are place-based accounts of the lived experiences of generations of Onsleys, who lived and worked in this urban borderland, shifting between its villages and farms and the neighborhoods of Providence. These stories are about powwows on the Tillinghast estate near Hipses Rock where they gathered with other Native people, mostly Narragansetts and Wampanoags with whom they shared common ancestry, on the first Monday of September in the 1930s to reinforce a sense of community that transcended rural-urban binaries. On these occasions, the Onsleys and other Indians confronted challenges to their authenticity raised by Euro-Americans' stories of place and implications that to be "real" Indians they had to eschew modernity and all of its trappings by their sheer presence. Donning regalia and using indigenous names, they performed their Indianness and asserted their identity and culture to a white audience on their own terms. Their regalia, displays of skills, and reenactments of cultural practices might have appealed to how many Euro-Americans gauged

Native American authenticity, but they, as well as elected officials, knew that participation in these events created a platform for airing concerns and bringing about certain political and economic gains.

Although Rhode Island's Native Americans did not form a sizable voting bloc, Senator Jesse H. Metcalf (1860-1942) sought their votes and appealed to them as fellow citizens, pledging not to raise or squander their tax dollars or increase their monthly rents. He was praised by Newport's mayor for having stood up against "the wrongs being done to the red men" and for advocating that they had "a right to live in certain sections" of the country.[122] For Senator Metcalf, who donated the tent in which a turkey dinner was served to several hundred people at the 1931 powwow, real Indians belonged on reservations or tribal land, rather than everywhere. Yet those listening to him were proof that the entire modern world belonged to them as much as anyone else, as Philip Deloria argues.[123] Other politicians gave assurances that conditions would improve—one even predicting that by next powwow the Great Depression would be over. Despite promises of good times ahead, Ernest Onsley reminded everyone that one of the purposes of the 1931 powwow was to raise funds to obtain land where a home could be built for poor and orphaned Native children. Rev. Leroy Perry took a moment to say that there were only "110 Indians in Rhode Island, 550 in Massachusetts, and 342,000 on 161 reservations in the country."[124] Amid the investitures, exchanges of gifts, passing of the peace pipe, and other activities, the powwow ground below Hipses Rock had become a place of new memories, where Native people spoke about issues that mattered to them hoping that their voices would be heard and understood.

These stories of Providence's borderlands, like those of its other homelands, are also about Native people whose life histories were intimately entangled in an unspoken narrative of marginalized men and women laboring at menial jobs and of children dying prematurely. They tell about colonialism's dispersals and indentures that brought Native people to sites on the colonized landscape that were part of a new social order in which household space was shared with non-Natives in exchange for a nonnegotiable term of service. But they are also about Native-owned homes, urban jail cells, a gallows, a family burying ground, a steatite quarry mostly rendered to rubble and partially removed by small-scale economic development that occurred on the edges of an increasingly urbanized Native landscape, and the complicated histories of the scattering of material objects made and used there.

These place-based stories that comment on the diversity of Native peoples' lives contradict what Paige Raibmon has called the "binaries of authenticity."[125] These oppositional alignments that supposed that real Indians could never be modern or urban convinced European settler colonists, capitalist developers, and occasional tourists that Natives had vanished from this borderland. They had to reckon with this contention every time they came face-to-face with a Native neighbor hauling excrement from their privies, doing their wash, sharing a meal, riding a wagon through town, or dancing at the annual powwow. These were neighbors they might have met on trolley cars or passed by on Providence streets. They were not the Indians who still roamed the woods after King Philip's War, though the presence of those who might have as mostly unseen neighbors did not prevent early European settler colonists from building more permanent homes to replace their smaller dwellings and makeshift shelters.[126] These later Indians were the Indians next door. Some lived in mill housing. Their children played with and celebrated birthdays with white children, as Louis McGowan, a lifelong resident and historian of Johnston, remembered.[127] At times, the oppositions between being indigenous and being modern might have seemed "neither absolute nor without contradiction," as Raibmon puts it.[128] But even when they overtly reinforced their Indianness with regalia, names, and exhibitions, as they did at the Morgan Avenue powwows, Johnston's Native people challenged their exclusion from modernity and doubts about their authenticity. Indian history and urban history were no more separate at this urban borderland than they were in the inner homelands of Providence.

Epilogue

Imagining Past, Present, and Future Urbanity

Donald Fixico (Shawnee, Sac and Fox, Muscogee Creek, and Seminole), author of *The Urban Indian Experience in America*, notes that one of the most important challenges for researchers is locating and identifying Native people in cities.[1] I could not agree more. But after finding them, the larger challenge is writing about them, especially in a way that is deeply human, intimate, and richly textured. The place-based stories of Native people that I have pieced together are the heart of this book, and the very heartbeat of the urban homelands I have written about. Most of these people went unnoticed, not only because of the myth that Indians were vanishing, but also because their lives did not seem to matter. But they did matter and they still do today, to their descendants and to researchers like me, intent on reframing the history of a settler-colonial city through Native experiences and on revising the venues of Native history. These stories of survivance reinforce Native people's connections within a web of relationships that centered on home, even if home was paved with sidewalks, crossed by streetcar lines, overshadowed by factory buildings, and crowded with strangers.

"Urban," as Terry Straus and Debra Valentino insist, "is not a kind of Indian."[2] It is a kind of experience, or a diversity of lived experiences, that most Native people have today and have had in the past. Louise Erdrich, who writes about the Twin Cities of Minneapolis–St. Paul, Minnesota, in her acclaimed novel *Love Medicine*, says that "every foot and inch" of those cities that Indians are "standing on, even if it's on top of the highest skyscraper," belongs to them.[3] Every foot and inch of Providence also belongs to Indians, as does every foot and inch of other U.S. cities.[4] They were more than sojourners in this so-called thoroughfare town, and European settler-colonists' dispossessions did not entirely displace them. Some who remained did so under conditions that were not of their making. Others, warned out by town officials, kept coming back. Providence was their home. It was where they could find companionship and comfort among family and friends. Many continued to gravitate to the city from their tribal reservations during the nineteenth century and after, though some returned to those homelands and places nearby. But mostly they created new urban homelands with inexact boundaries that reimagined New England's Indian Country in such a way that the finely drawn lines of colonial possession in city atlases and cadastral maps were made to seem meaningless.

Panoramas drawn from an imaginary overhead vantage at about the time that these homelands were being inscribed in the urban landscape portray Providence as a place of possibilities. Coveted by the middle class and those who aspired to join its ranks, these bird's-eye views were considered a democratic art form that could help educate and assimilate the newly arrived (fig. 31).[5] Yet much of what the new residents needed to know about the city was missing. Animal carcasses and industrial waste floating in the Cove, construction debris clogging ponds, and chemicals infiltrating groundwater could not be seen on the maps. Nor could one see Native men standing at the city's crossroads, docks, and bridges hoping to find work, Native laundresses laboring over vats of boiling water, and the houses of Providence Indians that might serve as safe havens for relatives and tribal kin who were adjusting to urban life or had fallen on hard times. That these maps were not made using information collected from the city's Native residents seems obvious. They would have had their own maps. Their maps would not have resembled the conjectural maps made by antiquarians using toponyms recorded by "early white scribes who knew nothing about Indian tongues," in the estimation of Frank Speck, who compared the task of interpreting these place names to attempting to "juggle sand," let alone to making any sense of indigenous place-worlds.[6] Unpublished and not usually drawn on paper, their maps would have been guides to everyday urban living in a landscape that no longer belonged to them. They would have shown places in the city where you could find other Native people, homes where you could probably stay for a while and get a hot meal, where rents were reasonable and accommodations not half bad, where an employer was looking to hire, where a preacher might welcome you from the pulpit, and where there was still good fishing. These storied maps would have also identified places of tension that whites considered off-limits to Indians, though the Indians might not have agreed: orchards where jumping a fence or picking fruit was condemned as trespassing, bars and clubs where there were unwritten codes about socializing, and residential streets where Native people were not supposed to be unless they drove a team or were employed as a housekeeper. Native people might have also been unwelcome at art galleries and gaming parlors, given that they were not expected to possess talents that could be showcased or that measured up to those of a different race or class. Some whites discretely wrote about their prejudices and nervousness in diaries, recording their innermost thoughts about a chance encounter in a carriage or at a party, as Susan Lear did, or after hearing shots fired in an altercation in which "a colored man shot two women and himself," as did Bessie Rose Paine, a resident of South Providence.[7] Others expressed such sentiments when speaking publicly, or by showing their uneasiness at finding an Indian standing close to them at a public event.

It is difficult to visualize in any dynamic way the immediacy of the interactions that occurred in places where Native people mingled and in places they had been told to avoid during the nineteenth and early twentieth centuries. The variety of experiences that accrued—and that have never stop accruing—contribute to an enduring affinity for known localities and ways of life, as Keith Basso writes.[8] Yet while finishing this book I wondered if visualizations of individuals' experiences of place could be better approximated. In May 2018 at the opening of an exhibition at the Haffenreffer Museum of Anthropology in Providence, *Drone Warriors: The Art of Surveillance and Resistance at Standing Rock*, about the use of drones as tools of surveillance and resistance on the Standing Rock Sioux Reservation, I was struck by sweeping panoramas that revealed incredible details of the landscape. The aerial photographs were taken from April 2016 to February 2017, when thou-

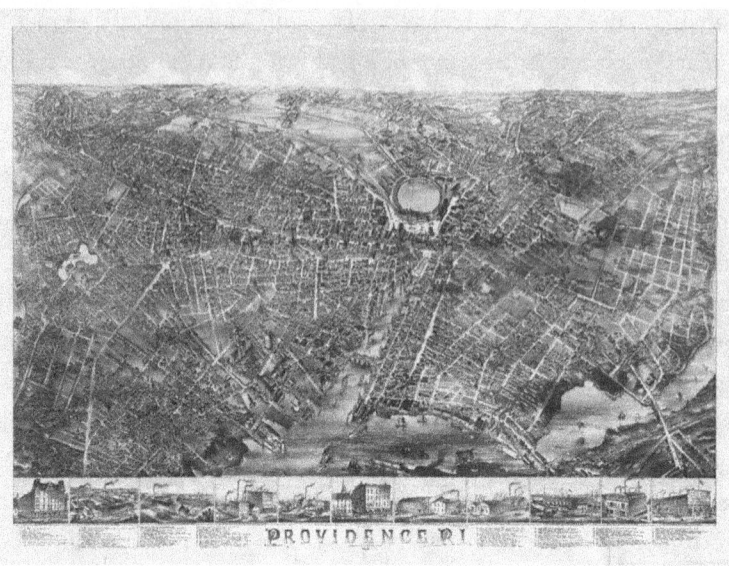

Fig. 31. *Providence, R.I.*, a bird's-eye view from the southeast, published by O. H. Bailey & Co., 1882. Courtesy of the Norman B. Leventhal Map & Education Center at the Boston Public Library.

sands of Natives and non-Natives gathered on the northern plains to oppose the Dakota Access Pipeline, which threatened Lakota cultural and sacred sites and the Standing Rock Sioux Nation's sovereignty. The introductory panel for the exhibit stated that the photographs "illuminated spaces hidden from the public, unmasked the face of force, and showed the world the beauty of the landscape that was threatened by construction and potential contamination." This statement on the wall of the gallery could not have been more accurate. I returned to the museum after the opening to take a closer look. What I saw so clearly was not a cityscape but a vaster and less densely populated landscape, despite the presence of the protestors. Why did these images resonate with my project on Providence's Native homelands? Was it because they showed chaotic confrontations or because they afforded me the ability to see interconnectedness? Or was it because they allowed me to see what had happened on land where I had not walked and where others were prevented from setting foot?

Most commonly associated with targeted killings in modern warfare and with collecting and updating information to make better maps for moving across space in real time, drones (also called unmanned aerial vehicles, or UAVs) were used at Standing Rock as tools of social activism. In cities they are increasingly used in upgrading projects, while efforts are made to align the benefits of the technology with values of participation, empowerment, accountability, transparency, and equity, to allay concerns about security and privacy.[9] Obviously drones were not available in earlier centuries for gathering geospatial information on the interactions of everyday life in Providence's Native homelands. But what if they had been? Could they have detected invisible lines of ownership? Would they have provided more precise measurements of how these homelands were gradually encroached on by urban development and contaminated by environmental pollution, or helped to evaluate the material conditions of neighborhoods slated for renewal? Could they have shown all that went on at urban powwows? Could they have revealed interactions on city streets and in more private spaces during the daytime and in after hours when they became a "landscape of the night," a different space in its own right, as Denis Byrne remarks, where other rules of behavior might have applied?[10] Could these images have been used to locate Native men and women? Ethical issues about infringing on the privacy of space are beside the point, because drones did not fly over nineteenth- and early twentieth-century landscapes still replete with Native people. And if they had, they could not have documented what went on inside the houses, courtrooms, jail cells, livery stables, checkers parlors, and beauty salons. Forewarned of impending flights, residents would have had the power to camouflage sweat houses in backyards that they considered culturally sensitive or to remove rubbish that parties collecting geospatial information could construe as indicting. And yet, other evidence of their presence in the urban landscape on land that European settler-colonists did not view as theirs might have been hard to hide or disguise.

In the museum, a wall with text and a large map of the world separated *Drone Warriors: The Art of Surveillance and Resistance at Standing*

Rock from a companion installation, *Sacred Is Sacred: The Art of Protecting Bears Ears*, about a storied indigenous landscape in Utah at risk of losing its status as a national monument and the associated protections against extractive development. Visitors were asked to tag a place on the map that they wanted to protect because it was meaningful to them and endangered. The tags, strips of colored paper that identify places by name, were meant to raise awareness about sites of spiritual, historical, and cultural significance threatened by development, and to encourage social and environmental engagement to prevent violations of human rights to land and resources. As I glanced at the map, I thought about Providence's Native homelands and the many houses that have been destroyed, burial grounds that have been desecrated, and ponds that have been contaminated by urban development. Native people had complained about the destruction of their homes, neighborhoods, and sacred sites, though their protests had been ignored. Would the availability of this sophisticated new technology have helped broadcast images of these homelands and the looming threats to them and rallied public opinion in favor of protecting such meaningful places? Is it even reasonable to consider this possibility? Cities, after all, are works in progress where continuous dissolution and increasing improvements invade place-worlds. Dislocating powers indifferent to already extant positive values sweep away old buildings, even good ones, to make room for new ones, as the anthropologist Nancy Munn writes, and in the process swap the rich for the poor, and non-Natives for Natives.[11] But in the unending process of growing, renewing, and encompassing, replacements are never total; pasts are unearthed, the poor are not eliminated, and not all Native people are dislocated.

Looking more closely at the map, I noticed that one of the tags identified "Broad Street, Prov, RI" as an endangered place that should be protected (fig. 32). The street runs through Upper South Providence and was home to Narragansett, Wampanoag, and Nipmuc families in the nineteenth and early twentieth centuries. Some probably still live there today. Off of Broad Street, there were other streets filled with Native people. Yet their histories were ignored and their lives were considered

Fig. 32. Broad Street tag on the map of endangered sites at the *Drone Warriors* and *Sacred Is Sacred* exhibits, Haffenreffer Museum of Anthropology. Photograph by Patricia E. Rubertone.

as dispensable as those of homeless families and the individuals today who find emergency shelter at Crossroads, a nonprofit organization at Broad and Seekel Streets, within close sight of where Interstate 95 removed part of this homeland. Because of civic engineering projects and less far-reaching changes, this stretch of the urban landscape would be largely unrecognizable to Native people who lived there during the nineteenth and early twentieth centuries. Nevertheless, Broad Street is still a meaningful place to the anonymous person who cared enough to tag it on the map in the gallery, and to others.

There are no drones hovering over Broad Street to record images of what is at risk from further development in a homeland where the evidence of destruction inflicted earlier is all too apparent. There is virtually nothing left to see of the homeland's deep past and less and less that remains visible of its more recent Native past, as is true of Providence's

Epilogue 331

other Native homelands. New technologies cannot reanimate these past landscapes, at least not the ancestries and shared experiences that shaped them. These histories, victims of documentary genocide and what Coll Thrush has termed the narrative estrangement of indigenous history from urban history, exist if one looks or listens closely.[12] The Broad Street tag is a reminder that Native stories about this place and its people and those about other homelands in the city have not disappeared and are ongoing. These stories are not only buried below the ground or in fleeting references in archives both large and small, waiting to be discovered by chance or by diligent research. They also exist in memories kept by those who know the meaning of these places.

Providence, like other European settler-colonial cities in the United States, Australia, Canada, New Zealand, and beyond, has an indigenous past that is foundational to its existence. As I have argued in this book, it also has a more recent indigenous past. Native people were part of the city's emerging modernity. As symbols of disorderliness, their very presence was a reason for adopting a modern city government. Some withstood being completely driven from their homes in the colonial town. Others flocked to the newly incorporated city to make new homes for themselves, defying settler colonialism's racialized and segregated geographies. Generations were born, married, and died here, long before the 1934 Indian Reorganization Act and the Bureau of Indian Affairs Relocation Act of 1956. Some came to start over after the Civil War or returned after serving in World War I. They found one another, jobs, and houses that they rented or bought, sent their children to school, went to church and to powwows, and visited back and forth with friends and relatives who had not moved too far away from tribal reservations. They experienced disappointment, satisfaction, doubt, and, I suspect, everything in between, in an urban landscape where they belonged as much as, if not more than, anyone else. Existing in plain view, regardless of how they might have been counted or what they were called, Native people were not given a place in the modern history of the city, though they are part of its past, present, and future. Like histories of other contemporary cities, this is an unfinished history. Its uncertainties open new interpretive spaces for telling other stories of Native survivance and for unsettling understandings, rooted in settler colonialism, about Native people's place in the urban narrative.

> Home,
>   the place of the Ancestors.
> Layers of usurpation—seen
>   as street upon street
>   pollution upon pollution.
> How have you taken so much
>   when you have cared
>   so little.
> The people cry.
>
> Twilight's Hour
> Time to contemplate
> The future[13]

Appendix

Native Residents of Providence Homelands

Name	Fox Point	Lippitt Hill	Upper South Providence	Lower South Providence	The Ponds	Federal Hill	Johnston
Ammons, Alexander	x		x				
Apess, William		x					
Babcock, Estella						x	
Babcock, Melvenia			x			x	
Bannister (Babcock), Christiana	x				x		
Baxter, Sarah		x	x				
Bell, Lillian					x		
Bent, Ida				x	x		
Bent, William H.				x	x	x	
Blunt, Maria	x	x			x		
Booth, Martha A.			x	x			
Bourne (Cheats), Glendora					x		
Bourne (Cheats), Harriet					x		
Bourne (Cheats), Harvey					x		
Bourne (Cheats), Jean					x		
Bourne (Cheats), Jerome					x		
Bourne (Cheats), Joyce					x		
Bourne (Cheats), Philip					x		
Bourne (Cheats), Rodman					x		
Bourne (Cheats), Ruell					x		
Bourne (Cheats), Vivian					x		
Brewster, Amos	x		x				
Brown (Taylor), Ida					x		
Brown, Isabella E.			x				
Brown, John E.			x				

Name	Fox Point	Lippitt Hill	Upper South Providence	Lower South Providence	The Ponds	Federal Hill	Johnston
Brown (Taylor), Lillian					x		
Brown, Sarah E.					x		
Brown, William J.	x	x					
Brown, William R. (Ross)			x				
Buscher (Elderkin), Isabella				x			
Buscher (Elderkin), Joseph				x			
Carl, Araminta					x		
Carl, Arthur					x		
Carl, Arthur V.					x		
Carl, Elizabeth					x		
Carl, Franklin					x		
Carl, Frederick					x		
Carl, Howard					x		
Carl, Lena					x		
Carl, Lloyd Emerson					x		
Carl (Ingram), Maxine					x		
Carpenter, Mary			x				
Cesar, Joan		x					
Champlin, Benjamin R.			x				
Champlin, Blanch			x				
Champlin, Christopher	x		x				
Champlin, Ellen M.			x				
Champlin, Jane R.			x				
Champlin (Helm), Mary			x				
Champlin, Walter G.			x				
Cheeves (Noka), Nancy	x						
Chinn (Wheeler), Barbara						x	
Ciscoe, Sarah M.					x		
Clarke, Mary J.				x			
Cone, Anna Maria						x	
Cone, Charles H.	x	x				x	x
Cone, Edward S.	x	x				x	x

Name	Fox Point	Lippitt Hill	Upper South Providence	Lower South Providence	The Ponds	Federal Hill	Johnston
Cone, Frederick	x						
Cone, Frederick F.					x		
Cone, Frederick H.	x						
Cone, Henrietta						x	
Cone, John			x	x			
Cone, Mary J.	x	x	x				
Cone, Sarah	x	x	x	x	x		
Congdon, George			x				
Cooper, Nettie			x				
Clarke, Mary J.				x			
Creighton, Charles H.		x					
Creighton, John A.			x				
Creighton, Martha		x	x				
Creighton, Pauline	x		x				
Creighton, Thomas H.		x	x				
Dailey, Charles E.	x		x	x		x	
Dailey, Moses P.					x	x	
Dailey, Nettie					x	x	
Davis, Lorenz	x						
Davis, Abbey E.			x				
Davis, Mary E.			x				
Dwight (Daniels), Roxanna				x			
Dwight (Daniels), Theodolphus				x			
Edwards, Clara			x				
Edwards, William			x			x	
Elderkin, Agatha			x				
Elderkin Arthur			x				
Elderkin, Charlotte				x	x		
Elderkin, Claude		x			x		
Elderkin, Earl A.		x			x		
Elderkin, Earl E.				x	x		
Elderkin, Earl E., Jr.				x	x		

Appendix 337

Name	Fox Point	Lippitt Hill	Upper South Providence	Lower South Providence	The Ponds	Federal Hill	Johnston
Elderkin, Edwin				x	x		
Elderkin, Esther			x	x			
Elderkin, Harvey			x		x		
Elderkin, Leona				x	x		
Elderkin, Kenneth				x	x		
Elderkin, Marcus			x	x	x		
Elderkin, Marcus, Jr.			x	x	x		
Elderkin, Neotah				x	x		
Elderkin, Oscar				x			
Ellis (Chace), Mary J.		x					
Ellston, Ann E.	x						
Ellston, Walter B.	x						
Fearson, Caleb Rodman		x				x	
Fenner, Susan						x	
Ford (Weeden), Ruth M.			x				
Ford (Weeden), Ruth M., Jr.			x		x		
Ford (Weeden), William P.			x				
Fox, Elizabeth						x	
Freeman, Clarence	x		x			x	
Gardner, Benjamin G.			x		x		
Gardner, Dhowusk Lovel				x			
Gardner, Hannah			x			x	
Gardner, Mary		x					
Greene (Elderkin), Beatrice				x			
Greene (Elderkin), Myrtle				x			
Greene, William S.			x				
Guiles, Frederick D.		x					
Guy, Clifford				x	x		
Guy, Clifford, Jr.				x			
Guy (Weeden), Esther				x	x		
Guy, Ida				x			

Name	Fox Point	Lippitt Hill	Upper South Providence	Lower South Providence	The Ponds	Federal Hill	Johnston
Guy, John				x			
Guy, Malcolm				x			
Guy, Walter S.				x			
Guy, Walter S., Jr.				x			
Harker (Malbone), Sarah M.			x		x		
Harris (Thomas), Lydia			x				
Harry, Louis			x				
Hazard, Grace			x				
Hazard, Carrie			x				
Hazard, Hannah M.	x		x		x		
Hazard, Howard B.				x		x	
Hazard, Mercy Ann			x				
Hazard, Minnie B.						x	
Hazard, Sarah E.					x	x	
Hazard, Sarah M.						x	
Helm, Frank			x				
Henries, Perry E.			x				
Henries, Auguette		x					
Henries, Edith		x					
Henries, Elizabeth		x					
Henries, Elsie		x					
Henries, Ethel		x					
Henries, Winfred		x					
Henry, James			x				
Henry (Nichols), Olive			x				
Hilton (Thomas), Clarence			x		x		
Hilton (Thomas), Eliza	x		x		x		
Holden, Lloyd		x					
Holden, Susan			x	x			
Howard, Frank A.	x						
Jackson, Amy			x	x			

Name	Fox Point	Lippitt Hill	Upper South Providence	Lower South Providence	The Ponds	Federal Hill	Johnston
Jackson, Minnie		x					
Jackson, Oling		x					
Jackson, Oling, Jr.		x					
Jackson, Prudence	x	x					
Jandes, Jacob				x			
Johnson, Charles						x	
Johnson, Howard H.			x				
Kendall, Albertina			x			x	
Kendall, Fannie			x		x	x	
Kendall, Franklin E.			x				
Kendall, Louisa						x	
Kendall, Stephen			x		x	x	
Lee, Lillian R.			x	x			
Lee, Margaret R.				x			
Lee, Robert E.				x			
Lowling/Loring, Frank						x	
Lowling/Loring, Joseph						x	
Lowling/Loring, Maria						x	
Lowling/Loring, Mary						x	
Lowling/Loring, Nancy						x	
Lowling/Loring, Newell						x	
Lowling/Loring, Thomas						x	
Malbone, Charles			x			x	
Malbone, Jessie			x				
Malbone, Mary A.					x		
Malbone, Nancy			x				
Malbone, Susie			x				
Malbone, William			x				
Marley, Mary						x	
Marley, Susan						x	
Mars, Harold					x		

Name	Fox Point	Lippitt Hill	Upper South Providence	Lower South Providence	The Ponds	Federal Hill	Johnston
Mars, Laura					x		
Marsh, Mabel					x	x	
Maurelle, Lorenz	x						
Melville (Daniels), Jane				x			
Melville (Daniels), Jerome				x			
Michael, Edward	x	x		x			
Mitchell (Chace), Benjamin		x					
Morris (Profit), Alice A.			x				
Morris (Profit), Cornelia			x				
Morris (Profit), Ezra, Jr.			x				
Morris (Profit), Lucy A.			x				
Nichols, Anna F.			x				
Nichols, Anstriss	x						
Nichols, Benjamin	x				x	x	
Nichols, Charles E.		x	x				
Nichols, David			x	x		x	
Nichols, Florence		x					
Nichols, Frank E.		x	x	x	x		
Nichols, Frank M.		x					
Nichols, Georgianna		x	x				
Nichols, Georgianna F.			x				
Nichols, Gertrude		x					
Nichols, Grace E.		x					
Nichols, Harriet	x						
Nichols, Hannah			x				
Nichols, Mabel			x				
Nichols, Priscilla			x			x	
Nocake, Joshua				x		x	
Noka, Benjamin	x						
Noka, Christopher		x					
Noka, Daniel		x					

Name	Fox Point	Lippitt Hill	Upper South Providence	Lower South Providence	The Ponds	Federal Hill	Johnston
Noka, Edward	x				x	x	
Nokey, Alice						x	
Northrup (Chace), Alice		x	x	x			
Northrup (Chace), Charles		x	x	x			
Northrup (Chace), Clark				x			
Northrup (Chace), David		x					
Northrup (Chace), Edward		x		x			
Northrup (Chace), James		x	x	x			
Northrup (Chace), Mercy Ann						x	
Onsley, Annie							x
Onsley, Benjamin F.							x
Onsley, Dolly							x
Onsley, Eldridge							x
Onsley, Emma							x
Onsley, Ernest P.							x
Onsley, Ethel							x
Onsley, Josephine							x
Onsley, Julia							x
Onsley, Louisa							x
Onsley, Mary Jane							x
Onsley, Nellie							x
Onsley, Susan							x
Ownsley, Harriet			x				x
Ownsley, Phebe					x		
Ownsley, Willis A. K.	x		x			x	
Parker, Mary A.		x					
Peckham, Mary E.			x				
Perry, Angelina		x					
Perry, Arthen		x					
Perry, Beatrice					x		
Perry, Earl C.					x		

Name	Fox Point	Lippitt Hill	Upper South Providence	Lower South Providence	The Ponds	Federal Hill	Johnston
Perry, Hazel L.					x		
Perry, Herman					x		
Perry, Leroy C.					x		
Perry, Louise		x					
Perry, Nada					x		
Perry, Percy		x					
Perry, Royal					x		
Perry, Sarah		x					
Perry, Susie		x					
Perry, William C.		x					
Perry, William C., Jr.		x					
Philips, Ruth				x			
Post, Mary A.				x			
Potter, Joan		x					
Price, John A.			x			x	
Proffitt, Nancy Elizabeth		x		x		x	
Proffitt, William		x	x			x	
Prophet, Alice J.	x						
Prophet, Florence L.	x						
Prophet, George	x						
Prophet, Joseph N.	x						
Prophet, Moses	x						
Prophet, Moses B.	x	x					
Randolph, Mary			x				
Reckling, Bertha			x				
Reed, Flavius				x			
Rocker, Catalina	x						
Rocker, Emily	x						
Rocker, Eunice			x				
Rocker, Harry W.	x		x				
Rocker, Johanna	x						

Name	Fox Point	Lippitt Hill	Upper South Providence	Lower South Providence	The Ponds	Federal Hill	Johnston
Rocker, Lawrence	x	x					
Rocker, Mary	x						
Rocker, Nellie Josephine			x				
Rocker, Walter W.					x		
Rocker, William	x						
Rodman, Caleb		x		x	x	x	
Rodman, Frances	x						
Rodman, Joshua						x	
Rodman, Samuel	x		x	x		x	
Rosser, Dorcas			x				
Scott, George Ross		x			x		
Smith (Noka), Abigail		x					
Smith (Noka), Frederick W.	x	x					
Smith (Noka), Roland		x					
Steppo, Melvin							x
Stockett, James M.			x				
Stockett, James M., Jr.	x						
Storms (Crank), Rachel			x	x	x		
Sullivan (Thomas), Mary			x		x		
Taylor, Alfred H.					x		
Taylor, Anna					x		
Taylor, Charles					x		
Taylor, Fred W.					x		
Taylor, Hannah					x		
Thomas, Annie		x					
Thomas, Benjamin F.			x	x			
Thomas, Cora D.			x				
Thomas, Early			x				
Thomas, Elizabeth			x				
Thomas, Frank				x			
Thomas, Frederick D.			x	x	x	x	

Name	Fox Point	Lippitt Hill	Upper South Providence	Lower South Providence	The Ponds	Federal Hill	Johnston
Thomas, William H.			x				
Walmsley, Elizabeth		x					
Wamsley, Betsey	x						
Wamsley, George L.	x						
Wamsley, William G.	x						
Wamsley, William H.	x						
Warmsley, Judson			x				x
Watson, Rosella					x		
Weeden, Andrew			x				
Weeden, Clarence O.				x	x		
Weeden, Dorothy					x		
Weeden, Esther M.					x		
Weeden, Everett G.			x	x			
Weeden, Everett G., Jr.				x			
Weeden, Frederick H.						x	
Weeden, Frederick H., Jr.						x	
Weeden, Georgianna					x		
Weeden, Gladys						x	
Weeden, James					x		
Weeden, Mary			x				
Weeden, Otis E.			x		x	x	
Weeden, Otis E., Jr.			x		x		
Weeden, William	x						
Wheeler, A. A.	x				x		
Wheeler, Ann M.			x				
Wheeler, Caroline E.			x			x	
Wheeler, Edwin			x				
Wheeler, Hannah			x				
Wheeler, Pauline E.			x			x	
Wheeler, Thomas P.			x	x	x	x	
Williams, Atwood I., Jr.					x		

Appendix 345

Name	Fox Point	Lippitt Hill	Upper South Providence	Lower South Providence	The Ponds	Federal Hill	Johnston
Williams, Joseph		x					
Williams, Mary		x					
Woodson (Elderkin), Wilfred				x			
Young (Weeden), Georgianna						x	
Young, Mary E.						x	
Young, Walter H.	x					x	

Notes

Abbreviations

JHS	Johnston Historical Society
ND	*Narragansett Dawn*
PCA	Providence City Archives
PCD	Providence City Directory (various years)
RIBHS	Rhode Island Black Heritage Society
RIBR	Rhode Island State Birth Register
RI Census	Rhode Island State Census (various years)
RIDR	Rhode Island State Death Register
RIHPHC	Rhode Island Historic Preservation and Heritage Commission
RIHS	Rhode Island Historical Society
RIMR	Rhode Island State Marriage Register
RISA	Rhode Island State Archives
U.S. Census	U.S. Census records (various years)

Introduction

1. "By Golly, 'Twas an Indian; a Real Narragansett Too!" *Providence Evening Bulletin*, March 30, 1943, 25.
2. Stevens, "Tomahawk."
3. Veracini, *Settler Colonialism* and *The Settler Colonial Present*; Glenn, "Settler Colonialism as Structure"; Wolfe, "Settler Colonialism and the Elimination of the Native"; Kauanui, "A Structure, Not an Event."
4. O'Brien, *Firsting and Lasting*, xiv.
5. Smith, "The Archaeological Study of Neighborhoods and Districts"; see also Rothschild, "Colonial and Postcolonial New York," 132.
6. Warf and Arias, *The Spatial Turn*.
7. For criticism of the term "urban Indian," see Straus and Valentino, "Retribalization in Urban Indian Communities."
8. Glenn, "Settler Colonialism as Structure."
9. See Edmunds, *Urbanizing Frontiers*; Fixico, *The Urban Indian Experience in America*; Krouse and Howard, *Keeping the Campfires Going*; Lapier

and Beck, *City Indian*; Lobo and Peters, *American Indians and the Urban Experience*; McBride, *Molly Spotted Elk*; Ramirez, *Native Hubs*; Rosenthal, *Native American Migration and Identity*; Thrush, *Native Seattle* and *Indigenous London*; and Weaver, *The Red Atlantic*.

10. For exceptions, see Guillemin, *Urban Renegades*; and Welburn, *Hartford's Ann Plato and the Native Borders of Identity*.
11. Thrush, *Indigenous London*, 14.
12. Mandell, *Tribe, Race, History*, 4–5.
13. Rhode Island, [*First*] *Annual Report*, appendix C.
14. Mandell, *Tribe, Race, History*, 4–5; Den Ouden, *Beyond Conquest*; Herndon and Sekatau, "The Right to a Name"; Plane and Button, "The Massachusetts Indian Enfranchisement Act."
15. Earle, *Report to the Governor*.
16. "The Indians of Providence," *Providence Journal*, May 31, 1914, 2:4.
17. See U.S. Census 1830.
18. Williams, "To [Robert Williams?], 1 April 1676," in Williams, *Correspondence*, 2:722.
19. Williams, "To Governor Henry Vane and Deputy Governor John Winthrop, 1 May 1637," in Williams, *Correspondence*, 1:72.
20. Williams, "To Governor John Winthrop, 30 June 1637" and "To John Winthrop, 31 July 1637," in Williams, *Correspondence*, 1:88, 109, 110n5.
21. Calloway, "Introduction," in Calloway, *After King Philip's War*, 4.
22. Ulrich, *Age of Homespun*; Williams, "To Governor John Leverett or Governor Josiah Winslow, 16 October 1676," in Williams, *Correspondence*, 2:728.
23. Williams, "To [Robert Williams?], 1 April 1676," in Williams, *Correspondence*, 2:721–22.
24. Staples, *Annals of the Town of Providence*, 170–71.
25. Fisher, "'Why Shall Wee Have Peace'"; Newell, *Brethren by Nature*; Sainsbury, "Indian Labor in Early Rhode Island"; Warren, *New England Bound*; Rogers and Field, *The Early Records of the Town of Providence*.
26. Stone, *Life and Recollections of John Howland*, 25–26.
27. Rogers, Carpenter, and Field, *The Early Records of the Town of Providence*, 33–36.
28. RIHS, Items 16959 and 16960, June 1715, Providence Town Papers, MSS 214, subgroup 1, series 1, vol. 39, 6.
29. RIHS, Item 16879, June 4, 1711, Providence Town Papers, MSS 214, subgroup 1, series 1, vol. 39, 127.
30. Newell, *Brethren by Nature*.
31. Herndon, *Unwelcome Americans*, 62–66 (quote at 62).

32. RIHS, Susanna Lear Diary, 1788, MSS 9001-L; "Notes and Queries," 377; Lancaster, "'By the Pens of Females,'" 73–75.
33. "The Indians of Providence."
34. "The Indians of Providence."
35. Deloria, *Indians in Unexpected Places*.
36. Doughton, "Unseen Neighbors," 207–30; Gonzales, "Racial Legibility," 57–67; Handsman, "First Whalers"; Jobe, "Native Americans and the U.S. Census," 66–80; Shoemaker, *American Indian Population Recovery*; Mancini, "Beyond Reservation"; Mihesuah, "American Indian Identities."
37. Rubertone, *Grave Undertakings*, xii.
38. Vizenor, "Aesthetics of Survivance," 1.
39. Deloria, *Indians in Unexpected Places*, 232.
40. Campbell and La Fantasie, "Scattered to the Winds of Heaven."
41. Mihesuah, *Natives and Academics*; Smith, *Decolonizing Methodologies*; and Wilson and Yellow Bird, *For Indigenous Eyes Only*.
42. Trouillot, *Silencing the Past*, 25.
43. Simmons, *Spirit of the New England Tribes*.
44. For example, see *Narragansett Dawn*, a magazine published by the Narragansett tribe in 1935 and 1936; Apess, *On Our Own Ground*; Senier, *Dawnland Voices*.
45. Fenn, *Encounters at the Heart of the World*; see also Brooks, *Our Beloved Kin*; and DeLucia, *Memory Lands*.
46. Basso, *Wisdom Sits in Places*.
47. Lipsitz, "The Racialization of Space and Spatialization of Race."
48. Thrush, *Indigenous London*, 14.
49. Wolf, *Europe and the People without History*. For a discussion of Wolf's thesis for critical readings of urban history, see Susie McFadden-Resper and Brett Williams, "Washington's People without History."
50. Jacobs, *Life and Death of Great American Cities*.
51. O'Connell, "Introduction," xxv.
52. Brooks, "Continental Shifts"; Brooks, DeCorse, and Walton, *Small Worlds*; Lepore, "Historians Who Love Too Much"; Spector, *What This Awl Means*.
53. For a discussion of the "unhoused" see Duneier, *Sidewalk*.
54. Lobo, "Urban Clan Mothers."
55. Clifford, "Indigenous Articulations," 478.

1. Fox Point

1. Arnold, *History of the State of Rhode Island*, 40.

2. Rubertone, *Grave Undertakings*, 30–31. For meanings of Tuncowoden, see O'Brien, "American Indian Place Names in Rhode Island"; Rider, *The Lands of Rhode Island*, 275.
3. Brigham, *Seventeenth-Century Place-Names of Providence Plantations*, 10.
4. Williams, "To Major John Mason and Governor Thomas Prence, 22 June 1679," in Williams, *Correspondence*, 2:610.
5. Basso, *Wisdom Sits in Places*; Brooks, *Common Pot*.
6. Arnold, *History of the State of Rhode Island*; Cady, *Civic and Architectural Development*.
7. Ingold, "The Temporality of Landscape."
8. RIHPHC, Archaeological Site Files; Cook, *The Rhode Island Burial Survey, Part 2*, 89–91; Rubertone, "Grave Remembrances"; Parsons, "Indian Relics."
9. Brooks, *Common Pot*.
10. Snow, *Statistics and Causes of Asiatic Cholera*.
11. Campbell, *A Community Apart*, 5.
12. Brown, *The Life of William J. Brown of Providence*; Sullivan, "Reconstructing the Olney's Lane Riot," 50.
13. Brown, *The Life of William J. Brown of Providence*, 52.
14. Brown, *The Life of William J. Brown of Providence*, 1.
15. Brown, *The Life of William J. Brown of Providence*, 18.
16. Beck, *Manny Almeida's Ringside Lounge*, 38.
17. Lobo, "Urban Clan Mothers," 5.
18. "Transcript of Interview with Yvonne Smart," 2009, Fox Point Project, Brown Digital Repository, Brown University Library, https://repository.library.brown.edu/studio/item/bdr:147920/.
19. Boissevain, *The Narragansett People*, 79.
20. Rhode Island, *[First] Annual Report*, 85.
21. PCA, Record of Marriages, book 5, 319.
22. *U.S., Find a Grave Index*.
23. PCA, Record of Deeds, book 68, 51.
24. U.S. Census 1840 lists her as the head of a household that included one free colored male under the age of ten (Benjamin), one free colored female age ten to twenty-three (Harriet), and one free colored female age fifty-five to ninety-nine, whose identity is unknown.
25. U.S. Census 1850.
26. RIHS, PCD 1856, 254.
27. PCA, Record of Marriages, book 8, 209.
28. RI Census 1865; RIHS, PCD 1867, 147.
29. RIHS, Dexter Asylum Records, MS 67, series 1, vol. 3.

30. PCA, Record of Deeds, book 65, 178; book 71, 200; book 74, 113; book 67, 119; book 74, 146. Record of Deeds, book 66, 368, concerns a strip of land about seven inches wide "on a street leading from Arnold to Transit Street" sold to William S. Nichols for one dollar by Luther Pearson in 1835, presumably to settle a boundary of the Nichols home lot.
31. PCA, Probate No. A 6049, Providence Probate Records.
32. PCA, Record of Deeds, book 74, 113; book 85, 317-19.
33. PCA, Probate No. A 6049, Providence Probate Records.
34. PCA, Probate No. A 6049, Providence Probate Records.
35. PCA, Probate No. A 6049, Providence Probate Records.
36. PCA, Probate No. A 6049, Providence Probate Records.
37. Horton, "The Making of a Kentucky Counterpane."
38. Anderson, *Mahogany*.
39. Schoelwer, "Form, Function, and Meaning."
40. McMullen, "Looking for People in Woodsplint Basketry Decoration"; Turnbaugh and Turnbaugh, "Weaving the Woods."
41. Ulrich, *Age of Homespun*, 342.
42. Simmons, "From Manifest Destiny."
43. PCA, Probate No. A 13812, Providence Probate Records.
44. Mann, *Features of Society in Old and in New England*, 60.
45. Among Benjamin Nichols's creditors were Joel F. Raynesford and John P. Gale; see PCA, Probate No. A 6835, Providence Probate Records. Raynesford, who sold Nichols a horse for $100 and a cab and harness for $85, owned a livery stable in Fall River. Fall River MA City Directory, 1853, 85, in *U.S. City Directories*. Gale, listed as a merchant in Fall River in the 1850 U.S. Census, was paid $7 for clothing.
46. In her sworn testimony to the Indian Affairs Commission during the detribalization hearing, Anstriss Nichols gave her mother's name as Mary M. Jackson. When her name was registered as a claimant, she was identified as "the daughter of Henrietta Jackson." Rhode Island, [*First*] *Annual Report*, 75, 72.
47. Rhode Island, [*First*] *Annual Report*, 34, 85, 100, 117, 120, 122, 124, 125, 128, 170.
48. Scott, *Seeing Like a State*.
49. "Lineage of Theodore Dennis Brown," ND 1, no. 2 (June 1935): 9-10; "In and about Peacedale," ND 1, no. 11 (March 1936): 263-64.
50. RIHS, PCD 1841, 186; 1844, 200.
51. U.S. Census 1850; RIHS, PCD 1852, 213.
52. Rodman, *Memorial*.
53. U.S. Census 1860.

54. RIHS, PCD 1864, 133; 1866, 151; 1867, 167.
55. U.S. Census 1870.
56. RIHS, PCD 1869, 194; 1872, 231.
57. RIHS, PCD 1873, 230.
58. Bristol, "From Outposts to Enclaves"; Mandell, *Tribe, Race, History*.
59. Lyons, *X-Marks*.
60. Weibel-Orlando, "Introduction."
61. U.S. Census 1850.
62. U.S. Census 1860.
63. *U.S., Civil War Draft Registrations Records*.
64. For a discussion of soldiers in the Twenty-Ninth Regiment of the Connecticut Colored Infantry from Nipmuc, Mashantucket, Eastern Pequot, and other tribal communities in Windham and New London Counties, see Naumec, "From Mashantucket to Appomattox."
65. Historical Data Systems, comp. *U.S., Civil War Soldier Records and Profiles, 1861–1865*.
66. King and Rivello, "Amos Brewster," 57–59.
67. King and Rivello, "Amos Brewster," 58–59.
68. Rose and Brown, *Tapestry*, 55.
69. RI Census 1865.
70. U.S. Census 1870.
71. RIHPHC, Building Data Sheet, 72 John Street, file 0000284, 1975, Rhode Island Statewide Survey. The lot at 70 John St. measures 2,835 square feet and has two wood-frame structures, one fronting the north side, on John St., and a smaller building at the east end of the lot. See Hopkins, *City Atlas of Providence*. The same configuration appears in the 1882 city atlas; see Hopkins, *Atlas of the City of Providence, R.I.* The footprint was the same in 1895, though the street number had been changed to 72 John St.; see Everts & Richards, *Atlas of Rhode Island*.
72. Beck, *Manny Almeida's Ringside Lounge*.
73. U.S. Census 1880.
74. For discussion of "anchor" households in urban Indian communities see Lobo, "Urban Clan Mothers," 11–12.
75. RIHS, PCD 1867, 53.
76. Rhode Island, [*First*] *Annual Report*, 104.
77. Rhode Island, [*First*] *Annual Report*, 33.
78. U.S. Census 1880. During the detribalization hearings, Louisa Weeden was described as "not married." She had married Dwight Weeden, who

was also born in Griswold, in the village of Wakefield in South Kingstown on February 22, 1865. RISA, RIMR vol. 1865, 702.
79. Rhode Island, [*First*] *Annual Report*, 33, 103.
80. RISA, RIMR, vol. 1881, 1270. Weeden's husband continued to live in Narragansett Pier with their daughter Bertha (married name Reckling) and her children until his death in 1900. Bertha Reckling later moved to Providence. Her name and those of other Recklings appear in the pages of *Narragansett Dawn*; see, for example, "Graduates of Yester-Years and Today," ND 1, no. 3 (July 1935): 7; "Be Careful What You Say," ND 1, no. 5 (September 1935): 118; "Sunrise New Items to the Narragansett Dawn," ND 1, no. 5 (September 1935): 128; "Trail of Daniel Harry in 1839," ND 1, no. 10 (February 1936): 237; "The Rag Sociable," ND 1, no. 11 (March 1936): 263; "News from Charlestown, R.I.," ND 2, no. 3 (July 1936): 55.
81. RI Census 1885.
82. Rhode Island, [*First*] *Annual Report*, 33, 102.
83. Doughton, "Unseen Neighbors"; O'Connell, "Introduction," lxiii.
84. PCA, Record of Marriages, book 16, 10.
85. Rhode Island, [*First*] *Annual Report*, 53, 57.
86. Rhode Island, [*First*] *Annual Report*, 71.
87. RIHS, PCD 1874, 64.
88. Frederick Harry Augustus Cone was born on November 24, 1885, and died on February 3, 1886. Sarah C. Cone is the only parent listed on his birth and death records. PCA, Record of Births, book 13, 138; PCA, Record of Deaths, book 16, 326.
89. Herndon and Sekatau, "The Right to a Name," 128; Simmons, *Spirit of the New England Tribes*, 152–53.
90. PCA, Record of Deaths, book 14, 128, 225; book 16, 186.
91. Basso, *Wisdom Sits in Places*, 147.
92. RI Census 1865.
93. "Data on Old Indian Church," ND 1, no. 6 (October 1935): 153.
94. U.S., *Colored Troops Military Service Records*.
95. Rhode Island, [*First*] *Annual Report*, 73.
96. RIHS, PCD 1882, 31; 1883, 31. For Eliza Hilton, see RIHS, PCD 1876, 176; 1878, 171; 1879, 168.
97. Beck, *Manny Almeida's Ringside Lounge*, 51.
98. PCA, Record of Deaths, book 16, 236.
99. "Charlestown's Indians, the Last of the Narragansetts and Their Shrines," *Providence Sunday Journal*, August 11, 1889 (for "Uncle Gid"); Gideon Ammons is registered in the customs district of Newport, Cer-

tificate No. 86, 12/29/1832, Seamen's Protection Certificate Register Database, Rosenfeld Collection, Mystic Seaport, Mystic CT. His name appears on the crew list of the *Roman*, registered in New Bedford for a whaling voyage in the Indian Ocean that left on July 17, 1843 and returned April 27, 1847. He was discharged at Maui on September 19, 1844. Whaling Collection Archives, New Bedford Free Public Library, New Bedford MA. A "Gideon Ammer" is listed on the crew of the ship *Adeline* in 1843 for an "attachment on at Oahu 10/9/1845," Whaling Crew Database, New Bedford Whaling Museum, New Bedford MA. For other information about his whaling exploits, see "A Memorial Service," *Narragansett Times*, March 2, 1900.

100. Rhode Island, *Narragansett Tribe of Indians*, 71. For discussions of Native New England whalers and mariners abroad, see O'Connell, "'Once More Let Us Consider'"; Shoemaker, "Race and Indigeneity in the Life of Elisha Apess"; Shoemaker, *Native American Whalemen*.
101. "Gideon Ammons Dead: Body of the Last of the Narragansett Chiefs Found in the Woods," *Westerly Sun*, December 4, 1899.
102. "Charlestown's Indians: The Last of the Narragansetts and Their Shrines," *Providence Sunday Journal*, August 11, 1889.
103. RISA, RIDR, vol. 1899, 652.
104. RI Census 1865.
105. *Massachusetts, Birth Records*.
106. U.S. Census 1910.
107. RIHS, PCD 1862, 112; 1863, 110.
108. Rhode Island, [*First*] *Annual Report*, 75; *Rhode Island, Marriage Index*. For George Cheves, see RIHS, PCD 1864, 39; 1865, 40; 1866, 43.
109. Mandell, *Tribe, Race, History*, 169; "Data on Old Indian Church," ND, 153.
110. RIHS, PCD 1836, 132; 1841, 185; U.S. Census 1840. Peter Nocake, born in Charlestown about 1813, was issued seamen's protection certificates in Newport and Providence. Seamen's Protection Certificate Register Database, Rosenfeld Collection, Mystic Seaport, Mystic CT; RIHS, "Index to the Register of Seamen's Protections: 1796–1883." He was also listed on the crew of the *Big Enterprise*, which left Providence for Havana on November 29, 1836. On August 8, 1838, he sailed on the schooner *Morning Star* for Pictou, Nova Scotia, and the following year he was on the *Big Arkansas* bound for the same destination. See RIHS, "Crew Lists and Shipping Articles," series 13, subseries A, box 9, folders 163, 167, and 171, respectively.
111. "Squaw Hollow," *Providence Sunday Journal*, January 1891, 16.
112. "The Ship That Never Made Port," ND 1, no. 9 (January 1936): 208.

113. U.S. Census 1880. (Her surname is spelled Cheeves [mostly], Cheves, and Chieves.)
114. Rhode Island, [First] Annual Report, 58.
115. Rhode Island, [First] Annual Report, 75.
116. Rhode Island, Acts and Resolves Passed, 228.
117. RISA, RIDR, vol. 1889, 569.
118. Rhode Island, Historical Cemetery Commission Index.
119. RIHS, PCD 1863, 110.
120. U.S. Census 1910; 1920; RI Census 1925; Washington, Enrollment and Allotment Applications of Washington Indians, 1911–1919; Lange, "Native Americans Force Settlers to Leave Whidbey Island."
121. Note from Mary Brewster and A. A. Wheeler to Thomas Bicknell, June 2, 1925, Bicknell Scrapbook, Haffenreffer Museum of Anthropology, Brown University, 125.
122. "Graduates of Yester-Years and Today," ND 1, no. 3 (July 1935): 7; "Sunrise News," ND 1, no. 7 (November 1935): 172; "James M. Stockett, Jr., Attorney and Counselor at Law" (advertisement), ND 1, no. 7 (November 1935): 174; "Editorial," ND 2, no. 3 (July 1936): 38.
123. Daniel and Mary Freeman (aka Ida Mary Proffitt) are identified as Clarence's parents in his marriage record (June 26, 1889). They married in 1856 or 1854 and divorced in 1869. *Massachusetts, Marriage Records*; Brown and Rose, *Black Roots*, 137; Pasay, *Full Circle*, 183, 438; Knox and Ferris, *Connecticut Divorces*, 314.
124. U.S. Census 1880.
125. Brown, *Games of the Restricted Match*; "Checker Board Champions: The Remarkable Contest Now Going on at Providence," *New York Times*, September 14, 1890.
126. The 1860 U.S. Census shows Clarence living with Elizabeth Profit, forty, and Thomas Profit, thirteen. In the 1870 federal census, Clarence is in the household of Elizabeth Williams, fifty-seven, who is presumably Elizabeth Profit. Other Profits lived next door, including Thomas Profit, who was married and had a blacksmith shop. See Brown, *Games of the Restricted Match*.
127. Williams, *Key into the Language of America*, 177.
128. "Checker Player of the Past," ND 1, no. 7 (November 1935): 160.
129. Brown, *Games of the Restricted Match*; "Checker Board Champions," *New York Times*, September 14, 1890.
130. PCA, Record of Deaths, book 23, 153; "Clarence Freeman Dead," *Providence Daily Journal*, May 22, 1909.

131. Bhahba, "Signs Taken for Wonders."
132. Jacobs, *Life and Death of Great American Cities*.
133. Duneier, *Sidewalk*; Jacobs, *Life and Death of Great American Cities*.
134. Barnd, *Native Space*, 58.
135. Simister, *Streets of the City*, vol. 1, 29. Benjamin West, a self-taught astronomer who observed and recorded the 1769 event in Providence, describes the it in *Account of the Observation of Venus upon the Sun*.
136. Campbell, *A Community Apart*, 5.
137. Beck, *Manny Almeida's Ringside Lounge*, 69.

2. Lippitt Hill

1. Kennedy, "Native Americans, African Americans," 198.
2. Sullivan, "Reconstructing the Olney's Lane Riot," 51; Brown, *The Life of William J. Brown of Providence*, 50.
3. *Hardscrabble Calendar*, 15-16.
4. RIBHS, *Creative Survival*, 47; Sullivan, "Reconstructing the Olney's Lane Riot," 52.
5. Cady, *Civic and Architectural Development*; Rubertone, "Urban Land Use and Artifact Deposition."
6. Lippard, *Lure of the Local*, 204-5.
7. *Official Redevelopment Plan Lippitt Hill*, 3.
8. *Official Redevelopment Plan Lippitt Hill*, 3, 6.
9. "Surplus Army Tank Demolishing Houses," *Providence Evening Bulletin*, March 27, 1960; "Little by Little, Lippitt Hill Fades Away," *Providence Journal*, May 4, 1986.
10. "Where Are Lippitt Hill Negroes Now?", *Providence Evening Bulletin*, September 26, 1960; Rhode Island Commission against Discrimination, *Relocation of Families from the Lippitt Hill Area*, 5-6.
11. Lippard, *Lure of the Local*; Mayne and Lawrence, "Ethnographies of Place."
12. RIHS, John Howland letter, November 24, 1838, MSS 499; Dorr, *Planting and Growth of Providence*, 235.
13. John Howland letter, November 24, 1838.
14. Dorr, *Planting and Growth of Providence*, 235.
15. Deloria, *Playing Indian*.
16. John Howland letter, November 24, 1838.
17. Allen, *Bi-centenary of the Burning of Providence in 1676*; DeLucia, *Memory Lands*, 151.
18. Allen, *Memorial to Roger Williams*, 5.
19. Artemel et al., *Providence Cove Lands Phase III Report*.

20. Thrush, *Indigenous London*, 14.
21. Dorr, *Planting and Growth of Providence*, 235.
22. "Archaeological Gathering Hears Tally of Uncovered Remains," *Providence Journal*, October 29, 2002.
23. Simmons, *Spirit of the New England Tribes*, 161.
24. Basso, *Wisdom Sits in Places*, 147.
25. Brown, *The Life of William J. Brown of Providence*, 9, 14-16.
26. RIBHS, *Creative Survival*, 40.
27. Brown, *The Life of William J. Brown of Providence*, 28-30.
28. Brown, *The Life of William J. Brown of Providence*, 3-4; Melish, "Introduction," xxv. Tall Oak Weeden suggests that Chloe Prophet was buried somewhere in Cranston; personal communications, July 2 and October 30, 2015.
29. Simmons, *Spirit of the New England Tribes*, 162-71.
30. Melish, "Introduction," xxxvi.
31. Dubuque, *Fall River Indian Reservation*, 37.
32. Earle, *Report to the Governor*, appendix, l.
33. RIBHS, *Creative Survival*, 43.
34. MacGunnigle, "Icabod Northrup"; RIBHS, *Creative Survival*, 57.
35. Brown, *The Life of William J. Brown of Providence*, 48.
36. Campbell, *A Community Apart*, 5; Snow, *Statistics and Causes of Asiatic Cholera*.
37. Dubuque, *Fall River Indian Reservation*, 62, 66 (quotation).
38. Dubuque, *Fall River Indian Reservation*, 93-94.
39. Pierce, *Indian History, Biography and Genealogy*, 218-19.
40. Simmons, "From Manifest Destiny," 132.
41. Earle quoted in Dubuque, *Fall River Indian Reservation*, 91.
42. Pierce, *Indian History, Biography and Genealogy*, 219.
43. Pierce, *Indian History, Biography and Genealogy*, 218-19; Simmons, "From Manifest Destiny."
44. Scott, "The Last of the Wampanoags."
45. Mandell, *Tribe, Race, History*, 167.
46. RIHS, PCD 1860, 112; U.S. Census 1860; PCA, Record of Deaths, book 10, 194.
47. Snow, *Report upon the Sanitary Effects*.
48. "Unholy Stench of 1890 Providence Still Recalled by Shipping Veteran," *Providence Evening Bulletin* March 5, 1940, 15; Snow, *Report upon the Sanitary Effects*, 5.
49. RISA, RIDR, vol. 1860, 854 (Cato), 866 (Edward); RIHS, Dexter Asylum Records, MS 67, vols. 1, 2, 4.

50. PCA, Record of Deaths, book 10, 159.
51. Dubuque, *Fall River Indian Reservation*, 95–96.
52. Simister, *Streets of the City*, vol. 2, 97.
53. Allen, *Bi-centenary of the Burning of Providence in 1676*, 11.
54. PCA, Record of Deaths, book 15, 912.
55. Little, "The Nantucket Indian Sickness," 184; Speck, *Territorial Subdivisions and Boundaries*, 113.
56. Crèvecoeur, *Letters from an American Farmer*, 122.
57. Karttunen, "Dorcas Honorable"; Simmons, "The Earliest Prints and Paintings"; Turano, "Taken from Life."
58. PCA, Record of Deaths, book 15, 912.
59. Crèvecoeur, quoted in Silverman, "The Impact of Indentured Servitude," 645.
60. Mandell, *Tribe, Race, History*, 65; Karttunen, *The Other Islanders*.
61. Hudson, *The Making of "Mammy Pleasant"*, 22.
62. Philbrick, *Away Off Shore*, 46.
63. William Baxter was a crew member on the *Laurel*, a 167-ton brig that sailed from Providence to Pictou, Nova Scotia, on May 12, 1837. A resident of Providence, born in Philadelphia, Baxter was described as twenty-six years old and six feet tall, with a black complexion and black hair. RIHS, "Crew Lists and Shipping Articles, 1792–1884," MSS 28, series 13, subseries A, box 9, folder 163 (January–May 1837).
64. RIHS, PCD 1853, 58; U.S. Census 1840. The census lists three free colored persons in William Baxter's household: two males, one between ten and twenty-three and another between twenty-four and thirty-five years old (presumably William), and a female between twenty-four and thirty-five (presumably Sarah).
65. Sullivan, "Reconstructing the Olney's Lane Riot," 50; Brown, *The Life of William J. Brown of Providence*, 52–55.
66. Sullivan, "Reconstructing the Olney's Lane Riot," 51, 57.
67. PCA, Record of Deaths, book 9, 169.
68. Silverman, "The Impact of Indentured Servitude," 653.
69. Steele, "Reduced to Images," 46.
70. Mithlo, *"Our Indian Princess."*
71. The image was reproduced from a photograph using leggotyping. For discussion of the technique, see Burant, "The Visual World in the Victorian Age"; McIntosh, "W. A. Leggo and G. E. Desbarats."
72. Mithlo, *"Our Indian Princess."*
73. *Massachusetts Register and Business Directory*, 857.

74. PCA, Probate No. A 13375, Providence Probate Records.
75. Brunton, *Health and Wellness in the 19th Century*.
76. Ihlder, *The Houses of Providence*, 15; Speck, "Medicine Practices of the Northeastern Algonquians"; Tantaquidgeon, *Folk Medicine*.
77. The Brown University Herbarium, an important depository of plants from Rhode Island collected from the middle of the nineteenth century through the early twentieth century, is organized by a combination of phylogeny, geography, and alphabetization. The files of preserved dried and pressed plants, searched at the Herbarium in 2015, can now be accessed online through the Consortium of Northeast Herbaria, a large-scale digitization project for plant specimens from across the Northeast and eastern Canada, http://portal.neherbaria.org/portal/.
78. Speck, "Medicine Practices of the Northeastern Algonquians," 320; Tantaquidgeon, *Folk Medicine*, 77.
79. Artemel et al., "Providence Cove Lands Phase III Report."
80. Mithlo, *"Our Indian Princess"*, 16.
81. PCA, Record of Marriages, book 8, 277.
82. Rhode Island, *Narragansett Tribe*, 134.
83. Robinson, "A Narragansett History," 85.
84. "Councilman: Charles Babcock," *ND* 1, no. 2 (June 1935): 10–11.
85. While in Charlestown, Wilder and his wife recorded gravestones in known Narragansett cemeteries and exhumed ten graves, mostly of children, in the Royal Indian Burial Ground at Fort Neck. The remains were taken to Smith College, where they were displayed at the Anthropological and Zoological Museum. Bruchac, "Historical Erasure and Cultural Recovery," 177; Wilder Papers, Smith College Archives.
86. U.S. Census 1870.
87. *U.S., Colored Troops Military Service Records*.
88. PCA, Record of Marriages, book 10, 65; Wilder Papers, Smith College Archives.
89. Rhode Island, *Narragansett Tribe*, 37; Rhode Island, *[First] Annual Report*, 95; Wilder Papers, Smith College Archives.
90. Rhode Island, *Narragansett Tribe*, 37.
91. Rhode Island, *Narragansett Tribe*, 39; PCA, Record of Deaths, book 16, 374.
92. RISA, Petition of Thomas Taylor to sell Indian land, 1855, Narragansett Indian Records Collection, 1746–1978.
93. Rhode Island, *[First] Annual Report*, 105; PCA, Record of Births, book 7, 4.
94. PCA, Record of Births, book 7, 4, 157; book 8, 59, 195; PCA, Record of Deaths, book 10, 179; 13, 22.

95. Rhode Island, [First] Annual Report, 104.
96. "A True Narragansett," Providence Daily Journal, April 14, 1907, 4, 8.
97. "A True Narragansett," Providence Daily Journal.
98. U.S. Census 1910.
99. U.S. Census 1910.
100. U.S. Census 1930.
101. Sterling, North Burial Ground.
102. Rhode Island, Fourth Annual Report of the Commission, 8, 19; Rubertone, "Memorializing the Narragansett."
103. RIHS, Canonicus Memorial, 3.
104. Office of the Commissioners of the North Burial Ground, Providence, annual report for year ending December 31, 1899, in Providence City Documents for the Year 1900, 8; RIHS, Canonicus Memorial, 3, 9, 29.
105. RIHS, Canonicus Memorial, 9.
106. Thrush, Native Seattle.
107. Rubertone, "Memorializing the Narragansett," 208.
108. U.S. Census 1860; 1880; 1900; 1910.
109. Byrne, "Nervous Landscapes," 169.
110. O'Brien, Firsting and Lasting, 159; Rubertone, "Memorializing the Narragansett."
111. Fawcett, Medicine Trail, 43, 45.
112. "Algonquin Indian Council of New England, Third Annual Meeting, Mason's Hall, 132 Benefit Street, Providence," announcement, Bicknell Scrapbook, Haffenreffer Museum of Anthropology, Brown University.
113. McMullen, "What's Wrong with This Picture?", 113–50; Rubertone, "Monuments and Sexual Politics."
114. Welburn, "A Most Secret Identity," 313.
115. U.S. Census 1900; RIHS, PCD 1901, 656; 1903, 543; 1904, 560; 1905, 214.
116. U.S. Census 1920; PCA, Record of Deaths, book 27, 186.
117. Robinson, "A Narragansett History," 86; cf. Rhode Island, [First] Annual Report, 23.
118. The meeting at Cross Mills was held on August 13, 1879. Rhode Island, Narragansett Tribe, 5. See also J. Earl Clauson, "These Plantations," Providence Evening Bulletin, January 10, 1933, 19.
119. RIHS, PCD 1896, 250; U.S. Census 1900.
120. U.S. Census; 1910; 1920, 1930; Clauson, "These Plantations," 19.
121. For a discussion of Edward Michael's participation at public events, see "Chief Sachem Night Hawk Speaks," ND 1, no. 4 (August 1935): 100; "Indians Open Pow-Pow at Shannock," ND 1, no. 5 (September 1935):

126–27 (excerpted from *Westerly Sun*, August 12, 1935); *The Day* (New London), August 12, 1936, 6; "The Tercentenary Celebration of the Coming of Roger Williams to the Lodge of Canonicus by the Narragansett Tribe of Indians in Rhode Island, Program, July 4th and 5th, 1936, Camp Ki-Yi, Glasko's Farm, Oakland, Rhode Island," *ND* 2, no. 3 (July 1936): 46; Clauson, "These Plantations," 19; "Governor (White Buffalo) Green Signs on Indian Bill," *ND* 2, no. 2 (June 1936): 22.

122. "The Scattering of Narragansetts," *Providence Daily Journal*, January 3, 1915, 5, 2.
123. Clauson, "These Plantations," 19.
124. "By Golly, 'Twas an Indian," *Providence Evening Bulletin*, 25.
125. Deloria, *Indians in Unexpected Places*, 9.
126. "Tea at Sunset Cottage," *ND* 1, no. 1 (May 1935): 19–20.
127. "Tea at Sunset Cottage," *ND* 1, no. 1 (May 1935).
128. "Tea at Sunset Cottage," *ND* 1, no. 1 (May 1935): 19.
129. Ihlder, *The Houses of Providence*, 36.
130. "Chief Sunset, 88, Dies in Hospital," *Providence Journal*, June 14, 1949, 14.
131. "Little by Little, Lippitt Hill Fades Away," *Providence Journal*, May 4, 1986.
132. "Little by Little, Lippitt Hill Fades Away," *Providence Journal*, May 4, 1986.
133. "Squaw Hollow, What Remains of a Notorious Part of the City," *Providence Sunday Journal*, January 18, 1891, 16.
134. "Squaw Hollow, What Remains of a Notorious Part of the City," *Providence Sunday Journal*, January 18, 1891, 16.

3. Upper South Providence

1. Cady, *Civic and Architectural Development*; Sweet, *Bodies Politic*.
2. "'Soul Liberty' Square," *Providence Journal*, August 22, 1909, S4, 1.
3. Byrne, "Nervous Landscapes," 185.
4. "'Soul Liberty' Square," *Providence Daily Journal*, August 22, 1909, 4, 1.
5. Barnd, *Native Space*, 69–70.
6. Pratt, *Imperial Eyes*, 7.
7. "Change in Name of Square Sought," *Providence Journal*, March 12, 1921, 5.
8. "Change in Name of Square Sought," *Providence Journal*, March 12, 1921, 5.
9. "Canonicus Square to Retain Name," *Providence Journal*, March 18, 1921, 18.
10. *Official Redevelopment Plan, Central-Classical*, 2; "Condemnation Set for Classical Area Project," *Providence Evening Bulletin*, September 21, 1961, 30.
11. "Central Classical Project Begun: 67 Acres Condemned," *Providence Evening Bulletin*, January 2, 1962, 1.

12. "Three Churches in Project Area Plan Expansion," *Providence Evening Bulletin*, January 2, 1962, 18; "Four Churches Tie Future to Survey Results," *Providence Evening Bulletin*, January 12, 1962, 23.
13. "Urges Slower Evacuation from Project Area," *Providence Evening Bulletin*, February 12, 1962, 34.
14. "Where Can the Remains of 80 Buildings Be Put?", *Providence Evening Bulletin*, September 18, 1963, 34.
15. Sterling, *North Burial Ground*, xxvi; Grant Dulgarian, personal communication, July 30, 2003.
16. Rubertone, "Memorializing the Narragansett."
17. Kari Lang, West Broadway Neighborhood Association, Providence, personal communication, October 29, 2003.
18. Kari Lang, West Broadway Neighborhood Association, Providence, personal communication.
19. Rubertone, "Memorializing the Narragansett," 210.
20. RI Census 1865; RIHS, PCD 1864, 38; 1865, 44; 1866, 42; 1868, 49; 1871, 61; 1872, 70; 1873, 69; 1874, 73; 1875, 78; 1876, 81; 1877, 80; 1878, 80; 1879, 78; 1880, 86; 1881, 89; 1882, 92; 1883, 97; 1884, 102; 1887, 115; 1900.
21. PCA, Probate No. A 2411, Providence Probate Records.
22. RIHS, PCD 1903, 185; 1908, 188; 1909, 187; 1911, 195; 1912, 196; 1914, 200; 1916, 202; 1919, 247; 1922, 247; RI Census 1915.
23. RISA, RIDR, vol. 1899, 785.
24. U.S. Census 1900.
25. RIHS, PCD 1905, 824; 1906, 155; 1908, 155; 1909, 66; 1910, 156; 1911, 159; 1920, 873.
26. U.S. Census 1930; RISA, RIDR, vol. 1934.
27. PCA, Record of Marriages, book 16, 10; U.S. Census 1900; 1910; RI Census 1915; 1925 U.S. Census; 1930.
28. U.S. Census 1880.
29. O'Connell, "Introduction," xxiv.
30. King and Rivello, "Amos Brewster," 59.
31. Warrior, "Afterword."
32. PCA, Record of Marriages, PCA, Record of Deaths, book 26, 82.
33. RIHS, PCD 1884, 437; 1903, 676; 1904, 690; 1906, 730; 1908, 588; 1909, 587; 1910, 599; 1911, 63; 1912, 639; 1914, 677; 1916, 687.
34. PCA, Record of Births, book 15, 11.
35. "Howard University in the War," *Howard University Record* 12, no. 4 (May 1918): 14; Scott, *Scott's Official History*, 133.

36. Rubertone, "Monuments and Sexual Politics."
37. "Exeter Unveils Indian Memorial," *Providence Journal*, October 29, 1923, 5.
38. U.S. Census 1900.
39. Leroy, *A Clashing of the Soul*, 56.
40. *Manual of the Pond St. Free Baptist Church*, RIHS; RIBHS, *Creative Survival*, 56–57.
41. Simister, *Streets of the City*, vol. 2, 24.
42. Boissevain, *The Narragansett People*, 79.
43. McMullen, "Culture by Design," 119n25.
44. RIBHS, *Creative Survival*, 66–67.
45. O'Connell, "Introduction"; Sweet, *Bodies Politic*.
46. "Council and Pow-wow of Native Indians of the New England Tribes of the Algonquin Nation at Providence, Thursday, December 13, 1923, at Pond Street Church," announcement, Bicknell Scrapbook, Haffenreffer Museum of Anthropology, Brown University.
47. "Council and Pow-wow of Native Indians of the New England Tribes of the Algonquin Nation at Providence, Thursday, December 13, 1923, at Pond Street Church," announcement, Bicknell Scrapbook, Haffenreffer Museum of Anthropology, Brown University.
48. RIHPHC, Roger Williams Park Historic District, National Register of Historic Places Nomination, March 20, 1974; *Curiouser: New Encounters with the Victorian Natural History Collection*, 2010–11 exhibit, Museum of Natural History and Planetarium, Roger Williams Park, Providence RI.
49. DeLucia, "Fugitive Collections in New England Indian Country," 14.
50. *Indian Tepee* 6, no. 2 (1924), Bicknell Scrapbook, Haffenreffer Museum of Anthropology, Brown University.
51. *Indian Tepee* 6, no. 2 (1924), Bicknell Scrapbook, Haffenreffer Museum of Anthropology, Brown University, 59.
52. Chapin, "Queen's Fort"; DeLucia, *Memory Lands*, 121; Rubertone, "Queen's Fort, North Kingstown, Rhode Island," 129–31.
53. Bourgaize, "Supernatural Folklore of Rhode Island"; Clausen, *These Plantations*, 99; Cole, *History of Washington and Kent Counties*, 47.
54. Bourgaize, "Supernatural Folklore of Rhode Island," 60–61.
55. Rhode Island, *Report of Committee on Marking Historical Sites*, 6; Rubertone, "Cocumscussoc, North Kingstown, Rhode Island."
56. Algonquin Indian Council of New England, October 14, 1925, Free Masons Temple, Benefit St., cor. of Cady St., Bicknell Scrapbook, Haffenreffer Museum of Anthropology, Brown University.

57. Letter from Leroy Perry to Thomas W. Bicknell, n.d., Bicknell Scrapbook, Haffenreffer Museum of Anthropology, Brown University, 75.
58. *Indian Tepee* 6, no. 2, Bicknell Scrapbook, Haffenreffer Museum of Anthropology, Brown University.
59. Basso, *Wisdom Sits in Places*, 146.
60. *Indian Tepee* 6, no. 1 (1924): 9, Bicknell Scrapbook, Haffenreffer Museum of Anthropology, Brown University, 57.
61. Newell, *Brethren by Nature*, 159.
62. Simmons, "The Pond Street Church."
63. Letter from Sarah Ciscoe to Thomas Bicknell, October 15, 1924, and letters from Chief Nonsuch to Thomas W. Bicknell, May 24 and 30, 1925, Bicknell Scrapbook, Haffenreffer Museum of Anthropology, Brown University.
64. Rhode Island, *Narragansett Tribe*, 35–38, 77, 89–90.
65. Rhode Island, *Narragansett Tribe*, 36.
66. Lobo, "Urban Clan Mothers"; Thrush, *Native Seattle*.
67. PCA, Record of Marriages, book 10, 65.
68. U.S. Census 1910; Westerly RI City Directory 1901, 134; 1903, 146 ;1906, 160; 1907, 179; 1908, 179; 1909, 178, in *U.S. City Directories*.
69. RI Census 1915.
70. Wilder Papers, Smith College Archives.
71. "Charlestown, Rhode Island, Summer 1912," Wilder Papers, Smith College Archives.
72. RISA, RIDR, vol. 1917, 31; Cemetery number 0016, Thomas Lot, Charlestown, *U.S., Find a Grave Index*. Emma Thomas, Frederick's wife, is also buried in the Thomas Lot.
73. PCA, Record of Marriages, book 11, 217; PCA, Record of Deaths, book 99, 791.
74. PCA, Record of Marriages, book 10, 17; RIBHS, *Creative Survival*, 57.
75. RIHS, PCD 1874, 289; 1875, 314; 1876, 335; 1877, 323; 1879, 318; 1880, 357; 1882, 390; 1883, 372; 1885, 459; 1887, 524; 1890, 266, 275.
76. Rhode Island, [*First*] *Annual Report*, 32.
77. Pond Street Baptist Church, "A Great Banquet."
78. U.S. Census 1910; 1920.
79. RISA, Rhode Island State Death Return, Benjamin Franklin Thomas, April 4, 1930.
80. Rhode Island, [*First*] *Annual Report*, 35.
81. PCA, Record of Marriages, book 11, 139; PCA, Record of Deaths, book 14, 6.
82. U.S. Census 1860; 1870; RI Census 1875.
83. RIHS, PCD 1876, 176; 1878, 171; 1879, 168; 1880, 168; 1882, 203; 1883, 195; 1884, 231; 1885, 236; 1890, 275.

84. RIHS, PCD 1916, 387; 1917, 382; 1918, 398; 1919, 399; U.S. Census 1920; RIHS, PCD 1921, 437.
85. RIHS, PCD 1922, 439; 1924, 457; 1928, 803; 1932, 848.
86. PCA, Record of Deaths, book 32, 387.
87. PCA, Record of Deaths, book 20, 2.
88. Plane, "Childbirth Practices among Native American Women," 13-24; Rockwell, "The Delivery of Power," 71-85; Rubertone, *Grave Undertakings*, 140-47; Williams, *Key into the Language of America*.
89. RI Census 1915.
90. Rhode Island, *[First] Annual Report*, 34.
91. PCA, Record of Deaths, book 11, 229.
92. Rhode Island, *[First] Annual Report*, 34.
93. Olive A. Henry, Brothertown Application No. 2884, November 29, 1901, Office of Indian Affairs, U.S. Department of Interior, Washington; Love, *Samson Occom and the Christian Indians of New England*, 353; Cipolla, *Becoming Brothertown*.
94. Rhode Island, *[First] Annual Report*, 37, 82.
95. *U.S., Civil War Draft Registration Records*; Chenery, *Fourteenth Regiment*.
96. "The Parade of the Colored Battalion," *Evening Bulletin*, August 28, 1863 (late edition of the *Providence Daily Journal*).
97. *U.S., Civil War Draft Registration Records*.
98. The early colonial records mention "an oake tree standing neer unto the corne field, this being the nearest corne field unto Patuxit." Bartlett, *Records of the Colony of Rhode Island*, 1. See also Ihlder, *The Houses of Providence*, 17.
99. Lobo, "Urban Clan Mothers," 12.
100. Byrne, "Nervous Landscapes," 181; Certeau, *The Practice of Everyday Life*.
101. See, for example, RIHS, PCD 1882, 165; 1884, 187; 1885, 191.
102. PCA, Record of Marriages, book 13, 63.
103. PCA, Record of Deaths, book 21, 187.
104. "The Last Narragansett," *New York Times*, August 10, 1896.
105. PCA, Record of Births, book 6, 96, 201; book 7, 86.
106. PCA, Record of Deaths, book 9, 195, 219; book 10, 111; book 6, 96.
107. U.S. Census 1900.
108. PCA, Record of Marriages, book 18, 335.
109. PCA, Record of Deaths, book 9, 195, 219; book 23, 144.
110. Pasay, *Full Circle*, 399.
111. RIHS, PCD 1852, 255.
112. Brown and Rose, *Black Roots*, 89, 422.

113. U.S. Census 1850.
114. *Massachusetts, State Census, 1855.*
115. U.S. Census 1860; 1870.
116. PCA, Record of Deaths, book 13, 172.
117. Ferrie and Trovesken, "Water and Chicago's Mortality Transition."
118. Winslow, "Statistical Study."
119. Winslow, "Statistical Study"; Robinson, "An Epidemic."
120. PCA, Record of Deaths, book 14, 146.
121. RIHS, PCD 1874, 231; 1875, 251; 1876, 269; 1877, 259; 1878, 259; 1879, 255.
122. PCA, Record of Deaths, book 17, 138; U.S. Census 1880.
123. Pasay, *Full Circle*, 94, 100. Connecticut, Hale Collection of Cemetery Inscriptions and Newspaper Notices; U.S., Find a Grave Index.
124. Pratt, *American Indians in British Art*, 87.
125. PCA, Record of Marriages, book 14, 124.
126. RIHS, PCD 1884, 133; 1885, 136.
127. PCA, Record of Deaths, book 20, 134.
128. U.S. Census 1900.
129. RIHS, PCD 1911, 234; PCA, Record of Marriages, book 22, 283.
130. RIHS, PCD 1924, 282; RI Census 1925.
131. PCA, Record of Deaths, book 27, 162.
132. Earle, *Report to the Governor*, appendix, l; U.S. Census 1870; 1880.
133. *Bartlett Chronicle Yearbook*, 1933, Bartlett High School, Webster, 56, E-Yearbook.com.
134. "Payne Henries' Walks through Town Recalled," *Worcester Telegram and Gazette*, February 11, 2010.
135. U.S. Census 1900.
136. Rhode Island, [*First*] *Annual Report*, 138.
137. RI Census 1865.
138. Pasay, *Full Circle*, 341.
139. U.S. Census 1910.
140. RISA, RIBR, vol. 1877, 360; *U.S., WWI Draft Registration Cards.*
141. Gonzales, "Racial Legibility."
142. Ciscoe to Bicknell, October 15, 1924, and Chief Nonsuch to Bicknell, May 24 and 30, 1925, Bicknell Scrapbook, Haffenreffer Museum of Anthropology, Brown University.
143. "Charlestown, Rhode Island, Summer 1912," Wilder Papers, Smith College Archives.
144. Mancini, "Beyond Reservation"; McMullen, "Blood and Culture," 265.
145. Rhode Island, [*First*] *Annual Report*, 85, 105.

146. Rhode Island, [*First*] *Annual Report*, 78, 37.
147. Rhode Island, [*First*] *Annual Report*, 101.
148. Rhode Island, [*First*] *Annual Report*, 34; RIBR PCA, Record of Marriages, book 11, 217; RISA, RIDR vol. 1899, 791.
149. Basso, *Wisdom Sits in Places*, 146.
150. PCA, Providence Redevelopment Photograph Collection.
151. Campbell, *A Community Apart*, 59.
152. Campbell, *A Community Apart*, 108, 146–49.

4. Lower South Providence

1. Conley and Campbell, *South Providence*, 7.
2. Conley and Campbell, *South Providence*, 8.
3. RIHPHC, "South Providence, Providence, Statewide Historical Preservation Report P-P-2, September 1978," 3.
4. "Dogtown, Once Section with Distinct Individuality, . . . Has Disappeared," *Providence Evening Bulletin*, January 4, 1928, 2, 3.
5. Cady, *Civic and Architectural Development*, 105.
6. "On the Tracks," *ND* 1, no. 11 (March 1936): 264–65.
7. Cady, *Civic and Architectural Development*, 105.
8. For discussion of railroads in expanding Native imaginaries, see Vizenor, *Blue Ravens*, 15.
9. Simmons, *Spirit of the New England Tribes*, 118, 161.
10. O'Brien, "Presidential Address."
11. Deloria, *Indians in Unexpected Places*, 136.
12. Russka, "Ghost Dancing and the Iron Horse."
13. Rhode Island, [*First*] *Annual Report*, 31, 101.
14. Providence Archaeology Collections, Roger Williams Park Museum of Natural History and Planetarium, Providence.
15. RIHS, PCD 1857, 200; 1861, 84; 1862, 83; 1863, 81; 1864, 86; 1865, 88; 1866, 97; 1869, 123; 1871, 138; 1872, 149; 1873, 148; 1875, 178; 1881, 209; 1882, 218; 1883, 233; 1884, 248; PCA, Record of Deaths, book 16, 80.
16. Rhode Island, [*First*] *Annual Report*, 101.
17. Rhode Island Historic Preservation and Heritage Commission, "South Providence, Providence, Statewide Historical Preservation Report P-P-2, September 1978," 4.
18. RIHS, PCD 1858, 108; 1862, 43.
19. Warrior, *People and the Word*, 27.
20. O'Connell, "Introduction," xxxiv, 47n46; Brown and Rose, *Black Roots*, 403; Gura, *Life of William Apess*, 35; Lopenzina, *Through an Indian's Looking Glass*.

21. RIHS, Item 004197, March 25, 1825, Providence Town Papers, MSS 214, subgroup 1, series 3, vol. 127, 26; Gura, *Life of William Apess*, 36; Sweet, *Bodies Politic*, 374. James Thurber, "justice of the peace," is listed at 221 North Main St. in RIHS, PCD 1824, 66; 1826, 78.
22. Lopenzina, *Through an Indian's Looking-Glass*, 161; Sweet, *Bodies Politic*, 374.
23. Koskela, "Discipline and Polity," 165
24. Apess, *A Son of the Forest*, in Apess, *On Our Own Ground*, 50.
25. Haynes, *Divine Destiny*, 31–32.
26. Schantz, *Piety in Providence*, 185 (for quotes); see also O'Connell, "Introduction"; Gura, *Life of William Apess*.
27. McDonald, *History of Methodism*, 66.
28. McDonald, *History of Methodism*, 63.
29. Miller, *Souvenir History of the New England Southern Conference*, 155.
30. Koskela, "Discipline and Polity," 166–67.
31. O'Connell in Apess, *On Our Own Ground*, 275.
32. *U.S. Army, Register of Enlistments*.
33. Rare Books Division, New York Public Library, "Mr. William Apes, a native missionary of the Pequot tribe of Indians," 1831 [frontispiece], New York Public Library Digital Collections, http://digitalcollections.nypl.org/items/0d68d6d0-5194-0132-75cf-58d385a7bbd0; Grolier Club, *Catalogue of an Exhibition of Early American Engraving upon Copper, 1727–1850*, 44; *Catalogue of the Gallery of Art of the New York Historical Society*, 186.
34. Apess, *A Son of the Forest*, in Apess, *On Our Own Ground*, 5; see also Warrior, *People and the Word*, 23.
35. O'Connell, "Introduction," xxvii; Warrior, *People and the Word*, 43.
36. O'Connell, "'Once More Let Us Consider,'" 5–6; Gura, *Life of William Apess*, xi–xiii.
37. Bicknell, *The History of the State of Rhode Island*; Shoemaker, *Native American Whalemen*.
38. Rhode Island, *[First] Annual Report*, 79.
39. *Massachusetts, State and Federal Naturalization Records*.
40. Taylor, *Runaways, Deserters, and Notorious Villains*, 60.
41. RISA, Certificate of Soldiers Metal Case, American Revolutionary War Files.
42. Fisher, *The Great Indian Awakening*, 196n40.
43. Mandell, *Tribe, Race, History*, 36.
44. RISA, *Report of Indian Committee*, no. 20 (June 1816), Narragansett Indians Records Collection, folder 57.
45. RISA, "Petition of Indian Council to have a R.I. Citizen Removed from Their Land," May 1815, Narragansett Indians Records Collection, folder 148.

46. RISA, "Report on Indian Affairs," 1816, Narragansett Indians Records Collection, folder 147.
47. A Frederick Bosemsdes, watchmaker or clockmaker, appears in the Boston city directories for 1820, 1821, and 1822, *UK and U.S. Directories, 1680–1830*; he died on the passage from Point Petre, Ontario, to Boston, November 27, 1824. *U.S., Newspaper Extractions from the Northeast*.
48. *U.S., Find a Grave Index*; Tarket-Arruda and Waite, *Charlestown, Rhode Island*.
49. U.S. Census 1850.
50. *Massachusetts, Marriage Records*; "Roxana" Melville's father is identified as Nocemodes, her mother as Francis [sic], and her spouse as Joseph Dewick. Both she and her husband are identified as residents of Providence.
51. U.S. Census 1860.
52. PCA, Record of Deeds, book 176, 476–68.
53. U.S. Census 1870; RI Census 1875.
54. U.S. Census 1850.
55. RISA, RIMR, vol. 1870, 626; vol. 1873, 832; vol. 1863, 228.
56. PCA, Record of Deeds, book 196, 371, 416.
57. Gilkeson, *Middle-Class Providence*.
58. "Says He Was Cheated by Wall Street Broker: Hartford Man Sues Jerome B. Melville for $1,314.36," *New York Times*, September 9, 1902.
59. "Last of Narragansett Chiefs: Thundercloud Accused of Being a Fagin in New York Court," *Providence Daily Journal*, March 7, 1910, 2; "'Dr. Thundercloud' Dies in Harlem Hut: 'Great Medicine Man' Had Treated Negroes with Herbs for Forty Years," *New York Times*, January 22, 1934, 3.
60. Gura, *Life of William Apess*, 134.
61. "Indians Pay Last Respect to Dead Chief," *Westerly Sun*, February 11, 1934; "Last Indian Line Will Sleep in R.I.: Chief Thundercloud Will Be Buried in South County," *Providence Journal*, February 4, 1934, 10.
62. Sanderson, *Mannahatta*, 110, 261.
63. Rhode Island, *[First] Annual Report*, 79.
64. RISA, RIMR, vol. 1887, 649.
65. PCA, Probate No. A 15278, Providence Probate Records.
66. *U.S., Find a Grave Index*; PCA, Record of Deaths, book 23, 325; book 26, 396.
67. RIHS, PCD 1905, 388; PCA, Record of Deaths, book 22, 142.
68. RIHS, PCD 1870, 236.
69. Earle, *Report to the Governor*, appendix, l.
70. U.S. Census 1870.
71. Earle, *Report to the Governor*, 83–85.

72. Dubuque, *Fall River Indian Reservation*, 97.
73. U.S. Census 1870.
74. *Massachusetts, Marriage Records*; U.S. Census 1880.
75. *U.S., Colored Troops Military Service*; *Massachusetts, Find a Grave Index*.
76. PCA, Record of Marriages, book 18, 384; "Mrs. Rachel E. Perry" is listed in RIHS, PCD 1890, 446; 1891, 477; 1892, 496.
77. PCA, Record of Marriages, book 18, 384.
78. U.S. Census 1900.
79. Faflik, *Boarding Out*.
80. RIHS, PCD 1908, 589; 1909, 588; 1922, 796; 1924, 833.
81. U.S. Census 1930.
82. RIHS, PCD 1896, 590; 1897, 600; U.S. Census 1900; RIHS, PCD 1930, 1131.
83. Krech, "Rudolf Haffenreffer and the King Philip Museum," 49.
84. *Fall River Herald News*, August 27, 1930. Quoted in McMullen, "Heart Interest," 173.
85. McMullen, "'Heart Interest,'" 173.
86. Apess, "Eulogy on King Philip," in Apess, *On Our Own Ground*, 277.
87. Munro, *The History of Bristol, R.I.*, 47; Krech, "Rudolf F. Haffenreffer and the King Philip Museum,", fig. 1–19; McMullen, "Heart Interest," fig. 4-1.
88. Mills, *Talking with the Elders of Mashpee*.
89. "Ousa Mequin," *ND* 1, no. 5 (September 1935): 121.
90. Leroy Perry's height would have been below the average height of 67.5 inches for World War I soldiers in 1918 (but above the 60-inch minimum requirement). Davenport and Love, *The Medical Department of the United States Army in the World War*, vol. 15, 46, 67; "Indians Open Pow-wow at Shannock," *ND* 1, no. 5 (September 1935): 126-27.
91. "The Tercentenary Celebration of the Coming of Roger Williams to the Lodge of Canonicus by the Narragansett Tribe of Indians in Rhode Island," *ND* 2, no. 3 (July 1936): 46; "First RI Indian Day," *ND* 2, no. 5 (September 1936): 2.
92. PCA, Record of Deaths, book 24, 99.
93. RIHS, PCD 1896, 590.
94. PCA, Record of Marriages, book 18, 86; RIHS, PCD 1897, 600.
95. U.S. Census 1920.
96. "Gay Head, Massachusetts, on Martha's Vineyard Island," *ND* 1, no. 10 (February 1936): 237–42; "Asks Educational Chance for Indian: Prophet Perry Declares Red Men Denied Economic Opportunities Given Aliens," *Providence Journal*, September 30, 1927, 18.
97. Guillemin, *Urban Renegades*.
98. *Life of John W. Johnson*, 04.02.

99. *Life of John W. Johnson*, 04.03, 04.04, 04.05.
100. *Life of John W. Johnson*, 04.04.
101. Lester, "'We Didn't Make Fancy Baskets,'" 42.
102. U.S. Census 1880.
103. Leah Morine Rosenmeier, research and interpretation specialist, Mi'Kmawey Debert Cultural Center, Nova Scotia, personal communication, October 19, 2009.
104. Byrne, "Nervous Landscapes," 172.
105. U.S. Census 1930.
106. PCA, Record of Marriages, book 26, 165; U.S. Census 1930.
107. *U.S., WWI Draft Registration Cards*; U.S. Census 1930; Conley and Campbell, *South Providence*, 60.
108. First Free Methodist Church, *Fiftieth Anniversary Historical Sketch Pamphlet*.
109. Moorehead, "My Grandfather's Wooden Chest."
110. U.S. Census 1940; *U.S., Social Security Death Index*.
111. Campbell, *A Community Apart*, 49-53.
112. Providence Housing Authority, *Second Annual Report, 1940-1941*, cited in Campbell, *A Community Apart*, 51.
113. For discussion of the idealized New England village, see Handsman, "Capitalism and the Center Village of Canaan."
114. Campbell, *A Community Apart*, 67.
115. Campbell, *A Community Apart*, 115.
116. "Sunrise News Items," *ND* 1, no. 9 (January 1936): 217; RIHS, PCD 1934, 523; 1937, 638; RI Census 1935.
117. "Governor (White Buffalo) Green Signs on Indian Bill," *ND* 2, no. 2 (June 1936): 22; "The Tercentenary Celebration of the Coming of Roger Williams to the Lodge of Canonicus by the Narragansett Tribe of Indians in Rhode Island," *ND* 2, no. 3 (July 1936): 48.
118. "Graduates of Yester-Years and Today," *ND* 1, no. 3 (July 1935): 8; "Lone Wolf," *ND* 1, no. 3 (July 1935): 1; "Indians Open Pow-wow at Shannock," *ND* 1, no. 5 (September 1935): 127; "Sunrise News Items," *ND* 1, no. 10 (February 1936): 246; "Sunrise News," *ND* 1, no. 11 (March 1936): 268; "The Tercentenary Celebration of the Coming of Roger Williams to the Lodge of Canonicus by the Narragansett Tribe of Indians in Rhode Island, Program, July 4th and 5th, 1936, Camp Ki-Yi, Glasko's Farm, Oakland, Rhode Island," *ND* 2, no. 3 (July 1936): 46-47.
119. Tall Oak Weeden, personal communication, July 2, 2015.
120. Goniwe, Tall Oak, Henry, and Heap of Birds, *Eagles Speak*.
121. Tall Oak Weeden, personal communication, September 18, 2014.

122. Campbell, *A Community Apart*, 115.
123. Handsman, "Being Indian in Providence," 15.
124. McMullen, "Blood and Culture," 280; "Summary under the Criteria and Evidence for Proposed Finding, Eastern Pequot Indians of Connecticut," prepared in response to a petition submitted to the secretary of the interior for federal acknowledgment, March 24, 2000, Office of Federal Acknowledgement, U.S. Department of Interior, Washington DC.
125. Guillemin, *Urban Renegades*; Talese, *The Bridge*, 130–34.
126. Deloria, *Indians in Unexpected Places*, 136.
127. Handsman, "Being Indian in Providence," 15.
128. Handsman, "Being Indian in Providence," 15.
129. Handsman, "Being Indian in Providence," 16.
130. Wallace, "Mazeway Disintegration," 23–27; Fullilove, "Root Shock."

5. Mashapaug Pond

1. Bartlett, *Records of the Colony of Rhode Island and Providence Plantations*, 28.
2. "Interview with Bill Simmons" (2011), *Mashapaug Pond*, Brown Digital Repository.
3. Chapin, "Indian Graves."
4. Hamell, "Mythical Realities and European Contact."
5. Hamell, "Mythical Realities and European Contact," 68.
6. Stone, *Life and Recollections of John Howland*, 25–26.
7. Ulrich, *Age of Homespun*, 41–74.
8. Stone, *Life and Recollections of John Howland*, 25.
9. Rhode Island, *Narragansett Tribe*, 85.
10. "Interview with Ed Hooks" (2012), *Mashapaug Pond*, Brown Digital Repository.
11. "The Black Bass," ND 2, no. 3 (July 1936): 59.
12. Dove and Ewald, *Through Our Eyes*.
13. Butler, "Sweat Houses in the Southern New England Area"; Williams, *Key into the Language of America*, 197; "Ancient Narragansett Bath Houses," ND 1, no. 11 (March 1936): 265. For a discussion of an urban sweat house, see Lobo, "Urban Clan Mothers," 12.
14. "The Goose Pond," ND 1, no. 9 (January 1936): 205; "Interview with Cliff Montiero" (2013), *Mashapaug Pond*, Brown Digital Repository.
15. Simmons, *Spirit of the New England Tribes*, 143–44; "John Onion," ND 1, no. 9 (January 1936): 206.
16. In 1637 "Saunkussecit alias Tom of Wauchimoqut" was authorized "to mark tress and set the bounds of the land" of Providence. Deed from

Ousamequin, chief of Paukanawket, to Roger Williams, Gregory Dexter, and the inhabitants of Providence, 1646. Bartlett, *Records of the Colony of Rhode Island*, 1:32.
17. "The 'Last of the Pequots,' a Resident of Providence," *Providence Sunday Journal*, November 2, 1913.
18. "Interview with Bill Simmons" (2011), *Mashapaug Pond*, Brown Digital Repository.
19. PCA, Record of Deaths, book 25, 176.
20. RIHPCH, "Elmwood, Providence, Statewide Historical Preservation Report P-P-3, June 1979," 3.
21. "Were Providence's Ponds Good or Bad for the City?," *Providence Sunday Journal*, October 15, 1922.
22. Simmons, "The Continuous Presence of Native People at Mashapaug Pond," 44.
23. "Were Providence's Ponds Good or Bad for the City?", *Providence Sunday Journal*, October 15, 1922.
24. Simmons, "The Continuous Presence of Native People at Mashapaug Pond," 44.
25. *Rhode Island, Death Index*; RIHS, PCD 1912, 149; 1920, 156; 1922, 160; 1924, 163. Maria Blunt is listed at 134 Dodge St. in the Upper South Providence neighborhood in RIHS, PCD 1916, 152.
26. RI Census 1915; 1920; PCA, Record of Deaths, book 27, 126.
27. U.S. Census 1910; Rhode Island, [*First*] *Annual Report*, 75.
28. RIHS, PCD 1869, 58; U.S. Census 1870.
29. PCA, Record of Births, book 10, 84; RIHS, PCD 1873, 259.
30. U.S. Census 1870.
31. PCA, Record of Marriages, book 10, 75.
32. RIHS, PCD 1890–1891; 1891–1892.
33. *Massachusetts, Marriage Records*; RISA, RIDR, vol. 1898, 551; U.S. Census 1880.
34. PCA, Record of Deaths, book 18, 76.
35. "Charlestown's Indians, the Last of the Narragansett and Their Shrines," *Providence Sunday Journal*, August 11, 1889.
36. Boissevain, *The Narragansett People*, 75, 78.
37. U.S. Census 1900.
38. Jane Bent Hazard, "Our Family Bible," *ND* 1, no. 2 (June 1935): 7.
39. Rhode Island, [*First*] *Annual Report*, 104.
40. Historical Data Systems, comp. *U.S., Civil War Soldier Records and Profiles, 1861–1865*; RIHS, PCD 1872, 203.

41. PCA, Record of Deaths, book 16, 470.
42. *U.S., Find a Grave Index*; National Park Service, *U.S. Civil War Soldiers, 1861–1865*; "Data on Old Indian Church," *ND* 1, no. 6 (October 1935): 153; Rhode Island, *[First] Annual Report*, 104.
43. RI Census 1875; U.S. Census 1880.
44. RIHS, PCD 1901, 920.
45. U.S. Census 1910.
46. *Rhode Island, Marriage Index*; U.S. Census 1900.
47. PCA, Record of Deaths, book 23, 280.
48. PCA, Record of Deaths, book 31, 345.
49. Everett "Tall Oak" Weeden, personal communication, July 2, 2015.
50. RISA, RIBR, vol. 1890, 23.
51. PCA, Record of Marriages, book 23, 138.
52. Kirschenbaum, "Nancy Elizabeth Prophet, Sculptor," 46.
53. Cullen, "Elizabeth Prophet," 204.
54. Nancy Elizabeth Prophet Diary (1922–1934), Digital Collection, John Hay Library, Brown University.
55. For discussions of the diaries of Charlotte Mitchell (1896) and Fidelia Fielding (1902–1905), see Simmons, "From Manifest Destiny." For Fielding's complete diary, see Speck, "Native Tribes and Dialects of Connecticut."
56. Nancy Elizabeth Prophet Diary (1922–1934), Digital Collection, John Hay Library, Brown University, August 11, 1922.
57. Nancy Elizabeth Prophet Diary (1922–1934), Digital Collection, John Hay Library, Brown University, November 11, 1925–May 3, 1926.
58. Nancy Elizabeth Prophet Diary (1922–1934), Digital Collection, John Hay Library, Brown University, June 26, 1926–July 19, 1935.
59. Amaki "Nancy Elizabeth Prophet," 53.
60. Leininger-Miller, *Negro Artists in Paris*, 65.
61. Amaki, "Nancy Elizabeth Prophet," 56.
62. "Negro Father, 88, Sees Famous Daughter's Work at Library," *Providence Journal*, April 23, 1945.
63. Leininger-Miller, *Negro Artists in Paris*, 18–19.
64. Leininger-Miller, *Negro Artists in Paris*, 48.
65. Amaki, "Nancy Elizabeth Prophet," 57.
66. Kirschenbaum, "Nancy Elizabeth Prophet," 49, 50.
67. Kirschenbaum, "Nancy Elizabeth Prophet," 57–58.
68. McBride, *Molly Spotted Elk*.
69. City of Providence, *Fourteenth Annual Report*, 10.

70. "City of Providence Wants State to Acquire Ponds," *Providence Journal*, August 10, 1951, 6.
71. "Major to Seek Advice on Curbing Dumping around Mashapaug Pond," *Providence Journal*, August 29, 1951, 8.
72. "Mashapaug Pond Called Peril to Health through Dumping," *Providence Journal*, April 22, 1952, 15.
73. "Interview with Ed Hooks" (2012), *Mashapaug Pond*, Brown Digital Repository.
74. RIHS, PCD 1956, 353.
75. "Pokanokut Spiritual Leader Elaborates on Thanksgiving," *Jamestown (RI) Press*, November 25, 2010.
76. Weeden, personal communication, July 2, 2015.
77. "Sunrise News," *ND* 1, no. 11 (March 1936): 268.
78. "News Items," *ND* 2, no. 1 (May 1936): 14.
79. McMullen, "Culture by Design," 137.
80. U.S. Census 1920; McMullen, "'Heart Interest,'" 170.
81. McMullen, "Culture by Design," 141.
82. "Sunrise News Items," *ND* 1, no. 8 (December 1935): 192; "Sunrise News Items," *ND* 1, no. 10 (February 1936): 242; "News Items," *ND* 2, no. 1 (May 1936): 13; "Governor (White Buffalo) Green Signs on Indian Bill," *ND* 2, no. 2 (June 1936): 22 and "Sunrise News," *ND* 2, no. 2 (June 1936): 34; McMullen "'Heart Interest,'" 170.
83. Weeden, personal communication, September 11, 2014.
84. Simmons, "The Continuous Presence of Native People at Mashapaug Pond."
85. U.S. Census 1910.
86. "Indian Graduates of South Kingstown High School," *ND* 1, no. 3 (July 1935): 4; U.S. Census 1930; 1940.
87. Simmons, "The Continuous Presence of Native People at Mashapaug Pond," 47; William Simmons in an unpublished interview by Harold and Laura Mars, early 1980s.
88. RIHS, PCD 1939, 604; 1941, 255; 1941, 255; 1943, 269.
89. RISA, RIDR, vol. 1938, 104.
90. *Massachusetts, Town and Vital Records, 1620–1988*.
91. U.S. Census 1900; 1910.
92. *U.S., WWI Draft Registration Cards*.
93. U.S. Census 1930; RIHS, PCD 1931, 464.
94. *U.S., WWII Draft Registration Cards*.
95. *Rhode Island, Marriage Index*; RIHS, PCD 1924, 170; 1928, 519; 1930, 490; RI Census 1925; U.S. Census 1930.

96. Pasay, *Full Circle*, 76, 77.
97. Harold Mars appears in Rochester city directories in the 1950s. In 1960 he was listed as the pastor of the Church of God. Rochester City Directory, 1953, p. 1193; 1975, 127; 1958, 145; 1960, 159, 737, in *U.S. City Directories*.
98. "Sunrise News," *ND* 2, no. 4 (August 1936): 75; Simmons, *Spirit of the New England Tribes*, 52.
99. Mills, *Talking with the Elders of Mashpee*.
100. Simmons, *Spirit of the New England Tribes*, 152, citing Stiles, *Extracts*, 145; Herndon and Sekatau, "The Right to a Name"; Rubertone, *Grave Undertakings*, 142.
101. Simmons, *Spirit of the New England Tribes*, 154–56.
102. Simmons, *Spirit of the New England Tribes*, 156–57.
103. Dove and Ewald, *Through Our Eyes*.
104. Byrne, "Nervous Landscapes," 180.
105. Providence Redevelopment Agency, "Mashapaug Pond Redevelopment Plan for the Huntington Expressway Industrial Park," 1960.
106. "Resolution Making an Appropriation for the Marking of Sites of Historic Interest in the State, No. 40, Passed on April 13, 1906," RIHS Archives, box 24, Minutes of the Committee on Marking Historical Sites.
107. Foote, *Shadowed Ground*.
108. Bicknell, *Addresses and Poem*; "Minutes of Fourteenth Meeting, March 19, 1908," Minutes of Committee on Marking Historical Sites, RIHS Archives, box 24.
109. Downes, "Cyrus E. Dallin, Sculptor," 4.
110. Downes, "Cyrus E. Dallin, Sculptor"; May, "Work of Cyrus E. Dallin," 408–15; "The *Appeal to the Great Spirit*, Cyrus Dallin."
111. Johnson and Francis, *Frontier to Fame*, 113.
112. "Registry of Local Art," 14.
113. Greenthal, Kozoi, and Ramirez, *American Figurative Sculpture*; Gorham Manufacturing Company, *Famous Small Bronzes*, 51.
114. Gorham Manufacturing Company, *Famous Small Bronzes*.
115. Phillips, *Trading Identities*, 74, 100–102, 208–9.
116. Krech, "Rudolf Haffenreffer and the King Philip Museum, 70."
117. Clark, "Indians on the Mantle and in the Park," 26.
118. May, "Work of Cyrus E. Dallin," 408.
119. Clark, "Indians on the Mantle and in the Park."
120. Providence Redevelopment Agency, "Application for an Environmental Protection Agency Brownfields Cleanup Grant"; Rudin, Murray, and Whitfeld, "Retrospective Analysis of Heavy Metal."

121. See Senier, *Dawnland Voices*, 313–16.
122. Valk and Ewald, "Bringing a Hidden Pond to Public Attention"; "Gorham Factory Site," Environmental Justice League of Rhode Island, http://ejlri.org/toxic-hazards/gorham-factory-site/.
123. Providence City Planning Commission, *Conditions of Blight*.
124. Providence City Planning Commission. *Conditions of Blight*.
125. "Human Values Stressed in Mashapaug Area Plan," *Providence Evening Bulletin*, September 20, 1960, 21.
126. Jennings, "The Wisdom of the Eagle Speaks to Us," 30.

6. Federal Hill

1. Rider, *The Lands of Rhode Island*, 279.
2. DeLucia, *Memory Lands*, 192.
3. "Federal Hill of Fifty Years Ago," *Providence Evening Bulletin*, April 11, 1928, 3.
4. Walking Tour, Georgiaville Village, Smithfield RI, blackstoneheritagecorridor.org.
5. "The Passing of Shoo Fly Village," *Providence Sunday Journal*, November 26, 1911, S4, 1C; King, *King's Pocket-Book of Providence, R.I.*, 40.
6. "The 'Last of the Pequots,' a Resident of Providence," *Providence Sunday Journal*, November 2, 1913.
7. RIHPHC, *Native American Archaeology in Rhode Island*, 56.
8. RIHPHC, Archaeological Site Files.
9. "The 'Last of the Pequots,' a Resident of Providence," *Providence Sunday Journal*, November 2, 1913.
10. Cady, *Civic and Architectural Development*, 10, 25–26; Greene, *The Providence Plantations*.
11. "The 'Last of the Pequots,' a Resident of Providence," *Providence Sunday Journal*, November 2, 1913.
12. "The 'Last of the Pequots,' a Resident of Providence," *Providence Sunday Journal*, November 2, 1913.
13. Banvard, *A Guide to the Providence River and Narragansett Bay*, 133.
14. Belcher, "Old Rocky Point"; Gilkeson, *Middle-Class Providence*, 222; Lemons, "Summer Times."
15. Rider, "More about Moses P. Dailey," 153.
16. PCA, Record of Marriages, book 12, 20; PCA, Record of Births, book 7, 26.
17. PCA, Record of Births, book 12, 131.
18. "The 'Last of the Pequots,' a Resident of Providence," *Providence Sunday Journal*, November 2, 1913.
19. Dundes, "The Vampire as Bloodthirsty Revenant."

20. Rider, "More about Moses P. Dailey," 153; "The 'Last of the Pequots,' a Resident of Providence," *Providence Sunday Journal*, November 2, 1913.
21. PCA, Record of Marriages, book 19, 141.
22. Rider, "The Last of the Pequot Indians," 150.
23. Rider, "More about Moses P. Dailey," 154.
24. Shoemaker, *Native American Whalemen*, 4; Gonzales, "Racial Legibility."
25. PCA, Record of Births, book 12, 131.
26. U.S. Census 1850; 1860; 1870; RI Census 1865; 1885.
27. Newport RI City Directory 1876, 161; 1879, 86; 1880, 100; 1881, 99; 1882, 142, in *U.S. City Directories*; U.S. Census 1880.
28. "The 'Last of the Pequots,' a Resident of Providence," *Providence Sunday Journal*, November 2, 1913; "Moses P. Dailey, Last Pequot Indian, Dead at 91," *Providence Daily Journal*, August 21, 1915; Simmons "The Mystic Voice," 245n28; Stark, *Groton, Conn. 1705-1905*. For discussion of summer migrations of basket makers and tourism, see Mt. Pleasant, "Salt, Sand, and Sweetgrass."
29. Turnbaugh and Turnbaugh, "Weaving the Woods."
30. PCA, Record of Marriages, book 17, 211.
31. U.S. Census 1900.
32. RIHS, PCD 1901, 885; 1903, 728; RIHPHC, National Register of Historic Places Nomination, Broadway-Armory Historic District, 1974.
33. Ihlder, *The Houses of Providence*, 38.
34. Cranston, RI, City Directory, 1916, 196; 1918, 188; U.S. Census 1920; 1930; 1940; Cranston, RI, City Directory 1932, 281; 1934, 290; RI Census, 1935; Cranston, RI, City Directory 1939, 251; 1941, 264; 1943, 267; 1945, 1296; 1947, 418; 1948, 419; 1954, 336, in *U.S. City Directories*.
35. "Frederick H. Weeden, 57, Died Sunday at Home in East Providence," *Providence Journal*, April 19, 1927, 10.
36. Rhode Island, *Narragansett Tribe*, 36.
37. *Massachusetts, Marriage Records*; U.S. Census 1860.
38. U.S. Census 1900; RIHS, PCD 1901, 432.
39. PCA, Probate No. A 10262, Providence Probate Records.
40. Shrum, *In the Looking Glass*.
41. PCA, Record of Marriages, book 9, 154.
42. PCA, Record of Births, book 9, 109, 184.
43. Rhode Island, [*First*] *Annual Report*, 134.
44. RIHS, PCD 1844, 199.
45. RIHS, PCD 1858, 279.
46. PCA, Record of Marriages, book 10, 75.
47. Cole, *History of Washington and Kent Counties*, 28; RI Census 1865.

48. PCA, Record of Births, book 7, 135; PCA, Record of Deaths, book 10, 56.
49. PCA, Record of Births, book 7, 201.
50. Brown and Rose, *Black Roots*, 89; Record of Births, PCA, book 8, 39.
51. PCA, Record of Deaths, book 11, 32.
52. RI Census 1865.
53. U.S. Census 1880.
54. RIHS, PCD 1838, 143. Manuel Fenner is also listed in the 1844 directory under "colored persons," 195.
55. RIHS, PCD 1847, 84, 1853, 127, 1854, 141, 1860, 191, 1861, 60, 1862, 58, 1863, 190; U.S. Census 1860; RI Census 1865.
56. RIHS, Dexter Asylum Records, MS 67, series 1, vol. 3.
57. PCA, Record of Deaths, book 19, 23.
58. McCallum, *Indigenous Women, Work, and History*.
59. G. Timothy Cranston, "The View from Swamptown: The Tale of a Painter, His Wife and Their Legacy," *The Independent*, July 16, 2015.
60. *Massachusetts, Town and Vital Records, 1620-1988*.
61. Lancaster, "'I Would Have Made Out Very Poorly,'" 108.
62. Block, "Respecting Hair"; Lancaster, "'I Would Have Made Out Very Poorly.'"
63. Gross, "The Negro and Events in Rhode Island, 1696-1968," cited in Lancaster, "Shampoos to Shelters,"14.
64. PCA, Record of Deaths, book 21, 103.
65. Lancaster, "'I Would Have Made Out Very Poorly,'" 118.
66. Ceremony of Rhode Island Secretary of State Commemorating the Unveiling of the Bronze Bust of Christiana Carteaux Bannister, Thursday, December 19, 2002, Capitol Rotunda, State House, Providence.
67. U.S. Census 1870.
68. *Massachusetts, State Census, 1865*; U.S. Census 1880.
69. RIHS, PCD 1906, 128; Lancaster, "'I Would Have Made Out Very Poorly,'" 118.
70. PCA, Record of Deaths, PCA, 131.
71. PCA, Probate No. 21981, Providence Probate Records.
72. For discussion, see Gill, "Civic Beauty."
73. Byrne, "Nervous Landscapes," 179.
74. Rhode Island Children's Friend Society, *Twenty-Seventh Annual Report*, 9; Ware, *Memoir of Harriet Ware*; "Federal Hill of 50 Years Ago," *Providence Evening Bulletin*, April 11, 1928.
75. Bender, "Landscapes on the Move."
76. The surname Lowling is variously transcribed as Loring, Loren, and Lorren in Providence records.
77. Neuman, "Basketry as Economic Enterprise," 93.

78. Pawling, "Wabanaki Homeland and Mobility," 623.
79. PCA, Record of Births, book 7, 156.
80. PCA, Record of Deaths, book 10, 158.
81. PCA, Record of Births, book 9, 32.
82. William S. Simmons, who was raised in Providence near Mashapaug Pond, said that his grandmother told him about Indian women from Maine who came to Rhode Island to work on farms. Personal communication, June 12, 2013; Prins, "Tribal Networks and Migrant Labor."
83. RIHS, Daniel Steadman Journal, 1829–1859, MSS 1129, 203.
84. Baker, "Glimpses of Ancient Sowams," 197.
85. Speck, *Penobscot Man*, 234n15. Cf. Baker, "Glimpses of Ancient Sowams," 197; Delabarre, "Chief Big Thunder."
86. Prins, "Chief Big Thunder," 144.
87. Baker, "Glimpses of Ancient Sowams," 198.
88. Prins, "Chief Big Thunder," 146–47.
89. Baker, "Glimpses of Ancient Sowams," 198.
90. Brooks, *Common Pot*, 8.
91. Nabokov, *Where the Lightning Strikes*, 3.
92. Delabarre, "Chief Big Thunder"; Siebert, *Penobscot Man*; but see Prins, "Chief Big Thunder."
93. O'Connell, "Introduction," xxv.
94. Lester, "'We Didn't Make Fancy Baskets,'" 53.
95. Pawling, "Wabanaki Homeland and Mobility," 636.
96. Caroline Masta (Abenaki), who sold baskets to tourists in the seaside town of Belmar, New Jersey around the turn of the century, used splints that were produced by her relatives in Quebec and sent to her in New Jersey to be woven into baskets along with braided sweet grass. See Handsman, "Stop Making Sense," 158, fig. 64.
97. Ulrich, *Age of Homespun*, 341.
98. Lester, "'We Didn't Make Fancy Baskets,'" 42; Nicholas, *Baskets of the Dawnland People*, 18.
99. Nicholas, *Baskets of the Dawnland People*, 18.
100. Consortium of Northeast Herbaria, http://portal.neherbaria.org/portal/; cf. Shebtiz, "Weaving Traditional Ecological Knowledge."
101. Richmond, "Spirituality and Survival in Schaghticoke Basket-Making."
102. Hauptman, *Between Two Fires*.
103. Naumec, "From Mashantucket to Appomattox," 631.
104. O'Brien, *Firsting and Lasting*.

105. The Fourteenth Rhode Island Heavy Artillery (Colored) was the name for Rhode Island's "colored" regiment during the Civil War prior to 1864. It was composed entirely of Black and colored enlisted men and white officers. In May 1864 the regiment was redesignated the Eleventh U.S. Colored Heavy Artillery. See Chenery, *Fourteenth Regiment*.
106. Speck, *Penobscot Man*, 234.
107. Speck, *Penobscot Man*, 228.
108. A Newell Loring, age twenty, of Old Town in Penobscot County, Maine, is listed in the 1870 U.S. Census, and a Newell Loring, age forty-nine and married to a basket maker, is recorded as living on Indian Island in the 1900 U.S. Census, though I cannot be certain that this is the same Newell Loring (Loren).
109. Dyer, *Annual Report of Adjutant General*.
110. State v. Thomas Loring, Providence Superior Court Case File No. 563, Record book, Digest of Case, October 1868, Judicial Records Center, Rhode Island Judiciary, Pawtucket.
111. PCA, Record of Deaths, book 12, 128.
112. *Narragansett Historical Register* 5 (1886–87): 346, 359; McKinney and Cook, *The Industrial Advantages of Providence, R.I.*, 86–87.
113. RIHPHC, National Register of Historic Places Registration Form, Broadway-Armory District, Amendment, 2007, 1–2; U.S. Census 1860.
114. RIHS, PCD 1875, 203.
115. Lester, "'We Didn't Make Fancy Baskets,'" 48, 51, 54–55. For a discussion of markings on other material objects, see Spector, *What This Awl Means*.
116. Nabokov, *Where the Lightning Strikes*, 16–17.
117. Ihlder, *The Houses of Providence*.
118. U.S. Census 1880.
119. Ihlder, *The Houses of Providence*, 17–18; Barbara Polichetti, "Memories and Dreams: The Changing Face of Federal Hill," *Providence Journal*, October 28, 1990, 7.
120. Des Jardins, "Federal Hill House."
121. Riis, "Merry Christmas in the Tenements," 175.
122. Barbara Polichetti, "Memories and Dreams: The Changing Face of Federal Hill," *Providence Journal*, October 28, 1990; William K. Gale, "The Way It Once Was for a Boy on Federal Hill," *Providence Journal*, October 9, 1972, 45; Lawrence M. Howard, "Flight from Federal Hill: Many See Crisis at Hand," *Providence Journal*, March 13, 1960, 1; Jonathan Karp, "The Hill: An Ethnic District Changes," *Providence Journal*, January 3, 1988, 1; Robert Chiappi-

nelli, "Families Pay Tribute to a Bygone Era: Simple Plaque to Pushcarts: 'This Was Their Life,'" *Providence Evening Bulletin*, December 24, 1979, 3.
123. Thrush, *Native Seattle*, 206.
124. Campbell, *A Community Apart*; "Mayor Goes on Tour with Mr. Aronovici," *Providence Daily Journal*, March 6, 1909; Providence Redevelopment Agency, "Land Utilization and Marketability Study, Federal Hill—South Providence, General Neighborhood Renewal Plan, Providence, Rhode Island," 1965.

7. Johnston

1. About one and a quarter square miles, including Olneyville and the eastern part of Neutaconkanut Hill, were reannexed to Providence in 1898. See Cady, *Civic and Architectural Development*, 185.
2. Jackson, *Report on the Geological and Agricultural Survey of the State*.
3. Thornton, "Highland Spring."
4. Hamell, "Trading in Metaphors," 25; Fawcett, *Medicine Trail*, 21
5. RIHPHC, Archaeological Site Files, Neutaconkanut Hill.
6. Neutaconkanut Hill Conservancy, "Voices from the Past."
7. Chapin, "Unusual Indian Implements Found in Rhode Island," 117.
8. Providence and Providence City Auditor, *Seventy-Sixth Annual Report of the City Auditor*, 163; "Catalogue of Portraits in the Picture Gallery of the Society," 85.
9. Chapin, "Unusual Indian Implements Found in Rhode Island," 117.
10. Chapin, "Unusual Indian Implements found in Rhode Island," 117.
11. Powers, *North American Burl Treen*.
12. For discussions of the social and cultural meanings of effigies in the Northeast, see Bradley, *Evolution of the Onondaga Iroquois*, 123; Goodby, "Technological Patterning and Social Boundaries"; Handsman, "Algonkian Women Resist Colonialism"; Wonderly, "Effigy Pipes, Diplomacy, and Myth."
13. Rider, *The Lands of Rhode Island*, 152.
14. Barnd, *Native Space*, 24.
15. James N. Arnold, "Locally Famous Rock in Johnston," newspaper clipping, Scrapbook, 149 (vertical file), Marian J. Mohr Memorial Library, Johnston RI.
16. Fawcett, *Medicine Trail*; Mavor and Dix, *Manitou*.
17. "Boulder out of Ice Age Pulverized for Safety," *Providence Journal*, November 21, 1954, 35.

18. Ellsworth and Kruse, *Making the Geologic Now*.
19. James N. Arnold, "Locally Famous Rock in Johnston," newspaper clipping, Scrapbook, 149 (vertical file), Marian J. Mohr Memorial Library, Johnston RI.
20. Workers of the Federal Writers' Project, *Rhode Island*, 453.
21. According to the 1930 U.S. Census, the Lee family lived at 360 Willard Avenue in Lower South Providence, not far from Rhode Island Hospital. Mary J. Clark, a "full-blood Wampanoag," lived at the same address with her nephew, Flavius Reed, a "mixed blood Wampanoag."
22. For details about the powwows, see "Seventh Annual Powwow of the National Algonquin Council Held on Estate of Col. Frank W. Tillinghast," *Providence Journal*, September 8, 1931; "Scenes during Annual Conference of National Algonquin Indians," *Providence Evening Bulletin*, September 5, 1933; "Col. Frank W. Tillinghast Host at 11th Annual Indian Pow-wow of Narragansett Council Yesterday," *Providence Journal*, September 3, 1935; JHS, Programs of the powwows.
23. "Political Leaders Play Prominent Part in Eighth Annual Indian Pow-wow," *Providence Journal*, September 6, 1932; "Scenes during Annual Conference of National Algonquin Indians," *Providence Evening Bulletin*, September 5, 1933; "Col. Frank W. Tillinghast Host at 11th Annual Indian Pow-wow of Narragansett Council Yesterday," *Providence Journal*, September 3, 1935.
24. Eschbach and Applbaum, "Who Goes to Powwows?"
25. Lerch and Bullers, "Powwows as Identity Markers."
26. Boissevain, "Narragansett Survival."
27. Boissevain, "Narragansett Survival," 357; Lerch and Bullers, "Powwows as Identity Markers."
28. "An Indian Pow-Wow," *Providence Journal*, September 26, 1893.
29. Buddle, "Media, Markets and Powwows"; Rice, "Witchery, Indigenous Resistance, and Urban Space."
30. Boissevain, "Narragansett Survival"; Buddle, "Media, Markets and Powwows"; McMullen, "Soapbox Discourse."
31. JHS, Chapman, "Just Smell the Seasons."
32. JHS, Interview with Mabel Sprague, July 7, 1997, Mabel Sprague folder.
33. *Massachusetts, Town and Vital Records, 1620–1988*.
34. U.S. Census 1850.
35. RIHS, PCD 1861, 116; 1862, 114; 1872, 208; 1877, 260; PCA, Record of Deaths, book 14, 146.
36. U.S. Census 1860; RIHS, PCD 1867, 150; RI Census 1875, 251.

37. RISA, RIDR, vol. 1879, 1230.
38. Dolly Onsley's parents were Ira Smith, an African American, and Sarah Hall, a Native American. See Pasay, *Full Circle*, 497.
39. JHS, Interview with Mable Sprague, March 7, 1996, Atwood folder.
40. JHS, Interview with Mabel Sprague, n.d., Mable Sprague folder.
41. U.S. Census 1870; 1880.
42. *Rhode Island, Marriage Index*; RISA, RIDR 86-117-16 (Ernest P. Onsley).
43. *U.S., WWI Draft Registration Cards*.
44. *Intentions and Returns of Marriage Recorded in the Town of Johnston*, book 2, Office of the Town Clerk, Johnston, 98.
45. RIHS, PCD 1908, 492; 1912, 532; 1914, 56.
46. RI Census 1915; 1925.
47. JHS, Chapman, "Just Smell the Seasons."
48. For discussions of Native use of fish as fertilizer, see Mrozowski, "The Discovery of a Native American Cornfield"; Nanepashemet, "It Smells Fishy to Me"; cf. Ceci, "Fish Fertilizer."
49. JHS, Chapman, "Just Smell the Seasons."
50. "News Items," *ND* 1, no. 4 (August 1935): 91-92.
51. "Indians Open Pow-wow at Shannock," *ND*, 1, no. 5 (September 1935): 127.
52. "Sunrise News," *ND* 1, no. 7 (November 1935): 172.
53. "First RI Indian Day," *ND* 2, no. 5 (September 1936): 3.
54. *U.S., WWII Draft Registration Cards*.
55. "Ernest P. Onsley," *Providence Journal*, October 25, 1960, 31.
56. JHS, Interview with Mrs, [Mable] Sprague and Mrs. Eastwood, 1978, Mable Sprague folder.
57. Change of Name Petition-Order-Decree, No. 338, June 10, 1919, Office of the Town Clerk, Johnston.
58. For a discussion of a medicine man conferring Indian names on children at modern Narragansett powwows "in a fashion similar to a Protestant baptism," see Boissevain, "Narragansett Survival," 354.
59. Cady, *Civic and Architectural Development*, 61 ; RIHS, PCD 1832, 133.
60. RIHS, PCD; 1836, 133; 1838, 147; 1841, 187; 1844, 202.
61. PCA, Record of Deaths, book 6, 81; book 7, 158, 192, 195, 200; book 8, 128, 296; book 11, 160.
62. PCA, Record of Deaths, book 13, 165; book 7, 120.
63. PCA, Record of Deaths, book 9, 139.
64. Walmsley, *Life and Confession*, 3.
65. D'Agostino and Nicholson, *Legends, Lore, and Secrets of New England*, 38-40.

66. Campbell, Gutterl, and Lee, *Race, Nation, and Empire*; Chambers, "'Neither Justice nor Mercy'"; Fabian, *The Unvarnished Truth*; Kahn, *Punishment, Prisons, and Patriarchy*.
67. Walmsley, *Life and Confession*. For discussions of gallows confessions, see Cohen, *Pillars of Salt*; *Sermons, Slavery, and Scandal in Early Boston*.
68. Walmsley, *Life and Confession*, 4.
69. State v. Amasa E. Walmsley and Thomas J. Walmsley, March Term, 1832, Rhode Island Supreme Court, Judicial Records Center, Rhode Island Judiciary, Pawtucket.
70. Walmsley, *Life and Confession*, 10.
71. Walmsley, *Life and Confession*, 9, 4, 11.
72. Daniel Anthony Map, Town of Providence, 1823, locates the "Gaol" between Water and North Main Streets to the west and east, and between North and South Court Streets to the north and south; RISA, Gaol Plans, 1819.
73. Walmsley, *Life and Confession*, 12-13.
74. "Execution of Walmsley," *Providence Patriot*, June 6, 1832; "Execution," *Newport Mercury*, June 9, 1832.
75. King, *King's Pocket-Book of Providence, R.I.*, 105.
76. "Squaw Hollow: What Remains of a Notorious Part of the City," *Providence Sunday Journal*, January 18, 1891.
77. Simister, *Streets of the City*, vol. 3, 100-101; Simmons, *Spirit of the New England Tribes*, 160.
78. "Execution," *Rhode Island American*, June 5, 1832.
79. *Genealogy of the Fields of Providence*; RISA, Rhode Island General Treasurer Accounts, May-August 1832; 1832, 60.
80. "Execution," *Providence Daily Journal*, June 2, 1832.
81. "Execution," *Rhode Island American*, June 5, 1832; Walmsley, *Life and Confession*, 15.
82. "Execution," *Newport Mercury*, June 9, 1832; "Execution," *Providence Daily Journal*, June 2, 1832; "Execution of Walmsley," *Providence Patriot*, June 6, 1832; "Execution," *Rhode Island American*, June 5, 1832.
83. Chambers, "'Neither Justice nor Mercy,'" 437-39; "Execution," *Providence Daily Journal*, June 2, 1832.
84. "Execution," *Providence Daily Journal*, June 2, 1832.
85. Walmsley, *Life and Confession*, 5.
86. Gilkeson, *Middle-Class Providence*, 23-25.
87. Walmsley, *Life and Confession*, 4.

88. Walmsley, *Life and Confession*, 4.
89. For arguments that Walmsley's execution was an attempt to reinforce the authority of ruling elites following the Snowtown riots, see Chambers, "'Neither Justice nor Mercy.'"
90. RISA, *Report of Committee on Indian Tribe*, January 1831, Narragansett Indians Records Collection, folder 81; Mandell, *Tribe, Race, History*, 119–20.
91. The other person of color was Sarah Howland, who was reprieved because she was too sick to be transported to the execution site; she lingered in prison until she was finally pardoned and released. See "'Hanging in Rhode Island' (from the Boston Advocate)," *Rhode Island American*, April 13, 1832.
92. "Hanging in Rhode Island (from the Boston Advocate)," *Rhode Island American*, April 13, 1832; Stephen S. Wardell diary, No. 12, June 1, 1832, Beneficent Congregational Church, Providence, 93.
93. "Execution," *Providence Daily Journal*, June 2, 1832; "Execution," *Rhode Island American*, June 5, 1832.
94. Walmsley, *Life and Confession*, 15–16.
95. RISA, Rhode Island General Treasurer Accounts, May–August, 1832.
96. RIHS, PCD 1836, 133; 1838, 147; 1841, 187; 1844, 203; 1857, 360; PCA, Record of Deaths, book 10, 17.
97. "Grand Trunk's Shovel Opens Up Old Buried Graveyard," *Providence Evening Bulletin*, July 3, 1912.
98. Simister, *Streets of the City*, vol. 13, 69–69a.
99. Receiving Tomb Book, no. 3, North Burial Ground Records; Tomb Order, October 21, 1912, North Burial Ground Records.
100. Gilkeson, *Middle-Class Providence*; Sullivan, "Reconstructing the Olney's Lane Riot."
101. Cayleff, *Wash and Be Healed*.
102. RIHS, Angell, "Story of Ochee Spring," Towns folder, Johnston, 20.
103. RIHS, Angell, "Story of Ochee Spring," Towns folder, Johnston, 20.
104. Crook, *The Mineral Waters of the United States*, 241.
105. RIHS, "The Ochee Spring," advertising brochure (ca. 1916), Towns folder, Johnston, 20.
106. Varner, *Sacred Wells*, 47.
107. Dixon, "Surface Analysis."
108. Putnam, "The Manufacture of Soapstone Pots," 276.
109. Dixon, "Surface Analysis," 89.
110. Brooks, *Common Pot*, 3–8.

111. Turnbaugh, Turnbaugh, and Keifer, "Characterization of Selected Soapstone Sources."
112. *Proceedings of the Rhode Island Historical Society*, 37.
113. RIHS, "Providence Franklin Society, Record of Donations, 1826-1878," MSS 162, folder 8; RIHS, "Annual Reports, Cabinet Keeper, 1879-1887," MSS 162, folder 10.
114. RIHS Archives, vol. 26: *Records, 1862-1880*.
115. RISA, Report of the Committee of the Rhode Island Historical Society on the Old Indian Steatite Pottery, Preston Collection.
116. *Proceedings of the Rhode Island Historical Society*, 37-39.
117. RIHS Archives, vol. 26: *Records, 1862-1880*, 339.
118. Rhode Island, *Report of Committee on Marking Historical Sites*, 139-45.
119. "Arthur Ianelli Talks about the Johnston Soapstone Quarry and Ochee Springs, 6/26/2013," talk given at monthly meeting, YouTube video, 6:00, posted by "bethhurd1," June 26, 2013, www.youtube.com/watch?v=wFnLGpY4ItM.
120. Utley and Hemperly, *Placenames of Georgia*; Simpson, *A Provisional Gazetteer of Florida Place-Names*.
121. Rider, *The Lands of Rhode Island*, 207.
122. "Seventh Annual Powwow of the National Algonquin Council Held on Estate of Col. Frank W. Tillinghast," *Providence Journal*, September 8, 1931; "Political Leaders Play Prominent Part in Eighth Annual Indian Pow-wow," *Providence Journal*, September 6, 1932.
123. Deloria, *Indians in Unexpected Places*, 232.
124. "Seventh Annual Powwow of the National Algonquin Council Held on Estate of Col. Frank W. Tillinghast," *Providence Journal*, September 8, 1931.
125. Raibmon, *Authentic Indians*, 7.
126. "It's Rhode Island's Best 17th Century House," *Providence Sunday Journal*, June 29, 1941.
127. Johnston Historical Society, *Johnston: Volume II*, 106.
128. Raibmon, *Authentic Indians*, 7.

8. Epilogue

1. Fixico, *The Urban Indian Experience in America*, 44.
2. Straus and Valentino, "Retribalization in Urban Indian Communities," 86.
3. Erdrich, *Love Medicine*, 78.
4. Erdrich, *Love Medicine*, 278.

5. Reps, *Views and Viewmakers of Urban America*.
6. Dunlap and Weslanger, *Indian Place Names in Delaware*, viii.
7. RIHS, Bessie R. Paine Diaries, June 26[?], 1908, MSS 601.
8. Basso, *Wisdom Sits in Places*, 144.
9. Gevaert et al., "Evaluating the Societal Impact of Using Drones," 91.
10. Byrne, "Nervous Landscapes," 185.
11. Munn, "The 'Becoming-Past' of Places," 364.
12. Thrush, *Indigenous London*, 14.
13. Dove and Spears, "Home," 32. This poetry is taken from journals in which the indigenous authors reflected on Mashapaug Pond, Narragansett history, and art that envisions this urban homeland as it might have been when their ancestors lived there long ago and as it is today.

Bibliography

Archives and Manuscript Materials

Beneficent Congregational Church, Providence RI
    Stephen S. Wardell Diary
Brown Digital Repository, Brown University Library, Providence RI
    Fox Point Project
    Mashapaug Pond and Reservoir Triangle Collection
Digital Collection, John Hay Library, Brown University, Providence RI
    "A Great Banquet: In Union Hall, Broad Street, Providence, R.I., Given by the Ladies of the Pond Street Baptist Church." Broadside
    Nancy Elizabeth Prophet Diary
    Thornton, Frank L. "Highland Spring, Neutaconkanut Hill, Johnston, R.I."
Haffenreffer Museum of Anthropology, Brown University, Providence RI
    Bicknell Scrapbook. Thomas Bicknell Scrapbook of the Indian Council of New England, 1923–25
Johnston Historical Society, Johnston RI
    Mabel Sprague Interviews. Atwood and Mabel Sprague folders
    Myra Chapman, "Just Smell the Seasons," *Rambler*, 1983 (typescript)
Johnston Town Clerk's Office, Town Hall, Johnston RI
    Intentions and Returns of Marriage Recorded in the Town of Johnston
Judicial Records Center, Rhode Island Judiciary, Pawtucket RI
    Providence Superior Court case files
Marian J. Mohr Memorial Library, Johnston RI
    Rhode Island Historical Society Scrapbook
National Archives and Records Administration, College Park MD
    U.S. Census Records (various years)
    Federal Population Censuses (Records also accessed online at Ancestry.com, *U.S. Federal Census Collection*)
New Bedford Free Public Library, New Bedford MA
    Whaling Collection Archives
New Bedford Whaling Museum, New Bedford MA
    Whaling Crew Database
North Burial Ground Records, Providence RI

Providence City Archives, Providence RI
    City of Providence Record of Births; Record of Deaths; Record of Deeds; Record of Marriages
    Providence Probate Records
    Providence Redevelopment Photograph Collection
Rhode Island Historical Society, Providence RI
    Dexter Asylum Records, MSS 67
    Carl R. Gross, "The Negro and Events in Rhode Island, 1696–1968" (Bound typescript)
    John Howland Collection, MSS 499
    Susanna Lear Diary, MSS 9001-L
    Minutes of the Committee on Marking Historical Sites, Archives, box 24
    Bessie R. Paine Diaries, MSS 601
    Providence City Directory (various years), City Directories Collection (Records also accessed at Providence City Archives, the Providence Public Library, and online at Ancestry.com, *Rhode Island City Directories*)
    Providence Franklin Society Records, MSS 162
    Providence Town Papers, MSS 214, subgroup 1
    Records, 1862–1880, Archives, volume 26
    Records of the U.S. Customs House at Providence, MSS 28, subgroup 1
    Rhode Island Census, Rhode Island State Census (various years) (Records also accessed at Ancestry.com, *Rhode Island State Censuses, 1865–1935*)
    Daniel Steadman Journal, MSS 1129
    Streets of the City transcripts: Transcriptions of *Streets of the City* programs broadcast on station WEAN, Providence (Records also accessed at the Providence Public Library)
Manual of the Pond Street Free Baptist Church, Cor. of Pond and Angle Streets (Providence RI: Jas. R. Day, 1880), Rhode Island Towns, PR-5-B-289
Rhode Island Historical Preservation and Heritage Commission, Providence RI
    Archaeological Site Files
    National Register Nominations
    Statewide Surveys
Rhode Island State Archives, Providence RI (RISA)
    American Revolutionary War Files
    Narragansett Indian Records Collection
    Preston Collection
    Rhode Island State Birth Register (Records also accessed at the Rhode Island Historical Society)

Rhode Island State Death Register (Records also accessed at the Rhode Island Historical Society)

Rhode Island State Marriage Register (Records also accessed at the Rhode Island Historical Society)

Rosenfeld Collection. Mystic Seaport, Mystic CT

Seamen's Protection Certificate Register Database

Smith College Archives, Northampton MA

Wilder Papers: Harris Hawthorne Wilder Papers, Field Notebook 1, Charlestown, Rhode Island, Summer 1912, box 29, folder 9

Published Works

Allen, Zachariah. *Bi-centenary of the Burning of Providence in 1676: Defence of the Rhode Island System of the Treatment of the Indians and of Civil and Religious Liberty, an Address Delivered before the Rhode Island Historical Society, April 10th, 1876*. Providence RI: Providence Press, 1876.

———. *Memorial to Roger Williams: Paper Read before the Rhode Island Historical Society, May 18, 1860*. Providence RI: Cooke & Danielson, 1860.

Amaki, Amalia K. "Nancy Elizabeth Prophet: Carving a Niche at Spelman College." In *Hale Woodruff, Nancy Elizabeth Prophet, and the Academy*, edited by Amalia K. Amaki and Andrea Barnwell Brownless. Atlanta and Seattle: Spelman College Museum of Fine Art in association with University of Washington Press, 2007.

Anderson, Jennifer L. *Mahogany: The Costs of Luxury in Early America*. Cambridge MA: Harvard University Press, 2012.

Apess, William. *On Our Own Ground: The Complete Writings of William Apess, a Pequot*. Edited by Barry O'Connell. Amherst: University of Massachusetts Press, 1992.

"The *Appeal to the Great Spirit*, Cyrus Dallin" (frontispiece). *Art and Progress* 14, no. 8 (June 1913).

Arnold, Samuel Greene. *History of the State of Rhode Island and Providence Plantations*. Vol. 1: *1636–1700*. New York: D. Appleton, 1859.

Artemel, Janice G., et al. *Providence Cove Lands Phase III Report*, April 1984. Prepared for U.S. Department of Transportation, Federal Railroad Administration, Northeast Corridor Project. Providence: Rhode Island Historical Preservation and Heritage Commission.

Baker, Virginia. "Glimpses of Ancient Sowams." *Publications of the Rhode Island Historical Society* 2, no. 3 (1894): 196–202.

Barnd, Natchee Blu. *Native Space: Geographic Strategies to Unsettle Settler Colonialism*. Corvallis: Oregon State University Press, 2017.

Banvard, Joseph. *A Guide to the Providence River and Narragansett Bay from Providence to Newport.* Providence RI: Coggleshall & Stewart, 1858.

Bartlett, John Russell, ed. *Records of the Colony of Rhode Island and Providence Plantations in New England.* Vol. 1: *1636 to 1663.* Providence RI: A. Crawford Greene and Brothers, 1856; reprint, New York: AMS Press, 1968.

———, ed. *Records of the Colony of Rhode Island and Providence Plantations in New England.* Vol. 4: *1707 to 1740.* Providence RI: Knowles, Anthony, 1859.

Basso, Keith H. *Wisdom Sits in Places: Landscape and Language among the Western Apache.* Albuquerque: University of New Mexico Press, 1996.

Beck, Sam. *Manny Almeida's Ringside Lounge: The Cape Verdeans' Struggle for Their Neighborhood.* Providence RI: Gavea-Brown, 1992.

Belcher, Horace G. "Old Rocky Point." *Rhode Island History* 7, no. 2 (1948): 33–50.

Bender, Barbara. "Landscapes on the Move." *Journal of Social Archaeology* 1, no. 1 (2001): 75–89.

Bhahba, Homi K. "Signs Taken for Wonders: Questions of Ambivalence and Authority under a Tree outside Delhi, May 1817." *Critical Inquiry* 12, no. 1 (1985): 144–65.

Bicknell, Thomas W., ed. *Addresses and Poem in Commemoration of the Captain Michael Pierce Fight, March 26, 1676: Memorial Services at Central Falls, Rhode Island, October 15, 1904; Dedication of Monument, September 21, 1907.* N.p., 1908.

———. *The History of the State of Rhode Island and Providence Plantations: Biographical.* Vol. 8. New York: American Historical Society, 1920.

Block, Elizabeth L. "Respecting Hair: The Culture and Representation of American Women's Hairstyles, 1865–90." PhD dissertation, City University of New York, 2011.

Boissevain, Ethel. *The Narragansett People.* Phoenix: Indian Tribal Series, 1975.

———. "Narragansett Survival: A Study of Group Persistence through Adapted Traits." *Ethnohistory* 6, no. 4 (1959): 347–62.

Bourgaize, Eidola Jean. "Supernatural Folklore of Rhode Island." Open Access Master's Theses, Paper 909, DigitalCommons@URI, University of Rhode Island, 1956.

Bradley, James W. *Evolution of the Onondaga Iroquois: Accommodating Change, 1500–1655.* Lincoln: University of Nebraska Press, 1987.

Brigham, Clarence S., comp. *Seventeenth-Century Place-Names of Providence Plantations, 1636–1700.* Providence RI, 1903.

Bristol, Douglas. "From Outposts to Enclaves: A Social History of Black Barbers from 1750 to 1915." *Enterprise & Society* 4, no. 4 (2009): 595–606.
Brooks, James F. "Continental Shifts." *William and Mary Quarterly*, 3rd ser., 74, no. 3 (2017): 533–41.
Brooks, James F., Christopher R. N. DeCorse, and John Walton, eds. *Small Worlds: Method, Meaning, and Narrative in Microhistory*. Santa Fe NM: School of American Research Press, 2008.
Brooks, Lisa. *The Common Pot: The Recovery of Native Space in the Northeast*. Minneapolis: University of Minnesota Press, 2008.
———. *Our Beloved Kin: A New History of King Philip's War*. New Haven CT: Yale University Press, 2018.
Brown, Barbara W., and James M. Rose. *Black Roots in Southeastern Connecticut 1650–1900*. New London CT: New London County Historical Society, 2001.
Brown, Joseph. *Games of the Restricted Match between Clarence H. Freeman of Providence, R.I. and Charles F. Barker of Boston, Mass., for a Purse of $500*. Woonsocket RI: Joseph Brown and the press of W. H. Goodale, 1890.
Brown, William J. *The Life of William J. Brown of Providence, R.I., with Personal Recollections of Incidents in Rhode Island*. Durham: University of New Hampshire Press; Hanover NH: University Press of New England, 2006.
Bruchac, Margaret M. "Historical Erasure and Cultural Recovery: Indigenous People in the Connecticut River Valley." PhD dissertation, University of Massachusetts Amherst, 2007.
Brunton, Deborah. *Health and Wellness in the 19th Century*. Health and Wellness in Daily Life. Santa Barbara CA: Greenwood, 2014.
Buddle, Kathleen. "Media, Markets and Powwows: Matrices of Aboriginal Cultural Mediation in Canada." *Cultural Dynamics* 16, no. 1 (2004): 29–69.
Burant, Jim. "The Visual World in the Victorian Age." *Archivia* 19 (Winter 1984–85): 110–21.
Butler, Eva. "Sweat Houses in the Southern New England Area." *Bulletin of the Massachusetts Archaeological Society* 7, no. 1 (1945): 11–14.
Byrne, Denis R. "Nervous Landscapes: Race and Space in Australia." *Journal of Social Archaeology* 3, no. 2 (2003): 169–93.
Cady, John Hutchins. *The Civic and Architectural Development of Providence*. Providence RI: Book Shop, 1957.
Calloway, Colin G., ed. *After King Philip's War: Presence and Persistence in Indian New England*. Hanover NH: University Press of New England, 1997.
———. "Introduction: Surviving the Dark Ages." In Calloway, *After King Philip's War*.

Campbell, James T., Matthew Pratt Gutterl, and Robert G. Lee, eds. *Race, Nation, and Empire in American History*. Chapel Hill: University of North Carolina Press, 2007.

Campbell, Paul. *A Community Apart: A History of Public Housing in Providence*. Providence: Rhode Island Publications Society, 2007.

Campbell, Paul R., and Glenn W. La Fantasie. "Scattered to the Winds of Heaven: Narragansett Indians, 1676–1880." *Rhode Island History* 37, no. 3 (1978): 67–83.

Catalogue of the Gallery of Art of the New York Historical Society. New York: printed for the New York Historical Society, 1915.

"Catalogue of Portraits in the Picture Gallery of the Society." *Publications of the Rhode Island Historical Society*, n.s., 3, no. 2 (1895).

Cayleff, Susan E. *Wash and Be Healed: The Water-Cure Movement and Women's Health*. Philadelphia: Temple University Press, 1987.

Ceci, Lynn. "Fish Fertilizer: A Native American Practice?" *Science* 168 (1975): 26–30.

Certeau, Michel de. *The Practice of Everyday Life*. Translated by Steven F. Rendall. Berkeley: University of California Press, 1984.

Chambers, Stephen. "'Neither Justice nor Mercy': Public and Private Executions in Rhode Island, 1832–1833." *New England Quarterly* 82, no. 3 (2009): 430–51.

Chapin, Howard M. "Indian Graves: A Survey of Indian Graves That Have Been Discovered in Rhode Island." *Rhode Island Historical Society Collections* 20 (1927): 14–32.

———. "Queen's Fort." *Rhode Island Historical Society Collections* 24 (1931): 141–56.

———. "Unusual Indian Implements Found in Rhode Island." *Rhode Island Historical Society Collections* 19, no. 4 (1926): 117–28.

Chenery, William H. *The Fourteenth Regiment Rhode Island Heavy Artillery (Colored) in the War to Preserve the Union, 1861–1865*. Providence RI: Snow & Farnham, 1898.

Cipolla, Craig. *Becoming Brothertown: Native American Ethnogenesis and Endurance in the Modern World*. Tucson: University of Arizona Press, 2013.

City of Providence. *Fourteenth Annual Report of the Superintendent of Health of the City of Providence, for the Year Ending December 31, 1896*. Providence RI: Snow & Farnham, 1897.

Clark, Carol. "Indians on the Mantle and in the Park." In *The American West in Bronze, 1850–1925*, edited by Thayer Tholes and Thomas Brent Smith, 24–55. New York: Metropolitan Museum of Art; distributed by Yale University Press, 2013.

Clausen, J. Earl. *These Plantations*. With a foreword by Sevellon Brown and illustrations by Milton Halladay and Paule Loring. Providence RI: Roger Williams Press, E. A. Johnson, 1937.

Clifford, James. "Indigenous Articulations." *Contemporary Pacific* 13, no. 2 (2001): 468-90.

Cohen, Daniel A. *Pillars of Salt, Monuments of Grace: New England Crime Literature and the Origins of American Popular Culture, 1674-1860*. Amherst: University of Massachusetts Press, 2006.

Cole, J. R. *History of Washington and Kent Counties, Rhode Island, Including Their Early Settlement and Progress to the Present Time; A Description of Their Historic and Interesting Localities; Sketches of Their Towns and Villages; Portraits of Some of Their Prominent Men, and Biographies of Many of Their Representative Citizens*. New York: W. W. Preston, 1889.

Conley, Patrick T., and Paul Campbell. *Providence: A Pictorial History*. Norfolk VA: Donning, 1982.

———. *South Providence*. Images of America. Charleston SC: Arcadia, 2006.

Connecticut, Hale Collection of Cemetery Inscriptions and Newspaper Notices, 1629-1934. Ancestry.com. 2012.

Cook, Lauren J. *The Rhode Island Burial Survey*, part 2: *Data Base*. Office of Public Archaeology, Report of Investigation No. 28, 89-91. Providence RI: Center for Archaeological Studies, Boston University, 1985.

Crèvecoeur, J. Hector St. John. *Letters from an American Farmer and Sketches of Eighteenth-Century America*. Edited by Albert Stone. New York: Penguin, 1981. First published in 1782.

Crook, James K. *The Mineral Waters of the United States and Their Therapeutic Uses: With an Account of the Various Mineral Spring Localities, Their Advantages as Health Resorts, Means of Access, etc., to Which Is Added an Appendix on Potable Waters*. New York: Lea Brothers, 1890.

Cullen, Countee. "Elizabeth Prophet: Sculptress," *Opportunity*, July 1930, 204-5.

D'Agostino, Thomas, and Arlene Nicholson. *Legends, Lore, and Secrets of New England*. Charleston SC: History Press, 2013.

Davenport, Charles B., and Albert G. Love. *The Medical Department of the United States Army in the World War*. Vol. 15: *Statistics, Part One: Army Anthropology*. Washington DC: Government Printing Office, 1921.

Delabarre, Edmund G. "Chief Big Thunder: A Problematic Figure in Rhode Island Annals." *Rhode Island Historical Society Collections* 27, no. 4 (1935): 116-28.

Deloria, Philip J. *Indians in Unexpected Places*. Lawrence: University Press of Kansas, 2004.

———. *Playing Indian*. New Haven CT: Yale University Press, 1998.

DeLucia, Christine M. "Fugitive Collections in New England Indian Country: Indigenous Material Culture and Early American History Making at Ezra Stiles's Yale Museum." *William and Mary Quarterly*, 3rd ser., 75, no. 1 (2018): 109–50.

———. "The Memory Frontier: Uncommon Pursuits of Past and Place in the Northeast after King Philip's War." *Journal of American History* 98, no. 4: 975–97.

———. *Memory Lands: King Philip's War and the Place of Violence in the Northeast*. New Haven CT: Yale University Press, 2018.

Den Ouden, Amy E. *Beyond Conquest: Native Peoples and the Struggle for History in New England*. Lincoln: University of Nebraska Press, 2005.

Des Jardins, J. Ellyn. "Federal Hill House: Its Place in Providence and the Settlement Movement." *Rhode Island History* 54, no. 4 (1996): 99–122.

Dixon, Boyd. "Surface Analysis of the Ochee Spring Steatite Quarry in Johnston Rhode Island." *Man in the Northeast* 34 (1987): 85–98.

Dorr, Henry C. *The Planting and Growth of Providence*. Providence RI: S. S. Rider, 1882.

Doughton, Thomas. "Unseen Neighbors: Native Americans of Central Massachusetts, a People Who Had 'Vanished.'" In Calloway, *After King Philip's War*, 207–30.

Dove, Dawn, and Holly Ewald, eds. *Through Our Eyes: An Indigenous View of Mashapaug Pond*. Exeter RI: Tomaquag Indian Memorial Museum and Holly Ewald, 2012.

Dover, Dawn, and Lorén Spears. "Home." In *Through Our Eyes: An Indigenous View of Mashapaug Pond*, edited by Dawn Dove and Holly Ewald, 32. Exeter RI: Tomaquag Indian Memorial Museum and Holly Ewald, 2012.

Downes, William Henry. "Cyrus E. Dallin, Sculptor." *Brush and Pencil* 5, no. 1 (October 1899): 1–18.

Dubuque, Hugo Abelard. *Fall River Indian Reservation*. Fall River MA: n.p., 1907.

Dundes, Alan. "The Vampire as Bloodthirsty Revenant." In *The Vampire: A Casebook*, edited by Alan Dundes, 159–75. Madison: University of Wisconsin Press, 1998.

Duneier, Mitchell. *Sidewalk*. New York: Farrar, Straus and Giroux, 1999.

Dunlap, Arthur R., and Clinton A. Weslanger. *Indian Place Names in Delaware. With a Tribute to the Late Dr. Frank G. Speck*. Wilmington: Archaeological Society of Delaware, 1950.

Dyer, Elisha. *Annual Report of Adjutant General of the State of Rhode Island and Providence Plantations for Year 1865*. Providence RI: E. L. Freeman, 1893.

Earle, John Milton. *Report to the Governor and Council concerning the Indians of the Commonwealth under the Act of April 6, 1859*. Boston: William White, 1861.

Edmunds, Penelope. *Urbanizing Frontiers: Indigenous Peoples and Settlers in Nineteenth-Century Pacific Rim Cites*. Vancouver: University of British Columbia Press, 2010.

Ellsworth, Elizabeth, and Jamie Kruse, eds. *Making the Geologic Now: Responses to the Material Conditions of Contemporary Life*. Brooklyn NY: Punctum, 2012.

Erdrich, Louise. *Love Medicine*. Newly revised edition. New York: Harper Perennial/Modern Classics, 2013.

Eschbach, Karl, and Kalman Applbaum. "Who Goes to Powwows? Evidence from the Survey of American Indians and Alaska Natives." *American Indian Culture and Research Journal* 24, no. 2 (2000): 65-83.

Everts & Richards. *Atlas of Rhode Island*. Vol. 1: *Providence County, 1895*. Philadelphia: Everts & Richards, 1895.

Fabian, Ann. *The Unvarnished Truth: Personal Narratives in Nineteenth-Century America*. Berkeley: University of California Press, 2000.

Faflik, David. *Boarding Out: Inhabiting the American Urban Literary Imagination, 1840-1860*. Evanston IL: Northwestern University Press, 2012.

Faunce, William Herbert Perry. "Introduction." In *A Modern City: Providence, Rhode Island and Its Activities*, edited by William Kirk, 1-14. Chicago: University of Chicago Press, 1909.

Fawcett, Melissa Jayne. *The Medicine Trail: The Life and Lessons of Gladys Tantaquidgeon*. Tucson: University of Arizona Press, 2000.

Fenn, Elizabeth A. *Encounters at the Heart of the World: A History of the Mandan Peoples*. New York: Hill & Wang, 2014.

Ferrie, Joseph, and Werner Troveskin. "Water and Chicago's Mortality Transition, 1850-1925." *Explorations in Economic History* 45 (2008): 1-16.

First Free Methodist Church. *Fiftieth Anniversary Historical Sketch Pamphlet*. Seekonk MA, 1975.

Fisher, Linford D. *The Great Indian Awakening: Religion and the Shaping of Native Cultures in Early America*. Oxford: Oxford University Press, 2012.

———. "'Why Shall Wee Have Peace to Bee Made Slaves': Indian Surrenderers during and after King Philip's War." *Ethnohistory* 64, no. 1 (2017): 91-114.

Fixico, Donald L. *The Urban Indian Experience in America*. Albuquerque: University of New Mexico Press, 2000.

Foote, Kenneth E. *Shadowed Ground: America's Landscapes of Violence and Tragedy*. Austin: University of Texas Press, 2003.

Fullilove, Mindy Thompson. "Root Shock: The Consequences of African American Dispossession." *Journal of Urban Health* 78, no. 1 (2001): 72-80.

Genealogy of the Fields of Providence, Rhode Island, as Traced by Mrs. Harriet A. Brownell of Providence, R.I., Mainly from Records and Papers in Rhode Island. Providence RI: J. A. & R. A. Reid, 1878.

Gevaert, Caroline M., Richard Sliuzas, Claudio Persello, and George Vosselman. "Evaluating the Societal Impact of Using Drones to Support Urban Upgrading Projects." *International Journal of Geo-Information* 7, no. 3 (2018): article 91.

Gilkeson, John S. Jr. *Middle-Class Providence, 1820-1940*. Princeton NJ: Princeton University Press, 1986.

Gill, Tiffany M. "Civic Beauty: Beauty Culturists and the Politics of African American Female Entrepreneurship, 1900-1965." *Enterprise and Society* 5, no. 4 (2004): 583-93.

Glenn, Evelyn Nakano. "Settler Colonialism as Structure: A Framework for Comparative Studies of U.S. Race and Gender Formation." *Sociology of Race and Ethnicity* 1, no. 1 (2015): 54-74.

Goeman, Mishuana. "From Place to Territories and Back Again: Centering Storied Land in the Discussion of Indigenous Nation-Building." *International Journal of Critical Indigenous Studies* 1, no. 1 (2008): 23-34.

Goniwe, Thembinkosi, Mashantucket Pequot Tall Oak, David Henry, and Edgar Heap of Birds. *Eagles Speak: A New Project by Hachivi Edgar Heap of Birds*. Exhibition Notes (Rhode Island School of Design, Museum of Art) no. 17. Providence: RISD Museum of Art, 2002.

Gonzales, Angela A. "Racial Legibility: The Federal Census and the (Trans) Formation of 'Black' and 'Indian' Identity, 1790-1920." In *IndiVisible: African-Native American Lives in the Americas*, edited by Gabrielle Tayac, 57-67. Washington DC: Smithsonian Institution Books, 2009.

Goodby, Robert. "Technological Patterning and Social Boundaries: Ceramic Variability in Southern New England, AD 1000-1675." In *Technical Choices and Social Boundaries in Material Culture Patterning*, edited by Barbara Stark, 171-92. Washington DC: Smithsonian Institution Press, 1998.

Gorham Manufacturing Company, Bronze Division. *Famous Small Bronzes: A Representative Exhibit Selected from the Works of Noted Contemporary Sculptors*. New York: Gorham Manufacturing Company, 1928.

Greene, Welcome Arnold. *The Providence Plantations for Two Hundred and Fifty Years*. Providence RI: J. A. & R. A. Reid, 1886.

Greenthal, Kathryn, Paula M. Kozoi, and Jan Seidler Ramirez. *American Figurative Sculpture at the Museum of Fine Arts*. Boston: Museum of Fine Arts, 1986.

Grolier Club. *Catalogue of an Exhibition of Early American Engraving upon Copper, 1727-1850*. New York: De Vinne, 1908.

Guillemin, Jeanne. *Urban Renegades: The Cultural Strategy of American Indians*. New York: Columbia University Press, 1975.
Gura, Philip F. *The Life of William Apess, Pequot*. Chapel Hill: University of North Carolina Press, 2015.
Hamell, George R. "Mythical Realities and European Contact in the Northeast during the Sixteenth and Seventeenth Centuries." *Man in the Northeast* 33 (1987): 63–87.
———. "Trading in Metaphors: The Magic of Beads." In *Proceedings of the 1982 Glass Trade Bead Conference*, edited by Charles F. Hayes II, Research Records 16, 5–28. Rochester NY: Rochester Museum and Science Center, 1983.
Handsman, Russell G. "Algonquian Women Resist Colonialism." *Artifacts* 16, no. 3-4 (1988): 29–31.
———. "Being Indian in Providence." Research essay published for the exhibit *Pequot Lives in the Lost Century*. Mashantucket CT: Mashantucket Pequot Museum and Research Center, 2009.
———. "Capitalism and the Center Village of Canaan, Connecticut: A Study of Transformations and Separations." *Artifacts* 9 (1981): 1–21.
———. "First Whalers: Wampanoag Indian Communities and the New Bedford Whaling Industry." Research Report prepared for the New Bedford Whaling National Historic Park and the Northeast Regional Office, National Park Service, Boston, 2010.
———. "Stop Making Sense: Toward an Anti-Catalogue of Woodsplint Basketry." In McMullen and Handsman, *Language of Woodsplint Baskets*, 144–63.
Hardscrabble Calendar: Report of the Trials of Oliver Cummins, Nathaniel G. Metcalf, Gilbert Humes and Arthur Farrier Whoe Were Indicted with Six Others for a Riot and for Aiding in Pulling Down a Dwelling-house on the 18th of October, at Hard-Scrabble. Providence RI: n.p., 1824.
Hauptman, Laurence M. *Between Two Fires: American Indians in the Civil War*. New York: Free Press, 1995.
Haynes, Carolyn A. *Divine Destiny: Gender and Race in Nineteenth-Century Protestantism*. Jackson: University of Mississippi Press, 1998.
Herndon, Ruth Wallis. *Unwelcome Americans: Living on the Margins in Early New England*. Philadelphia: University of Pennsylvania Press, 2001.
Herndon, Ruth Wallis, and Ella Wilcox Sekatau. "Colonizing the Children: Indian Youngsters in Servitude in Early Rhode Island." In *Reinterpreting New England Indians and the Colonial Experience*, edited by Colin G. Calloway and Neal Salisbury, 137–73. Boston: Colonial Society of Massachusetts, 2003.
———. "The Right to a Name: The Narragansett People and Rhode Island Official in the Revolutionary Era." In Calloway, *After King Philip's War*, 114–43.

Historical Data Systems, comp. *U.S., Civil War Soldier Records and Profiles, 1861–1865*. Ancestry.com, 2009.

Hopkins, G. M. *Atlas of the City of Providence, R.I., and Environs: From Official Records, Private Plans and Actual Surveys*. Philadelphia: G. M. Hopkins, 1882.

———. *City Atlas of Providence, Rhode-Island, by Wards*. 3 vols. Philadelphia: G. M. Hopkins, 1875.

Horton, Laurel. "The Making of a Kentucky Counterpane." *Journal of Backcountry Studies* 8, no. 1 (2013): 1–13.

Hudson, Lynn M. *The Making of "Mammy Pleasant," a Black Entrepreneur in Nineteenth-Century San Francisco*. Urbana: University of Illinois Press, 2003.

Ihlder, John. *The Houses of Providence: A Study of Present Conditions and Tendencies, with Notes on the Surrounding Communities and Some Mill Villages*. Providence RI: Snow & Farnham, 1916.

Ingold, Tim. "The Temporality of Landscape." *World Archaeology* 25, no. 2 (1993): 152–74.

Jackson, Charles T. *Report on the Geological and Agricultural Survey of the State of Rhode Island, Made under a Resolve of Legislature in the Year 1839*. Providence RI: B. Cranston, 1840.

Jacobs, Jane. *The Life and Death of Great American Cities*. New York: Random House, 1961.

Jennings, Wesly. "The Wisdom of the Eagle Speaks to Us." In Dove and Ewald, *Through Our Eyes*, 30.

Jobe, Margaret M. "Native Americans and the U.S. Census: A Brief Historical Survey." *Journal of Government Information* 30: 66–80.

Johnson, Wendell B., and Rell G. Francis. *Frontier to Fame: Cyrus E. Dallin, Sculptor*. Edited by Denise Dallin Wheeler. Arlington MA: Cyrus Dallin Art Museum, n.d.

Johnston Historical Society. *Johnston*. Vol. 2. Images of America. Charleston SC: Arcadia, 1999.

Kahn, Mark E. *Punishment, Prisons, and Patriarchy: Liberty and Power in the Early Republic*. New York: New York University Press, 2005.

Karttunen, Frances Ruley. "Dorcas Honorable: The Life and Heritage of an Oft-Married Woman." *Historic Nantucket* 51, no. 3 (Spring 2002): 15–18.

———. *The Other Islanders: People Who Pulled Nantucket's Oars*. New Bedford MA: Spinner, 2005.

Kauanui, J. Kēhaulani. "'A Structure, Not an Event': Settler Colonialism and Enduring Indigeneity." *Lateral* 5, no. 1 (Spring 2016).

Kennedy, Virginia. "Native Americans, African Americans, and the Space That Is America: Indian Presence in the Fiction of Toni Morrison." In Miles and Holland, *Crossing Waters, Crossing Worlds*, 196–217.

King, Brooks, and David Rivello. "Amos Brewster (1840-1899), Fighting for His People's Freedom." In *Grace Church Cemetery Project: Stories*, edited by Tracy Breton, 57-59. Providence RI: privately printed, 2002.

King, Moses. *King's Pocket-Book of Providence, R.I.* Providence RI: Tibbitts & Shaw, 1882.

Kirschenbaum, Blossom S. "Nancy Elizabeth Prophet, Sculptor." *Sage* 4, no. 1 (1987): 45-52.

Knox, Grace Louise, and Barbara B. Ferris, comps. *Connecticut Divorces: Superior Court Records for the Counties of New London, Tolland and Windham, 1719-1910*. Bowie MD: Heritage, 1987.

Koskela, Douglas M. "Discipline and Polity." In *The Cambridge Companion to American Methodism*, edited by Jason E. Vickers, 156-70. Cambridge: Cambridge University Press, 2010.

Krech, Shepard III, ed. *Passionate Hobby: Rudolph Frederick Haffenreffer and the King Philip Museum*. Bristol RI: Haffenreffer Museum of Anthropology, Brown University, 1994.

———. "Rudolf Haffenreffer and the King Philip Museum." In Krech, *Passionate Hobby*, 49-90.

Krouse, Susan Applegate, and Heather A. Howard, eds. *Keeping the Campfires Going: Native Women's Activism in Urban Communities*. Lincoln: University of Nebraska Press, 2009.

Lancaster, Jane. "'By the Pens of Females': Girls' Diaries from Rhode Island, 1788-1821." *Rhode Island History* 57, nos. 3-4 (1999): 59-113.

———. "'I Would Have Made Out Very Poorly Had It Not Been for Her': The Life and Work of Christiana Bannister, Hair Doctress and Philanthropist." *Rhode Island History* 59, no. 4 (2001): 103-19.

———. "Shampoos to Shelters: Christiana Bannister 1819-1902." In "In Transit: Unmapped Territories of African-American Art, Relocation of Cultural Traditions: The Legacy of Edward Mitchell Bannister and Christiana Carteaux." Special issue, *FAS RIC* (newsletter of the Faculty of Arts and Sciences, Rhode Island College), no. 22 (2000): 11-16.

Lange, Greg. "Native Americans Force Settlers to Leave Whidbey Island in August, 1848." HistoryLink.org Essay 5246, February 2, 2003, www.historylink.org/File/5246.

Lapier, Rosalyn R., and David R. M. Beck. *City Indian: Native American Activism in Chicago, 1893-1934*. Lincoln: University of Nebraska Press, 2015.

Leininger-Miller, Theresa. *Negro Artists in Paris: African American Painters and Sculptors in the City of Light, 1922-1934*. New Brunswick NJ: Rutgers University Press, 2001.

Lemons, J. Stanley. "Summer Times, from Shore Resorts to Amusement Parks." In *What a Difference a Bay Makes*, 115–19. Providence: Rhode Island Historical Society and Rhode Island Department of State Library Services, 1993.

Lepore, Jill. "Historians Who Love Too Much: Reflections on Microhistory and Biography." *Journal of American History* 88 (2001): 124–44.

Lerch, Patricia Barker, and Susan Bullers. "Powwows as Identity Markers: Traditional or Pan-Indian?" *Human Organization* 55, no. 4 (1996): 390–95.

Leroy, Davis. *A Clashing of the Soul: John Hope and the Dilemma of African American Leadership and Black Higher Education*. Athens: University of Georgia Press, 1998.

Lester, Joan. "'We Didn't Make Fancy Baskets until We Were Discovered': Fancy-Basket Making in Maine." In McMullen and Handsman, *Language of Woodsplint Baskets*, 38–59.

Life of John W. Johnson. Transcribed and indexed by Ne-Do-Ba. Published online at www.nedoba.org, 1998. Original document in the collection of the Maine Historical Society, Portland.

Lippard, Lucy. *The Lure of the Local: Senses of Place in a Multicentered Society*. New York: New Press, 1997.

Lipsitz, George. "The Racialization of Space and Spatialization of Race: Theorizing the Hidden Architecture of Landscape." *Landscape Journal* 26, no. 1 (2007): 10–23.

Little, Elizabeth A. "The Nantucket Indian Sickness." In *Papers of the Twenty-First Algonquian Conference*, edited by William Cowan, 181–96. Ottawa: Carleton University Press, 1990.

Lobo, Susan. "Urban Clan Mothers: Key Households in Cities." In Krouse and Applegate, *Keeping the Campfires Going*, 1–21.

Lobo, Susan, and Kurt Peters, ed. *American Indians and the Urban Experience*. Lanham MD: Altamira, 2001.

Lopenzina, Drew. *Through an Indian's Looking Glass: A Cultural Biography of William Apess, Pequot*. Amherst: University of Massachusetts Press, 2017.

Love, W. DeLoss. *Samson Occom and the Christian Indians of New England*. Syracuse NY: Syracuse University Press, 2000.

Lyons, Scott Richard. *X-Marks: Native Signatures of Assent*. Minneapolis: University of Minnesota Press, 2010.

MacGunnigle, Bruce C. "Icabod Northrup, 'Soldier of the Revolution,' and His Descendants." *Rhode Island Roots* 34, no. 4 (2008): 169–88.

Mancini, Jason Richard. "Beyond Reservation: Indian Survivance in Southern New England and Eastern Long Island, 1713-1861." PhD dissertation, University of Connecticut, 2009.
Mandell, Daniel R. *Tribe, Race, History: Native American in Southern New England, 1780-1880*. Baltimore: Johns Hopkins University Press, 2008.
Mann, Henry. *Features of Society in Old and in New England*. Providence RI: Sidney S. Rider, 1885.
Massachusetts, Birth Records, 1840-1915. Ancestry.com. 2013.
Massachusetts, Find a Grave Index, 1620-2013. Ancestry.com. 2012.
Massachusetts, Marriage Records, 1840-1915. Ancestry.com. 2013.
Massachusetts Register and Business Directory, 1878. Boston: Sampson, Davenport, 1878.
Massachusetts, State Census, 1855 and 1865. Ancestry.com. 2014.
Massachusetts, State and Federal Naturalization Records, 1798-1950. Ancestry.com. 2011.
Massachusetts, Town and Vital Records, 1620-1988. Ancestry.com. 2011.
Mavor, James W. Jr., and Byron E. Dix. *Manitou: The Sacred Landscapes of New England's Native Civilization*. Rochester VT: Inner Traditions, 1989.
May, M. Stannard. "The Work of Cyrus E. Dallin." *New England Magazine* 48 (November 1912): 408-15.
Mayne, Alan, and Susan N. Lawrence. "Ethnographies of Place: A New Urban Research Agenda." *Urban History* 26, no. 3 (1999): 325-48.
McBride, Bunny. *Molly Spotted Elk: A Penobscot in Paris*. Norman: University of Oklahoma Press, 1995.
McCallum, Mary Jane Logan. *Indigenous Women, Work, and History: 1840-1980*. Winnipeg: University of Manitoba Press, 2014.
McDonald, William. *The History of Methodism in Providence, Rhode Island, from Its Introduction in 1787 to 1867*. Boston: Phipps & Pride, 1868.
McFadden-Resper, Susie, and Brett Williams. "Washington's 'People without History.'" *Transforming Anthropology* 13, no. 1 (2005): 3-17.
McGowan, Louis, and Daniel Brown. *Providence*. Postcard History Series. Charleston SC: Arcadia, 2006.
McIntosh, Teresa. "W. A. Leggo and G. E. Desbarats: Canadian Pioneers in Photomechanical Reproduction." *History of Photography* 20, no. 2 (1996): 146-49.
McKinney, James P., and George H. Cook. *The Industrial Advantages of Providence, R.I.: Together with an Account of Her Material Development and Progress, and a Series of Comprehensive Sketches of Her Representative Mercantile and Manufacturing Houses*. Providence RI: Jas. P. McKinney, 1889.

McManamon, Francis P., Linda S. Cordell, Kent G. Lightfoot, and George R. Milner, eds. *Archaeology in America: An Encyclopedia*. Vol. 1: *Northeast and Southeast*. Westport CT: Greenwood, 2009.

McMullen, Ann. "Blood and Culture: Negotiating Race in Twentieth-Century Native New England." In *Confounding the Color Line: The Indian-Black Experiences in North America*, edited by James F. Brooks, 261-91. Lincoln: University of Nebraska Press, 2002.

———. "Culture by Design: Native Identity, Historiography, and the Reclamation of Tradition in Twentieth-Century Southeastern New England." PhD dissertation, Brown University, 1996.

———. "'The Heart Interest': Native Americans at Mount Hope and the King Philip Museum." In Krech, *Passionate Hobby*, 167-85.

———. "Looking for People in Woodsplint Basketry Decoration." In McMullen and Handsman, *Language of Woodsplint Baskets*, 102-23.

———. "Soapbox Discourse: Tribal Historiography, Indian-White Relations, and Southeastern New England Powwows." *Public Historian* 18, no. 4 (1996): 53-74.

———. "What's Wrong with This Picture? Context, Conversion, and Development of Regional Native Culture and Pan-Indianism in Southeastern New England." In *Enduring Traditions: The Native People of New England*, edited by Laurie Weinstein, 113-50. Westport CT: Bergin & Garvey, 1994.

McMullen, Ann, and Russell G. Handsman, eds. *A Key into the Language of Woodsplint Baskets*. Washington CT: American Archaeological Institute, 1987.

Melish, Joanne Pope. "Introduction." In Brown, *Life*, xv-xliii.

Mihesuah, Devon A. "American Indian Identities: Issues of Individual Choices and Development." *American Indian Culture and Research Journal* 22, no. 2 (1998): 193-226.

———, ed. *Natives and Academics: Researching and Writing about American Indians*. Lincoln: University of Nebraska Press, 1998.

Miles, Tiles, and Sharon Holland, eds. *Crossing Waters, Crossing Worlds: The African Diaspora in Indian Country*. Durham NC: Duke University Press, 2006

Miller, Rennetts C., ed. *Souvenir History of the New England Southern Conference in Three Volumes*. Vol. 3: *Providence District*. Nantasket MA: published by the author, 1897.

Mills, Earl H. Sr. *Talking with the Elders of Mashpee: Memories of Earl H. Mills, Sr.* Hanover NH: University Press of New England, 2012.

Mithlo, Nancy Marie. *"Our Indian Princess": Subverting the Stereotype*. Santa Fe NM: School for Advanced Research Press, 2008.

Morehead, Deborah Spears.. "My Grandfather's Wooden Chest." *Cultural Survival Quarterly*, January 16, 2015.
Mrozowski, Stephen A. "The Discovery of a Native American Cornfield on Cape Cod." *Archaeology of Eastern North America* 22 (1994): 47–63.
Mt. Pleasant, Alyssa. "Salt, Sand, and Sweetgrass: Methodologies for Exploring the Seasonal Basket Trade in Southern Maine." *American Indian Quarterly* 38, no. 4 (2014): 411–26.
Munn, Nancy D. "The 'Becoming-Past' of Places: Spacetime and Memory in Nineteenth-Century, Pre-Civil War New York." *Journal of Ethnographic Theory* 3, no. 2 (2013): 359–80.
Munro, Wilfred H. *The History of Bristol, R.I.: The Story of the Mount Hope Lands from the Northmen to the Present Time*. Providence RI: J. A. & R. A. Reid, 1880.
Nabokov, Peter. *Where the Lightning Strikes: The Lives of American Indian Sacred Places*. New York: Viking, 2006.
Nanepashemet. "It Smells Fishy to Me: An Argument Supporting the Use of Fish Fertilizer by the Native People of Southern New England." In *Algonkians of New England: Past and Present: The Dublin Seminar for New England Folklife, Annual Proceedings: 1991*, edited by Peter Benes and Jane Montague Benes, 42–50. Boston: Boston University, 1993.
National Park Service. *U.S. Civil War Soldiers, 1861–1865*. Ancestry.com, 2007.
Naumec, David J. "From Mashantucket to Appomattox: The Native American Veterans of Connecticut's Volunteer Regiments and the Union Navy." *New England Quarterly* 81, no. 4 (2008): 596–635.
Neuman, Lisa K. "Basketry as Economic Enterprise and Cultural Revitalization: The Case of the Wabanaki Tribes of Maine." *Wicazo Sa Review* 25, no. 2 (2010): 89–106.
Neutaconkanut Hill Conservancy. "Voices from the Past: Mrs. Sprague & Mrs. Eastwood." Text from 1978 interview, published November 16, 2010, www.nhill.org/voices-from-the-past/.
Newell, Margaret Ellen. *Brethren by Nature: New England Indians, Colonists, and the Origins of American Slavery*. Ithaca NY: Cornell University Press, 2015.
Nicholas, Joseph A. *Baskets of the Dawnland People*. Edited by Stephanie Francis and Scott Francis, with assistance from Donald Soctomah. Old Town ME: Maine Indian Basketmakers Alliance, 1980.
"Notes and Queries." *Pennsylvania Magazine of History and Biography* 29, no. 3 (1905): 359–80.
O'Brien, Francis Joseph Jr. "American Indian Place Names in Rhode Island: Past and Present." Rhode Island USGenWeb (RIGenWeb) Project, 2003, https://sites.rootsweb.com/~rigenweb/IndianPlaceNames.html.

O'Brien, Jean M. *Firsting and Lasting: Writing Indians Out of Existence in New England*. Minneapolis: University of Minnesota Press, 2010.

———. "Presidential Address: Memory and Mobility: Grandma's Mahomen, White Earth." *Ethnohistory* 64, no. 3 (2017): 345–97.

O'Connell, Barry. "Introduction." In Apess, *On Our Own Ground*, xiii–lxxvii.

———. "'Once More Let Us Consider': William Apess in the Writing of New England Native American History." In Calloway, *After King Philip's War*, 163–77.

Orange, Tommy. *There There*. New York: Alfred A. Knopf, 2018.

Parsons, Usher. "Indian Relics." *Historical Magazine* 7, no. 2 (1863): 41–44.

Pasay, Marcella Houle. *Full Circle: Houle-Pasay Memorial Project—A Directory of Native and African Americans in Windham County, CT, and Vicinity, 1650–1900*. Bowie MD: Heritage, 2002.

Pawling, Micah. "Wabanaki Homeland and Mobility: Concepts of Home in Nineteenth-Century Maine." *Ethnohistory* 63, no. 4 (2016): 621–43.

Philbrick, Nathanial. *Away Off Shore: Nantucket Island and Its People, 1602–1890*. New York: Penguin, 1994.

Phillips, Ruth B. *Trading Identities: The Souvenir in Native North American Art from the Northeast, 1700–1900*. Seattle: University of Washington Press; Montreal: McGill—Queen's University Press, 1998.

Pierce, Ebenezer W. *Indian History, Biography and Genealogy Pertaining to the Good Sachem Massasoit of the Wampanoag Tribe*. North Abington MA: Zerviah Gould Mitchell, 1878.

Plane, Ann Marie. "Childbirth Practices among Native American Women of New England and Canada, 1600–1800." In *Medicine and Healing: The Dublin Seminar for New England Folklife, Annual Proceedings, 1990*, edited by Peter Benes, 13–24. Boston: Boston University Press, 1992.

Plane, Ann Marie, and Gregory Button, "The Massachusetts Indian Enfranchisement Act: Ethnic Context in Historical Context, 1849–1869." *Ethnohistory* 40, no. 4 (1993): 587–618.

Powers, Stephen S. *North American Burl Treen: Colonial and Native American*. Brooklyn NY: S. Scott Powers Antiques, 2005.

Pratt, Mary Louise. *Imperial Eyes: Travel Writing and Transculturation*. London: Routledge, 1992.

Pratt, Stephanie. *American Indians in British Art, 1700–1840*. Norman: University of Oklahoma Press, 2005.

Prins, Harald. E. L. "Chief Big Thunder (1827–1906): The Life History of a Maine Trickster." *Maine History* 37, no. 3 (1998): 144.

———. "Tribal Networks and Migrant Labor: Mi'kmaq Indians as Seasonal

Workers in Aroostock's Potato Fields, 1870-1980." In Calloway, *After King Philip's War*, 231-52.

Proceedings of the Rhode Island Historical Society, 1877-1878. Providence: printed for the Rhode Island Historical Society, 1878.

Providence and Providence City Auditor. *Seventy-Sixth Annual Report of the City Auditor Showing the Receipts and Expenditures of the City of Providence for the Year Ending September 30, 1922, with a Schedule of City Property.* Providence RI: City Auditor, 1922.

Providence City Documents for the Year 1900. Providence RI: Providence Press, Snow & Farnham, 1901.

Providence City Planning Commission. *Conditions of Blight in the Mashapaug Pond Redevelopment Project Area, a Study Prepared for the Providence Redevelopment Agency with the Assistance of Blair Associates, Appendix A of the Mashapaug Pond Redevelopment Plan for the Huntington Expressway Industrial Park.* Providence RI, 1960.

Providence Housing Authority. Second Annual Report, 1940-1941. Providence RI, *1941*.

Providence Redevelopment Agency. "Application for an Environmental Protection Agency Brownfields Cleanup Grant-Parcel C, Former Gorham Manufacturing Property." 2012.

———. *Land Utilization and Marketability Study: Federal Hill - South Providence General Neighborhood Renewal Plan, Prepared by W.H. Ballard Company, Boston, MA*. Providence RI, 1965.

———. "Mashapaug Pond Redevelopment Plan for Huntington Expressway Industrial Park with Plan Amendments." Providence RI, 1960.

———. *Official Redevelopment Plan, Central-Classical, Project No. R.I.-2.* Providence RI, 1961.

———. *Official Redevelopment Plan, Lippitt Hill, Project R.I. No. 3.* Providence RI, 1959.

Putnam, F. W. "The Manufacture of Soapstone Pots by the Indians of New England." *Annual Report of the Trustees of the Peabody Museum of American Archaeology and Ethnology* 2. Cambridge MA: John Wilson and Son, 1880.

Raibmon, Paige. *Authentic Indians: Episodes of Encounter from the Late-Nineteenth-Century Northwest Coast.* Durham NC: Duke University Press, 2005.

Ramirez, Renya K. *Native Hubs: Culture, Community, and Belonging in Silicon Valley and Beyond.* Durham NC: Duke University Press, 2017.

"Registry of Local Art: 'The Appeal to the Great Spirit.'" *Museum of Fine Arts Bulletin* 11, no. 61 (February 1913): 13-14, https://www.jstor.org/stable/4423583.

Reps, John W. *Views and Viewmakers of Urban America: Lithographs of Towns and Cities in the United States and Canada, Notes on the Artists and Publishers, and a Union Catalog of Their Work, 1825-1925*. Columbia: University of Missouri Press, 1984.

Rhode Island. *Acts and Resolves Passed by the General Assembly of the State of Rhode Island and Providence Plantations at the January Session, 1879. State of Rhode Island, etc., Office of the Secretary of State, May, 1879*. Providence RI: E. L. Freeman, 1879.

———. *[First] Annual Report of Commission on the Affairs of the Narragansett Indians Made to the General Assembly at Its January Session, 1881*. Providence RI: E. L. Freeman, 1881.

———. *Fourth Annual Report of the Commission on the Affairs of the Narragansett Indians, Made to the General Assembly at Its January Session, 1884*. Providence RI: E. L. Freeman, 1884.

———. *Narragansett Tribe of Indians: Report of the Committee of Investigation; A Historical Sketch and Evidence Taken, Made to the House of Representatives at Its January Session, A.D. 1880*. Providence RI: E. L. Freeman, 1880.

———. *Report of Committee on Marking Historical Sites in Rhode Island Made to the General Assembly at Its January Session, 1913*. Providence RI: E. L. Freeman, 1914.

Rhode Island Black Heritage Society. *Creative Survival: The Providence Black Community in the 19th Century*. Providence: Rhode Island Black Heritage Society, 1985.

Rhode Island Children's Friend Society. *Twenty-Seventh Annual Report*. Providence RI: K. A., 1862.

Rhode Island Commission against Discrimination. *Relocation of Families from the Lippitt Hill Area*. Report submitted December 15, 1960. Providence RI, 1960.

Rhode Island, Death Index, 1630-1930. Ancestry.com. 2000.

Rhode Island, Historical Cemetery Commission Index, 1647-2008. Ancestry.com. 2016.

Rhode Island Historical Preservation and Heritage Commission. *Native American Archaeology in Rhode Island*. Providence: Rhode Island Historical Preservation and Heritage Commission, 2002.

Rhode Island Historical Society. *Canonicus Memorial: Services of Dedication, under Auspices of the Rhode Island Historical Society, September 21, 1883*. Providence RI: Providence Press, 1883.

Rhode Island Historical Society. "Catalogue in Picture Gallery of the Society." *Publications of the Rhode Island Historical Society*, n.s. 3, no. 2 (1895): 85.

Rhode Island, Marriage Index, 1851-1920. Ancestry.com. 2000.

Rhode Island State Censuses, 1865–1935. Ancestry.com. 2013.

Rice, David A. "Witchery, Indigenous Resistance, and Urban Space in Leslie Marmon Silko's *Ceremony*." *Studies in American Indian Literatures* 17, no. 4 (2005): 114–43.

Richmond, Trudie Lamb. "Spirituality and Survival in Schaghticoke Basket-Making." In McMullen and Handsman, *Language of Woodsplint Baskets*, 126–43.

Rider, Sidney S. *The Lands of Rhode Island: As They Were Known to Caunounicus and Minatunnomu When Roger Williams Came in 1636.* Providence RI: published by the author, 1904.

———. "The Last of the Pequot Indians, the Worst Tribe That Ever Lived in New England." *Book Notes* 32, no. 18 (August 28, 1915): 150.

———. "More about Moses P. Dailey and His Life Here in Providence." *Book Notes* 32, no. 20 (September 25, 1915): 153–54.

Riis, Jacob A. "Merry Christmas in the Tenements." *Century Magazine* 55, no. 2 (December 1897): 163–82.

Robinson, George R. "An Epidemic, Simulating Typhoid, Caused by a Paragaertner Organism." *Journal of Infectious Diseases* 16, no. 3 (1915): 448–55.

Robinson, Paul A. "A Narragansett History from 1000 B.P. to the Present." In *Enduring Traditions: The Native Peoples of New England*, edited by Laurie Weinstein, 79–89. Westport CT: Bergin & Garvey, 1994.

Rockwell, Susan L. "The Delivery of Power: Reading American Indian Childbirth Narratives." *American Indian Culture and Research Journal* 19, no. 3 (1995): 71–85.

Rodman, Samuel. *Memorial; To the Honorable General Assembly of the State of Rhode Island, January Session, A.D., 1867.* Tribe and Council of the Narragansett Indians, 1867.

Rogers, Horatio, George Moulton Carpenter, and Edward Field. *The Early Records of the Town of Providence.* Vol. 7. Providence, RI: Snow & Farnham, 1894.

Rogers, Horatio, and Edward Field. *The Early Records of the Town of Providence.* Vol. 15. Providence RI: Snow & Farnham, 1899.

Rose, James M., and Barbara W. Brown. *Tapestry: A Living History of the Black Family in Southeastern Connecticut.* New London CT: New London County Historical Society, 1979.

Rosenthal, Nicholas G. *Native American Migration and Identity in Twentieth-Century Los Angeles.* Chapel Hill: University of North Carolina Press, 2012.

Rothschild, Nan A. "Colonial and Postcolonial New York: Issues of Size, Scale, and Structure." In *Urbanism in the Preindustrial World*, edited by Glenn R. Storey, 121–38. Tuscaloosa: University of Alabama Press, 2006.

Rubertone, Patricia E. "Cocumscussoc, North Kingstown, Rhode Island." In McManamon et al., *Archaeology in America: An Encyclopedia*. Vol. 1, 126-29.

———. "Grave Remembrances: Enduring Traditions among the Narragansett." In "Reshaping Traditions: Native Americans and Europeans in Southern New England." Special issue, *Connecticut History* 35 (1994): 22-45.

———. *Grave Undertakings: An Archaeology of Roger Williams and the Narragansett Indians*. Washington DC: Smithsonian Institution Press, 2001.

———. "Memorializing the Narragansett: Placemaking and Memory Keeping in the Aftermath of Detribalization." In *Archaeologies of Placemaking: Monuments, Memories, and Engagement in Native North America*, edited by Patricia E. Rubertone, 195-216. Walnut Creek CA: Left Coast, 2008.

———. "Monuments and Sexual Politics in New England Indian Country." In *The Archaeology of Colonialism: Intimate Encounters and Sexual Effects*, edited by Barbara L. Voss and Eleanor Conlin Casella, 232-51. Cambridge: Cambridge University Press, 2012.

———. "Queen's Fort, North Kingstown, Rhode Island." In In McManamon et al., *Archaeology in America: An Encyclopedia*. Vol. 1, 129-31.

———. "Urban Land Use and Artifact Deposition: An Archaeological Study of Change in Providence, Rhode Island." In *Archaeology of Urban America: The Search for Pattern and Process*, edited by Roy S. Dickens, 117-42. New York: Academic Press, 1982.

Rudin, Sofia M., David W. Murray, and Timothy J. S. Whitfeld. "Retrospective Analysis of Heavy Metal Contamination in Rhode Island Based on Old and New Herbarium Specimens." *Applications in Plant Sciences* 5, no. 1 (2017), doi: 10.3732/apps.1600108.

Russka, Alan. "Ghost Dancing and the Iron Horse: Surviving through Tradition and Technology." *Technology and Culture* 52, no. 3 (2011): 574-97.

Sainsbury, John A. "Indian Labor in Early Rhode Island New England." *New England Quarterly* 48 (1975): 378-93.

Salwen, Bert. "Archaeology in Megalopolis." In *Research and Theory in Current Archaeology*, edited by Charles L. Redman, 151-63. New York: John Wiley & Sons, 1973.

Sanderson, Eric W. *Mannahatta: A Natural History of New York City*. New York: Abrams, 2009.

Schantz, Mark Saunders. *Piety in Providence: Class Dimensions of Religious Experiences in Antebellum Rhode Island*. Ithaca NY: Cornell University Press, 2000.

Schoelwer, Susan Prendergast. "Form, Function, and Meaning in the Use of Fabric Furnishings: A Philadelphia Case Study, 1700–1775." *Winterthur Portfolio* 14, no. 1 (1979): 25–40.

Scott, Charles T. "The Last of the Wampanoags." *New England Magazine* 33, no. 4 (1905): 392–97.

Scott, Emmett J. *Scott's Official Hisotry of the American Negro in the World War*. Chicago: Homewood, 1919.

Scott, James C. *Seeing Like a State: How Certain Schemes to Improve the Human Condition Have Failed*. New Haven CT: Yale University Press, 1998.

Senier, Siobhan. *Dawnland Voices: An Anthropology of Indigenous Writing from New England*. Lincoln: University of Nebraska Press, 2014.

Sermons, Slavery, and Scandal in Early Boston: Printed Works 1660–1830. Exhibition catalogue. Boston: University of Massachusetts, Boston, and Department of Rare Books and Manuscripts, Boston Public Library, 2009, https://www.umb.edu/editor_uploads/images/centers_institutes/center_library_partnerships/Von_Morze_Exhibit_Catalog.pdf.

Shebtiz, Daniela. "Weaving Traditional Ecological Knowledge into the Restoration of Basketry Plants." *Journal of Ecological Anthropology* 9 (2005): 51–68.

Shoemaker, Nancy. *American Indian Population Recovery in the Twentieth Century*. Albuquerque: University of New Mexico Press, 1999.

———. *Native American Whalemen and the World: Indigenous Encounters and the Contingency of Race*. Chapel Hill: University of North Carolina Press, 2015.

———. "Race and Indigeneity in the Life of Elisha Apess." *Ethnohistory* 60, no. 1 (2013): 27–50.

Shrum, Rebecca K. *In the Looking Glass: Mirrors and Identity in Early America*. Baltimore: Johns Hopkins University Press, 2017.

Siebert, Frank T. "*Penobscot Man: The Life History of a Forest Tribe in Maine*," review. *American Anthropologist* 43, no. 2 (1935): 278–80.

Silverman, David J. "The Impact of Indentured Servitude on the Society and Culture of Southern New England." *New England Quarterly* 74, no. 4 (2001): 622–66.

Simmons, William S. "The Continuous Presence of Native People at Mashapaug Pond." In Dove and Ewald, *Through Our Eyes*, 44–47.

———. "The Earliest Prints and Paintings of New England Indians." *Rhode Island History* 41, no. 3 (1982): 73–81.

———. "From Manifest Destiny to the Melting Pot: The Life and Times of Charlotte Mitchell, Wampanoag." In *Anthropology, History, and American*

Indians: Essays in Honor of William Curtis Sturtevant, edited by William Merrill and Ives Goddard, 131-38. Smithsonian Contributions to Anthropology 44. Washington DC: Smithsonian Institution Scholarly Press, 2002.

———. "The Mystic Voice: Pequot Folklore from the Seventeenth Century to the Present." In *The Pequots in Southern New England: The Fall and Rise of an American Nation*, edited by Laurence M. Hauptman and James D. Wherry, 114-75. Norman: University of Oklahoma, 1990.

———. "The Pond Street Church." Unpublished manuscript.

———. *Spirit of the New England Tribes: Indian History and Folklore, 1620-1984*. Hanover NH: University Press of New England, 1986.

Simpson, J. Clarence. *A Provisional Gazetteer of Florida Place-Names of Indian Derivation Either Obsolescent or Retained Together with Others of Recent Application*. Edited by Mark F. Boyd. Special Publication 1. Tallahassee: Florida Geological Survey, 1956.

Smith, Linda Tuhiwai. *Decolonizing Methodologies*. London: Zed, 1999.

Smith, Michael E. "The Archaeological Study of Neighborhoods and Districts in Ancient Cities." *Journal of Anthropological Archaeology* 29, no. 2 (2010): 137-54.

Snow, Edwin M. *Report upon the Sanitary Effects of Filling the Cove Basin in the City of Providence*. Providence RI: Providence Press, 1868.

———. *Statistics and Causes of Asiatic Cholera, as It Prevailed in Providence, in the Summer of 1854: Being a Letter Addressed to the Mayor of Providence*. Providence RI: Knowles, Anthony, 1855.

Speck, Frank G. "Medicine Practices of the Northeastern Algonquians." In *Proceedings of the Nineteenth International Congress of Americanists, Held at Washington, D.C., December 27-31, 1915*, edited by F. W. Hodge, 303-21. Washington DC: n.p., 1917.

———. "Native Tribes and Dialects of Connecticut: A Mohegan-Pequot Diary." In *Forty-Third Annual Report of the Bureau of American Ethnology, 1925-1926*, 199-287. Washington DC: Government Printing Office, 1928.

———. *Penobscot Man: The Life History of a Forest Tribe in Maine*. New York: Octagon, 1940.

———. *Territorial Subdivisions and Boundaries of the Wampanoag, Massachusett, and Nauset Indians*. Edited by F. W. Hodge. Indian Notes and Monographs 14. New York: Museum of the American Indian, Heye Foundation, 1928.

Spector, Janet D. *What This Awl Means: Feminist Archaeology at a Wahpeton Dakota Village*. St. Paul: Minnesota Historical Society Press, 1993.

Staples, William R. *Annals of the Town of Providence from Its First Settlement to the Organization of the City Government, in June, 1832*. Providence RI: Knowles and Vose, 1843.

Stark, Charles Rathbone. *Groton, Conn. 1705-1905*. Stonington CT: Palmer, 1922.

Steele, Jeffrey. "Reduced to Images: American Indians in Nineteenth-Century Advertising." In *Dressing in Feathers: The Construction of the Indian in American Popular Culture*, edited by S. Elizabeth Bird, 45-64. Boulder CO: Westview, 1996.

Sterling, John E. *North Burial Ground, Providence, Rhode Island: Old Section, 1700-1848*. Greenville: Rhode Island Genealogical Society.

Stevens, Scott Manning. "Tomahawk: Materiality and Depictions of the Haudenosaunee." *Early American Literature* 53, no. 2 (2018): 475-511.

Stiles, Ezra. *Extracts from the Itineraries and Other Miscellanies of Ezra Stiles, D.D., LL.D., 1755-1794*, edited by Franklin Dexter. New Haven CT: Yale University Press, 1916.

Stone, Edwin M. *The Life and Recollections of John Howland, Late President of the Rhode Island Historical Society*. Providence RI: George H. Whitney, 1857.

Straus, Terry, and Debra Valentino. "Retribalization in Urban Indian Communities." In Lobo and Peters, *American Indians and the Urban Experience*, 85-94.

Sullivan, Joseph W. "Reconstructing the Olney's Lane Riot: Another Look at Race and Class in Jacksonian Rhode Island." *Rhode Island History* 65, no. 2 (2007): 49-60.

Sweet, John Wood. *Bodies Politic: Negotiating Race in the American North, 1730-1830*. Philadelphia: University of Pennsylvania Press, 2003.

Talese, Gay. *The Bridge: The Building of the Verrazano-Narrows Bridge*. New York: Bloomsbury, 2014.

Tantaquidgeon, Gladys. *Folk Medicine of the Delaware and Related Algonkian Indians*. Anthropological Series 3. Harrisburg: Pennsylvania Historical and Museum Commission, 1977.

Tarket-Arruda, Lorraine, and Gayle E. Waite. *Charlestown, Rhode Island, Historical Cemeteries*. Hopkinton RI: G. E. Waite, 2008.

Taylor, Maureen Alice. *Runaways, Deserters, and Notorious Villains from Rhode Island Newspapers*. Vol. 1: *The Providence Gazette, 1762-1800*. Rockland ME: Picton, 1994.

Thrush, Coll. *Indigenous London: Native Travelers at the Heart of Empire*. New Haven CT: Yale University Press, 2016.

———. *Native Seattle: Histories from the Crossing-Over Place*. Seattle: University of Washington Press, 2007.

Trouillot, Michel-Rolfe. *Silencing the Past: Power and the Production of History*. Boston: Beacon, 1995.

Turano, Jane Van Norman. "Taken from Life: Early Photographic Portraits of New England Algonkians, ca. 1844-1865." In *Algonkians of New*

England: Past and Present, edited by Peter Benes, 114-43. Dublin Seminar for New England Folklife, Annual Proceedings, 1991. Boston: Boston University, 1993.

Turnbaugh, Sarah Peabody, and William S. Turnbaugh. "Weaving the Woods: Tradition and Response in Southern New England Splint Basketry." In McMullen and Handsman, *Language of Woodsplint Baskets*, 76-93.

Turnbaugh, W. A., S. P. Turnbaugh, and T. H. Keifer. "Characterization of Selected Soapstone Sources in Southern New England." In *Prehistoric Quarries and Lithic Production*, edited by Jonathan E. Ericson and Barbara A. Purdy, 129-38. Cambridge: Cambridge University Press, 1984.

UK and U.S. Directories, 1680-1830. Ancestry.com. 2003.

Ulrich, Laurel Thatcher. *The Age of Homespun: Objects and Stories in the Creation of an American Myth*. New York: Alfred A. Knopf, 2001.

U.S. Army, Register of Enlistments, 1798-1914. Ancestry.com. 2007.

U.S. City Directories, 1822-1995. Ancestry.com. 2011.

U.S., Civil War Draft Registrations Records, 1863-1865. Ancestry.com. 2010.

U.S., Colored Troops Military Service Records, 1863-1865. Ancestry.com. 2007.

U.S., Find a Grave Index, 1600s-Current. Ancestry.com. 2012.

U.S., Newspaper Extractions from the Northeast, 1704-1930. Ancestry.com. 2014.

U.S., Social Security Death Index, 1935-2014. Ancestry.com. 2014.

U.S., World War I Draft Registration Cards, 1917-1918. Ancestry.com. 2005.

U.S., World War II Draft Registration Cards, 1942. Ancestry.com. 2010.

Utley, Frances Lee, and Marian R. Hemperly, eds. *Placenames of Georgia: Essays of John H. Goff*. Athens: University of Georgia Press, 1975.

Valk, Ann, and Holly Ewald. "Bringing a Hidden Pond to Public Attention: Increasing Impact through Digital Tools." *Oral History Review* 40, no. 1 (2013): 8-24.

Varner, Gary R. *Sacred Wells: A Study in the History, Meaning, and Mythology of Holy Wells*. New York: Algora, 2009.

Veracini, Lorenzo. *The Settler Colonial Present*. Basingstoke UK: Palgrave Macmillan, 2015.

———. *Settler Colonialism: A Theoretical Overview*. Basingstoke UK: Palgrave Macmillan, 2010.

Vizenor, Gerald. "Aesthetics of Survivance: Literary Theory and Practice." In *Survivance: Narratives of Native Presence*, edited by Gerald Vizenor, 1-24. Lincoln: University of Nebraska Press, 2008.

———. *Blue Ravens*. Middletown CT: Wesleyan University Press, 2014.

Wallace, Anthony F. C. "Mazeway Disintegration: Human Perception of Socio-Cultural Disorganization." *Human Organization* 16 (1957): 23-27.

Walmsley, Amasa E. *Life and Confession of Amasa E. Walmsley*. Providence RI: n.p., 1832.

Ware, Harriet. *Memoir of Harriet Ware*. Providence RI: George H. Whitney, 1850.

Warf, Barney, and Santa Arias, eds. *The Spatial Turn: Interdisciplinary Perspectives*. Oxford: Routledge, 2009.

Warren, Wendy. *New England Bound: Slavery and Colonization in Early America*. New York: W. W. Norton, 2016.

Warrior, Robert. "Afterword." In Miles and Holland, *Crossing Waters, Crossing Worlds*, 321–26.

———. *The People and the Word: Reading Native Nonfiction*. Minneapolis: University of Minnesota Press, 2005.

Washington, Enrollment and Allotment Applications of Washington Indians, 1911–1919. Ancestry.com. 2013.

Weaver, Jace. *The Red Atlantic: American Indigenes and the Making of the Modern World, 1000–1927*. Chapel Hill: University of North Carolina Press, 2014.

Weibel-Orlando, Joan. "Introduction." In "Keeping the Campfires Going: Urban American Indian Women's Community Work and Activism," edited by Susan Applegate Krouse and Heather Howard-Bobiwash. Special issue, *American Indian Quarterly* 27, no. 3–4 (2003): 491–504.

Welburn, Ron. *Hartford's Ann Plato and the Native Borders of Identity*. Albany: State University of New York Press, 2015.

———. "A Most Secret Identity: Native American Assimilation and Identity Resistance in African America." In *Confounding the Color Line: The Indian-Black Experience in North America*, edited by James F. Brooks, 292–320. Lincoln: University of Nebraska Press, 2002.

West, Benjamin. *Account of the Observation of Venus upon the Sun, the Third Day of June, 1769, at Providence, in New-England, With Some Account of the Use of Those Observations*. Providence RI: printed by John Carter, at Shakespeare's Head, 1769.

Williams, Roger. *The Correspondence of Roger Williams*. Edited by Glenn La Fantasie. 2 vols. Providence RI: Brown University Press; Hanover NH: University Press of New England; for the Rhode Island Historical Society, 1988.

———. *A Key into the Language of America*, 5th ed. Providence: Rhode Island and Providence Plantations Tercentenary Committee, 1936. First published 1643.

Wilson, Waziyatawin Angela, and Michael Yellow Bird, eds. *For Indigenous Eyes Only: A Decolonization Handbook*. Santa Fe NM: School of American Research Press, 2005.

Winslow, C. E. A. "A Statistical Study of Fatality of Typhoid Fever at Different Seasons." *Publications of the American Statistical Association* 8, no. 59 (1902): 103–25.

Wolf, Eric. *Europe and the People without History*. Berkeley: University of California Press, 1982.

Wolfe, Patrick. "Settler Colonialism and the Elimination of the Native." *Journal of Genocide Research* 8, no. 4 (2006): 387–409.

Wonderly, Anthony. "Effigy Pipes, Diplomacy, and Myth: Exploring Interaction between St. Lawrence Iroquoians and Eastern Iroquois in New York State." *American Antiquity* 70, no. 2 (2005): 211–40.

Wood, Joseph S. *The New England Village*. Baltimore: Johns Hopkins University Press, 1997.

Workers of the Federal Writers' Project of the Works Progress Administration for the State of Rhode Island. *Rhode Island: A Guide to the Smallest State*. American Guide Series. Boston: Houghton Mifflin, 1937.

Index

Page numbers in italic indicate illustrations

Abrams, Sarah Ann Elizabeth (Mrs. B. Gardner), 140
activism, 235-36; social, 31
Addison's Hollow, 71-72, 77, 106
advertisements, 87-92, *89*, *256*
African Americans: churchgoing, 122-23; intemperance of, 312; intermarriage of, 16, 33-35, 86; and looking glasses, 253; Methodism of, 160-61; and racial tensions, 54-55, 71-72, 150; surnames of, 44
African Grays, 81
Alger, Asel (Albe), 300, 303
Allen, Zachariah, 75, 85, 319
American Indian Federation, 171, 222, 296
American Negro Art (Dover), 217
American Screw Company, 85
Ammons, Alexander, 57-59
Ammons, Gideon, 57-59, 198, 353-54n99
Ammons, Henrietta, 119
Ammons, John, 119
Ammons, Mary, 119
Angell, Arthur P. and Horatio N., 313-20
Angle Street, 120-22, 141, 150-51
Apess, Elisha, 166
Apess, Leonard, 166
Apess, Lillias, 166

Apess, William, 160-66, 301
Appeal to the Great Spirit (Dallin), 230-34
Aquinnah Cliffs, 180
archaeological evidence: in Blackstone Park, 241; effigies, 285-86; at Fox Point, 31-32; Indian remedies, 92; at Johnston, 284-86, 315-19; at Lippitt Hill, 74-76, 106-8; at Lower South Providence, 159-59; and manufacturing traditions, 158-59; at Mashapaug Pond, 195-96; taskscapes, 30-32
Arnold, James N., 288
artisan-entrepreneurs, 169-70
Assawompset Pond, 83
August Meeting, 35-36, 51, 123, 178
authenticity, 16, 286, 291, 320-23
Axum, James "Uncle Jimmie" and Hannah, 33

Babcock, Charles, 93
Babcock, Estelle, 259-60
Babcock, Melvenia, 258-60
Baker, Virginia, 263
Balanced Rock, 287
Banks, Ann Elizabeth (Mrs. C. Cone), 254
Bannister, Edward M. and Christiana, 257-59
Banvard, Joseph, 242-43

Barker, Charles, 65
Bark Street, 84–87, 90–92
Barnd, Natchee Blu, 113
Bartlett Chronicle Yearbook, 147
basket making and selling, 40–41, 180–84, 247–48, 260–75, 380n96
Basso, Keith, 18, 56, 76, 151, 227, 327
Bates Street, 93–96, *95*, 103–5
Baxter, Sarah, 84–92
Baxter, William, 86–87, 358n63
Benedict Pond, 202, 206–8, 218–20
Benedict Street, 135, 208, 215–18
Bent, Alice, 204
Bent, Betsey, 204
Bent, Ida F., 203–5, 254
Bent, Joseph (Joe), 204–5
Bent, Prince, 204
Bent, William Henry, 204–5
Betty's Neck, 82–83
Bhabha, Homi, 67
Bicknell, Thomas, 114, 124–29
binaries of authenticity, 323
birchbark maps *(awikhiganak)*, 264
Blackstone Canal, 84
Blackstone Park, 241
Blunt, Maria, 50–53, 202
Blunt, Robert, 50–51
Boissevain, Ethel, 35, 291
Book Notes (newsletter), 245
Booth Street, 119, 146
Bosemsdes, Fanny (née Daniels), 166–68
Bosemsdes, Frederick, 166–68
Bosemsdes, Roxanna (Mrs. J. Dwight), 166–69, 172–73
Boston's Metropolitan Improvement League, 230
Bourgaize, E. J., 127
Bourne (Cheats), Hattie, 225

bowls. *See* steatite pots
Braxton, John, 124, *125*
Brewster, Amos, 48–54, 119–20
Brewster, Mary, 62, 119–22
Brewster, Olive (née Cross), 48
Brewster, Sarah, 50–51
Bristol RI, 176–77
Broad Street tag, 330–32, *331*
bronzes and statuettes, 229–35
Brooks, Lisa, 32, 317
Brothertown Indians, 137
Brown, Cudge, 77
Brown, Ellison ("Tarzan"), 222
Brown, Isabella (wife of John E.), 151
Brown, J. M., 304
Brown, John, 93
Brown, John E., 151
Brown, Marion (Princess Minnetonka), 104
Brown, Max, 76–77
Brown, Moses, 77, 242
Brown, Nicholas, 11
Brown, Noah, 77
Brown, William J., 33–34, 77–81
Brown Garcia, Nancy, 76–77
Brown University Herbarium, 91, 219, 267, 359n77
Bucklin Park, 201
Buffum, William, 301
Bureau of Indian Affairs (BIA) relocation program, 2, 22, 48, 332
Burgess Cove, 156–58
Burke, John, 300–312
Burlingame, Daniel, 300–301
Busher, Isabella (née Elderkin), 184
Byrne, Denis, 140, 184, 228, 329

Calendar Street, 175
Calloway, Colin, 7

Campbell, Paul, 155, 186
"Can I Become a Sculptor?" (Leininger-Miller), 215–17
Canonicus, 19, 30, *31*, 97, 100, 112, 113–14, 127, 195, 239, 283
Canonicus Branch of Indians, 62
Canonicus Monument, 97–102, *99*, 117–18, *118*
Canonicus Square. *See* Hoyle Square
Carmichael, George, Jr., 98
Carpenter's Point, 75
cars and automobiles, 191–93; dream rides, 191
Central-Classical Redevelopment Project, 115–16, 152, 223
Central High School, 115–16
Chace, Alice (Mrs. C. Northrup), 80–84, 159–60
Chace, George, 300–301
Champlain, Mary, 103
Champlin, Christopher R., 59, 119
Champlin, Hazard, 151
Chapin, Howard M., 285
Chapman, Myra, 296
Chapelle, Mary, 124
Charlestown RI, 46, 52–54, 93–94, 130–32, 166–73, 204–6, 222
checkers, 63–68
Cheeves, Nancy (née Noka), 60–62, 122
Chestnut Street Methodist Church. *See* Second Methodist Meeting House
Chief Big Thunder (Frank Loring), 262–65
Chief Gray Eagle (Frank M. Nichols), 102–3
Chief Great Owl (Benjamin Franklin Onsley), 292–93
Chief Night Hawk, 288

Chief Nonsuch, 126
Chief Occum (Lemuel Fielding), 126
Chief Ochee's "chair," 316
Chief Pine Tree (William L. Wilcox), 104–5, 222–23
Chief Rainbow (Ernest P. Onsley), 292–98, 322
Chief Robert Clark, 126–27, 128
Chief Silver Star (Atwood I. Williams), 222, 289
Chief Strong Horse, 124, 126–27
Chief Strong Wolf, *125*, 128
Chief Sunset (Edward Michael), 1–2, 103–6, 171
Chief Thundercloud (Frank Wicks), 170–72
childbirth, 134–35
cholera, 81
Christianity, 123, 163
churchgoing, 122–23, 223
cities, 2–5, 23, 149, 205; as assemblages of neighborhoods, 3, 23; settler colonial, 5, 20; ambitions, 25, 149, 205; and rural-urban binary, 26, 84, 149–50, 297, 321
citizenship, 44, 123, 130–31, 149
Citizens Savings Bank, 114
Civil War, 48–49, 138, 207, 268–69
clairvoyants, 169, 313–14, 316
Clark, Carol, 233
Classical High School, 115–16, *116*
Clauson, J. Earl, 127
Clifford, James, 26
Cocumpaug (aka Schoolhouse) Pond story, 199
Codding Court Project, 152
Cole, J. R., 127
colonial justice, 299–313
colonization. *See* settler colonialism

Index 419

Commission of the Affairs of the Narragansett Indians, 52, 207
Committee on Marking Sites in Rhode Island, 319
common pot metaphor, 32
Cone, Anna, 45
Cone, Charles H., 203, 254
Cone, Edward S., 54–55, 61, 203
Cone, George, 45
Cone, John F., 160
Cone, Mary, 45
Cone, Mary Jane, 55, 93
Cone, Sarah C., 55–56, 160
Congdon, George, 142
Congdon, Hannah, 143
Congdon, Henrietta (née Warmsley), 143
Congdon, Mary Louise, 145
Congdon, Moses C., 143
Congdon, Stephen, 143, 255
Conley, Patrick, 155, 188
Cooper, Nettie, 148
Courtland Street, 200, 240, 244, 249–50
Cove Basin (Great Salt Cove), 75, 84, 240, 284
Crank, Julia, 173
Crank, Rachel (Mrs. G. Storms), 173–76, 178–80
Crank, Sarah, 174
Crank, Thomas, 173–74
Cranston RI, 78–79, 115, 127, 134, 155, 200, 258, 357n28
Creighton, Hamilton. *See* Creighton, Thomas H.
Creighton, Martha, 94–95
Creighton, Thomas H., 94, 101–2
Crèvecoeur, J. Hector St. John, 85
Cross, John O., 48–49

Croud, Priscilla, 148
Crying Rocks legend, 56, 131, 225–26
Cullen, Countee, 209
cultural practices: basket making, 40–41, 180–84, 247–48, 260–75, 380n96; childbirth, 134–35; effigies, 286; games, 64–65; green corn thanksgivings, 35, 221, 290; and identity, 128–29; medicinal knowledge, 84–92, 219–20; and modernity, 277–78; powwows, 124–26, 288–98, 321–23; sharing, 317–18; sweat lodges, 65, 139, 199, 329

Dailey, Benjamin West, 145–46, 158, 242
Dailey, Charles, 146
Dailey, Dorcas, 200, 247–48
Dailey, Frances (Fannie) (Mrs. C. Dailey), 146
Dailey, Jeanette (Nettie), 243–45, 247
Dailey, Moses P., 200, 240–50, 241, 279
Dallin, Cyrus, 126, 229–34
Daniels, Fanny (Mrs. F. Bosemsdes), 166–68
Daniels, John, 166–67
The Death and Life of Great American Cities (Jacobs), 67
deed to Providence (1638), 30, *31*
Deloria, Philip J., 13, 74, 191, 322
Denison, Frederic, 98, 319
detribalization, 46, 51–54, 57, 94–99, 150
Devil's Foot Rock, 127
Dickson, Maria Madelena (Mrs. M. P. Dailey), 243–44
discrimination, 53, 189, 193
dockworkers, 57–58
documentation. *See* written history
Dorr, Henry, 76

Douglass, Frederick, 94
Dover, Cedric, 217
Doyle, Thomas, 55, 75
Drone Warriors (installation), 327–32
drum rocks, 287
Du Bois, W. E. B., 217
Duck Pond, 201–2, 206–7
Dundes, Alan, 244
Dwight, Joseph, 168
Dwight, Roxanna (née Bosemsdes), 166–69, 172–73
Dwight, Theodolphus, 168–73
Dyer, Betsey, 138
Dyer, Elisha, 98

Earle, John Milton, 6, 80, 82–83, 147, 173–74
Eddy Street, 183–84, 190–91
effigies, 285–86
Elderkin, Earl (son of Marcus Aurelius), 184–85, 224
Elderkin, Marcus Aurelius, 224
Elderkin, Oscar (son of Marcus Aurelius), 224
Eleazer, Sarah, 57
Eliot, John, 163
Ellis, Mary J. (Alice Northrup's granddaughter), 83
environmental contamination, 20–21, 115, 186, 220, 222, 235–36, 329, 333
Environmental Justice League of Rhode Island, 235
"Epic of the Indian" (Dallin), 230–34
Erdrich, Louise, 325
ethnic diversity, 34–35, 240
"Eulogy on King Philip" (Apess), 162–63
executions, public, 9, 301, 303, 304, 305–6, 307–8, 310, 312, 385n89, 385n91

Exeter Hill Monument, 121
expansionist colonialism, 75, 76

Fall River Herald News, 177
Fall River MA, 43, 80, 173–74, 176
Fall River Tribe (Troy Watuppa), 80–84, 173–76
Famous Small Bronzes (catalog), 231–32
Farrow, Annie (née Perry), 288
Federal Hill, 239–80; and basket making, 260–75; hair doctresses and ladies' hairdressers in, 255–60; home ownership in, 250–55; landscape of, 239–40; map of, *238*; and Native occupation, 240–50; Pequots at, 240–50
Federal Hill House, 277
Federal Urban Renewal Project, 236
Fenn, Elizabeth, 18
Fenner, Arthur, 196–97
Fenner, Manuel, 255
Fenner, Susan, 255–58
Field, Ellen, 305
Fielding, Lemuel (Chief Occum), 126
Field's Point, 158–59, 304–5
First Free Methodist Church, 185
Fixico, Donald, 325
Football Rock, 287
Fort Ninigret, 98
Fourteenth Rhode Island Heavy Artillery (Colored), 380n105
Foxes Hill, 29–32
Fox Point, 29–69; home ownership in, 35–47; map of, *28*; maritime industries of, 57–62; Native occupation of, 30–35; and settler creation story, 29–30; as stopping-over place, 47–56; and Transit of Venus, 68, 145, 356n135; urban passages, 63–69

Index 421

Frank, Hannah, 300–312
Freeman, Clarence Herbert, 63–69, 65
Free Will Colored Church, 81
Frog's Hollow, 186

Gardner, Anna (Mrs. B. Gardner), 146
Gardner, Benjamin G., 138–40
Gardner, Stephen, 140
Garrison, Lloyd, 148
Gaspee Street, 45, 75, 80, 83–84, 92, 309
gentrification, 69
George, John, 222
Glasko, Mary Congdon (Princess Red Wing), 104–5, 296
Glover, Thomas G., 169
Gorham Manufacturing Company, 227–37
Gorton, Charles, 318–19
Great Salt Cove (Cove Basin), 75, 84, 240, 284
Griswold CT, 48–49, 150, 207, 249, 254, 304, 352n78
Grove Street, 254, 276
Guillemin, Jeanne, 181
Guy, Clifford, Jr., 188–89, 221
Guy, Clifford, Sr., 188, 221
Guy, Esther (née Weeden), 188

Haffenreffer, Rudolf, 176–77, 232–33
hairdressing and restoration, 255–60
Hall, Wealthy (née Stockett), 121
Hall, William, 120–21, 203
Halton Street, 207–8
Hamell, George, 196
Harris, Lydia (née Thomas), 132, 151
Harris Homestead, 242
Hawkings, Stephen, 9–10
Hazard, Ben, 159

Hazard, Bessie, 134
Hazard, Carrie, 122, 134
Hazard, Edith, 134
Hazard, Grace, 134
Hazard, Hannah M., 132–35, 208, 250–54
Hazard, Howard B., 173
Hazard, Jane Bent, 206
Hazard, John B., 250–54
Hazard, John P., 250–54
Hazard, Leonard and Rowland, 252–54
Hazard, May, 134
Hazard, Mercy, 151
Hazard, Sarah E. (née Nichols), 250–54
Hazard, Walter G., 134–35, 250–54
Hazard Mills, 95–96
Heathman, W. A., 126
Heaton, David, 243–44, 246
Helme, Frank V., 142–43
Helme, Marth (née Noka), 142
Henries, Edith, 97
Henries, Elizabeth, 97
Henries, Elsie, 97
Henries, Ethel, 97
Henries, Lemuel, 146–47
Henries, Lydia Sprague, 147
Henries, Perry, 146–47
Henries, Winfred and Augenette, 97
Henry, James, 137
Henry, Olivia (Olive) (née Nichols), 122, 137
Highland Spring brand name, 284
Hilton, Clarence, 133
Hilton, Edward Burns, 133
Hilton, Eliza, 132–34, 208
Hipses Rock, 282, 283, 286–92
historic preservation, 22, 49–50, 69, 106, 279–80
History of Methodism in Providence, Rhode Island, 161

History of Washington and Kent Counties (Cole), 127
Histrionic Club, 257
Holden, Susan, 148
home, concept of, 72, 262
Home for Aged Colored Women, 258
Honorable, Dorcas, 85
Hopkins, John, 309
Howard, Frank, 62
Howland, John, 196
Howland, Sarah, 385n91
Hoyle Square, 111–18
Hoyle Tavern, 112
Hoyt, David W., 319–20
Huntington Expressway Industrial Park, 236

identity: challenges to, 53, 217; expressions of, 92, 266; indigenous, 90, 128, 297; individual, 253; intertribal, 129; Native, 53, 62, 79–80, 82, 264–65, 297; racial, 48, 51, 100, 149–50, 192, 246–47, 269; sharing practice, 317; tribal, 51, 54–55, 129, 149–50, 192, 246
Ihlder, John, 139, 249
"The Increase of the Kingdom of Christ" (Apess), 165
Indian Council of New England, 62, 101–3, 124–30, *125*, 149–50, 288
Indian Day in Rhode Island. *See* Rhode Island Indian Day
Indian doctresses, 87–90, 255–60
Indian Hill. *See* Federal Hill
Indian medicine, 66, 79, 84–92, 243–47, 159, 170, 255–57, 275
Indianness: discrimination, 174; loss of, 226; Native identity, 265; placehood, 150; powwows, 290–91, 321; 323; and racial classifications, 13; and white space, 286
Indian-playing, 74, 92
Indian relics, 74, 318
Indian Reorganization Act, 296
Indian Rock. *See* Hipses Rock
Indian Run, 226–27
"Indian Sickness," 85–86
Indians in Unexpected Places (Deloria), 13
Indian Tammany Society, 74
Indian Tepee, 126–27, 129
Indian-themed street names, 113–14, 117
India Point, 58–60
indigeneity: and Christianity, 163; expansionist colonialism, 75–76; identity, 90, 128, 297; knowledge, 84–92; *vs.* modernity, 248, 323; powwows, 291; rural/urban binary, 84, 149–53, 297, 321; scholarly attention, 4–5; street names as appropriating, 68; survivance, 106–8
industrialization, 72–73, 84, 186, 235–36. *See also* urban renewal
intemperance, 81–82, 301, 307, 312
intermarriage, 16, 34–35, 86, 89, 102, 166–73, 190
inventories, 9–10, 37–43, 63, 90–91, 252–53

Jackson, Amy, 158, 159
Jackson, Florence (Mrs. Benjamin Dailey), 146
Jackson, Henrietta, 36
Jackson, John E., 43–44
Jackson, Mary M., 36
Jackson, Oling, 97
Jacobs, Jane, 67
Jandes, Jacob, 183

Index 423

Jenks, J. W. P., 316, 319–20
Jessamine Street. *See* Benedict Street
Johnson, Howard E., 121
Johnson, John W., 181–83
Johnson, Oliver, 271
Johnson, William S., 269–72
Johnston, 283–323; colonial geographies, 283; colonial justice, 299–313; natural landforms, 283–88; Ochee Springs Quarry, 313–20; powwows, 288–98, 290, 321–23
John Street, 49–54
Jones, Debra Sebastian, 190–92
Jones's Hill, 239–40
Kendall, Fannie, 144–45, 254–55, 256

Kendall, Albertina, 155
Kendall, Franklin Edison, 255
Kendall, Louisa, 255
Kendall, Stephen, 144, 255
Kendall, William B., Jr., 255
King, Dan, 308
King, Samuel W., 285–86
King Philip, 7–8, 162–63, 177
King Philip Museum, 176, 232–33
King Philip's Chair, 177
King Philip's War, 7–9
King's Church, 242
kinship network, 44, 136, 138, 299
Kitka, Alice, 147
Knowles, Joseph, 254
Koskela, Douglas, 160

LaFlesche, Francis, 233–34
Lamoreux, Alfred E., 166
Lancaster, J., 258
land deals, 77–78
landscape of the moral imagination, 151

Lear, Susanna, 11–12
Lee, Margaret R., 288–89
legibility, 14, 67
Leininger-Miller, Theresa, 215–17
Leroy, Davis, Jr., 122
Life and Confession (Walmsley), 300–309
Lippitt Hill, 71–108; Chief Sunset, 103–6; indigenous knowledge, 84–92; map of, 70; Native occupation of, 93–103; place-based stories, 76–84; reverse migrations, 80–84; transformed landscape, 106–8
Lockwood Street, 173, 176
lodging houses, 175
Lone Wolf (Lawrence W. Wilcox), 157
Long Pond, 201–4, 206
looking glasses, 253
Loquer, Mary F. (Mrs. Fred Weeden), 249
Loren, Joseph, 261
Loring, Frank (Chief Big Thunder), 262–65
Lower South Providence, 155–93; alternative pathways, 173–85; Apess, 160–66; development and industry, 155–59; intermarriage, 166–73; map of, 154; Native mobility, 191–93; Native occupation, 159–60; urban passages, 186–92
Lowling/Loring, Nancy, 262, 272–74
Lowling/Loring, Newell, 268–69, 381n108
Lowling/Loring, Thomas, 269–72
Lowling/Loring family, 260–62, 265–75
Lull, H. C., 313–14

Malbone, Caroline, 148
Malbone, Charles, 148
Malbone, Hannah, 148
Malbone, Rhuahammer, 148
Manchester, Abram, 244
maritime industries, 57–62, 180
Market Square, 81, 129
Mars, Christian, 132, 223
Mars, Harold, 223–27
Mars, Laura, 225Mars, Rosebud (née Thomas), 132–33, 223
Mashapaug Pond, 195–237, *198*; condition of, 220; and conflicted urbanisms, 290–20; Gorham Manufacturing Company, 228–35; map of, *194*; as Native homeland, 195–97; pollution, 234–36; urban pond lands, 197–208
Mashpee Revolt of 1833, 161
mazeway disintegration, 192
McDonald, William, 161
McGowan, Louis, 323
McMullen, Ann, 123
The Medicine Man (Dallin), 230, 234
Melish, Joanne Pope, 80
Melville, Jane (Jennie), 168
Melville, Jerome, 168–73
memory: collective, 162; cultural, 212; and memory-keeping sites, 79, 118, 280; and photographs, 17–18, 62,185, 253; and politics of commemoration, 100; and settler colonialism, 20
Metacom. *See* King Philip
Metcalf, Jesse H., 322
Methodism, 160–62
Miantonomo, 7, 30, *31*, 98, 121, 195, 239, 283
Michael, Brister, 54, 103

Michael, Edward (Chief Sunset), 1–2, 103–6, 171
Michel, Edwin E. *See* Michael, Edward
Mi'kmaqs, 181, 183
miniaturization, 232
mishoonémese, 199, 229
Mitchell, Charlotte, 82–83
Mitchell, Melinda, 82
Mitchell, Thomas, 83
Mitchell, Zerviah Gould, 82–83
mixed ancestry, 48, 129–30, 150, 291
modernity: authenticity, 321, 323; cities as representation of, 2; and indigeneity, 105, 247–48, 323; Ochee Springs Soapstone Quarry, 313; Providence, 332; railroads, 157–58; tradition binary, 88, 218, 228, 296
Mohawk Lane, 68
Mohegans, 91–92, *125*
Mollie Flynn's Hill, 239
Moorehead, Deborah Spears, 185
Moorehead, Warren K., 177
Morris, Louisa, 180–84
Mosby, Alice, 122
Mosby, Isaac B., 204
Moshassuck River, 29–30, 32, 71–72, 75, 77, 81, 84, 239
Mount Hope, 176–77, 263
Mowry, William G. R., 319
Mumford, H. G., 309
Munn, Nancy, 330
music, 191–92

Nabokov, Peter, 273–74
Narragansett Bay, 34, 239, 283–84
Narragansett Dawn (newspaper), 66–67, 121, 178, 199, 206, 222, 257, 296

Index 425

Narragansett Indian Church, 57, *179*, 225, 297

Narragansett Indian Council, 131–32, 167–68

Narragansett Pier, 52, 142, 247–48

Narragansetts: Canonicus Monument, 97–101, 117–18; Chief Sunset, 103–6; citizenship, 130–31; Cocumpaug (Schoolhouse Pond) story, 199; Crying Rocks story, 56, 131, 225–26; cultural knowledge, 78–79; destruction of Providence, 8; detribalization, 47, 51–54, 57, 98–99; Federal Hill, 252–54; Fox Point, 35, 47; games, 64–65; Indian Run story, 226–27; John Onion story, 199, 226–27; Lippitt Hill, 93–103; Lower South Providence, 166–73; Mashapaug Pond, 205–8; and Pequots, 222, 245; phenotypes, 149–50; place-names, 113; Pond Street Church, 122–23; powwows, 288–91, 297; retribalization, 296; settler creation story, 30; stonemasonry, 132–33; storied places, 127–28; Sugarloaf Hill story, 226; Tercentenary Celebration, 178, 188–89; tribal membership, 35–36, 46, 51–55; Upper South Providence, 137–44; White Dog Swamp story, 157; Wilder's field notes, 131–32. *See also* August Meeting; Canonicus; Indian Council of New England; Miantonomo; quitclaim agreement

National Algonquin Indian Council (NAIC), 102–3, 171, 288, 292, 295, 297

National Register of Historical Places, 279–80, 320

Native people: agency, 4; and churches, 57, 60, 149, 150–51, 161–62, 178–79, 185, 192–93, 207, 223, 225, 297; dress and representation, 88–89, 145–47, 163–64, 172, 249, 258; and employment, 58, 63, 57–58, 130, 133, 169–70, 257–59; identity, 53, 62, 79–80, 82, 264–65, 297; involuntary servitude, 9–11, 151, 161, 189, 300–301; "last of", 85, 147, 240; legibility, 14, 67; military service of, 48–49, 121, 138, 207, 268–69, 332; mobility, 135, 148, 180, 191–93, 260, 283; and and public events, 101, 104–05, 108, 126, 178, 188–89, 222, 295–96, 288–89, 297; surnames, 44, 62; taskscapes, 31–32, 280; Upper South Providence occupation, 119–22. *See also* settler colonialism; *individual tribes*

Nelson, Molly "Spotted Elk," 218–19

Neptune, Joseph, 126

Neutaconkanut Hill, 283–87, 314, 321

Neutaconkanut Hill Conservancy, 284–85

Newell, Harriet (Mrs. W. Onsley), 143–45

New Guinea, 86

Newport RI, 58, 168, 182, 208, 214, 247–48, 322, 353n99, 354n110

New York, New Haven, and Hartford Railroad, 156, 204, 207, 236, 249, 260

Nicholas, Joseph A., 267

Nichols, Anstriss, 35–47, 351n46

Nichols, Benjamin, 351n45

Nichols, Charles (brother of Frank E.), 136

Nichols, Charles (son of Frank E.), 136
Nichols, David, 136
Nichols, Frank E., 103, 136, 206-7
Nichols, Frank M. (Chief Gray Eagle), 102-3
Nichols, George (brother of Frank E.), 136
Nichols, Georgianna, 137
Nichols, Georgianna (daughter of Frank E.), 136
Nichols, Grace (daugher of Frank E.), 136
Nichols, Hannah, 137
Nichols, Harriet Frances, 36-37, 42, 46-47
Nichols, Mabel (daughter of Frank E.), 136
Nichols, Olivia (Olive) (Mrs. J. Henry), 122, 137
Nichols, Priscilla, 136, 137, 250
Nichols, Sarah E. (Mrs. J. Hazard), 250-54
Nichols, William S., 36-38, 43
Niles, James, 137
Niles, Samuel, 122
Niles, Sarah, 94
Nipmucs, 147
Nocabulabet, 239, 275-76, 280
Nocake, Joe, 304
Nocake, Peter, 304, 354n110
Noka, Abby Perry, 96
Noka, Abigail (Mrs. A. Smith), 95-96
Noka, Alice, 60
Noka, Edward, 207, 254
Noka, Jeremiah, 138
Noka, John, 95
Noka, Nancy (Mrs. G. Cheves), 60-62, 122
Noka, Peter, 60-61
Noka, Samuel, 60
North Burial Ground, 97-102, 106, 200, 311
Northrup, Alice (née Chace), 80-84, 159-60
Northrup, Cato, 80-84, 159-60
Northrup, David, 81
Northrup, Edward, 84
Northrup, James, 81
Northrup, Mary, 83

O'Brien, Jean, 2, 157, 268
Ochee Spring Bottling Company, 314
Ochee Springs Quarry, 313-20
O'Connell, Barry, 23, 120, 162-63, 166, 266
Odeon, 162-65
Old Blood's Mine story, 79
Oliver, Mary Jane (Mrs. O. Weeden), 207
Oliver Johnson & Company, 271
Olney, Betsey (née Brewster), 49, 52
Olney's Lane Riot, 72
Olney Street, 71-73, 77-79, 94, 103, 214, 243, 298
one-family house/cottage, 104, 105
Onsley, Benjamin, 292
Onsley, Benjamin (Ben) Franklin (Chief Great Owl), 292-93
Onsley, Chester Benjamin Martin, 298
Onsley, Dolly (née Smith), 292-93, 294
Onsley, Ernest P. (Chief Rainbow), 292-98, 322
Onsley, Louisa, 293
Onsley, Nellie M. (Princess Flaming Arrow), 292-98
Onsley, Samuel, 293
Onsley family, 288-98
Onsley home, 294
Opportunity, Journal of Negro Life, 209

oral narratives, 17–18, 101–2, 123–24, 200, 225–28
Orange, Tommy, xvii
Ousa Mekin, Yellow Feather (Leroy Perry), 128, 174, 176–80, 202, 203, 288, 289, 322
Ownsley, Benjamin, 143, 295, 299
Ownsley, Harriet (née Newell), 143–45
Ownsley, Phebe, 143–44
Ownsley, Willis A. K. (Willis A. R.), 143–44, 254–55

P. P. Caproni and Brother, 234
Paine, Bessie Rose, 135, 327
Paine, Joseph, 300–301
Paradise, John, 163–64
Paris, France, 209–19
Parsons, Usher, 32
Passamaquoddies, 126, 267, 275
Pawling, Micah, 262
Pawtuxet River, 284
Pawtuxet Turnpike, 156
Peckham, Clara (Nokomis), 288
Peckham, Clara (Sweetheart or Teppekathita), 288
Peckham, Harry (Yellow Feather), 288
Peckham, Mary, 150
Peckham, Mary (Sweetgrass), 288
Peckham, Philip (Chief Night Hawk), 288
Penobscots, 219, 263–65, 274
Pequot Path, 241
Pequots, 200, 222, 240–50
Pequot War, 245
Perry, Alfred A. C., , 124, 125, 127, 128, 288, 290
Perry, Commodore, 174
Perry, Caroline (Mrs. T. P. Wheeler), 142

Perry, Eunice (wife of A. C. Perry), 288
Perry, Fannie L., 176
Perry, Leroy (Ousa Mekin, Yellow Feather), 128, 174, 176–80, 202, 203, 322
Perry, Royal, 174, 178
pésuponck, 199
phenotypes, 16, 54–55, 149–50
Pike, Nancy, 303–4
Pine Grove, 260–62
place(s): ancestral, 2, 3, 177, 264; attachments to, 15, 82–83, 100, 138; scents of, 261, 267, 296; sense of, 78, 128, 150–51, 321; storied, 83, 100–101, 100, 128, 139, 152–53, 226, 229, 264
"Poison in the Pond" (Savageau), 235
place-based knowledge, 264
place-based stories, 49–50, 56, 76–84, 139, 225–28, 312–13, 321–23
placehood, 78, 128, 150–51, 223, 311
place-names, 32, 113–14, 156, 159, 239, 275, 320–21
pollution. *See* environmental contamination
pond lands, 197–208
Pond Street Church, *125*: Cato Northrup, 81, 122; churchgoing, 122–24, 223; Ladies of the Pond Street Church banquet, 132; urban renewal, 115
powwows, 124–26, 288–98, 321–23
Pratt, Mary Louise, 113
Princess Corn Blossom (Ethel Steppo), 292
Princess Flaming Arrow (Nellie M. Onsley), 292–98
Princess Minnetonka (Marion Brown), 104

Princess Red Wing (Mary Congdon Glasko), 104-5, 296
Proffitt, Emma (Mrs. B. Nichols), 37
Proffitt, Nancy Elizabeth, 208-20, *211*
Proffitt, William H., 208, 215-19, *216*
Prophet, Chloe, 78-79
Prophet, Moses B., 98-101
Prophet, Nancy Elizabeth. *See* Proffitt, Nancy Elizabeth
The Protest (Dallin), 230
Providence, R.I. (bird's-eye view), *328*
Providence City Planning Commission, 235-36
Providence Daily Journal (newspaper), 250, 305-7
Providence Directory, 88-90; advertisements, 87-90; listings for Colored Persons, 44, 312; omissions, 63; street numbers, 272
Providence Evening Bulletin (newspaper), 236
Providence Gazette (newspaper), 16
Providence-Hartford-New Haven Railroad, 261, 276
Providence Housing Authority, 152, 186-87
Providence Journal (newspaper), 13, 96, 106, 112, 138, 200
Providence Parks Department, 284
Providence Redevelopment Agency, 73
Providence River, 239
Providence-Stonington railroad, 156-58
Providence Sunday Journal (newspaper), 106, 204-5, 240, 242, 244
public characters, 23, 67
public housing, 152, 186-92
Public Street, 200, 240, 244

pulpit rocks, 287
Putnam, Frederick Ward, 316-20

Quary, Abram, 85
Queen's Fort, 127
Quiaipen, 127
quitclaim agreement, 130

race: censuses, 13-14, 246; ethnic diversity, 34-35; identity, 48, 51, 100, 149-50, 192, 246-47, 269; intermarriage, 190; looking glasses, 253; mixed ancestry, 129-30; naming practices, 87; phenotypes, 16, 54, 149-50; prejudice, 81, 161; tribal identity, 149-50; unrest, 11-12, 54-55, 71-72
Raibmon, Paige, 323
railroads, 156-58, 180, 260, 309-11. *See specific railroads*
remedies. *See* Indian medicine
Report of the Commission on the Affairs of the Narragansett Indians, 136
Report to the Governor and Council under the Act of April 6, 1859, 147
representation, 113, 234-35, 280
research practices, decolonizing, 16-20
reservations and reserves, 3, 5-6, 14-15, 22, 24-25, 47, 59, 102, 149-50, 226, 248, 266, 322, 326, 332
retribalization, 104, 296
reverse migrations, 80-84, 191
revival meetings (Hoyle Square), 112-13
Rhode Island American (newspaper), 305
Rhode Island Children's Friend Society, 261
Rhode Island Department of Environmental Management, 284

Index 429

Rhode Island General Assembly, 35, 61, 167, 229, 283, 308
Rhode Island Historical Preservation and Heritage Commission, 201, 285
Rhode Island Historical Society (RIHS), 126, 177, 196, 229, 318–19
Rhode Island Indian Day, 178, 297
Richmond, France (Mrs. E. Cone), 45
Richmond, Trudie Lamb, 267
Richmond Street, 166–69, 172
Rider, Sidney, 245–47, 321
Rocker, Emily, 60
Rocker, Harry, 59–60
Rocky Point, 242–43
Rodman, Caleb, 43–45
Rodman, Caroline, 57
Rodman, Esther, 95
Rodman, Frances, 62
Rodman, Mollie, 105
Rodman, Samuel, 44, 96, 159
Roger Williams Homes, 186–92, *187*
Roger Williams Park, 318–19
Roger Williams Park Museum, 126
Roger Williams Trading House, 127
rolling rocks, 287
rural/urban binaries, 149–53, 297, 321

Sacred Wells (Varner), 315
Sassamon, John, 163
Savageau, Cheryl, 235
Schantz, Mark, 161
Scout (Dallin), 231–32
Sebastian, Alfred C. and Alice R., 190
Second Freewill Baptist Church. *See* Pond Street Church
Second Methodist Meeting House, 160–62, *164*
Seekonk River, 29–30, 241

Sekatau, Ella, 93
settler colonialism: advertisements, 92; agendas of, 232; archaeological evidence, 74–76; Canonicus Monument, 100; cities, 2, 20–21; corrupting influences, 241; cultural heritage, 267; effects on Native American space, 235; expansionist colonialism, 75–76; indigenous naming practices, 44; Narragansett experiences, 226; Native mobility, 192–93; Neutaconkanut Hill, 284–88; pow-wows, 291; representation, 113; spatial erasure, 22; urban narrative, 332–33
Sheldon, Martha, 10
Sherwood, Herbert, 128
Shoemaker, Nancy, 166, 246
Shoo Fly Village, 240, 277
Shrum, Rebecca, 253
A Signal of Peace (Dallin), 230
Simister, Florence Parker, 122, 304–5, 310–11
Simmons, William S., 17, 196, 202, 379n82
slaughterhouses, 155–56
Slocum, Emma, 94
slum clearance project, 186–87
Smart, Yvonne, 34–35
Smith, Abigail (Abby) (née Noka), 95–96
Smith, Alice (née Cooper, Mrs. B. Dailey), 146
Smith, Archibald, 96
Smith, Dolly Eaton. *See* Onsley, Dolly (née Smith)
Smith, Fidelia, 302–3
Smith, Michael E., 3

Smith, William Elmer, 185
Smith (Noka), Frederick, 96
Smith (Noka), Roland, 96
Snowtown, 71–72
Snowtown Riot. *See* Olney's Lane Riot
Sockbeson, Nicholas, 124–26
A Son of the Forest (Apess), 160–61, 163–65
South Kingstown RI, 48–50
Sowams, 263–64
spatial erasure, 20–22, 72
spatial segregation, 139–40
Speck, Frank, 263, 269, 273, 326
Spirit of the New England Tribes (Simmons), 17
Sprague, Mabel, 292–93
Sprague House, 277
Spring Street, 84, 137–40, 144, 148, 151, 255
Spurlock, Emma, 132
Spurlock, John, 132
Squaw Hollow, 106, 304–5
Standing Rock Sioux Reservation, 327–29
Stanton, Nancy, 204
Stanton, Patience, 150
statuettes, 231–34, 286
Steadman, Daniel, 263
steatite pots, 316–19
Steele, Minnie, 124, *125*, 127, 288
Steppo, Ethel (Princess Corn Blossom), 292
Steppo, Melvin, 292
Stockett, James M., 121
Stockett, James M., Jr., 62, 121, 126
Stockett, Mary E., 121
Stockett, Wealthy (Mrs. W. Hall), 121
Stone, Thomas, 309
stonemasonry, 132–33

Storms, George, 175
Storms, Rachel (née Crank), 173–76, 178–80
Straus, Terry, 325
Sugarloaf Hill story, 226
sweetgrass, 267

Tantaquidgeon, Gladys, *125*, 127
taskscapes, 31–32
Taubabwahhoman, Joe, 10
Taylor, Anna F., 310
Taylor, M. Sales, 171
Tell Street, 252, 271–73
temperance movement, 307
tenement houses, 138, 239–40
texts of intelligibility, 67
Thayer Street, 36–38, 43, 46–47
Thomas, Albert, 132
Thomas, Annie, 94, 98–99, 101, 102, 130–31
Thomas, Benjamin Franklin, 132–33
Thomas, Benjamin, Sr., 130
Thomas, Cora (Carrie), 132, 141
Thomas, Elizabeth (Lizzie), 132, 141
Thomas, Frank, 180–84
Thomas, Frederick (Fred) D., 93–94, 130–33, 150, 173, 208
Thomas, Lorenzo (Early), 132
Thomas, Nancy, 180–84
Thomas, William (Willie), 132
Thornton, Frank I., 284
Thrush, Coll, 5, 332
Tillinghast, Frank W., 288–89
Tillinghast farm, 289
tipping rocks, 287
Todd, William A., 297
The Torch Still Burns (Weeden), 251
tradition, 218, 228, 296. *See also* cultural practices

Index 431

Transit of Venus, 68, 145, 356n135
Transit Street, 63, 66, 68–69, 120, 258
transportation, 156–58, 191–93
trash fish, 295–96
Treaty of Buffalo Creek, 137
tribes: detribalization, 5–6, 46, 51–54, 57, 94–99, 150; identity, 51, 54–55, 129, 149–50, 192, 246; membership, 35–36, 46, 51–55, 57, 93–96, 132, 136, 142; retribalization, 104, 296; tribal relations, 6, 117; tribal sovereignty, 296. *See also individual tribes*
tricksters, 170, 172
Trouillot, Michel-Rolph, 17
Troy-Watuppas. *See* Fall River Tribe
Tuncowoden, 29–30. *See also* India Point
Tuntiachchee, Hannah, 10, 26–27
two-family house, 104, 120, 133, 146, 207, 228, 249, 252
Tyler Street, 223–25
typhoid fever, 143–44

Upper South Providence, 111–53; Canonicus Rock, 112–18; churchgoing, 123; community building, 123–30; home ownership, 130–48; map of, *110*; as Native homeland, 111–12; Native occupation, 119–22; urban passages, 148–53
urban gardening, 139–40, 218
urban geographies, 20–21
urban histories, 2, 76, 183, 297, 332
urban homelands, 3, 15–16, 35, 46, 97, 123, 148–51, 228, 276–77
"urban Indian" as term, 4, 347n7
urban imaginary, 192, 325–26

urban pond lands, 197–208
Urban Pond Procession, 235
urban renewal, 122, 201–2; Canonicus Monument, 117–18; Central-Classical Redevelopment Project, 115; Federal Hill, 279–80; Fox Point, 32, 69; Lippitt Hill, 73–74; Lower South Providence, 186–88; Mashapaug Pond, 236–37; spatial erasure, 20–22; Upper South Providence, 152–53
U.S. Census: Indian as category in, 6; and population count of Providence 1910, 13; racial categories, 13–14, 246–47, 269; and urban renewal, 73
U.S. Indian policy, 6, 163, 296

Valentino, Debra, 325
Varner, Gary, 315
Vinton Street, 250–55, 279
Vizenor, Gerald, 15

Wabanakis, 261–73
Wallace, Anthony, 192
Walmsley, Amasa, 299–313
Walmsley, Benjamin (B. F. Onsley's grandfather), 292
Walmsley, Betsey, 298
Walmsley, George, 298
Walmsley, Louisa, 299
Walmsley, Patience, 298–99, 309
Walmsley, Sarah, 298
Walmsley, Stephen, 309
Walmsley, Thomas, 298, 301–3, 311–12
Walmsley, Uriah, 309
Walter Thurston Gentleman's Lounge, 233

Wampanoags, 60, 82, 177–80, 184–85, 200, 263–65, 288–89, 295–96
Ware, Harriet, 261
warnings out, 10–11, 326
Watson, Rosella, 202–3
Watuppa Water Commission, 176
Weber, Max, 161
Weeden, Alice and Bertha (Louisa Brewster's daughters), 52
Weeden, Clarence (son of Otis and Mary), 208
Weeden, Everett G., Jr., 189
Weeden, Everett "Tall Oak," 208, 221, 249–50
Weeden, Frank, 249
Weeden, Frederick H., 249–50, 251
Weeden, George (son of Otis and Mary), 208
Weeden, Georgianna (Mrs. W. Young), 207–8
Weeden, Gladys (daughter of Otis and Mary), 208
Weeden, James (son of Otis and Mary), 208
Weeden, Louisa, 52, 352n78
Weeden, Mary, 221–22
Weeden, Otis (son of Otis and Mary), 208
Weeden, Otis and Mary Jane Oliver, 207–8
Weeden, Ruth (daughter of Otis and Mary), 208
Weeden, Sarah (née Brewster), 49
Weeden, Toby, 189
Weeden, William C., 50
Welburn, Ron, 102
West Burial Ground, 159
Westerly RI, 13, 221–22
Westerly Sun (newspaper), 171
Weybosset Point, 111–12, 242
whaling business, 58
What Cheer Paint Works and Drug Depot, 272
Wheeler, Amelia, 62
Wheeler, Ann (daughter of Thomas and Hannah), 141
Wheeler, Edwin (son of Thomas and Hannah), 141
Wheeler, Hannah, 141–42
Wheeler, Sarah (daughter of Thomas and Hannah), 141
Wheeler, Thomas, 141, 159, 207
Wheeler, Thomas Franklin, 141
Wheeler, Thomas P., 141–42
Where Lightning Strikes (Nabokov), 273–74
White, John, 87–88
White Dog Swamp, 157
Wickendon Street, 55–56
Wicks, Frank (Chief Thundercloud), 170–72
Wilcox, Lawrence W. (Lone Wolf), 157
Wilcox, Lewis, 221–22
Wilcox, William L. (Chief Pine Tree), 104–5, 222–23
Wilder, Harris Hawthorne, 94, 131–32, 150, 359n85
Williams, Atwood I. (Chief Silver Star), 222, 289
Williams, James and Rachel, 259
Williams, Roger, 7–9, 29–30, 64–65
Wilmarth, Stephen, 300–301
Winslow, Benjamin S., 81–82, 84
Winslow, Edward, 29
Winter Street, 133, 141–42
Winthrop, John, 29, 86
Wisdom Sits in Places (Basso), 18

Wolf, Eric, 22, 349n49
Woonasquatucket River, 75, 239–40, 260–61, 283–84
Worcester Telegram and Gazette (newspaper), 147
Works Progress Program, 225
written history, 16–17, 33, 120–22, 159, 200, 265–66

Yellow Feather. *See* Ousa Mekin, Yellow Feather (Leroy Perry)
Young, Andrew (son of Bessie Hazard), 135
Young, Georgianna (née Weeden), 207–8
Young, Walter, 207–8

www.ingramcontent.com/pod-product-compliance
Lightning Source LLC
Chambersburg PA
CBHW022000041225
36326CB00018B/449